Global Politics

Global Politics

A Toolkit for Learners

Roni Kay M. O'Dell and Sasha Breger Bush

LEXINGTON BOOKS
Lanham • Boulder • New York • London

Published by Lexington Books
An imprint of The Rowman & Littlefield Publishing Group, Inc.
4501 Forbes Boulevard, Suite 200, Lanham, Maryland 20706
www.rowman.com

6 Tinworth Street, London SE11 5AL, United Kingdom

Copyright © 2021 by The Rowman & Littlefield Publishing Group, Inc.

All rights reserved. No part of this book may be reproduced in any form or by any electronic or mechanical means, including information storage and retrieval systems, without written permission from the publisher, except by a reviewer who may quote passages in a review.

British Library Cataloguing in Publication Information Available

Library of Congress Control Number: 2020948470

ISBN 978-1-7936-0476-7 (cloth)
ISBN 978-1-7936-0477-4 (electronic)

Contents

Dedication and Acknowledgments ... ix
Introduction: Taking Responsibility for Learning ... xi
    Learning about Global Politics ... xii
    Thinking about Learning (Research and Resources) ... xiii
    Overview of this Learner-Centered Book on Global Politics ... xv
    Learners and Learning Environments ... xvi
    Learning Practices ... xix
    The Learner-Centered Challenge ... xx
    Reading Recommendations on Learning, Learner-Centered Teaching, and Teaching Global Politics ... xxi

1 Understanding Global Politics ... 1
    1.A: Bloom's Taxonomy and Chapter Organization ... 3
    1.B: Primary Source on Global Politics ... 6
    1.C: Learning How to Study Global Politics ... 9
    1.D: Recommended Readings to Use Along with This Book (If You So Choose) ... 19

2 What Does That Mean? Definitions, Terminology, and Jargon ... 21
    2.A: Tools and Techniques for Defining Terms and Concepts ... 22
    2.B: Primary Sources on Capitalism ... 25
    2.C: Defining, Identifying, and Using Capitalism in Context ... 30
    2.D: Recommended Readings on Capitalism and Academic Skills ... 37

3	Who? Actors, Positions, Perspectives, and Interests	41
	3.A: Active Reading and Credible Internet Sources	42
	3.B: Primary Source on International Trade	44
	3.C: Free Trade, Agriculture, and Anti-globalization Movements	45
	3.D: Recommended Readings on Global Food and Agricultural Politics	55
4	What or What is? Identifying What Matters	59
	4.A: Internet Search Engines and Search Tools and Skills	60
	4.B: Primary Source on Global Governance	62
	4.C: The United Nations and Global Governance	64
	4.D: Recommended Readings on the United Nations	72
5	Where? Assessing Geographic Location and Influence	77
	5.A: Handwritten, Generative Note-Taking, and Consistent Study Methods	78
	5.B: Primary Source on International Agreements	80
	5.C: Geopolitics and International Agreements	81
	5.D: Recommended Readings on Geopolitics	90
6	Why? How Things Work in Global Politics	93
	6.A: Avoiding Harmful Procrastination	94
	6.B: Primary Sources on Containment Policy	95
	6.C: Diplomacy and US Foreign Policy	98
	6.D: Recommended Readings on Foreign Policy and Diplomacy	107
7	When? Outlining Chronology	111
	7.A: Logical Reasoning, Fallacies, and Timelines	112
	7.B: Primary Source on Development	114
	7.C: Global Poverty and Development	115
	7.D: Recommended Readings on Development	124
8	What's the Point? Isolating Main Ideas	129
	8.A: Identifying Main Ideas and Thesis Statements	129
	8.B: Primary Source on the International System	132
	8.C: Sovereignty, Subjugation, and the International System	136
	8.D: Recommended Readings on US-Haiti Relationship and Debt	146
9	Making Connections: Applying Knowledge across Global Political Contexts	149
	9.A: Recall and Retrieval Rather than Re-reading	150
	9.B: Primary Source on War	151
	9.C: Inequality and Working-Class Politics during World War I	153
	9.D: Recommended Readings on Debs, Inequality, and the Iran-Iraq War	164

10	Breaking It Down: Categorizing and Analyzing Topics	167
	10.A: Chunking and Navigating Propaganda	168
	10.B: Primary Sources on Rationales for War	170
	10.C: Going to War	172
	10.D: Recommended Readings on Propaganda, Rhetoric, War, and Genocide	180
11	Compare and Contrast: Clarifying and Distinguishing Concepts and Ideas	185
	11.A: Brainstorming with Mindmaps and Using Writing Tips	186
	11.B: Primary Sources on Peace	189
	11.C: Making Peace	193
	11.D: Recommended Readings on Peace and Learning	197
12	Tying the Pieces Together: Synthesizing Information about Global Politics	199
	12.A: Goal Setting, Adaptation, and Self-reflection	200
	12.B: Primary Sources on Collective Goods	201
	12.C: Collective Action Problems and the Environment	205
	12.D: Recommended Readings on Collective Action Problems and the Environment	212
13	Determining Value: Evaluation and Assessment	217
	13.A: Be a Teacher!	218
	13.B: Primary Source on Human Rights	218
	13.C: The International Human Rights Regime	222
	13.D: Recommended Readings on Human Rights	233
Conclusion: Creating and Negotiating the Future		237
Problem-Posing Education, Research, and Writing		238
The Future of Global Politics		242
Recommended Readings on Creativity		244
Bibliography		245
Index of Primary Sources		261
Subject Index		263
About the Authors		269

Dedication and Acknowledgments

We are blessed to have had incredible support as we created this book. The idea for the book began in 2012, five years before we even started writing it. We had been laboring to teach international relations (IR) to our students, to make the subject matter as exciting as it was to us, but we had noticed that there was a lack of focus on real people in the way that most IR textbooks and resources presented the material. We longed to see people's actions and ideas come alive to students, and we began a conversation that took years to come to fruition and we are grateful to many people for their help and support along the way. First, we would like to acknowledge the individual people whose works we quote in this book as primary sources that reflect how people think and act in IR—we are grateful to them and to the organizations that gave us permission to reprint their works. We are also thankful to our colleagues in learning and teaching pedagogy whose works have strongly influenced us and who also connect pedagogy with justice. Finally, as we researched and wrote this book we received support from our families and friends, our colleagues and our library staff, our editor and their support staff, and especially from our students.

RONI KAY M. O'DELL

I would specifically like to thank my immediate family members, Matt Bates and José M. B. O'Dell, for their continual support and love. Major thanks to my colleagues and the librarians and administration at Seton Hill University who supported the research and writing of this book. I cannot thank my students enough for helping me conceptualize and finalize this project, specifically Paris Szalla, who carried out focus group sessions to obtain feedback from students in one iteration of my Introduction to International Relations course, and Charles Stull, who supported Paris in that process. Thank you to all my students for their excellent feedback during this process.

SASHA BREGER BUSH

I would especially like to thank Bill and Will Bush, and Debra Breger, for their love and support. I also want to profusely thank my students, who graciously and patiently worked with me over the years as I experimented, sometimes failing and sometimes not, and then tried again. Their feedback and willingness to try new things was indispensable as I developed and refined many of the techniques and practices included in this book.

Introduction

Taking Responsibility for Learning

This book invites readers to take responsibility for their own learning and to consider themselves lifelong *learners*. To be responsible for one's own learning means being curious about the world and seeking to understand life's mysteries. A commitment to learning supports building the knowledge, skills, and self-confidence necessary to make your life, the lives of others, and the world a better place. Intelligence is not an innate ability; it is learned. Developing intelligence and acquiring knowledge take time, practice, and a toolkit of learning techniques and approaches. Neither instructors, mentors, or guides, nor any book will be able to give individuals intelligence and knowledge, though they may be useful; rather, *individual learners* make use of them to gather, interpret, and synthesize knowledge for themselves. This book is written to support and encourage learners in global politics.

As opposed to a typical book that focuses on providing substantive knowledge around the subject area, this book invites learners to employ their curiosity and develop skills, practices, techniques, and habits of mind that are useful for engaging in knowledge-building and action around global politics. As children, we have unlimited curiosity and continually ask the question *why?* of those we trust: Why is the sky blue? Why do I have to eat vegetables? Why do I have to go to school? Many of the answers to such questions from trusted parents or elders ended with "just because" or "because I say so." Over the years we tend to lose our original curiosity, especially after being offered unsatisfying answers to our questions. This book challenges learners to *reclaim* their curiosity and interest in the world.

LEARNING ABOUT GLOBAL POLITICS

This book has a particular way of viewing and thinking about global politics. All books on global politics are written from a particular viewpoint or attitude, and it is important for both the author and the reader to recognize that perspective so as to identify different ways of thinking about the issues that other perspectives might provide. While the chapters avoid editorializing, readers may notice particular orientations in the text (related in the bullet points below).

- This book uses the terminology of *global politics*, not just *international relations or international politics* (for more on the conceptual difference, see chapter 1). The world is a complex place with dynamic and shifting power relations. Identifying and analyzing global problems or issues requires learners to build on a basic understanding of *nation-states* and their interactions with each other (as is implied in the term *international*) by considering global actors and relationships of all kinds, and identifying and exploring other levels of analysis that intersect with the global (e.g., household/individual, domestic, foreign policy, and international).
- Contemporary discussions of global politics are monopolized by academics from North America and Europe. This book encourages learners to think about global politics using both academic and non-academic sources of information from people and communities all over the world, as evidenced in the primary sources chosen to set the discussion and topics for many of the chapters.
- This book highlights matters of justice, freedom, and equality, and considers possibilities for social transformation in the global arena. This orientation is embedded in the learner-centered and critical pedagogy, highlighted for example in Paulo Freire's book and described as: "Education's role is to challenge inequality and dominant myths rather than socialize students into the status quo. Learning is directed toward social change and transforming the world, and 'true' learning empowers students to challenge oppression in their lives."[1]
- A concern with democratic dialogue and civic discourse, along with the democratic values of justice, equality, and freedom, underlies every chapter of this book. Dialogic interactions with other people prove transformative and allow for real understanding and learning to occur. The authors of this text, as instructors themselves, support creating democratic environments in the world and in the classroom that allow for dialogue and engagement, following Stephen Brookfield's advice that "good classrooms are inherently democratic" and that teaching impacts students for better or worse: "What we do as teachers makes a difference in the world. In our classrooms students learn democratic or manipulative behavior."[2]

THINKING ABOUT LEARNING (RESEARCH AND RESOURCES)

The discussion in this section is about the pedagogy and philosophy of learning that underpins this book on learning about global politics. Each of the chapters in this book offers ideas and advice about learning tools, habits, and approaches grounded in pedagogical and scientific evidence about best learning methods. The first subsection below on *Learner-Centered Teaching* (LCT) reviews the important pedagogical reasons for encouraging learners to teach themselves about a new subject matter rather than relying on others for that knowledge. The learner-centered rationale is important for understanding some of the content and organization of this book, especially since the format of this book differs greatly from the average introductory book on global politics. The second subsection reviews the basics from the scientific literature about how the brain learns. Although scientists have much left to research and understand, the evidence thus far points to important practical tools and techniques learners can use to study new information, including constant practice. Finally, the third subsection reviews the format of this book and other books that encourage the reader to take responsibility for their learning, providing a guide on how to successfully use the text and navigate the format.

Learner-Centered Learning and Teaching

This book supports learners of all sorts. It builds on books and resources on teaching and learning, books that would be excellent companions to this text, depending on the goals of the reader. Some resources, for instance, review effective teaching techniques and classroom instruction that an instructor might find helpful.[3] Additional excellent sources focus on the learner and on how to be a better learner and take responsibility for one's own learning, and are specifically geared to lifelong learners who are no longer learning in a classroom at a college or university.[4] Educational resources that review how to use learning tools and techniques for specific subject areas might also be beneficial to use along with this book, such as those supporting language learning, or how learners can understand math and science better.[5]

The pedagogy, or philosophy of teaching and learning, to which this book ascribes is called *Learner-Centered Teaching* (LCT).[6] LCT considers learning as both a communal and an individual process. Learning is communal because most humans learn well through connection, collaboration, and in dialogue with others.[7] Learning is individual because ownership of the learning process will result in knowledge and skill acquisition, and ultimately assist in an individual's ability to engage in dialogue, debate, and social transformation. LCT and other learning and teaching pedagogies recognize the importance of supportive environments for successful learning.[8] What sets LCT apart from other pedagogies is that it focuses on the learner more than the instructor or even the content, carefully transforming the classroom or learning environment to highlight the importance of individual motivation for knowledge acquisition.

LCT argues that the learner should be at the center of teaching techniques. LCT techniques have been a part of higher education discussions for many years, and research shows that students who are responsible for their own learning retain the information and master the skills to a greater extent and at a higher competency.[9] In a classroom context, the instructor's role is to empower the student to learn; the instructor serves as a guide and facilitator.[10] In contrast, higher education rules and processes generally center on the instructor more than the student in ways that limit knowledge acquisition. Consider for a moment how a classroom is typically set up, both in physical space and in social structure: Who is the focus of attention? Who does most of the talking? Who makes the decisions? If the answer is that the instructor is the focus of attention and talks and makes decisions, then you are thinking of an *instructor-centered* teaching and learning environment. In contrast, the LCT environment puts the student or learner at the center, and puts the responsibility for learning on the student, not on the instructor. To be sure, the LCT instructor still has a major responsibility for guiding the learner; indeed, the task of teaching is made much more difficult, but more rewarding, using LCT techniques. Not only does the LCT instructor have to be competent in their field, know a lot of information, and excel in analytical skills associated with the discipline, but they have to be able to guide students to discover knowledge and develop skills for themselves, rather than just tell students about knowledge or skills.

As a learner, whether in the context of a classroom or as a lifelong learner reading this book to gain a better understanding of global politics and issues, it is crucial to understand why taking responsibility for your own learning is important. LCT encourages transparency on the part of those guiding instruction because it allows learners to consider the rationale for learning a subject matter or completing an assignment, and it allows learners to decide for themselves whether the rationales and strategies presented connect with learning goals. The next section discusses the scientific foundation for the pedagogy described here, emphasizing how to be a lifelong learner and learner-centered methods of knowledge acquisition and application.

Research on Learning

Research on learning and the brain reveals that the brain changes over the course of a human being's lifetime and is capable of lifelong learning and development.[11] Research on how the brain works shows us that *intelligence* can be grown, developed, and refined over time, but learners must cultivate and nurture their brain with supportive learning tools, and lots of practice, in order to make full use of the brain's capacity. One foundational concept of LCT is that consistent practice and repetition is essential for long-term memory retention. Theories of brain function suggest that the more the practice and repetition of a thought-process, the stronger the relevant neural connections in the brain, allowing knowledge to move from short-term memory to long-term memory.[12] Neural pathways weaken without consistent use, and are ultimately eliminated to make way for newer and stronger connections, a process called *synaptic pruning*.[13]

The phrase "if you don't use it, you lose it" captures the theory in relation to memory and knowledge acquisition. Consider learning another language: no matter how hard one tries to keep the grammatical and syntax knowledge, limited practice speaking and writing in that language means that one becomes less adept in that language over time. The technique of *spaced repetition*, or practicing knowledge repeated over time, helps overcome the lack of memory retention.[14] The typical methods of teaching used in higher education are problematic from this perspective, because they encourage passivity among students, rather than the more active and independent learning processes that substantially change and improve memory retention.[15]

Learning new knowledge and skills can be difficult and may make new learners uncomfortable because the brain is not used to thinking in new ways or about new subject matter, especially when that subject matter challenges what a person already knows or believes. In addition, new knowledge can confront one's worldview and be very disorienting, if not downright disturbing (consider the famous controversy about whether or not the earth is round).[16] Further, new knowledge that challenges old knowledge can produce *cognitive dissonance*, where ideas or beliefs contradict each other and produce mental discomfort in a person.[17] However, exposure to new things is critical for learning: our brains continually change in response to stimuli. If the learning feels difficult or uncomfortable, it is actually a sign that knowledge acquisition is occurring. Challenging oneself to think about the lifelong learning process as a series of exciting and meaningful puzzles and mysteries can help overcome the feelings of discomfort that arise when confronted with new information.

OVERVIEW OF THIS LEARNER-CENTERED BOOK ON GLOBAL POLITICS

This book fills a gap in that it connects LCT with global politics. It is written for the learner, to help them accept and take responsibility for their learning.

Books and resources available for implementing LCT in global politics teaching and learning are limited, although there are a few exceptions, especially those that incorporate active learning models.[18] Typical books tend to focus on the subject matter, giving overviews, syntheses, basic facts, and broad generalizations of information. Yet this book is distinct from such books (especially other introduction to global politics or international relations texts) because while this book provides structure for learning about global politics, the format focuses on the learner. Each chapter offers advice and ideas for how to be prepared for the challenges encountered in the learning process.

In addition, this book is grounded in the idea that it is more interesting and engaging to learn about global politics when hearing directly from people about their lives and experiences and ideas, rather than learning about people's lives and ideas through second-hand descriptions and inevitably dry prose. Therefore, *primary documents* chosen for each chapter incorporate the ideas and experiences of people from around the world living at various times in history. The primary documents reveal the lives and ideas of politicians and policymakers, social leaders and activists, idealists and visionaries, pragmatists and critics, and pariahs and malcontents. The discussions following each of the primary documents encourage learners to think about global politics for themselves, to think about the voices and events represented in the primary documents, and to make their *own* determinations about what ideas, values, ideologies, and facts are important for understanding the world. The text provides guidance and suggestions but offers no dictates or dogma.

LEARNERS AND LEARNING ENVIRONMENTS

Throughout their lives, human beings have the opportunity to learn in all kinds of different ways. This book is written to be used by anyone who wishes to learn more about global politics and refine their learning skills so that they do not have to rely on others (like instructors) for knowledge acquisition. The rest of this section is broken down to address the two main kinds of learners who might use this text: (1) independent and lifelong learners who are learning on their own and (2) students in a college or university setting.

Independent and Lifelong Learners (Learning Everywhere)

This book may appeal to people who wish to learn about global politics but do not have the time or resources to learn in the traditional way (from an instructor in a classroom). The concept of LCT and the way that this book is structured is perfect for such learners because it directly supports them in accumulating knowledge on their own by giving guidance on where to look for that knowledge and what questions might be asked in determining how to gather that knowledge, and in describing skills, tools, and techniques that may be useful in analyzing and synthesizing such knowledge. The format of this text may also appeal to adult learners because they may take the information and utilize it in ways that are specific to their idiosyncratic ways of learning, developed based on their own past experience.[19]

For all learners, and especially for those without the benefit of a classroom or instructor, the LCT experience may feel uncomfortable because it is designed to take learners out of their comfort zone, reaffirm their own responsibility in learning, and engage them with deep and meaningful dialogue about the material: "The goal of learner-centered teaching is the development of students as autonomous, self-directed, and self-regulating learners."[20] When confronted with requests and expectations of personal responsibility, learners often engage in *passive* or *active* resistance.[21] As a learner, it is important to be able to recognize feelings and behaviors of *resistance* because the resistance behavior will obstruct deep learning of the subject matter. Once learners overcome the first feelings of resistance, the difficult task of taking responsibility for learning ensues and it challenges our preconceived notions of how to learn. Learning requires a lot of work and demands reflection and action.

Lifelong learners who are reading this book outside of the context of a classroom are in exactly the right place because this book is written for people who are willing to take responsibility for their own learning. In addition to using this book to learn, talking about what one is learning with others is an excellent way to boost learning capacity, whether that means talking about the information at the dinner table with family members, finding a friend to read with and discuss with in a regular format (perhaps over lunch), or forming a book club that meets regularly to discuss readings and ideas. The Shakespearian phrase, "the world is your oyster," signifies that an individual is able to take advantage and control of their surroundings and living situations in order to be the person they wish to be and change the world into the one they want to have. The best advice for learners who do not have the advantage of the classroom or an instructor is to utilize the world as the classroom, and everyone in life as instructors, for each person has experience and knowledge to add to the conversation.

Student Learners (Learning in a Classroom)

Students in an LCT classroom will be challenged to approach learning in ways they have not likely seen before even while universities desire to focus on learning over instruction.[22] In the typical classroom the style of learning is sometimes called the *banking* style in which instructors have knowledge and they *deposit* that knowledge into students through a lecture-style classroom setup, asking students to memorize the material and reiterate it back to the instructor through a variety of assignments.[23] While the banking style might support memorization, it does not encourage deeper understanding and assessment of the material, or allow for application in different contexts. The LCT classroom requires that students work on memorization outside of class, in their own study time as part of their daily practice in order to prepare for classroom discussion. Classroom time, then, is used to actively engage students in thinking about problems through assignments that ask students to reflect on and assess what they are learning to help them achieve a deeper understanding of the material and encourage them to learn independently.

The LCT classroom instruction style may make students feel uncomfortable and their first response may be *resistance* to the teaching style, resistance that they will have to constantly work to overcome.[24] Students might resist at first because LCT asks them to do a lot more work than the typical course they may have taken in college, and it asks them to take responsibility for their own learning. Students cannot rely on their instructor to tell them everything they need to know about the subject matter. Rather, the instructor is there as a guide, an *instructor-guide*, to give students advice as they approach new material. The instructor-guide sends students in the right direction, just as a mountain climbing guide or sports coach would do, and tells students about all the tools and skills they need along the way. Their instructor-guide gives them examples and helps them understand how to use the tools and skills, and how to approach the new material. But the instructor-guide will not do the work for students, and that may be frustrating because it is what many students have come to expect from their previous educational experience.

Students demonstrate *passive resistance* by nonverbally refusing to cooperate or only partially cooperating with an assignment, begrudgingly doing it just because they were told to do it by the authority figure, in this case, the instructor. Nonverbal *passive resistance* has many forms, but may include not taking the assignment seriously, withdrawing and wishing not to do the assignment, rolling one's eyes or placing one's head on the desk, dragging one's feet in team assignments or even being the free-rider in the team assignment, letting others do the work, and avoiding work by texting friends or surfing the internet. Students may demonstrate *active resistance* by openly questioning the instructor on the assignment and attempting to demand that the instruction be done in the banking style. A student may say to their instructor: Why don't you just tell us the answer? or What exactly will be on the midterm? or Isn't this what you get paid for?[25]

Whenever learners recognize they are engaging in *resistance* behavior, it is an opportunity to take a moment to ask themselves why, as in, "What is it about the learning experience that is causing me to feel uncomfortable?"

To address resistance, learners might consider writing or talking about their feelings. Writing about uncomfortable feelings may help learners identify the source of the feelings and may help to overcome them. Thinking deeply about the rationale behind the assignment is another tool for overcoming resistance (the instructor may have explained it, or the rationale may be somewhat hidden, but there is a reason for the assignment). Talking to the instructor about the feelings of resistance, especially asking the instructor in a respectful way the rationale for instruction method and assignments, will help learners understand the bigger picture. Classroom assignments are meant to prepare students for their later career possibilities and life-long learning practices (especially in honing critical thinking skills that are important in everyday interaction), so understanding the meaning behind classroom assignments is the starting point for lifelong learning and overcoming resistance.

LEARNING PRACTICES

This book is partly designed to help learners assemble a toolkit of learning practices for themselves, full of approaches, techniques, and habits useful for lifelong learning in global politics and beyond. Below we begin this conversation with a discussion of self-reflection and evaluation (both key practices to enhance *metacognition*) and dialogue (a central practice for social learning and for making social change).

Evaluating the Learning Experience

Constant practice, reflection, and self-evaluation allow learners to make the most of their learning experience. The key is to consider not only the *content* of learning but also the *process* of learning and whether one's learning is efficient, effective, and meaningful.

- *Reflective Journaling about the Learning Experience.*[26] Challenge yourself to journal about your learning experience since journaling provides a valuable outlet to reflect on what is going well and what needs to be improved in the learning process. On a regular basis (perhaps weekly) answer one or all of the following questions:
    - What were my learning goals this week?
    - What have I learned this week about myself as a learner?
    - What have I learned this week about my emotional responses to learning?
    - What learning tasks did I respond to most easily this week?
    - What learning tasks gave me the greatest difficulties this week?
    - What difficulties might I be having with learning tasks?

- *Short Essay Responses to Open-Ended Questions.* An excellent learning practice is to reflect in writing on lectures or readings shortly after listening or reading. The reflection process allows the mind to grapple more deeply (and actively) with the information and supports the skill of *retrieval* (or *recall*).[27] Creating questions to answer is an excellent way to challenge yourself, or you might respond to the following questions after reading or listening to a lecture:
  - What is the main idea or argument in the reading or lecture?
  - How does the reading or lecture connect with what I have learned thus far in my life experience?
  - What words or ideas or events do I need to know more about?

Dialoguing about Learning with Others

Learning that internalizes and applies knowledge and skills is consolidated when learners are engaged, alert, active, and in dialogue (an interactive, purposeful, cooperative exchange of ideas) with others: "Education should not be viewed as the transmission of knowledge by trained technicians, but rather as an interactive process through which problems are posed and answers collaboratively sought."[28] Independent, individual time for reading, reflection, and memorization is crucial to the learning experience, but so is dialoguing with others about the content, and these two practices are interdependent. If you are a classroom learner, be ready in advance to engage substantively in group discussions (reading and taking notes on readings, engaging in recall and reflection, and also critically reviewing and setting the information to memory in some way). Doing the work on learning in advance allows for deeper dialogue with others and may produce surprising results, like coming up with ideas for solving difficult social and political problems. The challenge to prepare for dialoguing with others applies to book clubs, discussion or study sessions with one partner, and the classroom experience.

THE LEARNER-CENTERED CHALLENGE

This book challenges learners to engage in practices and habits of mind when learning about global politics, learning practices that are mostly rushed through or ignored by the contemporary learner. We live in a fast-paced world where information is easily accessible through electronic technology, and therefore we are not often challenged to memorize or think deeply about new information and knowledge application. The general idea is that since the information is constantly at our fingertips, we needn't spend precious time putting it to memory. However, that sentiment does a disservice because it does not allow for long-term memory retention, blocks application of the information to other areas of our lives (because it is not stored in long-term memory and we therefore forget it), and impedes our ability to collectively create solutions to serious societal problems. This book challenges the global politics learner to utilize deep learning tools and techniques to be able to make the world a better place.

READING RECOMMENDATIONS ON LEARNING, LEARNER-CENTERED TEACHING, AND TEACHING GLOBAL POLITICS

On Learning

Brown, Peter C., Henry L. Roediger III, and Mark A. McDaniel. *Make it Stick: The Science of Successful Learning.* Cambridge, Massachusetts: Belknap Press of Harvard University Press, 2014.

Carey, Benedict. *How We Learn: The Surprising Truth About When, Where, and Why it Happens.* New York: Random House, 2015.

McGuire, Saundra Yancy. *Teach Yourself How to Learn: Strategies You Can Use to Ace Any Course at Any Level.* Sterling, VA: Stylus Publishing, 2018.

Oakley, Barbara. *A Mind for Numbers: How to Excel at Math and Science.* New York: Penguin Random House, 2014 (and free companion Coursera Course: *Learning How to Learn*).

Zull, James E. *The Art of the Changing Brain.* Sterling, VA: Stylus, 2002.

On Learner-Centered Teaching

Barkley, Elizabeth F. *Student Engagement Techniques: A Handbook for College Faculty.* San Francisco: Jossey-Bass, 2015.

Benassi, Victor A., Catherine E. Overson, and Christopher M. Hakala, eds. *Applying Science of Learning in Education: Infusing Psychological Science into the Curriculum.* Division 2, American Psychological Association, 2014. http://teachpsych.org/ebooks/asle2014/index.php

Brookfield, Stephen D. *Becoming a Critically Reflective Teacher.* 2nd ed. San Francisco: Jossey-Bass, 2017.

Doyle, Terry. *Learner-Centered Teaching: Putting the Research on Learning into Practice.* Sterling, VA: Stylus Publishing, 2011.

Freire, Paulo. Pedagogy of the Oppressed. Translated by Myra Bergman Ramos. London: Penguin Press, 1996.

Kaufman, Peter and Janine Schipper. *Teaching with Compassion: An Educator's Oath to Tech from the Heart.* Lanham, MD: Rowman & Littlefield, 2018.

Lang, James M. *Small Teaching: Everyday Lessons from the Science of Learning.* San Francisco: Jossey-Bass, 2016.

Noel, Terry W. "Lessons from the Learning Classroom." Journal of Management Education 28, no. 2 (April 2004): 188–206.

Seidel, Shannon B. and Kimberly D. Tanner. ""What is Students Revolt?"— Considering Student Resistance: Origins, Options and Opportunities for Investigation," Cell Biology Education—Life Sciences Education 12, no. 4 (Winter 2013): 586–95.

Shor, Ira. *Empowering Education: Critical Teaching for Social Change.* Chicago, IL: University of Chicago Press, 1992.

Weimar, Maryellen. *Learner-Centered Teaching: Five Key Changes to Practice.* 2nd Edition. San Francisco: Jossey-Bass, 2013.

On Teaching Global Politics

Breger Bush, Sasha and Roni Kay M. O'Dell. "Teaching About Poverty and Inequality: Critical Pedagogy and Personal Experience in the Learner-Centred Classroom." International Journal of Pluralism and Economics Education 9, no.1-2 (June 2018): 81–105.

Gormley-Heenan, Cathy and Simon Lightfoot, Eds. *Teaching Politics and International Relations.* New York: Palgrave MacMillan, 2012.

Lantis, Jeffrey S., Lynn M. Kuzma, and John Boehrer. *The New International Studies Classroom: Active Teaching, Active Learning.* Boulder; London: Lynne Rienner Publishers, 2000.

NOTES

1. Frances K. Stage, Patricia A. Muller, Jillian Kinzie, and Ada Simmons, *Creating Learning Centered Classrooms. What Does Learning Theory Have To Say?* (Washington, DC: ASHE-ERIC Higher Education Report, 1998), 57; quoted also in Maryellen Weimar, *Learner-Centered Teaching: Five Key Changes to Practice*, 2nd ed. (San Francisco: Jossey-Bass, 2013), 18.

2. Stephen D. Brookfield, *Becoming a Critically Reflective Teacher*, 2nd ed. (San Francisco: Jossey-Bass, 2017), 5, 92.

3. E.g., Lorin W. Anderson and David R. Krathwohl, *A Taxonomy for Learning, Teaching, and Assessing,* Abridged ed. (Boston, MA: Bacon, 2001); Benjamin Bloom, *Taxonomy of Educational Objectives: The Classification of Educational Goals, Handbook I: Cognitive Domain* (New York: Longmans, Green, 1956); James M. Lang, *Small Teaching: Everyday Lessons from the Science of Learning*, 1st ed. (San Francisco, CA: Jossey-Bass, 2016).

4. E.g., Anders Ericsson and Robert Pool, *Peak: Secrets from the New Science of Expertise*, First Mariner Books ed. (Boston: Mariner Books/Houghton Mifflin Harcourt, 2017); Barbara A. Oakley, *Mindshift: Break through Obstacles to Learning and Discover Your Hidden Potential* (New York: TarcherPerigee, 2017).

5. E.g., Benny Lewis, *Fluent in 3 Months: How Anyone at Any Age, Can Learn to Speak Any Language from Anywhere in the World*, 1st ed. (San Francisco:

HarperOne, 2014); Barbara Oakley, *A Mind for Numbers: How to Excel at Math and Science* (New York: Penguin Random House, 2014).

6. Weimer, *Learner-Centered Teaching*, 41. Wiemer specifically notes how LCT is different than *active learning* and other well-known teaching techniques because of its focus on student responsibility in learning.

7. Paulo Freire. *Pedagogy of the Oppressed*, trans. Myra Bergman Ramos (London: Penguin Books, 1996).

8. Richard E. Nisbett, *Intelligence and How to Get It: Why Schools and Cultures Count* (New York: W.W. Norton and Co., 2009).

9. E.g., Terry Doyle, *Learner-Centered Teaching: Putting the Research on Learning into Practice* (Herndon, VA: Stylus, 2011).

10. Weimer, *Learner-Centered Teaching*, 10–11.

11. James E. Zull, *The Art of the Changing Brain* (Sterling, VA: Stylus, 2002).

12. Oakley, *A Mind for Numbers*, 11–26; 42–43 (and free companion Coursera Course: Learning How to Learn). Oakley provides a very accessible overview of neuroscientific research, along with references to the scientific studies, off of which our discussion is based.

13. Sarah-Jayne Blakemore. *The Learning Brain: Lessons for Education* (New York: Blackwell, 2005).

14. Oakley, *A Mind for Numbers*, 43 (and free companion Coursera Course: Learning How to Learn). See also Oakley's references in footnote 22 on p. 276 for neuroscientific research specific to using spaced repetition.

15. E.g., Larry Cuban, *How They Taught: Constancy and Change in American Classrooms, 1890-1990*, 2nd ed. (New York: Teachers College Press, 1993).

16. Dava Sobel, *A More Perfect Heaven: How Copernicus Revolutionized the Cosmos* (London: Bloomsbury, 2011).

17. Horace Miner, "Body Ritual among the Nacerima," *American Anthropologist* 58, no. 3 (1956): 503–07.

18. E.g., Jeffrey S. Lantis, Lynn M. Kuzma, and John Boehrer, *The New International Studies Classroom: Active Teaching, Active Learning* (Boulder; London: Lynne Rienner Publishers, 2000); Cathy Gormley-Heenan and Simon Lightfoot, Eds., *Teaching Politics and International Relations* (New York: Palgrave MacMillan, 2012).

19. E.g., Malcolm S. Knowles, Elwood F Holton, and Richard A. Swanson. *The Adult Learner: The Definitive Classic in Adult Education and Human Resource Development*, 6th ed. (Amsterdam: Elsevier, 2005). Theories of adult learning focus on the different ways that learning may be incentivized or implemented based on longer history and deeper knowledge than younger people have had the chance to acquire.

20. Weimer, *Learner-Centered Teaching*, 10.

21. Weimer, *Learner-Centered Teaching*.

22. Robert B. Barr and John Tagg, "From Teaching to Learning--A New Paradigm for Undergraduate Education," *Change* 27, no. 6 (November/December 1995): 12–25.

23. Freire. *Pedagogy of the Oppressed*, 64.

24. Shannon B. Seidel and Kimberly D. Tanner. ""What Is Students Revolt?"— Considering Student Resistance: Origins, Options and Opportunities for Investigation,"

Cell Biology Education—Life Sciences Education 12, no. 4 (Winter 2013): 586–95; Weimer, *Learner-Centered Teaching,* 71–72. Brookfield, *Becoming a Critically Reflective Teacher,* 123; 137. Several works note that student resistance is to be expected in the LCT classroom and can be overcome, especially when instructors explain why they are engaging in teaching techniques with which students are unfamiliar.

25. Weimer, *Learner-Centered Teaching*, 155–210.

26. Brookfield, *Becoming a Critically Reflective Teacher,* 98–99; Weimer, *Learner-Centered Teaching,* 133–37. Brookfield provides a list of these questions and more when he discusses his journaling assignments. Weimer calls her assignments "learning logs."

27. Peter C. Brown, Henry L. Roediger III, and Mark A. McDaniel. *Make It Stick: The Science of Successful Learning* (Cambridge, MA: Belknap Press of Harvard University Press, 2014), 23–45.

28. Antonia Darder, Marta P. Baltodano, and Rodolfo D. Torres, Eds. *The Critical Pedagogy Reader,* 2nd ed. (New York: Taylor and Francis, Routledge, 2009), 312–13.

Chapter 1

Understanding Global Politics

To learn about global politics is to engage with matters of wealth, power, order, freedom, and justice at the global level. It is about how human beings interact with one another and the earth, across, through, and beyond borders. Learning about global politics also means thinking about *your* place in the world and the many ways in which the global system touches down in your own life, and also about how you live relative to others and how your life connects to the lives of others. In today's interconnected and interdependent world, almost every decision made by individuals, companies, or governments has global repercussions.[1] The 2008 financial crisis, for example, began as a household debt crisis in the United States and was felt in every corner of the world as markets shrunk and investments faltered.[2] In another example, as this book was being finalized in 2020, the coronavirus pandemic and associated disease (COVID-19) was realigning economies and politics as businesses shut down and supply chains were disrupted throughout the world. Most of us engage with global politics on a daily basis. Consider the global politics involved in working for a multinational corporation, in which knowledge of other cultures and religions is often a necessary job skill, or the way in which global politics shapes the choices available to you at the supermarket, or the global political consequences of who you vote for in a national election. Global politics is for everyone because we all live in the world together.

There are multiple ways to refer to the study of global issues: global politics, global studies, international relations, international politics, world politics, or the like. While this book favors the term *global politics*, it is a useful *international relations* (IR) tool in that it spends significant time discussing IR concepts, dynamics, and structures. The term IR refers to the academic discipline, developed in the United States and other western countries, dedicated to thinking about relationships between nation-states, more commonly referenced as states (i.e., governments that exercise control over territory and people), such as through war, peace, or trade.[3] An example of such an interaction would be the United States, Canada, and Mexico working together in the 1990s to create the North American Free Trade Agreement, or NAFTA, which was renegotiated in 2018–2019 and pending with a new name of the United States-Mexico-Canada agreement, or USMCA.[4]

In contrast to IR, the term *global politics* connotes a broader field of inquiry because it considers many kinds of actors (entities, whether individuals or groups) including, but not limited to, states. *International* literally means *between nations*, while *global* is a geographic category, that is, the *globe*, the whole world and all of the many actors and relationships that populate it. For example, multinational corporations (MNCs) like Apple and Coca Cola impact governments around the world and influence individual daily lives. Intergovernmental organizations (IGOs) like the United Nations support collaboration between governments. Nongovernmental organizations (NGOs) like Amnesty International conduct global research and report their findings. And transnational movements, like the global environmental justice movement, include individuals, civil society, and groups, coordinating to challenge the status quo. *Global politics* garners participation from academics across the social sciences and humanities, business and marketing, public health, and law, to name a few connected disciplines.

To further explore the meaning, content, and boundaries of *global politics*, this chapter includes and expounds upon a primary document (i.e., a text revealing a first-hand account of an issue): US president Harry Truman's 1949 Inaugural Address. Truman delivered the speech at a time in history when global politics were massively changing due to the end of World War II, one of the worst wars in history up to that time because of the number of state parties involved in the conflict and the number of deaths associated with the violence. Truman's speech outlined the terms of the new world order that would follow the war and was influential globally due to his position as President of the United States, the world's strongest state at the time and the most prominent state in leading negotiations on ending World War II.[5] In his speech, Truman challenged preconceived notions about how state governments relate to each other and built a normative foundation (based on *values* and *beliefs*) for state interactions for much of the latter twentieth century.

1.A: BLOOM'S TAXONOMY AND CHAPTER ORGANIZATION

This book is organized to meet its primary goal: to teach learners *how* to think about global politics, not *what* to think about global politics. Learners include anyone interested in understanding and assessing global politics, from students studying at a university to professionals seeking to expand their knowledge of how global issues affect their daily lives and jobs. As such, chapters are ordered to help learners *scaffold* the tools and techniques of knowledge acquisition, and bolster practices and habits of mind that contribute to effective analytical and critical thinking about global politics. Chapters are layered on top of one another, with each chapter building off the skills discussed in the previous chapter, as shown in Textbox 1.1. This book uses the basic framework first discussed by Benjamin Bloom (commonly known as Bloom's Taxonomy) and updated by Anderson and Krathwohl, to organize information.[6] Bloom's Taxonomy reveals the necessary levels of knowledge acquisition and consolidation that learners need when approaching a new subject matter in order to gain mastery in the subject.

TEXTBOX 1.1: LETTERED SECTIONS OF EACH CHAPTER IN THIS VOLUME

Each chapter includes the following lettered sections:

A. Suggestions about general skills, practices, tools, approaches, techniques, and habits of mind that may be useful to lifelong independent learners;
B. Primary source reading(s) in global politics;
C. Conversations about cognitive skill development rooted in the global political context provided by the primary sources, along with opportunities for learners to think, research, and participate;
D. Suggested additional readings and resources.

Table 1.1 shows Bloom's Taxonomy and how it informs the book's organizational scheme. The column labeled "cognitive skills framework" illustrates that learning is a dynamic and evolutionary process that involves multiple skill sets and types of knowledge that complement, support, and reinforce each other as a learner's knowledge and skills improve. For learners, building cognitive skills suggests the importance of focusing on basic knowledge and skill development early on when trying to master a new subject.

4 Chapter 1

Table 1.1 Bloom's Taxonomy of Cognitive Skills and Chapter Organization

Cognitive Skills Framework	Associated Chapter	Chapter Overview	Learning Tools in Chapter Section A
Overview: Remembering, Understanding, Applying, Analyzing, Synthesizing, Evaluating, Creating	Chapter 1: Understanding Global Politics	Provides a succinct overview of the critical thinking framework and questions for learners of global politics to pursue.	• Bloom's Taxonomy
Remembering—identifying and recalling new information Understanding—organize and categorize facts and ideas	Chapter 2: What Does That Mean? Definitions, Terminology and Jargon	Reviews how to study definitions (including etymology and history of words) in order to use and assess them appropriately in context.	• Global Politics Terminology • Annotated Bibliographies • T-Charts • Specialized Resources for Research
	Chapter 3: Who? Actors, Positions, Perspectives, and Interests	Relates how to go about identifying actors and their interests.	• Active Reading • Credible Internet Sources • Intercultural Competency
	Chapter 4: What or What is? Identifying What Matters	Identifies how to ask about important ideas, concepts, and facts in a situation under study.	• Tools for Using and Searching Internet Sources
	Chapter 5: Where? Assessing Geographic Location and Influence	Examines the importance of place to a situation under study.	• Taking Notes During Lectures • The Cornell Method of Note-Taking
	Chapter 6: Why? How Things Work in Global Politics	Reviews critical thinking skills for assessing parts of a whole.	• Memorizing Techniques • The Pomodoro Technique as a Study Method

	Chapter 7: When? Outlining Chronology	Examines the importance of chronology in a situation under study.	• Assessing Logical Reasoning • Creating Timelines
	Chapter 8: What's the Point? Isolating Main Ideas	Isolates main ideas of a situation under study and how to think about them.	• Techniques for Writing and Interpreting Thesis Statements
Applying—apply knowledge to new situations and compare between situations under study	Chapter 9: Making Connections: Applying Knowledge Across Global Political Contexts	Reviews how to determine what you are studying and why it is significant.	• Techniques for Recalling and Retrieving Information, not re-reading
Analyzing—breaking down information into components to more clearly understand complex social phenomena	Chapter 10: Breaking It Down: Categorizing and Analyzing Topics	Identifies how to break down large topics into smaller, more manageable pieces to study.	• Chunking as Study Method • Navigating Propaganda
	Chapter 11: Compare and Contrast: Clarifying and Distinguishing Concepts and Ideas	Provides tools and techniques for how to compare a situation under study to another situation.	• Creating Mindmaps • Tools and Techniques for Writing Efficiently
Synthesis—connecting ideas and concepts into a whole argument or clarifying position.	Chapter 12: Tying the Pieces Together: Synthesizing Information about Global Politics	Examines how to use information to infer ideas or understanding about global politics.	• Goal Setting and Adaptation • Self-Reflection Learning Tools
Evaluating—determining the value of an idea, concept, or event	Chapter 13: Determining Value: Evaluation and Assessment	Reviews questions to ask when determining the value of a situation under study.	• Being One's Own Teacher
Creating—combining ideas in new ways that reveal more about a situation under study	Conclusion: Creating and Negotiating the Future	Reviews how to come up with new ideas (built on old ones) and future thinking in global politics.	• Review • Problem-Posing Education, Research, and Writing

Organization and chapter development inspired by Lorin W. Anderson and David R. Krathwohl, *A Taxonomy for Learning, Teaching, and Assessing*, Abridged ed. (Boston, MA: Bacon, 2001); Benjamin Bloom, *Taxonomy of Educational Objectives: The Classification of Educational Goals, Handbook I: Cognitive Domain* (New York: Longmans, Green, 1956).

1.B: PRIMARY SOURCE ON GLOBAL POLITICS

Inaugural Address of Harry S. Truman, 33rd President of the United States (excerpt, 1949)[7]

Mr. Vice President, Mr. Chief Justice, fellow citizens:

I accept with humility the honor which the American people have conferred upon me. I accept it with a resolve to do all that I can for the welfare of this Nation and for the peace of the world.

In performing the duties of my office, I need the help and the prayers of every one of you.

I ask for your encouragement and for your support. The tasks we face are difficult. We can accomplish them only if we work together.

Each period of our national history has had its special challenges. Those that confront us now are as momentous as any in the past. Today marks the beginning not only of a new administration, but of a period that will be eventful, perhaps decisive, for us and for the world.

It may be our lot to experience, and in a large measure bring about, a major turning point in the long history of the human race. The first half of this century has been marked by unprecedented and brutal attacks on the rights of man, and by the two most frightful wars in history. The supreme need of our time is for men to learn to live together in peace and harmony.

The peoples of the earth face the future with grave uncertainty, composed almost equally of great hopes and great fears. In this time of doubt, they look to the United States as never before for good will, strength, and wise leadership.

It is fitting, therefore, that we take this occasion to Proclaim to the world the essential principles of the faith by which we live, and to declare our aims to all peoples. . . .[8]

We are moving on with other nations to build an even stronger structure of international order and justice. We shall have as our partners countries which, no longer solely concerned with the problem of national survival, are now working to improve the standards of living of all their people. We are ready to undertake new projects to strengthen a free world.

In the coming years, our program for peace and freedom will emphasize four major courses of action.

First, we will continue to give unfaltering support to the United Nations and related agencies, and we will continue to search for ways to strengthen their authority and increase their effectiveness. We believe that the United Nations will be strengthened by the new nations which are being formed in lands now advancing toward self-government under democratic principles.

Second, we will continue our programs for world economic recovery.

Understanding Global Politics 7

This means, first of all, that we must keep our full weight behind the European recovery program. We are confident of the success of this major venture in world recovery. We believe that our partners in this effort will achieve the status of self-supporting nations once again.

In addition, we must carry out our plans for reducing the barriers to world trade and increasing its volume. Economic recovery and peace itself depend on increased world trade.

Third, we will strengthen freedom-loving nations against the dangers of aggression.

We are now working out with a number of countries a joint agreement designed to strengthen the security of the North Atlantic area. Such an agreement would take the form of a collective defense arrangement within the terms of the United Nations Charter.

We have already established such a defense pact for the Western Hemisphere by the treaty of Rio de Janeiro.

The primary purpose of these agreements is to provide unmistakable proof of the joint determination of the free countries to resist armed attack from any quarter. Every country participating in these arrangements must contribute all it can to the common defense.

If we can make it sufficiently clear, in advance, that any armed attack affecting our national security would be met with overwhelming force, the armed attack might never occur.

I hope soon to send to the Senate a treaty respecting the North Atlantic security plan.

In addition, we will provide military advice and equipment to free nations which will cooperate with us in the maintenance of peace and security.

Fourth, we must embark on a bold new program for making the benefits of our scientific advances and industrial progress available for the improvement and growth of underdeveloped areas.

More than half the people of the world are living in conditions approaching misery. Their food is inadequate. They are victims of disease. Their economic life is primitive and stagnant. Their poverty is a handicap and a threat both to them and to more prosperous areas.

For the first time in history, humanity possesses the knowledge and skill to relieve the suffering of these people.

The United States is pre-eminent among nations in the development of industrial and scientific techniques. The material resources which we can afford to use for assistance of other peoples are limited. But our imponderable resources in technical knowledge are constantly growing and are inexhaustible.

I believe that we should make available to peace-loving peoples the benefits of our store of technical knowledge in order to help them realize their aspirations for a better life. And, in cooperation with other nations, we should foster capital investment in areas needing development.

Our aim should be to help the free peoples of the world, through their own efforts, to produce more food, more clothing, more materials for housing, and more mechanical power to lighten their burdens.

We invite other countries to pool their technological resources in this undertaking. Their contributions will be warmly welcomed. This should be a cooperative enterprise in which all nations work together through the United Nations and its specialized agencies whenever practicable. It must be a worldwide effort for the achievement of peace, plenty, and freedom.

With the cooperation of business, private capital, agriculture, and labor in this country, this program can greatly increase the industrial activity in other nations and can raise substantially their standards of living.

Such new economic developments must be devised and controlled to the benefit of the peoples of the areas in which they are established. Guarantees to the investor must be balanced by guarantees in the interest of the people whose resources and whose labor go into these developments.

The old imperialism—exploitation for foreign profit—has no place in our plans. What we envisage is a program of development based on the concepts of democratic fair-dealing.

All countries, including our own, will greatly benefit from a constructive program for the better use of the world's human and natural resources. Experience shows that our commerce with other countries expands as they progress industrially and economically.

Greater production is the key to prosperity and peace. And the key to greater production is a wider and more vigorous application of modern scientific and technical knowledge.

Only by helping the least fortunate of its members to help themselves can the human family achieve the decent, satisfying life that is the right of all people.

Democracy alone can supply the vitalizing force to stir the peoples of the world into triumphant action, not only against their human oppressors, but also against their ancient enemies-hunger, misery, and despair.

On the basis of these four major courses of action we hope to help create the conditions that will lead eventually to personal freedom and happiness for all mankind.

If we are to be successful in carrying out these policies, it is clear that we must have continued prosperity in this country and we must keep ourselves strong.

Slowly but surely we are weaving a world fabric of international security and growing prosperity.

We are aided by all who wish to live in freedom from fear—even by those who live today in fear under their own governments.

We are aided by all who want relief from lies and propaganda—those who desire truth and sincerity.

We are aided by all who desire self-government and a voice in deciding their own affairs.

We are aided by all who long for economic security—for the security and abundance that men in free societies can enjoy.

We are aided by all who desire freedom of speech, freedom of religion, and freedom to live their own lives for useful ends.

Our allies are the millions who hunger and thirst after righteousness.

In due time, as our stability becomes manifest, as more and more nations come to know the benefits of democracy and to participate in growing abundance, I believe that those countries which now oppose us will abandon their delusions and join with the free nations of the world in a just settlement of international differences.

Events have brought our American democracy to new influence and new responsibilities. They will test our courage, our devotion to duty, and our concept of liberty.

But I say to all men, what we have achieved in liberty, we will surpass in greater liberty.

Steadfast in our faith in the Almighty, we will advance toward a world where man's freedom is secure.

To that end we will devote our strength, our resources, and our firmness of resolve. With God's help, the future of mankind will be assured in a world of justice, harmony, and peace.

1.C: LEARNING HOW TO STUDY GLOBAL POLITICS

Learning about global politics requires learners to collect and remember facts about politics, history, society, culture, economy, and ecology around the world and then to understand facts by organizing them in meaningful ways. This section provides an overview of the skills learners will build—based in Bloom's Taxonomy—throughout the rest of the book. Chapters 2–8 support learners in building lower-order thinking skills by practicing tools and techniques in *remembering* and *understanding* that identify, categorize, and assign meaning to important facts, concepts, issues, patterns, relationships, and dynamics necessary for a basic understanding of global politics. The chapters cover basic tools and techniques for studying using the following questions: *What Does That Mean?* (chapter 2), *Who?* (chapter 3), *What or What Is?* (chapter 4), *Where?* (chapter 5), *Why and How?* (chapter 6), *When?* (chapter 7), and *What's the Point?* (chapter 8). Chapters 9–14 then build higher-order thinking skills of *applying* (chapter 9), *analyzing* (chapter

10–11), *synthesizing* (chapter 12), *evaluating* (chapter 13), and *creating* (chapter 14).

What Does That Mean? Definitions, Terminology, and Jargon

Learners inevitably encounter words, phrases, and terms that are unfamiliar when learning a new subject, including words that seem familiar but that the author is using in an unfamiliar way or context. When such definitional and conceptual questions occur, it is important to *look up the unfamiliar terms using dictionaries and encyclopedias*. In Truman's speech, key terms like *freedom, democracy, communism,* and *international order* seem important to his overall perspective on the United States' role in the world at the beginning of the Cold War in 1949 and are worth investigating. Chapter 2 provides tools and resources to help learners with such tasks and includes a discussion of credible sources of information and the appropriate number of sources to consult.

Who? Actors, Positions, Perspectives, and Interests

The question *who?* is one of the most important questions learners might ask of anything they study in global politics because the answer helps identify who is involved in a situation and what their interests may be. A primary document, such as Truman's inaugural address, does not provide an overview or insight into the *actors* or people involved with the text and the situation it represents: rather, learners must identify what is missing from the text and knowledge, fire up their curiosity, and then find the answers to questions in order to fill in the missing information. Answering the question *who?* gives learners important hints about why the author writes and speaks as they do and provides insights into the author's perspective and how their text or speech would be received by their audience. Chapter 3 provides guidance on the process of thinking about actors, positions, perspectives, and interests.

Thus, questions to ask of President Truman's speech would be: Who was the individual person (Truman) who gave this inaugural address? Did Truman act and speak primarily from his perspective and experience as a man, an American citizen, or a president? In answer, we know Truman was President, but he had become so after serving as Vice President (VP) for the beloved President Franklin D. Roosevelt (FDR) even though his nomination as VP at the 1944 Democratic National Convention was contentious—how might that information help clarify the meaning of the language or ideas included in the inaugural address? In addition, one might ask what roles Truman filled during his adult life that may shed light on his ideas (consider, for instance, where he grew up and what perspective he had about the world and politics).[9] Further, considering how the office of the president and the legacy of the previous presidents—such as FDR, the most recent US president in this case—would offer additional information that illuminates our understanding of the speech.

In addition, an important practice to implement when considering a written piece of work is identifying the intended or unintended audience, because the author was, in a sense, performing for that audience. In the case of Truman's speech one might ask: *Who* was the intended audience? Truman wrote his inaugural speech to deliver to the United States Congress and to the American people, not only to signify his plans for the executive office but also to convince Congress to distribute funds to Europe for redevelopment. Knowing his audience was Congress, we might ask how Truman might have crafted his speech in such a way as to specifically target and influence members of Congress? For instance, every reference he made to the United States was a positive one, invoking American *exceptionalism* as a standard for everyone else in the world to follow, a rhetorical device that might have appealed to particular members, especially those not of Truman's Democratic Political Party. Consider one of the first phrases where Truman says, "The peoples of the earth . . . look to the United States as never before for good will, strength, and wise leadership." Are there other places in the speech where Truman explicitly or implicitly signifies American *exceptionalism*? Why would using American *exceptionalism* rhetoric help Truman achieve his goals of having Congress approve funding for his development project? Asking such questions helps learners identify the influence that an audience has on a piece of written work.

What or What Is? Identifying What Matters

The question *what?* focuses on identifying, defining, and understanding relationships, patterns, dynamics, structures, and institutions central to thinking about global politics. Many *what?* questions—as in, *what is this?*—appear first as ideas, terms, or concepts in need of definition, and then as global political phenomena at work in the world. Thus, chapter 2 reviews important tools and practices in learning and defining key terms, and chapter 4 builds on definitional tools to identify and assess relationships, patterns, dynamics, structures, and institutions indicated by conceptual definitions.

For example, before reading the primary document in this chapter, one might need to answer the following question: w*hat is* an inaugural address? An *inaugural address* is a speech given at an inauguration ceremony when a person is inducted into a specific job or post. In this case the US presidential inaugural address is a tradition in which the new president gives a speech to Congress to signify to Congress (and to the American people) the policies of the new presidential administration and the major ideas, concepts, and beliefs the president holds that will guide executive office decision-making in the years to come. With such initial definitions in mind, a learner might consider finding other instances for comparison and contrast. For instance, Truman's inaugural address made a huge impact on foreign policy for the subsequent four decades—see chapter 6 for more on that influence—but considering it in comparison to the first US presidential inaugural address by George Washington will provide important information on differences in theme and environment.[10] A key question about meaning might arise that shows the connection from remembering to understanding in Bloom's Taxonomy: why does an *inaugural address* have meaning?

To give another example, Truman's speech references the term *nation* when he refers to the "welfare of this Nation," yet there are multiple terms that are used interchangeably to mean different things in alternate contexts related to the term nation: *nation, nation-state, nationalism, tribe, state, patriotism, or country*.[11] Additionally, definitions might not fit with the way that one thinks or uses the term in popular vernacular, and definitions may be interchangeable in some respects. The term *nation* can mean shared territory, as in the nation of the United States (the citizens connected to the territory and government as the nation). Alternately, the term may be used to discuss governments and representation, especially when used as a conjunction: nation-state. Further, the term may reference a group of people who share a similar history, culture, or other identifying characteristic. The problem, then, is that all of the applications of the term *nation* are correct, depending on context. What does Truman mean when he says "this *Nation*" (emphasis added)? Does he mean the American people, the US government, territorial boundaries, or some other group of individuals? It would appear that he means American citizens as holding a shared history, but does he also mean territory or government representation? Go through the speech and find every instance of the terms associated with the ideas of *nation* or *nationalism*, assess the meaning and consider the implications for how people relate to and organize with one another around the world.

What other entities exist and have an impact on a large geographic area or on multiple groups of people? Truman refers to a group of institutions that were quite new at the delivery of this speech but have since proliferated in the world with multiple categories under which they might fall: *international organizations (IOs), intergovernmental organizations (IGOs), nongovernmental organizations (NGOs), transnational interest groups,* etc. Consider the institutions that Truman refers to in his speech and how they might impact the world: the United Nations (UN) and the "joint agreement designed to strengthen the security of the North Atlantic area" that later became the collective security organization called the North Atlantic Treaty Organization (NATO). In order to get a better grasp of *what* is being discussed, investigate the definition, and then find out more about the history and function of that entity. Both the entities mentioned here, the UN and the NATO, continue to exist and have a large impact in global politics.[12]

Where? Assessing Geographic Location and Influence

Assessing *where* a situation under study is located in the world helps one think about physical and spatial relationships between actors and the political significance of geographic positioning (in the case of geography, positionality refers to how the spatial and physical positioning of actors in relation to each other impacts their influence in the world and access to power and resources).[13] Asking *where?* allows learners to assess geopolitics, that is, how the physical locale and associated characteristics intersect with and influence political interests, motivations, and decisions. The next step is to identify history associated with that place (whether the territory was historically independent or colonized, for instance), the people who live there (present and past) and their interests and cultures, and the resources and animals of the area (size, ease of accessibility, domesticated or wild, etc.). Finally, assessing what all those characteristics mean politically in the situation under study is crucial. For more depth, see chapter 5.

Where did Truman deliver his inaugural address? Pomp and circumstance surround the presidential inaugural address. Since the address is such an important speech (delivered to the US Congress, and heard by American citizens and people worldwide who derive clues about the ideology and planned policies of the new presidential administration) the customs surrounding it are important to review.[14] Truman delivered his inaugural address at the east portico of the US Capitol after taking the oath of office administered by the Chief Justice of the Supreme Court. Consider the significance of delivering the address in front of the US Capitol. Take some time to look up some pictures of the US Capitol building: What do you notice about the architecture and the sense of awe that it creates? Where and when in the world does the architecture come from (consider the Roman and Greek roots and the significance therein)? While the variation on place of delivery of the inaugural address has not significantly changed, note how it has changed over time and why; consider, for example, that since Ronald Reagan's inauguration in 1981 the location of the delivery has been the west front of the US Capitol rather than the east portico.[15]

Where in the world does Truman refer to in his inaugural address? Notice how often Truman refers to places beyond the United States, indicating an *expansionist* rather than *isolationist* policy.[16] It is not only American citizens who are the subjects of Truman's speech but the "peoples of the earth," and Truman says that "we take this moment to Proclaim to the world . . . and to declare our aims to all peoples" [*sic*]. It is evident from the speech that Truman means to be engaged in world politics rather than merely focus on national concerns. Further, recall that part of Truman's goal with this address was to secure monetary support from the US Congress to provide aid for redevelopment in Europe after the end of World War II. He references Greece, Turkey, the Soviet Union, the nations of Europe, among others—why are those areas of the world so important? Do those areas have specific kinds of resources that would influence US policy toward them (i.e., incentivize US support)? Geopolitical considerations are prominent in the speech, especially when Truman discusses the collective security organization that became known later as the North Atlantic Treaty Organization.

Why? How Things Work in Global Politics

The question *why?*—as in *why is it like this?*—further helps learners to explore the meaning of a situation under study by encouraging curiosity, that is, not accepting information or actions at face value and investigating the reasons for social and political behavior. Part of the goal in answering the question *why?* is to fill in the question of *how?* as in *how does this work?* Describing a situation under study gives learners a sense of what is going on and supports assessing *why* it happens in the first place and why it is important to study. When a learner arrives at the point in their studies where they are assessing the meaning behind an issue or event—answering the question *why*—it is important to have already answered basic identifying questions of *who?*, *what?* or *what is?*, and *where?* Basic knowledge is necessary for making informed causal or correlational statements and to help identify the *why?* or *how?* questions to ask. Chapter 6 provides additional tools and resources on these points.

Consider a *why?* or *how?* question one might ask of Truman's speech after amassing initial basic information. *Why is an inaugural address important?* Consider that at the time of Truman's speech the United States had just emerged as one of the leading countries in the world, still strong in military might in the aftermath of World War II (and arguably because of World War II), and acting as main negotiator in crafting the postwar world order by, for example, hosting the negotiations for the creation of intergovernmental organizations, for example, the Bretton Woods Institutions. Countries, and people who do not have as much military or economic might or influence, will look to those who do for guidance, formation of alliances, or out of fear for what might befall them at the hands of stronger and richer powers. This suggests the importance of what a US president might say in the inaugural address, especially at a time in history when the United States was in the process of becoming a *hegemonic power*. One might also ask a *how?* question such as, how does a US president make decisions and impact policy? Truman's goal with his inaugural address was indeed to impact policy by incentivizing the US Congress to support his goals in the world, especially with the monetary support that Truman needed to engage in the *expansionist* or *liberal internationalist* policies that were the hallmarks of his administration's foreign policy.

When? Outlining Chronology and Historical Context

Asking *when?* of a text is to ask about the historical context of an event or issue that one is studying. Knowing chronological context provides crucial information necessary for understanding what is going on in the situation under study, but also for applying one's knowledge to similar situations in other contexts. Asking *when* the situation under study occurred historically in relation to other events, either at a local or national level or at a global level, gives insight into why the situation under study happened at all, and why people acted in the way they did. Chapter 7 reviews the skills important to answering chronological questions and embedding analysis in historical context.

Identifying international events and context helps to illuminate the importance and meaning behind Truman's inaugural address. For example, Truman delivered his inaugural address a few years after the end of World War II, a major event that affected people all over the globe, and which Truman himself was involved in resolving (by participating in negotiations to end the war after President FDR died). World War II was named this because it extended around the world and had an indelible effect on many people and communities, and more troops and citizens were killed in this war than any other war up to that point (approximately 60 million dead; compare that with 15 million dead in World War I). The devastation of World War II had a lasting effect on the perspectives of people who ended the war and who went on to become new government leaders. How does the context of World War II (1939–1945) ending impact the way Truman wrote and delivered his speech in 1949, and what textual evidence shows he was thinking about the end of the war?

Local or national events and context further elucidate meaning and provide depth to understanding Truman's inaugural address, to which he even refers in his speech when he says, "Each period of our national history has had its special challenges. Those that confront us now are as momentous as any in the past." Consider that Truman's speech was delivered after he won a national election that was fraught with contention, especially in the aftermath of the death of one of the most beloved US presidents of history. FDR was elected to four terms as president, even though no president before him had served more than two terms. Partially because of FDR's untimely death, Congress revised the US Constitution to limit the number of terms a president may serve to two terms. Truman stepped into FDR's position and led in a very different manner, making many people uneasy across the nation and in the Congress. Studying the US national historical political context will help make Truman's speech more understandable because the context helps bring together an assessment of the individual (and his perspective and interests) with the audience (and their interests) and can help interpret particular ideas that might not mean the same thing or make sense in today's context.

What's the Point? Isolating the Main Idea

The series of basic questions (i.e., *who? what? where? why?* and *when?*) encourages learners to increase their knowledge and understanding of global politics, leading to a crucial question: *What's the point?* as is covered in chapter 8. Sometimes when we ask this question we are asking what the *author's* main idea is; that is, the central message that they wanted their audience to understand. On the surface Truman's main point is support for peace, democracy, trade, and the social good at home and abroad. But politics are not often straightforward, and speeches like Truman's are laden with subtext closely linked to historical events. Indeed, Joseph Stalin, leader of the Union of Soviet Socialist Republics (USSR) in 1949, might have had a different understanding altogether of Truman's main idea. Stalin, perceiving the United States as his main rival on the world stage in the wake of World War II, might have seen this speech as a show of strength and determination to fight against Soviet communism and also as an attempt to buy the loyalty of other countries who had not yet chosen a side in the bourgeoning Cold War. (Notice Truman's commitment to foreign aid to fight poverty. Might this aid also be used to curry favor with other countries and create alliances against the USSR?)

Applying

Crucially, the next step in studying a given situation is to investigate *how* your learning applies to other areas of study, or even to your own life. Indeed, IR started as an academic discipline with scholars analyzing historical intergovernmental exchanges in order for them to apply their knowledge of past exchanges to present and future foreign policy problems. Learning how to apply knowledge to new contexts allows learners to figure out *why* they are studying a particular situation or text and builds upon basic knowledge and expertise. Global political analysts often apply theoretical concepts to practical experience, the experiences of one country or community to those of another, and existing methodological techniques to new data sets, among other forms of *applying* in the field. Chapter 9 reviews the skills to apply existing knowledge to new situations or contexts.

There is always a reason for studying a text or a situation. A central question to ask of anything you are learning is: *How is this situation under study relevant?* The answer may be hard to find (it may take some time to understand, it may require developing critical thinking skills, it may take a lot of thinking and writing and exposure to new ideas and contexts), but it is worth it. In order to apply knowledge to a new context, learners might use a conceptual heuristic (chapter 9 uses the heuristic of *inequality*), or might simply *compare and contrast* different types of situations (chapter 11 reviews the compare and contrast technique in the context of analysis or breaking down a whole into smaller parts), asking how they relate to each other and whether one situation can inform interpretation of another.

Analyzing

After going through the stages of remembering, understanding, and applying, deeper *analysis* of the situation under study becomes possible. When *analyzing* something, learners take apart the whole and dig deeper into some of the main ideas already identified, drawing connections and making comparisons. Chapter 10 reviews tools useful for breaking down main ideas into their various parts, ensuring comprehension of those components in the interests of having a better picture of the whole. Taking apart the concept so as to understand the component parts in relation to the whole is an important part of analytical capabilities.

Chapter 11 reviews how to compare and contrast between two situations, primary documents, or other global political phenomena. An excellent way to analyze a situation is to identify a component of that situation and study it at length, comparing and contrasting the component within the situation under study, and against other like or unlike situations. When you compare, you consider a component of a whole in juxtaposition with itself or another example. For instance, Truman's inaugural address could be compared with other presidential inaugural addresses throughout US history, or compared with similar inaugural addresses by Truman's contemporaries, such as Joseph Stalin. In comparing, we would continue by asking whether the histories, cultures, and mindsets of the different people who wrote the two documents impacted how they thought of democracy and human rights. Further, in addition to comparing, contrasting takes particular notice of concepts or situations that are very similar but bear a striking difference from each other. Noting difference and what it entails will help learners assess what is important in a particular context.

Tying the Pieces Together: Synthesizing Information about Global Politics

Synthesis occurs when learners combine bits and pieces of information about global politics into a meaningful whole that helps explain or clarify the situation under study, reviewed in detail in chapter 12. A synthesis marries disparate pieces together when appropriate in order to illuminate a significant trend, pattern, or dynamic in global politics. For instance, a learner might ask of the document or situation under study: *Of which whole is this piece of information a part?* Considering Truman's speech and seen in the light of its historical context, the concepts and ideas in the speech (democracy, communism, containment, etc.) all fit into a discussion of Cold War politics.

Determining Value: Evaluation and Assessment

One of the most important elements of higher-order learning is that of evaluation, determining the value or importance of a concept, idea, situation under study, or other. It is important to note that all of us engage in evaluation every day, making unconscious decisions based on habit, and making conscious decisions based on individual desires and valuation ordering (for instance, whether you choose to eat pizza or salad at lunch may be based on your desire for taste or health or need for calories). The evaluation discussed in chapter 13 is conscious evaluation based on internal consistency or external performance standards or other criteria, rather than on egocentric values.

Create: Negotiating the Future of Global Politics

Becoming a force for social transformation in global politics requires one to draw on all of the lower- and higher-order skill sets discussed in this book, leveraging existing knowledge and skills to create something new. Creating something new in global politics might mean looking at an old problem in a new way or addressing a new problem with an innovative solution. It might mean that you borrow tools from other disciplines to intervene in debates about global politics in the social sciences. Creating something new might mean that learners invent a new technology or program or policy to help address a pressing social problem.

Above all else, creating is an *imaginative* process in which you take what you already know and manipulate it and play with it and add to it so as to do or say something new. It may be new to the world or it may just be new to you. Creativity is an essential attribute for learners of all kinds, and absolutely necessary to enact positive change in the world. Chapter 14 introduces you to the process of creating new ideas and solutions in global politics.

What Comes Next?

This chapter presented a shortened version of the tools necessary to build basic knowledge and cognitive skills, as shown in Bloom's Taxonomy. Chapters 2–8 provide learners with tools and techniques that help amass basic knowledge and understanding, and practice basic analytical and critical thinking skills, asking and answering the questions *who?*, *what?* or *what is?*, *where?*, *why?* or *how?*, and *when?* Once a learner acquires depth and breadth of understanding on a subject area, it is possible to delve into deeper and higher-order critical thinking skills, covered in chapters 9–14: *applying*, *analyzing*, *synthesizing*, *evaluating*, and *creating*.

1.D: RECOMMENDED READINGS TO USE ALONG WITH THIS BOOK (IF YOU SO CHOOSE)

This book is best used alone because it encourages learners to take responsibility for their own learning and find the information they need to know about global politics on their own (see the Introduction for the rationale). However, some learners may want to build learner-centered education into their practice gradually while continuing to use some of the excellent books that already exist for global politics courses. The list below provides a good starting point for books that cover the field of global politics and international relations with breadth and depth.

Art, Robert J., and Robert Jervis, eds. *International Politics: Enduring Concepts and Contemporary Issues.* New York: Longman (Division of Pearson), 2017.
Baylis, John, Steve Smith, and Patricia Owens. *The Globalization of World Politics: An Introduction to International Relations.* Oxford: Oxford University Press, 2017.
Bova, Russell. *How the World Works: A Brief Survey of International Relations.* Pearson: New York, 2011.
Campbell, Patricia J, Aran MacKinnon, and Christy R Stevens. *An Introduction to Global Studies.* Somerset: Wiley, 2010.
Frieden, Jeffrey, David Lake, and Kenneth Schultz. *World Politics: Interests, Interactions, Institutions.* New York, London: W. W. Norton & Company, 2010.
Lamy, Steven L, John Scott Masker, John Baylis, Steve Smith, and Patricia Owens. *Introduction to Global Politics.* 5th ed. New York: Oxford University Press, 2019.
Kinsella, David, Bruce Russett, and Harvey Starr, Eds. *World Politics: The Menu for Choice.* 10th ed. Boston: Wadsworth, Cengage Learning, 2013.
Mingst, Karen and Ivan M. Arreguin-Toft. *Essentials of International Relations.* New York; London: W. W. Norton & Company, 2016.
Nau, Henry. *Perspectives in International Relations: Power, Institutions, and Ideas.* 7th ed. Thousand Oaks, CA: CQ Press/Sage, 2020.
Pevehouse, Jon C., and Joshua S. Goldstein. *International Relations.* Pearson: New York, 2017.

NOTES

1. Manfred Steger, *Globalization: A Very Short Introduction*, 4th ed. (Oxford: Oxford University Press, 2017).
2. Adam Tooze, *Crashed: How a Decade of Financial Crisis Changed the World* (New York: Penguin Books, 2019).
3. Robert Keohane, *Neorealism and Its Critics* (New York: Columbia University Press, 1986).
4. E.g., Maxwell A. Cameron and Brian W Tomlin. *The Making of NAFTA: How the Deal Was Done* (Ithaca, NY: Cornell University Press, 2000).
5. E.g., "Harry S. Truman: A Resource Guide," The Library of Congress, Web Guides. Last modified October 20, 2015. https://www.loc.gov/rr/program/bib/presi

dents/truman/bibliography.html; Robert Ferrell, *Harry S. Truman: A Life* (Columbia: University of Missouri Press, 1994); David McCullough, *Truman* (New York: Simon & Schuster, 1992). For more on the creation of the post–World War II world order and the Bretton Woods Institutions, see Benn Steil, *The Battle of Bretton Woods: John Maynard Keynes, Harry Dexter White, and the Making of a New World Order* (Princeton: Princeton University Press, 2014).

6. Lorin W. Anderson and David R. Krathwohl, *A Taxonomy for Learning, Teaching, and Assessing*, Abridged ed. (Boston, MA: Bacon, 2001); Benjamin Bloom, *Taxonomy of Educational Objectives: The Classification of Educational Goals, Handbook I: Cognitive Domain* (New York: Longmans, Green, 1956). There are many updates and criticisms to Bloom's Taxonomy, especially in the cognitive psychology research on the levels of cognition. This text does not engage in that discussion; rather, it uses Bloom's taxonomy as a framework to show learners how to engage in knowledge acquisition and critical thinking of global politics, assuming learners are learning about the subject for the first time.

7. Harry S. Truman, "Inaugural Address of Harry S. Truman" (speech, Washington, D.C., January 20, 1949), The Avalon Project, Yale Law School (reproduced based on fair use doctrine from Section 107 of US Copyright Law), https://avalon.law.yale.edu/20th_century/truman.asp.

8. The section of Truman's speech in which he compares democracy and communism is excised in this reprinting but is important to read in order to understand how Truman and his administration thought about global politics.

9. The Harry S. Truman Presidential Library and Museum is an excellent place to start finding the answers to such questions.

10. All presidential inaugural addresses are public domain, meaning that the public owns and can have easy access to them because they are produced by the federal government. There are several online databases that post them, including the Avalon Project by Yale University https://avalon.law.yale.edu/subject_menus/inaug.asp, the Library of Congress Web Guides https://www.loc.gov/rr/program/bib/inaugurations/, and they are usually also published online on the website for each of the presidential libraries.

11. Anthony D/ Smith, *Nationalism: Key Concepts* (New York: Polity, 2013).

12. As do reliable sources on the internet, the United Nations and NATO both include a page on their respective websites that is titled *About* or *What is . . .* where you are able to access a short overview of the organization's history and function: https://www.un.org/en/about-un/ and https://www.nato.int/nato-welcome/index.html; See also the *Very Short Introductions* series from Oxford University Press that include an introduction to the United Nations and NATO: https://global.oup.com/academic/content/series/v/very-short-introductions-vsi/?cc=us&lang=en&.

13. Saul Bernard Cohen, *Geopolitics: The Geography of International Relations*, 3rd ed. (Lanham, MD: Rowman & Littlefield, 2013).

14. Karlyn Kohrs Campbell and Kathleen Hall Jamieson. *Presidents Creating the Presidency: Deeds Done in Words* (Chicago: University of Chicago Press, 2013).

15. "Inauguration at the U.S. Capitol," Architect of the Capitol, accessed July 14, 2020, https://www.aoc.gov/what-we-do/programs-ceremonies/inauguration

16. Joyce P. Kaufman, *A Concise History of US Foreign Policy* (Lanham, MD: Rowman & Littlefield, 2014), 5.

Chapter 2

What Does That Mean?

Definitions, Terminology, and Jargon

Conversations about global politics are often riddled with terminology, that is, words that are defined and applied in specific ways in global politics. The major arc of this chapter is to encourage learners to look up, define, and think deeply about important terms that provide foundations for global politics studies. As learners develop expertise, it is crucial to practice integrating new terminology and jargon into their thinking and analysis of global politics. Indeed, understanding new material requires humility and a willingness to investigate familiar and unfamiliar words to ensure mastery of the issues and concepts being discussed in context, as well as the ability to apply new terms (and the ideas and dynamics they represent) to other global politics issues. As learners become experts in the field of global politics, they may even come to create terms of their own, based on new understandings and analyses.

Three types of terms are important to watch for:

1. Unknown terminology: Terms not necessarily central to the study of global politics (for example, *patrician*, *antagonism*, and *transmuting* found in the primary source excerpts in Section 2.B).
2. Expert terminology: Terms (or *jargon*) forged in specific disciplines and theoretical traditions that signify context-specific concepts, ideas, and dynamics, that is, terms that someone new to global politics may not have heard before (for example, *welfare capitalism* found in the primary source excerpts in Section 2.B).
3. Common terminology: Terms that a new learner of global politics has likely heard and read, may be accustomed to using, and might even

be confident about the definitions, such as commonly used terms like *democratic, market, communism,* and *exploitation,* or often misused and abused terms like *liberal, socialist,* and *sustainable.*

Section 2.A discusses tools and techniques useful for defining and thinking about new terms in global politics. The rest of the chapter then provides an example of how to go about studying expert terminology through the use of an example term: *capitalism.* Section 2.B includes primary sources that discuss and describe the term *capitalism* in various ways; Section 2.C uses tools and techniques to rigorously define capitalism in global political context; finally, Section 2.D provides a list of recommended readings for learning more about capitalism.

2.A: TOOLS AND TECHNIQUES FOR DEFINING TERMS AND CONCEPTS

Utilizing specific tools, techniques, and habits of mind to approach defining key terms helps learners become more adept at and astute in building foundational knowledge that allows for greater expertise in a subject. This section includes an overview of some important techniques, including annotated bibliographies, T-charts, and using dictionaries, journal articles, and specialized encyclopedias as resources to help with understanding terminology.

Annotated Bibliographies

An annotated bibliography is a useful way to take notes on multiple sources, and helps in describing, understanding, organizing, analyzing, and criticizing information. The main idea behind an annotated bibliography is that it helps summarize and compare several different texts in order to gain a broader understanding of an issue, rather than relying on just one interpretation.[1] An annotated bibliography is distinct from a regular bibliography in that the latter is simply a list of properly formatted citations relevant to the research topic under study. An annotated bibliography adds to a regular bibliography by including notes on each source, with the content and organization of one's notes written purposefully toward a goal(s) in completing and interpreting the texts. Note taking is more productive, and notes are more useful, if notes are created *with a purpose*, or a goal, in mind. For example, the annotated bibliography in Section 2.C of this chapter is organized around findings from the primary sources about *capitalism* (from Section 2.B) with a goal to understand and define *capitalism* as expert terminology in global politics. Textbox 2.1 provides key ideas for how to construct an annotated bibliography.

TEXTBOX 2.1: KEY ELEMENTS OF AN ANNOTATED BIBLIOGRAPHY

- *Citation*: Cite the source with specific and consistent formatting. Academia has developed several standard formatting types that are used within and across disciplines including the Chicago Manual of Style (used in this text), the Harvard Referencing Style, the Modern Language Association (MLA) Formatting and Style Guide, and the American Psychological Association (APA) Formatting and Style Guide.[1] The most important element in citing sources is consistency and accuracy in formatting so that the reader is easily able to find a source (consult project or assignment requirements for formatting guidelines to follow correct citation formatting and style). Writing the citation additionally provides an opportunity to think about the author(s) of the text you are citing, creating an opportunity to do some brief research on the author.
- *Annotation*: Annotations come in all different forms, and individuals eventually create their own way of recording, analyzing, and synthesizing information from a source. As an example, consider including the following four sections for each entry in the annotated bibliography, categories that are useful for organizing annotations oriented specifically toward defining terms in context (also review the example annotated bibliography in Section 2.C):

  1. *Definitions and Quotations*: Identify important definitions, with quotes or evidence to support them, and page numbers. Quoting with relevant citation information allows for an easier transition from notes to the final output (e.g., exams, papers, or presentations).[2]
  2. *Associated Concepts*: Include lists and definitions of concepts related to the concept being defined, ones that come up in the text, that come to mind, or that are in other texts. Reflect on the connections and meanings across texts.
  3. *Associated Events*: Identifying historical connections will help immensely in understanding the text and the context in which a particular definition is offered, for writings are embedded in the historical setting and meanings of a particular era.
  4. *Associated Dynamics*: Identify and record central interactions and relationships, changes in concepts or ideas, or how concepts are affecting and changing ideas, environments, and/or historical events.

- *Personal Reflection*: Most importantly, reflect on the text with personal comments and ideas about its main arguments and definitions throughout the annotation. Make notes in each entry that reflect your own personal attempts to disambiguate, clarify, and explain terms, questions raised while reading and taking notes, or questions that also make excellent fodder for discussion with others.

[1] For an excellent overview of formatting and style types, along with additional writing support, seek out a campus library website or online guides including the Online Writing Lab (OWL) by Purdue: https://owl.purdue.edu/owl/purdue_owl.html

[2] Note that quoting a source is different form citing a source; to quote means to include direct language in quotation marks in the text with a citation in the text and bibliography, while to cite means to reference the source in the text and in the bibliography.

T-Charts

A T-chart involves distilling information into two columns with headings that allow a learner to efficiently compare information and ideas across different thinkers and contexts. One of the major benefits of a concise T-chart is that it forces readers to think about main points, and only main points. It's called a T-chart because it looks like a "T" with two columns with headings and two bold lines to divide, as described in Textbox 2.2 and seen in Figure 2.1.

TEXTBOX 2.2: KEY ELEMENTS OF A T-CHART

- Two headings/categories to compare (use the T-chart for note taking, for comparing different texts on a definition or arguments, for comparing historical events, for trying to make a decision between two options, etc.).
- Columns with different definitions, arguments, ideas, or associations.
- Summary of the comparison results: identification of similarities and differences across the information gathered.

Specialized Resources for Defining Expert Terminology

Learning expert terminology (that is often highly specialized) is a gateway to learning about the concepts, ideas, and dynamics that the terminology signifies. Expert terminology is a bit like secret code: once you have deciphered the code, the meaning and significance of the message become clearer. Steady accumulation of expert terminology, using such terminology appropriately, and integrating it into one's working vocabulary are crucial tasks for learners in all disciplines. Generally, there are two kinds of resources that will be useful to learners in defining expert terminology in global politics, in addition to original sources of the term.

- *Peer-Reviewed Journal Articles*: Academic journal articles are written by scholars and are published (both in print and online) to encourage discussion and debate among experts. Such articles may be useful in providing background and analysis of certain terms that can bolster understanding. If a given term is central to an author's argument, they will define the term in their article. Often, scholars take some time developing the definition, using multiple sources to help clarify, explain, disambiguate, and apply.
- *Specialized Encyclopedias*: The second kind of resource useful for defining jargon is a specialized encyclopedia that includes entries and articles written by experts to elaborate and provide overviews on specific terms or subjects. Such specialized resources may by be accessed through a library, either online or in the reference book stacks.

2.B: PRIMARY SOURCES ON CAPITALISM

"Capitalism, n.2" from the *Oxford English Dictionary* (excerpt, 2019) [2]

> Pronunciation: Brit. /ˈkapɪtlɪzm/, /ˈkapɪtəlɪzm/, U.S. /ˈkæpədlˌɪzəm/
> Origin: Formed within English, by derivation. Etymons: capital n.2, -ism suffix.
> Etymology: < capital n.2 + -ism suffix, after capitalist n.
> Compare French capitalisme possession of capital (1753), economic system based on capital investment (1842), German Kapitalismus possession of capital (1787 or earlier), economic system (K. Marx 1863 or earlier).
> Compare earlier capitalism n.1
> The possession of capital or wealth; an economic system in which private capital or wealth is used in the production or distribution of goods and prices are determined mainly in a free market; the dominance of private owners of capital and of production for profit. Cf. capitalist n., socialism n. 2.
> Sometimes used *depreciatively*.
> Frequently with modifying term; for *anarcho-, anti-, market, monopoly, popular, pro-, state, venture, welfare capitalism*: see the first element.
> 1833 *Standard* 23 Apr. Whatever tended to paralyse British industry could not but produce corresponding injury to France; when the same tyranny of capitalism which first produced the disease would be at hand to inflame the symptoms by holding out promises of loans, &c.
> 1848 *Caledonian Mercury* 25 Sept. That sweeping tide of capitalism and money-loving which threatens our country with the horrors of a plutocracy.

1884 *Pall Mall Gaz.* 11 Sept. 6/1 A loophole for capitalism to creep in upon the primitive Christian communism.

1894 S. Gompers in J. Swinton Striking for Life 318 When the time comes, if it does come, for the displacement of the barbarity of capitalism to make way for humane conditions it will be accomplished by men whose heads are as cool as their hearts are warm.

1908 *Polit. Sci. Q.* 23 670 Socialism . . . will step into its heritage when capitalism . . . has created a thoroughly proletarized, class-conscious and revolutionary population.

1919 *Amer. Jrnl. Sociol.* 24 371 The beginnings of capitalism in England are to be traced to the thrifty manufacturing middle class.

1969 Listener 28 Aug. 267/1 Can capitalism . . . achieve the rate of growth that planning in a really publicly-owned economy has achieved?

1986 H. J. Maroney Feminism at Work in J. Mitchell & A. Oakley What is Feminism? 119 Kinship networks have also traditionally provided a support base for working-class struggles. Their steady disintegration in late capitalism thus has a mixed import for class-based politics.

2010 N.Y. Times (National ed.) 15 June a25/3 The rivalry between democratic capitalism and state capitalism is not like the rivalry between capitalism and communism.

The Manifesto of the Communist Party by Karl Marx and Friedrich Engels (excerpt, 1848)[3]

The history of all hitherto existing society is the history of class struggles.

Freeman and slave, patrician and plebeian, lord and serf, guild-master and journeyman, in a word, oppressor and oppressed, stood in constant opposition to one another, carried on an uninterrupted, now hidden, now open fight, a fight that each time ended, either in a revolutionary reconstitution of society at large, or in the common ruin of the contending classes . . .[4]

The modern bourgeois society that has sprouted from the ruins of feudal society has not done away with class antagonisms. It has but established new classes, new conditions of oppression, new forms of struggle in place of the old ones. Our epoch, the epoch of the bourgeoisie, possesses, however, this distinct feature: it has simplified class antagonisms. Society as a whole is more and more splitting up into two great hostile camps, into two great classes directly facing each other: Bourgeoisie and Proletariat . . .

The discovery of America, the rounding of the Cape, opened up fresh ground for the rising bourgeoisie. The East-Indian and Chinese markets, the colonisation of America, trade with the colonies, the increase in the means of exchange and in commodities generally, gave to commerce, to navigation, to industry, an impulse never before known, and thereby, to the revolutionary element in the tottering feudal society, a rapid development . . .

Meantime the markets kept ever growing, the demand ever rising. Even manufacturer no longer sufficed. Thereupon, steam and machinery revolutionised industrial production. The place of manufacture was taken by the giant, Modern Industry; the place of the industrial middle class by industrial millionaires, the leaders of the whole industrial armies, the modern bourgeois . . .

The bourgeoisie cannot exist without constantly revolutionising the instruments of production, and thereby the relations of production, and with them the whole relations of society. Conservation of the old modes of production in unaltered form, was, on the contrary, the first condition of existence for all earlier industrial classes. Constant revolutionising of production, uninterrupted disturbance of all social conditions, everlasting uncertainty and agitation distinguish the bourgeois epoch from all earlier ones. All fixed, fast-frozen relations, with their train of ancient and venerable prejudices and opinions, are swept away, all new-formed ones become antiquated before they can ossify. All that is solid melts into air, all that is holy is profaned, and man is at last compelled to face with sober senses his real conditions of life, and his relations with his kind.

The need of a constantly expanding market for its products chases the bourgeoisie over the entire surface of the globe. It must nestle everywhere, settle everywhere, establish connexions everywhere . . .

In proportion as the bourgeoisie, i.e., capital, is developed, in the same proportion is the proletariat, the modern working class, developed—a class of labourers, who live only so long as they find work, and who find work only so long as their labour increases capital. These labourers, who must sell themselves piecemeal, are a commodity, like every other article of commerce, and are consequently exposed to all the vicissitudes of competition, to all the fluctuations of the market.

Owing to the extensive use of machinery, and to the division of labour, the work of the proletarians has lost all individual character, and, consequently, all charm for the workman. He becomes an appendage of the machine, and it is only the most simple, most monotonous, and most easily acquired knack, that is required of him. Hence, the cost of production of a workman is restricted, almost entirely, to the means of subsistence that he requires for maintenance, and for the propagation of his race. But the price of a commodity, and therefore also of labour, is equal to its cost of production. In proportion, therefore, as the repulsiveness of the work increases, the wage decreases. Nay more, in proportion as the use of machinery and division of labour increases, in the same proportion the burden of toil also increases, whether by prolongation of the working hours, by the increase of the work exacted in a given time or by increased speed of machinery, etc.

Modern Industry has converted the little workshop of the patriarchal master into the great factory of the industrial capitalist. Masses of labourers, crowded into the factory, are organised like soldiers. As privates of the industrial army they are placed under the command of a perfect hierarchy of officers and sergeants. Not only are they slaves of the bourgeois class, and of the bourgeois State; they are daily and hourly enslaved by the machine, by the overlooker, and, above all, by the individual bourgeois manufacturer himself. The more openly this despotism proclaims gain to be its end and aim, the more petty, the more hateful and the more embittering it is . . .

The General Theory of Employment, Interest and Money by John Maynard Keynes (excerpt, 1936)[5]

The outstanding faults of the economic society in which we live are its failure to provide for full employment and its arbitrary and inequitable distribution of wealth and incomes . . .

For my own part, I believe that there is social and psychological justification for significant inequalities of incomes and wealth, but not for such large disparities as exist today. There are valuable human activities which require the motive of money-making and the environment of private wealth-ownership for their full fruition. Moreover, dangerous human proclivities can be canalised into comparatively harmless channels by the existence of opportunities for money-making and private wealth, which, if they cannot be satisfied in this way, may find their outlet in cruelty, the reckless pursuit of personal power and authority, and other forms of self-aggrandisement. It is better that a man should tyrannise over his bank balance than over his fellow-citizens; and whilst the former is sometimes denounced as being but a means to the latter, sometimes at least it is an alternative. But it is not necessary for the stimulation of these activities and the satisfaction of these proclivities that the game should be played for such high stakes as at present. Much lower stakes will serve the purpose equally well, as soon as the players are accustomed to them. The task of transmuting human nature must not be confused with the task of managing it. Though in the ideal commonwealth men may have been taught or inspired or bred to take no interest in the stakes, it may still be wise and prudent statesmanship to allow the game to be played, subject to rules and limitations, so long as the average man, or even a significant section of the community, is in fact strongly addicted to the money-making passion . . .

Furthermore, the modern classical theory has itself called attention to various conditions in which the free play of economic forces may need to be curbed or guided. But there will still remain a wide field for the exercise of private initiative and responsibility. Within this field the traditional advantages of individualism will still hold good.

Let us stop for a moment to remind ourselves what these advantages are. They are partly advantages of efficiency—the advantages of decentralisation and of the play of self-interest. . . . But, above all, individualism, if it can be purged of its defects and its abuses, is the best safeguard of personal liberty in the sense that, compared with any other system, it greatly widens the field for the exercise of personal choice. It is also the best safeguard of the variety of life, which emerges precisely from this extended field of personal choice, and the loss of which is the greatest of all the losses of the homogeneous or totalitarian state . . .

Interview with Milton Friedman from Playboy Magazine (excerpt, 1973)[6]

PLAYBOY: Even if a consensus of right and left could be achieved on a modified version of your flat-rate tax proposal, there are many critics—particularly among the young—of what they feel are your basic assumptions. How would you answer those who claim that capitalism cannot foster a just and orderly society, since it's based on the emotion of greed?

FRIEDMAN: What kind of society isn't structured on greed? As a friend of mine says, the one thing you can absolutely depend on every other person to do is to put his interests ahead of yours. Now, his interests may not be greedy in a narrow, selfish sense. Some people's self-interest is to save the world. Some people's self-interest is to do good for others. Florence Nightingale pursued her own self-interest through charitable activities. Rockefeller pursued his self-interest in setting up the Rockefeller Foundation. But for most people, most of the time, self-interest is greed.

So the problem of social organization is how to set up an arrangement under which greed will do the least harm. It seems to me that the great virtue of capitalism is that it's that kind of system. Because under capitalism, the power of any one individual over his fellow man is relatively small. You take the richest capitalist in the world; his power over you and me is trivial compared with the power that a Brezhnev or a Kosygin has in Russia. Or even compared in the United States with the power that an official of the Internal Revenue Service has over you. An official of the IRS can put you in jail. I doubt that there is a person in the United States who couldn't be convicted of technical violation of some aspect of the personal income tax. One of the great dangers I see in the American situation is that there is a strong temptation in Government to use the income tax for other purposes. It's been done. When gangsters couldn't be convicted under the laws they had really violated they were gotten on income-tax evasion. When John F. Kennedy threated to steel executives in 1962 to get them to drive down their prices, there was the implicit threat that all their taxes would be looked at. Now, that is a much more serious threat—the power an official has in the pursuit of *his* self-interest—than anything Howard Hughes is capable of. We want the kind of world in which greedy people can do the least harm to their fellow men. That's the kind of world in which power is widely dispersed and each of us has as many alternatives as possible.

"Development as a New Project of Western Patriarchy" by Vandana Shiva, in *Reweaving the World: The Emergence of EcoFeminism* (excerpt, 1990)[7]

"Development" was to have been a postcolonial project. It was to have been a choice for accepting a model of progress in which the entire world remade itself following the example of the colonizing modern West without being subjected to the subjugation and exploitation that colonialism entailed. The assumption was that Western-style progress was possible for all. Development thus implied improved well-being of all and was equated with the Westernization of economic categories—of needs, of productivity, of growth. Concepts and categories about economic development and natural resource utilization that had emerged in the specific context of industrialization and capitalist growth in a center of colonial power were raised to the level of universal assumptions and applicability in the entirely different context of the need to satisfy basic needs for the people of the newly independent Third World countries. Yet, as the German socialist Rosa Luxembourg has pointed out, the early industrial development in Western Europe necessitated the permanent occupation of the colonies by the colonial powers and destruction of the local "natural economy." According to Luxembourg, colonialism is a constant necessary condition for capitalist growth. Without colonies, capital accumulation would grind to a halt. "Development" as capital accumulation and the commercialization of the economy of the generation of "surplus" and profits thus involved the reproduction of the associated creation of poverty and dispossession. A replication of economic development based on commercialization of resource use for commodity production in the newly independent countries created internal colonies. Development was thus reduced to a continuation of the process of colonization. It was an extension of modern Western patriarchy's economic vision based on the exploitation or exclusion of women (of the West and non-West), on the exploitation and destruction of nature, and on the exploitation and destruction of other cultures. That is why, throughout the Third World, women, peasants, and tribal peoples are struggling for liberation from development as they earlier struggled for liberation from colonialism.

2.C: DEFINING, IDENTIFYING, AND USING CAPITALISM IN CONTEXT

It is crucial for understanding global politics that a learner think and rethink about common terminology, that is, terms that may already be known and that are frequently used in global political conversations but may have a different meaning among experts. The bulk of this section is spent working with common terminology. As a term's usage becomes more ubiquitous, its meaning becomes fuzzier, increasing debate among participants in global political conversations about what it means and how it should be used. Even experts define commonly used terms differently depending on the disciplinary and theoretical lens deployed by the person using them and depending on the context in which they appear. For example, anthropologists and economists may use the term *market* quite differently, for example, in conversations among anthropologists about the decline of wet markets in the Philippines versus theoretical economists discussing the vagaries of the efficient market hypothesis.[8] This section provides detailed suggestions about the practices, techniques, and habits of mind that will be useful to learners in their efforts to define key terms in context, focusing specifically on a central set of structures, dynamics, and relationships in the global political system that are signified by the term *capitalism*.

Definition and Identification

Almost all words have multiple definitions. Reading through *all* the definitions provided by a dictionary or other source can help a learner identify the definition that is most appropriate to the context at hand, even as one might be aware of different or competing definitions. For instance, two options come up (n.1 and n.2) for *capitalism* when entered into the *Oxford English Dictionary* (OED) online, referring to two separate definitions.[9] Because the two definitions are sufficiently different from one another, they are given different entries. The first definition of capitalism listed in the OED is limited historically to a form of centralized city-based government advocated specifically by the United Provinces of South America in the early nineteenth century, a definition that is clearly too limited for understanding the definitions of *capitalism* referenced in the primary documents included in Section 2.B. The second definition of *capitalism* from the OED is more appropriate to the inquiry.

It is also important to be attentive to different parts of speech when trying to identify the definition(s) that apply best to the situation under study. Different parts of speech may have the same root word, for example, *capitalism* is a noun, *capitalistic* is an adjective, and *capitalization* is a verb and a noun. All three of these terms come from the root word *capital*, which has its own extensive entry in the OED that is worth reading. It is important *not* to assume such variations on *capitalism* carry the same meaning. For example, while *capitalization* can indeed refer to the process by which an economy transitions to capitalism (the definition you might assume of this word), it can also refer to the size of a given marketplace, as with the *capitalization* of the US stock market.

Etymology and Context

Words have a historical lineage, changing over time. A word's *etymology* is its origin in history. A good dictionary, and any specialized encyclopedia, will discuss the history of the term (though this history will be more or less robust depending on the source). The OED provides a chronology of word usage that includes excerpts from works that use the word from different historical periods. Reading entries in the OED, like the entry for *capitalism*, allows a learner to contextualize a term, that is, to identify its initial use and track how the word is used over time. The meaning and usage of words can change significantly over time, and across different locales, contexts, and thinkers.

Take a moment to re-read the entry from the OED.

- What do you notice about the historical usage of the term *capitalism*?
- How does the historical use of the term change over time?
- Is there a core set of ideas about or associations with *capitalism* that do not change?

Based on the OED entry, one can see how different users of the term *capitalism* have contextualized its meaning, with the earliest example from 1833 using it to talk about the economic fortunes of England and France (at a time when both countries were industrializing and increasingly competing with one another), and the example from 1908 using the term in contrast to *socialism* (an increasingly important set of ideas and practices during the late nineteenth and early twentieth centuries, often discussed in contradistinction to capitalism). We would not expect *capitalism* to be used in 1833 in contrast to *socialism*, because socialist movements and ideas were only in their infancy and had not yet become a force to reckon with in Europe. Note how a close reading of the OED entry can help learners sketch a historical timeline for the development of *capitalism* via word usage. Thus, *capitalism* was first named as such in the context of industrialization and international economic competition in Europe, though its historical roots go back much further; and capitalist ideas conflict with socialist ideas in the decades preceding World War I.[10]

Capitalism as Expert Terminology

Pundits and public officials, activists and policymakers, titans of industry, spiritual leaders, and students, all use the term *capitalism* in a variety of different contexts and ways. Using the tools and techniques outlined in Section 2.A, it is possible to assess the definition of *capitalism*, put it into context, compare and contrast different definitions, and assign appropriate meaning to the term, especially in terms of the goal of this chapter: to understand the meaning of the term *capitalism* as used in the primary documents included in Section 2.B.

This section assesses how the five primary source excerpts in Section 2.B use the term *capitalism* by weighing and disambiguating between contrasting definitions from different authors and contexts. The organizational scheme in the annotated bibliography in Textbox 2.3 compares and contrasts definitions of capitalism between the five primary sources, allowing for development of short summaries of main ideas and arguments, definitions derived from context, interpretations of concepts or situations or historical events across different works, and questions and perspectives on the readings and definitions.

TEXTBOX 2.3: EXAMPLE ANNOTATED BIBLIOGRAPHY ON CAPITALISM

The following annotated bibliography was created by the authors as an example for how to analyze a primary or secondary source document. When the notes say "I think," it means that we, the authors, who created the annotation have recorded our thoughts and ideas and questions, but it is not meant as a definitive interpretation or definition of the primary documents covered. The annotated bibliography is only partially completed, on purpose. Two sources are not annotated (Marx and Engels, and Shiva) to give the learner a chance to annotate them in order to practice annotating with a guide and build expertise for later annotations on independent research projects.

"capitalism, n.2." *Oxford English Dictionary*, Oxford University Press, accessed August 1, 2019. https://www-oed-com.aurarialibrary.idm.oclc.org/view/Entry/27454?rskey=982XHj&result=2

1. *Definition(s) of capitalism*:
   "The possession of capital or wealth; an economic system in which private capital or wealth is used in the production or distribution of goods and services and prices are determined mainly in a free market; the dominance of private owners of capital and of production for profit" (OED 2019).
   - three different ideas here: having wealth <u>versus</u> an economic system organized privately by those with capital via free markets <u>versus</u> ideas about dominance (and inequality?) of private capital and profit motives.

2. *Associated concepts*: wealth, capital, profit, markets, economic growth, the working class, the middle class, "horrors of plutocracy"; a whole laundry list of concepts that include "capitalism" like "monopoly capitalism" and "state capitalism"; also, in conflict with "socialism" and "communism" and "a really publicly-owned economy."
   - Seems like a lot of the examples used to sketch out word usage over time are critical of "capitalism," describing "horrors" and "struggles" and "barbarity" and "tyranny"; that said, some are complementary, for example, about the "thrifty manufacturing middle class."
   - Also, are there different kinds of capitalism? The list of terms that include "capitalism" (e.g., "state capitalism") suggests this may be so; also, last example from 2010 talks about "democratic" vs. "state" capitalism.
3. *Associated events*: Industrial Revolution, "sweeping tide of capitalism."
4. *Associated dynamics*: trade between England and France, "working class struggles," disintegration of "kinship networks."

Friedman, Milton. "Playboy Interview: Milton Friedman." Playboy Magazine 20, no. 2 (February 1973).

1. *Definition(s) of capitalism*: "So the problem of social organization is how to set up an arrangement under which greed will do the least harm. It seems to me that the great virtue of capitalism is that it's that kind of system" (Friedman 1973).
2. *Associated concepts*: greed, self-interest (as with an interest in "charitable activities," and then also "in a narrow, selfish sense"), power (and power inequalities), income taxes.
   - He's obsessed with taxes, it seems. Why is he obsessed with taxes? I remember from my other class a quote by Weber, I think, about how modern governments have "monopolies" on violence and taxation. Is this related to Friedman's complaints about taxes and the IRS? Friedman seems to me to be setting up the market as a counterforce to the state . . . Is this right?
   - Also, I'm a little puzzled and mad about how he portrays charity . . . is charity compatible with self-interest? Is it right to think about Florence Nightingale in this way?
3. *Associated events*: The Cold War (he compares the US and Soviet systems in the context of power and who capitalism empowers), JFK's threat to steel executives in 1962.

- I think it's interesting that his ideas about capitalism combine the idea of "greed" and taming/harnessing greed, on the one hand, with ideas about power and freedom, on the other. Is he saying that markets "tame" greed *and* promote freedom? Is decentralizing power the same as promoting freedom?
- Also, he's obviously seriously opposed to the Soviet system. Says leaders there have too much power. In this context, is he comparing Brezhnev to IRS agents? Not sure how I feel about this.

4. *Associated dynamics*: power decentralization and centralization.

Keynes, John Maynard. *The General Theory of Employment, Interest and Money*. London: Macmillan, 1936.

1. *Definition(s) of capitalism*: There isn't just one definition or discussion here, lots of different ideas throughout, including "economic society," "private wealth-ownership," "money-making," and "private initiative and responsibility."
   - Some similar ideas to OED, like "private wealth."

2. *Associated concepts*: inequality, full employment, decentralization, individualism, tyranny and totalitarianism, "personal liberty" and "personal choice"; human nature.
   - I can't tell if he likes capitalism or not. He seems to agree with Friedman in places, especially in that capitalist systems and the markets that organize them are places that "tame" human nature somehow. Keynes says, "It is better that a man should tyrannise over his bank balance than over his fellow-citizens" (Keynes 1936). This is just like Friedman's discussion of those Soviet leaders. *But* Keynes also complains about capitalism's "failure to provide for full employment and its arbitrary and inequitable distribution of wealth and incomes" (Keynes 1936). Is Keynes a fan of capitalism or not?

3. *Associated events*: he doesn't mention any, but the date of his publication makes me think the Great Depression is important here. When he talks about everyone not having a job, it makes me think of how many people were out of work at this time. Ask about this in class, maybe?

4. *Associated dynamics*: "reckless pursuit of personal power and authority" vs. "money-making"; "transmuting" vs. "managing" human nature; "allow the game to be played."
   - I don't like the language Keynes uses in here, calling the economy a "game." I understand that he's trying to make a point here, but isn't this trivializing things a bit?

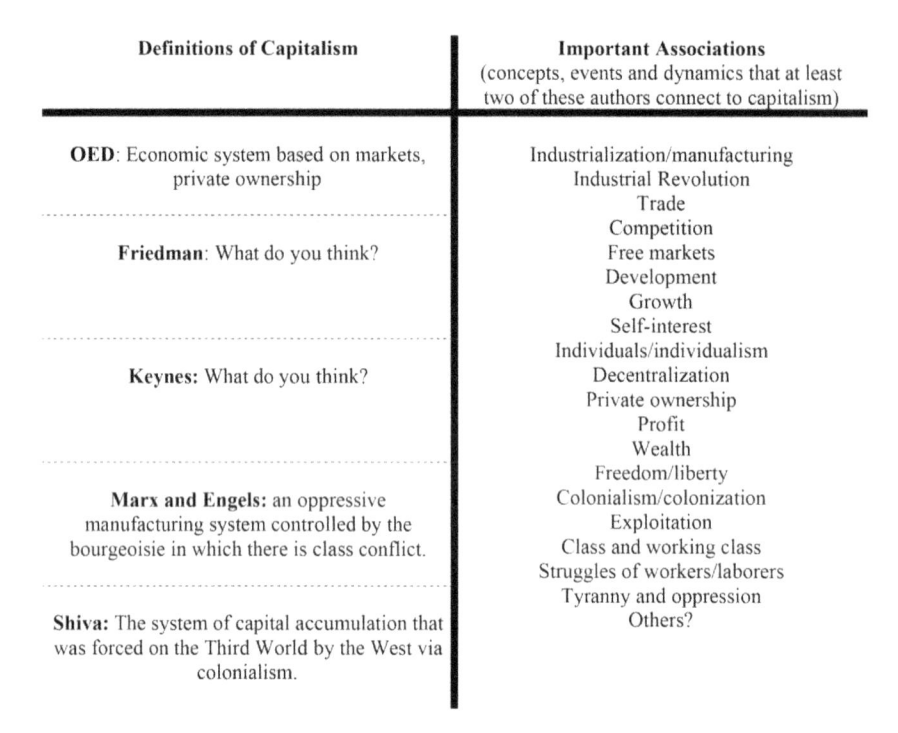

Definitions of Capitalism	Important Associations (concepts, events and dynamics that at least two of these authors connect to capitalism)
OED: Economic system based on markets, private ownership	Industrialization/manufacturing Industrial Revolution Trade Competition Free markets Development Growth Self-interest Individuals/individualism Decentralization Private ownership Profit Wealth Freedom/liberty Colonialism/colonization Exploitation Class and working class Struggles of workers/laborers Tyranny and oppression Others?
Friedman: What do you think?	
Keynes: What do you think?	
Marx and Engels: an oppressive manufacturing system controlled by the bourgeoisie in which there is class conflict.	
Shiva: The system of capital accumulation that was forced on the Third World by the West via colonialism.	

Figure 2.1   T-Chart: What Is Capitalism?

Having taken detailed notes on the readings in the form of annotated bibliography, as shown in Textbox 2.3, it is possible to clarify and summarize and condense knowledge gained in order to tentatively answer the question: *what does* capitalism *mean?* Figure 2.1 uses a T-chart to help think through the different definitions of capitalism derived from the primary sources. The T-chart in Figure 2.1 distills the notes from the annotated bibliography in Textbox 2.3. As with the annotated bibliography, the T-chart has blank spaces for the learner to complete using their individual interpretations of the texts.

What does "capitalism" mean, then? This chapter has discussed five possible definitions of capitalism derived from reading the primary sources in Section 2.B using a series of tools and approaches: annotated bibliographies, T-charts, and dictionaries. One surprising conclusion might be that all the different definitions are correct. Definitions, even of words that humans use all the time in global political conversations, are moving targets in a state of flux. That said, the five definitions provide some important points of agreement and convergence, especially in the context of the associations on the right-hand side of the T-chart. Based on the annotated bibliography and T-chart, one could adopt a working definition of capitalism. A *working definition* is one adopted by a learner/researcher in order to move forward in reaching one's goals on a project or assignment; working definitions are often revised as one continues to read and learn and think.

- How about this working definition, just for now? *Capitalism is an economic system based in private ownership and self-interest, organized via market institutions, and oriented toward the accumulation of profit and wealth, the virtues of which are debatable.*
- What do you think of this definition?
- How else could you refine and consolidate your notes to come up with a different working definition?

Other Possible Definitions to Assess. Other terms in the primary source documents, and to which a learner might apply annotated bibliography and T-chart approaches, or look up using specialized resources, so as to broaden their knowledge of global politics, include *class, competition, free market, wealth, development, inequality, industrialization,* and *colonialism.* Remember that even if a source does not use the actual term or phrase, it might still have something to say about it.

2.D: RECOMMENDED READINGS ON CAPITALISM AND ACADEMIC SKILLS

On Capitalism

DeMartino, George. *Global Economy, Global Justice: Theoretical Objections and Policy Alternatives to Neoliberalism.* Contemporary Political Economy Series. London: Routledge, 2000.

Friedman, Milton, and Rose D. Friedman. *Free to Choose: A Personal Statement.* New York: Avon, 1981.

Harvey, David. *Brief History of Neoliberalism.* Oxford: Oxford University Press, 2005.

Hayek, Friedrich A. *The Road to Serfdom.* London: Routledge & Kegan Paul, 1944.

Heilbroner, Robert L. *The Worldly Philosophers.* 7th ed. London: Penguin, 2000.

Marcuse, Herbert. *One-Dimensional Man: Studies in the Ideology of Advanced Industrial Society.* Routledge Classics. Hoboken: Taylor and Francis, 2013.

Polanyi, Karl. *The Great Transformation.* New York: Farrar & Rinehart, 1944.

Shiva, Vandana. *Oneness Versus the One Percent.* New Delhi: Women Unlimited 2018.

Skidelsky, Robert Jacob Alexander. 2013. *Keynes: The Return of the Master.* New York: Public Affairs, 2013.

Yergin, Daniel, and Joseph Stanislaw. *The Commanding Heights: The Battle for the World Economy.* New York: Free Press, 2008.

On Academic Skills

Baglione, Lisa A. *Writing a Research Paper in Political Science: A Practical Guide to Inquiry, Structure, and Methods.* 4th ed. Thousand Oaks, CA: CQ Press, an Imprint of SAGE Publications, 2020.

Burns, Tom, and Sandra Sinfield. *Essential Study Skills: The Complete Guide to Success at University.* 4th ed. London: Sage, 2016.

Galvan, José L., and Melisa Galvan. *Writing Literature Reviews: A Guide for Students of the Social and Behavioral Sciences.* 7th ed. New York: Routledge, Taylor & Francis Group, 2017.

Strunk, William and E.B. White. *Elements of Style.* 4th ed. New York: Longman, 2000.

Whitely, Bernard E. Jr. and Patricia Keith-Spiegel. *Academic Dishonesty: An Educator's Guide.* East Sussex, Psychology Press, 2012.

NOTES

1. Lisa A. Baglione, *Writing a Research Paper in Political Science: A Practical Guide to Inquiry, Structure, and Methods,* 4th ed. (Thousand Oaks, CA: CQ Press, an Imprint of SAGE Publications, 2020); José L. Galvan and Melisa Galvan, *Writing Literature Reviews: A Guide for Students of the Social and Behavioral Sciences* 7th ed. (New York: Routledge, Taylor & Francis Group, 2017).

2. "Capitalism, n.2," *Oxford English Dictionary* (OED) Online, accessed June 1, 2019 (all rights reserved; reproduced with permission of the Licensor through PLSclear), https://www-oed-com.aurarialibrary.idm.oclc.org/view/Entry/27454?rskey=982XHj&result=2.

3. Karl Marx and Friedrich Engels, "*The Manifesto of the Communist Party,*" from the English edition of 1888, edited by Friedrich Engels (originally published in February 1848, proofed and corrected against the 1888 English edition) last updated January 25, 2005, Project Gutenberg (all rights reserved, reproduced based on fair use doctrine from Section 107 of US Copyright Law) http://www.gutenberg.org/cache/epub/61/pg61-images.html.

4. We have only been able to reprint excerpts of the full documents in this volume in the C sections of each chapter (because of copyright or space constraints). Whenever you see an ellipsis (. . .), this is an indication that we have had to excise a section. Take the time to read the full document (usually, these documents may be found online—check the endnote citations for more detail).

5. John Maynard Keynes, *The General Theory of Employment, Interest and Money,* (London: Macmillan, 1936) (all rights reserved, reproduced based on fair use doctrine from Section 107 of US Copyright Law).

6. Milton Friedman, "Playboy Interview: Milton Friedman," *Playboy Magazine* 20, no. 2 (February 1973) (all rights reserved; reproduced with permission of the Licensor).

7. Vandana Shiva, "Development as a New Project of Western Patriarchy," In *Reweaving the World: The Emergence of EcoFeminism.* Edited by Irene Diamond and Gloria Feman Orenstein (New York: Zed, 1990), 189–200 (all rights reserved, reproduced based on fair use doctrine from Section 107 of US Copyright Law).

8. Robert L. Heilbroner, *The Worldly Philosophers,* 7th ed. (London: Penguin, 2000).

9. The *Oxford English Dictionary* is not an entirely free resource. Some entries are available for free at www.oed.com. Free dictionaries like *Cambridge Dictionary* online or *Merriam-Webster* online are good resources, though their entries are not typically as comprehensive or detailed as the OED.

10. Heilbronner, *Worldly Philosophers.* See also Daniel Yergin and Joseph Stanislaw, *The Commanding Heights: The Battle for the World Economy* (New York: Free Press, 1998).

Chapter 3

Who?

Actors, Positions, Perspectives, and Interests

Critical thinking is, at heart, a process of *questioning*: questioning others, questioning yourself, even questioning your questions. This chapter digs into the question *who?* Asking the question *who?* helps to probe and engage with key ideas, concepts, and frameworks that are useful for understanding and critically analyzing global politics. The primary document included in Section 3.B, Lee Kyung Hae's statement at the 2003 World Trade Organization (WTO) meeting in Cancun, Mexico, provides an excellent example of how to analyze a global politics issue by assessing who was involved. Lee's statement, which includes his perspectives on global agricultural trading, is a good context for thinking about *actors* in global politics and their positions, perspectives, and interests. Before moving to the primary document, Section 3.A introduces the practice of active reading and discusses how to locate credible sources of information that can help a learner engage with the reading and conceptually set the reading in context. Section 3.C provides learners with questions and ideas for how to find basic information about *actors* associated with Lee's speech, and Section 3.D provides a list of recommended readings about the concepts and ideas covered in the chapter.

Identifying actors, that is, asking and answering the question *who?*, in global politics is just one way to obtain depth and breadth on a given subject. As discussed in chapter 1, there are a series of questions to ask about a new subject in order to gather basic information and facts: *who? what* or *what is? when? where?* and *why/how?* Any of these basic analytical and critical thinking questions could act as the primary question and starting point for an investigation, but depending on the context, one might work better than another—the decision to focus on one question over others is up to the individual researcher to decide and investigate. No matter what the primary or starting question, the other basic questions will inevitably come up at some point, suggesting other potential avenues for additional research and study.

3.A: ACTIVE READING AND CREDIBLE INTERNET SOURCES

This chapter draws on three core skills for lifelong independent learning: (1) active reading, (2) the capacity to identify credible sources of information on the internet, and (3) intercultural competence (in this case, in international naming conventions).

Active Reading

Reading actively is crucial for general academic success, including success in global politics. Active reading helps with identifying and assessing main points from a text, integrating ideas from the text into one's own life, and better prepares learners to engage in dialogue with others, a practice that further ensures that the information gleaned moves from short-term to long-term memory.

Active reading tips:

- Read alone in a quiet place;
- Focus on one task: *reading*. Avoid using headphones or earbuds, television, and cellphones. If possible, turn off the cellphone and place it in a different location. People are not good at doing more than one thing at a time. *Multitasking* means efficient task prioritization, not doing many things at once;
- Avoid reading on a computer or cellphone, but if necessary, read in airplane mode or disable email and social media accounts while reading;
- Read with a satisfied/full stomach (i.e., don't read hungry). Have a snack. Snacks high in good quality protein improve cognition, focus, and attention (like peanut butter or yogurt). Snacks high in potassium are also beneficial (like bananas);
- Take a short walk before reading. Exercise improves cognition, focus, and attention;
- Read with a pen or pencil in hand to allow for writing all over the text (in the margins, in between the lines, on blank pages). Notations take many forms: highlighting, underlining, circling, enumerating, arrows to connect or to expand comments, defining, commenting, exclaiming. Identify key terms that need defining, important facts, central arguments or insights from the author, and include comments on, questions, and interpretations of the text;

- Talk to and argue with the text. Commiserate with or get mad at the text. Read the hardest parts of the text aloud. Ask the text questions and write questions in the margins;
- Be curious! Look things up! In the context of the primary source reading in Section 3.B, look up biographical information on Lee (the author), the WTO, and terms like *third world*, and *self-immolation*.

Credible Internet Sources

When using the internet to search for information, it is important to find and use credible sources. The following checklist is the bare minimum required in the context of seeking out definitions or basic information about an author or subject: depending on the specifics of the project, higher levels of verification may be necessary to ensure sources are credible and reliable.

Checklist for identifying reliable sources:

- Identify the author. If author is not identifiable, do not use the source/information (author can be a credible organization, government, or other source, such as the WTO as an author);
- Identify the author's credentials and ensure they are experts in the subject. Credentials need not be academic but could also include relevant life or work experience, or time spent researching the subject matter. Don't use source/information without good reason to trust the author's credentials;
- Identify source information. Does the author reveal where they get their information, such that their findings could be replicated? If not, don't use the source or the information provided;
- Identify the website/publisher. Do not use the source or information that cannot be traced to a reliable website or publisher;
- Identify possible interests or affiliations. Is the source affiliated with a company, interest group, political party, or political persona? If so, factor this into analysis of the author's/publisher's *bias* in conveying information in the text.

Intercultural Competency: Family Names in Global Context

Learners of global politics will find that one of the techniques important to their expertise is that of *intercultural competence* because it allows for empathetic understanding and awareness of other cultures, mores, norms, and ideologies that, when considered, will help to avoid misunderstanding and confusion. "Intercultural competence is the ability to develop targeted knowledge, skills and attitudes that lead to visible behaviour and communication that are both effective and appropriate in intercultural interactions."[1]

As an example of expanding intercultural competency, consider naming conventions related to the author of the primary source text in Section 3.B, Lee Kyung Hae, who was born in and grew up in Korea. As part of understanding the text, then, a learner will need to consider the Korean cultural conventions surrounding his name. Korean names do not follow the same conventions as English-speaking names in that the English language requires listing the given name first and the family name last. Korean convention is the opposite, but without a comma: family name first and given name last. Further, most Korean family names are one word, whereas the given name can be two words. In Lee Kyung Hae's case, Lee is the family name and Kyung Hae is the given name. This chapter cites his last name when referencing his speech as English-speaking academic convention dictates, as in "Lee's statement."

When reading a Korean name, or being introduced to a Korean person, remember that they will likely introduce themselves with their family name first. To avoid wrong assumptions or feeling self-conscious of making a mistake, ask the person what they would like to be called. Engaging with others in considerate and professional ways by recognizing differences in cultural conventions will help improve communication and refine the skill of intercultural competency.

3.B: PRIMARY SOURCE ON INTERNATIONAL TRADE

Statement of Lee Kyung Hae at the WTO Conference in Cancun, Mexico (excerpt, 2003)[2]

> I am 56 years old, a farmer from South Korea who has strived to solve our problems with the great hope in the ways to organize farmers' unions. But I have mostly failed, as many other farm leaders elsewhere have failed.
>
> Soon after the Uruguay Round Agreement was sealed, we Korean farmers realized that our destinies are no longer in our own hands. We cannot seem to do anything to stop the waves that have destroyed our communities where we have been settled for hundreds of years. To make myself brave, I have tried to find the real reason and the force behind those waves. And I reached the conclusion, here in front of the gates of the WTO. I am crying out my words to you, that have for so long boiled in my body:
>
> I ask: for whom do you negotiate now? For the people, or for yourselves? Stop basing your WTO negotiations on flawed logic and mere diplomatic gestures. Take agriculture out of the WTO system.
>
> Since (massive importing) we small farmers have never been paid over our production costs. What would be your emotional reaction if your salary dropped to a half without understanding the reasons?
>
> Farmers who gave up early have gone to urban slums. Others who have tried to escape from the vicious cycle have met bankruptcy due to accumulated debts.

For me, I couldn't do anything but just look around at the vacant houses. . . . Once I went to a house where a farmer abandoned his life by drinking a toxic chemical because of his uncontrollable debts. I could do nothing but listen to the howling of his wife. If you were me, how would you feel?

Widely paved roads lead to large apartments, buildings, and factories in Korea. Those lands paved now were mostly rice paddies built by generations over thousands of years. They provided the daily food and materials in the past. Now the ecological and hydrological functions of paddies are even more crucial. Who will protect our rural vitality, community traditions, amenities, and environment?

I believe that farmers' situation in many other developing countries is similar. We have in common the problem of dumping, import surges, lack of government budgets, and too many people. Tariff protection would be the practical solution.

I have been so worried watching TV and hearing the news that starvation is prevalent in many Less Developed Countries, although the international price of grain is so cheap. Earning money through trade should not be their means of securing food. They need access to land and water. Charity? No! Let them work again!

My warning goes out to all citizens that human beings are in an endangered situation. That uncontrolled multinational corporations and a small number of big WTO Members are leading an undesirable globalization that is inhumane, environmentally degrading, farmer-killing, and undemocratic. It should be stopped immediately. Otherwise the false logic of neoliberalism will wipe out the diversity of global agriculture and be disastrous to all human beings.

3.C: FREE TRADE, AGRICULTURE, AND ANTI-GLOBALIZATION MOVEMENTS

Which people, or groups or organizations of people, does Lee discuss in his statement? In other words, which *actors* are discussed in the text? Thinking about *actors* is an important step toward a critical analysis of global politics. In any situation under study it is typical to encounter multiple actors who occupy different social positions, have different perspectives on global politics, and have different interests that ground their actions and behaviors. There are different kinds of *who?* questions one might ask in thinking about Lee's statement and many good reasons for asking them:

- *Who* is the author? Researching and understanding biographical information about the author provides information about their life experiences, and thus also clues about their *position*, *perspectives*, and *interests*;
- *Who* is the intended or unintended audience of Lee's message? What affect does that audience have on the way that Lee crafted his message?

As discussed at more length in chapter 6, the substance, form, style, and tone of a thinker's message can change substantially, depending on their audience (that is, who they are trying to communicate with);
- *Who* does Lee talk about in his statement? Who Lee is thinking about tells us something about Lee's political perspective and worldview, and maybe also about his position and interests. This is the case in thinking about *any* kind of global political material: *who* a writer or speaker decides to focus on reveals something significant;
- Thinking about who is *not* mentioned or prioritized in a situation under study creates a partial basis for critique. Why does the thinker value one kind of actor but not others? What does the emphasis on one actor over others tell us about the author's ideas? What are the consequences of emphasizing one set of actors over others?

Who? Actors and Theories in International Relations

Theories of international relations (IR) are used extensively by academics and practitioners who study and work in global politics and can be partly distinguished from one another on the basis of *who* is prioritized in describing and explaining and criticizing global political events, relationships, and dynamics. There are a multitude of IR theories, built on philosophers' ideas about human nature and interaction, which are applied at the international level to explain why states act the way that they do, for example, why states would go to war with one another, or why states would engage in free trade or sign treaties with each other.[3] Such theories are discussed in most IR textbooks, debated by academics, and leveraged by policymakers and public officials, and include, for example, *realism*, *liberalism*, and *feminism*. Textbox 3.1 matches commonly taught IR theories with actor(s) and groups of actors, or *units of analysis*, that are typically prioritized within their theoretical frameworks.

TEXTBOX 3.1: PRIMARY UNITS OF ANALYSIS FOR COMMON THEORIES OF INTERNATIONAL RELATIONS

- *Realism* focuses primarily on nation-states, and their power and interests; when focused on individuals they are considered rational actors making decisions on the basis of cost/benefit analysis.
- *Liberalism* prioritizes thinking about individuals and their rights and interests, as well as institutions, understood in this tradition as collectives of individual actors collaborating to achieve mutual interests.

- *Marxism* is concerned with social classes and the relationships between them, for example in the capitalist era the "proletariat" (working class) and "bourgeoisie" (capitalist class).
- *Feminism* is concerned primarily with women, but also sometimes with children, gender nonconforming people, transgender people, and men.
- *Social Constructivism* considers society (as a whole) as a central actor, and how different societies in different times and places build and maintain different kinds of social realities.
- *Post-structuralism* considers actors with "power," how they express their power in diverse contexts, and the consequences of that power for how we think, how we communicate, and how we behave.

A Word of Caution: The identification of actors associated with international relations theories is not actually quite as simple as indicated above. IR theorists often focus in practice on multiple actors simultaneously. The trick is to think about emphasis and prioritization, about how certain kinds of actors are more central than others, and how the choice of focus on one actor over others impacts a thinker's ideas, perspectives, interests, and actions. You may personally decide to emphasize all the actors identified above, some of them, none of them, or a different set of actors entirely.

Who? Author Biography

Who is Lee Kyung Hae? What was his life like? Knowing the author of a text can provide valuable insights into its context, intent, meaning, and significance. When first finding out about an individual, it is important to research and think about many different dimensions of their life and how their life experiences may have impacted their thinking about global politics. Take the learner-centered challenge and find the answers to the following questions about Lee before reading on:

- Where was Lee born, where was he raised, who raised him, and what cultural influences may have affected Lee's interests and ideas?
- What kind of education did Lee attain and where did he attain that education? What degree did he achieve? How might his training have set his life on a particular course or influenced his decisions?
- What jobs and volunteer positions did Lee have after he completed his education and with which organizations or companies? How might those positions have affected Lee's life ambitions, interests, perspectives, and ideas?

- Is Lee still alive? If not, how and when and where did he die?

The time, place, and manner of an individual's death can be a very important piece of context for understanding their ideas and perspectives on global politics. This is certainly the case for Lee, who died by suicide only a few minutes after he distributed the statement in Section 3.B. The manner of a person's death may be significant for understanding a particular situation or primary document in context. Consider, for example, Dr. Martin Luther King, Jr., who was murdered in 1968, and whose 1967 speech is excerpted in chapter 11. King's leadership in the civil rights and poor peoples' movements put him in danger, and yet he was determined to support the movement. In like manner, assessing Lee's death—self-immolation—might help us better interpret the points he makes in his statement. Consider what it means to be a martyr or to die for a cause.

- Why would someone die for a cause?
- What are the morals or ethics surrounding the manner of Lee's death?[4]

Looking up biographical information about the author of a given text is a good first step in thinking about *positions*, *perspectives*, and *interests*, all central to asking *who?* and thinking critically about global political actors, and why people think and behave as they do.

Who Are the Subjects? Who Is the Audience?

Take a moment to identify all the actors listed in Lee's statement. One active reading and note-taking technique is to circle each named actor using a pen or pencil in the text itself. It is a good idea to make note of how Lee feels about these actors, along with other relevant information, perhaps using arrows to connect the circle to notes in the margins. Along with a consideration of the subjects of Lee's statement, also think about who might be the intended audience for his statement.

- *Farmers* (also in the text: "small farmers" and "Korean farmers"): an occupational category; *small* farmers meaning agricultural producers who farm relatively small plots of land;
- *Rural communities*: a geographically defined group, often used synonymously in global political conversations with *agricultural communities*, though rural and agricultural communities do not always reference the same groups. Rural communities are typically juxtaposed to *urban* ones, communities of people that Lee also mentions;

- *Korea*: a nation-state in East Asia. This is a good time to look up a map of East Asia to identify its location in the world and consider its neighbors and other geographical characteristics (proximity to ocean, connection to land mass, etc.);
- *Less developed countries* (LDCs): The term LDC is sometimes used to discuss countries with economies based in agriculture, that have relatively low average incomes, and/or in which relatively large portions of the population live in poverty. Many LDCs are now considered part of the *global south*, while during the Cold War most were lumped into the *third world*. (Before moving on, find out what these terms mean, who uses them, and when they are used. Start by reviewing how the United Nations and associated agencies define them and build from there.)[5]
- *World Trade Organization*: a *multilateral* or *international organization* (an IO), whose members are nation-states. The WTO is a forum for negotiating and establishing rules about international trade, and a forum for trade dispute resolution, among member states (take a moment to look up the WTO on the internet at www.wto.org).[6]

As Lee's statement indicates, thinking about global politics involves consideration of different kinds of actors and groups of actors, distinguished along multiple dimensions. Consider the following kinds of actor traits and characteristics used often in global political conversations to think about, understand, and categorize actors of different types:

- *Demographic characteristics*: Individual, community-level, and national demographic characteristics of the authors, actors, or audience of a situation under study (e.g., income level/class, ethnicity, gender/sex, religion, age, race, education, national origin, and language);
- *Geographic location*: Where in the world the actors involved live and the significance of that location (e.g., the *global south* or the *global north*, *Western* actors, the Middle East and North Africa (MENA), Sub-Saharan Africa (SSA), urban and rural communities, and metropoles and hinterlands);
- *Institutional type*: The nature and function of the actor, if it is an institutional or organizational one (e.g., public, quasi-public, or private institutions, nation-states, governments, political parties, corporations, state-owned enterprises, nonprofit organizations, religious institutions, multilateral organizations, schools, trade unions, and farmer cooperatives, but also functional types as with interest groups that advocate for the interests of their members or pressure groups that put pressure on policymakers);
- *Political-historical markers*: chronological markers that can help understand the actors identified, especially their perspectives and interests in

context of time/history (e.g., colonial and post-colonial states, empires and imperial powers, Bretton Woods institutions, and post–World War II collective security institutions);
- *Occupation and other socio-economic functions*: industrial workers, agricultural laborers, caregivers, teachers, nurses, civil servants, bankers, politicians and policymakers and public officials, debtors and creditors, consumers and distributors and producers, and core and peripheral actors.

In thinking critically about any writing or speech on global politics, it is also a good idea to think about *who is here?* and *who is missing?* These questions can help learners begin negotiating matters of position, perspective, and interest. Who a writer or speaker does *not* include is often as important, or even more important, than who *is* included in a text or statement.

Who? Position

Thinking about *positionality* is important in order to accurately describe, understand, analyze, and criticize global political events, actors, relationships, and dynamics. Concretely, positionality refers to one's *relative* position in global society compared to the positions of other social actors. Thinking about actor positions requires thinking about not only spatial and temporal locations but also actor locations within a variety of often overlapping local, national, and global social hierarchies, or *social positions*. Actor positions can change from context to context and over time and space. While some aspects of social positionality are relatively clear and objective (such as relative income level or level of formal education), others are more difficult to identify owing to conceptual and measurement difficulties (e.g., power).

Research the following questions when analyzing *positionality*:

- Where in time and space is this actor located?
- What is their position in the global social hierarchy?
- Which dimensions of the actor's position seem most relevant in context?

In the situation under study here, considering positionality helps decipher Lee's meaning and puts his obvious anger and frustration into context. Lee describes himself as a Korean farmer who has failed. He struggles to make a living in a world he sees as inhospitable, even deadly, for small-scale agriculture. He draws comparisons between himself and other Korean farmers, and then between Korean famers and farmers in other developing countries, noting that their experiences in the global economy over the past several decades have also been increasingly difficult. In this way, Lee sees himself occupying a similar position to others who have the same occupation (farmer) and live in countries that are developing. *Developing country* speaks to a complex position between nation-states, contrasting *developing* with *developed* countries. The term *developing*, then, references to relatively low national income and standards of living, national dependence on agriculture, geographic location in a developing region (Latin America, Asia, Africa or parts of Oceania, Eastern Europe, and the Middle East), and/or prior historical status as a colony.[7] Critical questions arise in the context of how Lee thinks about position:

- Is it appropriate for Lee to lump developing country farmers altogether?
- Do small farmers around the world see eye to eye on trade policy and the WTO?
- What about farmers from developed countries or city dwellers and their needs? Where do they fit into the story?
- Who is buying all the farmland in Korea and other developing countries, once farmers sell and move to the city? [8]

Lee also speaks about himself as someone whose life and fortunes are controlled by other actors, some of them in other parts of the world, who are more powerful than he is, and thereby points to issues related to *inequality*. He speaks bitterly about the fancy apartment buildings in which urbanites live, located on what used to be productive farmland. He rhetorically questions representatives to the WTO, accusing them of failing to represent farmers. He accuses a "small number of big WTO members" of sacrificing the well-being of citizens and farmers around the globe to their own interests. Lee is thus pointing to relatively different and unequal positions in the global political system, to *inequalities* that influence the outcome of the WTO meetings to the disadvantage of Lee and farmers like him. In his statement, Lee indicates that inequalities in negotiating power at the WTO stem from relative economic size/strength—in discussing the big WTO members, he is referencing the relatively wealthier and more industrialized (or *developed*) United States and European Union, actors that have historically had different ideas about agricultural trade than countries like Korea.

Now is a good time to briefly return to Lee's statement and find answers to the following additional questions about positionality and inequality:

- Where does Lee discuss inequalities in the text?
- Who is unequal to whom? And inequality of *what?* Income? Power? Something else?

Who? Perspective

An actor's perspective on the world is shaped by many factors, including social, geographic, and historical position, life experiences, formal and informal education, and cultural context, among others. The particular *lens* or *lenses* through which an actor views the world influences their ideas, interests, and behaviors. Put differently, *perspective* influences how an actor understands their role in the world and their obligations toward others, as well as how they interpret the behavior of other actors. Perspective identification may be as simple as pointing out profession or class position in society, or as deep as assessing a person's ideological belief system. Perspective is a window into *worldview* or *ideology* and can help us understand why actors think and behave the way they do.

- From what perspectives does Lee view and interpret the world?
- Which worldviews and ideologies does Lee disclose in his statement?

Even in Lee's short statement, differing perspectives are apparent. Lee's perspective is clearly informed by his experiences as a farmer himself and as an advocate for farmers for many decades. He also advocates for the earth. Part of Lee's concern for farmers is rooted in worry about who will steward the land and water after farmers sell their land to developers and move to the cities. Lee is also clearly opposed to the WTO, with its global advocacy and facilitation of free trade policies. In the final paragraphs, Lee takes a stand against multinational corporations (MNCs) and globalization in general.

The perspective that Lee articulates—an anti-free trade, anti-globalization, and anti-multinational corporation perspective—has been central to global protest and social movements since the 1990s.[9] The 1999 Battle in Seattle in protest against the WTO was followed by huge protests against the World Bank and International Monetary Fund in Washington DC in 2000, just three years before the massive WTO protests in Cancun, Mexico, at which Lee gave his statement and then died by suicide in protest. Globalization (a process of global integration that transcends national borders), free trade (a policy arrangement in which goods and services cross-national borders without government interference), and MNCs (entities that control operations in more than one country, even if they do not own them) are often grouped together by actors who embrace perspectives like Lee's.[10] Increasing global integration, growing hegemony of free trade policy and ideology, and increasing dominance of MNCs globally since the early 1970s have been central features of the global *neoliberal* period that is currently coming to a close. (Note: *neoliberalism* is another important and extensively debated term to investigate using the tools and techniques discussed in chapter 2.)[11]

If the WTO exists for the purpose of facilitating international free trade, and if Lee is clearly opposed to free trade in agriculture, then we can safely intuit on the basis of Lee's statement that Lee has a different perspective on trade than the WTO. We can also speculate that Lee and the WTO likely embrace different economic and political ideologies, though this is less clear from the text. While *ideologies* are collections of normative beliefs (i.e., beliefs about values and morals, about how we *should* look at the world and how the world *should* work), *perspective* indicates a broader outlook that may include ideological beliefs in addition to cultural, social, economic, and historical perspectives, likes and dislikes, and personal reflections and views, among other elements.[12] The primary source document in this chapter is too brief and specific to rush to conclusions about ideology—but can you connect some of the beliefs Lee might hold to ideologies you know about already?

When considering perspectives, a variety of critical questions arise in the context of Lee's statement and the WTO:[13]

- Why does the WTO support free trade between countries?
- Are there other perspectives on trade that are captured (or not captured) in Lee's statement?
- Does the government of Korea agree with Lee's anti-free trade stance?
- Why does Lee imply that the big members of the WTO have too much influence?
- Is anyone representing farmers at WTO negotiations?

It bears mentioning that perspective, and how perspectives align, is dependent on context, and that is also the case for *position* and *interests*.[14] Indeed, while Lee and the WTO have different perspectives on free trade, they may agree in other contexts. For example, they might agree that it is a bad idea to settle disputes on the Korean peninsula via nuclear standoff or on the likelihood of a bumper (or plentiful) rice crop next year.

- Does the text include evidence of how Lee interprets the world?
- Where and how does Lee criticize the WTO? Does Lee criticize anyone or anything else?

Who? Interests

Along with position and perspective, thinking about what an actor *wants* and *needs*—that is, their *interests*—in the situation under study can help make sense of their statements, writings, and other behaviors. Lee makes his primary interest rather clear in his statement: trade protections for agricultural products so that farmers can earn a decent living and take care of the earth. He seems to have a broader, and perhaps secondary, interest in halting and reversing globalization more generally.

- What does Lee want and need?
- How do Lee's interests help explain his behavior?

As Lee indicates, and as deeper research would verify, the interests of the WTO are different than his own, as are the interests of the big members Lee references. By the time Lee made his statement, the WTO had made great progress freeing trade in many industrial markets and in some services, but had made little progress freeing trade in agriculture, hence Lee's explicit criticism of the Uruguay Round negotiations of the General Agreement on Trade and Tariffs (GATT), the forerunner of the WTO.[15] The United States and the European Union (EU) maintain extensive systems of agricultural subsidies that work to lower agricultural prices abroad when US farmers export their subsidized crops. Freer agricultural trade would require the United States and the European Union to reduce or eliminate subsidies, policy changes that are very difficult for domestic political reasons in both places (not least because farmers in these countries who receive subsidies want to keep getting them). In part because of the unfair advantage subsidies give to developed countries, Lee thinks developing countries should be allowed to protect their agricultural trade too, so that farmers in developing countries can better compete with farmers from the United States and the European Union, on a more level playing field. By extension, Lee is also criticizing the power that the big members have to influence WTO negotiations, indicating a pivotal power inequality at the center of trade negotiations. Competing interests around agriculture remain a major issue for the WTO today.[16]

Considerations of government agricultural policy points to another great *who?* question, one that is especially useful for thinking critically about why a given actor may advocate or oppose a specific policy or outcome: *Cui bono?* Or *who benefits?*[17] Identifying who benefits can assist in critical thinking in many different contexts. Identifying beneficiaries can help learners question why a certain public official may support a specific policy in the legislature or can help them investigate why a certain country may vote as they do in the United Nations or the WTO.[18] And, analyzing who benefits in a given situation helps learners raise questions about conflicts of interest, from cases of public corruption to instances of suspicious journalism.

In various theoretical traditions in global politics, observers and scholars sometimes make general assumptions about the core interests that influence and frame individual worldviews, that is, assumptions about *human nature*.[19] For instance, *realists* assume humans all make decisions based on egocentric considerations. Thomas Hobbes theorized that people were generally motivated by "competition, diffidence, and glory," meaning that people are broadly interested in power, wealth, and social recognition (Hobbes recorded his theory in the sixteenth century, based on his observations of European society).[20] Hobbes' interpretation of human interests influenced his understanding of how society works and how nation-states behave. As another example, Karl Marx remarked that in capitalist systems a single interest in wealth and riches prevails: "Accumulate! Accumulate! This is Moses and the prophets."[21] This understanding of human nature under capitalism informs *Marxist* theoretical perspectives. Similarly, economists in the *neoclassical economics* tradition assume that humans are rational and are thus uniformly self-interested, though, unlike the Marxists, the neoclassical economists seem to be at peace with this. Other theories in global politics, like *liberalism*, take a different view of human nature. For example, Immanuel Kant thought that humans were inherently good and would get along with each other but for the negative influence and strictures of society.[22]

Critical questions come up when a thinker or writer makes big assumptions about what people want or what motivates their behavior. Lee argues that small farmers in developing countries have the same interests. Yet, Lee's interpretation of human nature is not clear cut: he advocates for himself and also for other farmers, and he sacrifices his life to support farmers around the world. Critical questions about human nature and Lee's own ideas might look something like the following, and learners would benefit from struggling with possible answers in this and other contexts:

- Do you agree with Lee that small farmers in developing countries have the same interests? Do they have similar interests beyond the limited context of farming and free trade?
- Are theories of human nature right in thinking that people have core interests that are relatively stable and unchanging (whether their interests are motivated by selfishness or a desire to cooperate)?
- Are people always self-interested as realists or neoclassical economists often suggest?
- Were Lee's statements and actions motivated by self-interest?
- Associated with Lee's manner of death, how do we understand interest in a context of death by suicide as a form of protest?

3.D: RECOMMENDED READINGS ON GLOBAL FOOD AND AGRICULTURAL POLITICS

Akram-Lodhi, Haroon. *Hungry for Change*. Halifax: Fernwood, 2013.
Bello, Walden. *The Food Wars*. London: Verso, 2009.
Bhagwati, Jagdish. *In Defense of Globalization*. London: Oxford, 2007.
Patel, Raj. *Stuffed and Starved*. Hoboken, NJ: Melville House, 2007.
Rosset, Peter. *Food Is Different!* Halifax: Fernwood, 2006.
Stringer, Lindsay, Twyman, Chasca and Gibbs, Leah. "Learning from the South: Common Challenges and Solutions for Small Scale Farming." *The Geographic Journal* 174, no. 3 (2008): 235–50.

NOTES

1. Darla K. Deardorff, "Identification and Assessment of Intercultural Competence As a Student Outcome of Internationalization," *Journal of Studies in International Education* 10, no. 3 (2006): 241–66.

2. Laura Carlsen, "WTO Kills Farmers: In Memory of Lee Kyung Hae," countercurrents.org, September 16, 2003, accessed April 4, 2020 (all rights reserved, reproduced based on fair use doctrine from Section 107 of US Copyright Law), http://www.countercurrents.org/glo-carlsen160903.htm.

3. Most international relations textbooks listed in the introductory chapter either include a chapter that discusses theories or extensively apply the theories of IR to the discussion of IR history and current events throughout the text. E.g., Henry Nau, *Perspectives on International Relations: Power, Institutions, and Ideas*, 7th ed (Thousand Oaks, CA: CQ Press/Sage, 2020). For a deeper analysis and review of the theories see Scott Burchill and Andrew Linklater. *Theories of International Relations*, 5th ed. (Hampshire, UK: Palgrave Macmillan, 2015).

4. Thinking about death and death by suicide may be difficult and even traumatic. Seek support from trusted mentors, colleagues, friends, and/or family if considering Lee's life and death cause stress. Counseling and mental health professionals also offer excellent outlets for talking about stress, when necessary and appropriate.

5. "Least Developed Countries," United Nations, accessed April 4, 2020, https://www.un.org/development/desa/dpad/least-developed-country-category.html.

6. In addition to World Trade Organization Website, https://www.wto.org/english/thewto_e/thewto_e.htm, consider the following for an overview of the WTO: Bernard M. Hoekman and Petros C Mavroidis, *World Trade Organization: Law, Economics, and Politics* (London: Routledge, Taylor & Francis Group, 2016); Amrita Narlikar, M. J. Daunton, and Robert Mitchell Stern, *The World Trade Organization: A Very Short Introduction* (New York: Oxford University Press, 2012).

7. United Nations "Least Developed Countries."

8. E.g., Raj Patel, *Stuffed and Starved* (Hoboken, NJ: Melville House, 2007); Haroon Akram-Lodhi, *Hungry for Change* (Halifax: Fernwood, 2013); Lindsay C. Stringer, Chasca Twyman, and Leah M. Gibbs. "Learning from the South: Common Challenges and Solutions for Small-Scale Farming." *Geographical Journal* 174, no. 3 (2008): 235–50.

9. Susan Ariel Aaronson, *Taking Trade to the Streets: The Lost History of Public Efforts to Shape Globalization* (Ann Arbor: University of Michigan Press, 2014).

10. On anti-globalization movements see, e.g., Joseph Stiglitz, *Globalization and Its Discontents* (New York: WW Norton, 2002); Jagdish Bhagwati, *In Defense of Globalization* (London: Oxford, 2007).

11. David Harvey, *A Brief History of Neoliberalism* (New York: Oxford University Press, 2005).

12. Matthew Festenstein and Michael Kenny, *Political Ideologies: A Reader and Guide*. (Oxford: Oxford University Press, 2005).

13. Hoekman and Mavroidis, *World Trade Organization: Law . . .*; Narlikar, *The World Trade Organization: A Very Short Introduction*.

14. Roger Fisher, William Ury, and Bruce Patton, *Getting to Yes: Negotiating Agreement Without Giving In*, 2nd ed. (New York: Penguin Books, 1991).

15. Jagdish N. Bhagwati and Mathias Hirsch, *The Uruguay Round and Beyond: Essays in Honor of Arthur Dunkel. Studies in International Economics* (Ann Arbor: University of Michigan Press, 2001).

16. E.g., Walden Bello, *The Food Wars* (London: Verso, 2009); Peter Rosset, *Food Is Different!* (Halifax: Fernwood, 2006).

17. The Latin legal phrase *Cui bono?* or *Who benefits?* is often used in International Political Economy (IPE) conversations.

18. For votes that are recorded, the UN provides voting records accessible to the public https://research.un.org/en/docs/find/voting.

19. For an excellent introduction to theories and theorists of human nature see Glenn Tinder, *Political Thinking: The Perennial Questions*, 6th ed. (New York: Longman Classics Series, 2004).

20. Hobbes, Thomas. *Leviathan*. A. D Lindsay, Everyman's Library. Philosophy and Theology (London: J.M. Dent, 1928, originally published 1651).

21. Marx, Karl. *Das Kapital, A Critique of Political Economy*. Chicago: H. Regnery, 1959.

22. Kant, Immanuel. *Perpetual Peace*. Project Gutenburg. Produced by Turgut Dincer, Ramon Pajares Box. https://www.gutenberg.org/files/50922/50922-h/50922-h.htm.

Chapter 4

What or What is?
Identifying What Matters

When approaching a new topic, subject, or situation, it is important to ask and answer the question *what?* or *what is?* Asking such questions allows a learner of a new subject to identify and understand the ideas, concepts, actors, relationships, dynamics, structures, institutions, and other political phenomena that are important in thinking about global politics. Global politics is about how people or other actors interact with one another around the world and how actors try to exercise power and control in their lives and the lives of others. This chapter examines some of the many social forms such interactions can take on the global political stage.

Essential to an understanding of global politics is identifying the basic functions and influence of global institutions within which people work and live, such as the United Nations (UN) on which this chapter focuses. The UN embodies the concept and practice of *global governance*, that is, the decision-making procedures, regulations, and institutions that facilitate political cooperation and policymaking over shared resources.[1] The UN is a global *intergovernmental organization* (IGO) through which states wield their influence and power on collective decisions and problems.[2] The primary source included in Section 4.B of this chapter is an excerpt from the UN's founding document, the *Charter of the United Nations*, that provides insight into the UN's mandate, goals, structure, and political dynamics, and also places the UN in its historical context. The *UN Charter*, and the UN as an IGO itself, is significant because it established the environment and rules that influence diplomatic engagement between states (led by individual delegates) on important collective action problems to this day.[3]

First, in what follows, Section 4.A reviews current best practices in internet searching because the internet is one of the most widely used resources for people who are learning about a new subject area. Section 4.B then includes an excerpt from the *UN Charter*, and Section 4.C guides learners on how to ask *what?* questions about global social interactions and processes. Finally, Section 4.D provides a recommended reading list for those who wish to learn more about the United Nations and global governance.

4.A: INTERNET SEARCH ENGINES AND SEARCH TOOLS AND SKILLS

Even while humans live their entire lives with some technologies, like the internet, we often take them for granted and think we know how to use them when we really only understand the basics. Lack of knowledge about methods of utilizing resources limits our productive capacities. This section seeks to support learners in overcoming such limitations by reviewing current (2019–2020) functions of internet search engines, along with several tools, skills, and practices that make internet research more efficient and productive. Even while such tools and practices are specific to the current structure of technological innovation, they are portable and may provide lifelong support for engaging in independent learning and especially for recognizing when to educate oneself on how technologies work in our lives.

The following discussion reviews searching new information using internet search engines by providing the specific example of learning more about the definition of a *charter* and searching for information on the primary document included in Section 4.B, the *Charter of the United Nations*. Anything that appears in brackets in the text below, like [this], is intended to give ideas about how learners can use terms to conduct searches, thus the words in the brackets should be entered into a search engine *without the brackets* to achieve the same results.

Searching with Search Engines

Search engines, card catalogs, or dictionaries and encyclopedias (whether printed or online) are written/collated and provided by their creators (and companies) to help optimize a researcher's ability to find unknown words or phrases by providing a list of the most reliable sources on the topic. Online search engines search internet websites for information on a topic, while online public access catalogs through a library search the books and journals to which a library has access.[4]

The internet has millions of entries on most subjects, and millions of sites to search; if we start our search on an internet search engine (Google is the most widely used in 2019) and type in the term [define charter], it is possible to limit the search results to definitions. The search provides millions of entries[5] and it is the researcher's job to identify reliable entries and decipher from a huge list of results. In almost every search engine, advertisements are first to appear and they are clearly identified. Researchers should ignore the advertisements because they are not reliable sources of information. To avoid advertisements, use search engines that cater to privacy, like SearchEncrypt or DuckDuckGo. After the advertisements, the search engine results will enumerate prioritized websites according to the search engine's algorithm and prior searches and indexing of the search term entered.[6] This list of prioritized websites may be an excellent start to a search, but, just because they are prioritized, does not mean they are reliable. It simply means that the search engine has identified them as being the most trusted sources on the term. It is up to the researcher to apply critical thinking and analytical skills to determine validity (see Section 3.B on reliable internet sources), and to use techniques to limit the searches to more reliable results, as is covered in the next section.

Limiting Searches

When a search produces millions of results, like the one conducted on [charter], the researcher has the difficult task of deciding which results to pursue and which to ignore, and that includes learning how to use keywords, filters, advanced search options, or quotations to create better search results. For instance, initial results for a term like *charter* do not provide history or definitions of government charters, but such information can be located by narrowing search results, for instance by adding new keywords or filters to the search.

As an example, using quotation marks or Boolean operators[7] to limit searches is helpful, such as in a search for [United Nations Charter] versus ["United Nations Charter"]. Without quotation marks most search engines will assume the Boolean operator OR in between each of the words and it will find every instance of the three words (not necessarily together), which may not yield the desired results. Limiting the search to the exact phrase will provide better results, that is, with the quotation marks, like so ["United Nations Charter"], or by adding the Boolean operator AND to limit to results that include all three of those words together like so [United AND Nations AND Charter]. Other search terms or shortcuts include [book "United Nations Charter"] to locate a book or [United Nations Charter filetype:PDF] to find a PDF on the phrase. Note that such conventions might change based on technological advances, or differ from search engine to search engine, and thus it is important to keep apprised of changes and educate oneself on best searching techniques; most search engines provide overviews of the best ways to use them.[8]

Identifying and Searching with Keywords and Phrases

The most frustrating part of searching may be when one is using words or phrases that are not returning the expected results. Along with search limitation tools, identifying the best keywords and phrases for a search is crucial.

- *Use many different possible terms, keywords, and phrases.* Make notes about the results received using different words or phrases because notes remind us to avoid repeating the same searches later and supports adaptation in using search terms in relation to earlier results (sometimes the first search is rather unproductive but provides ideas for a new set of words or phrases that may be useful in subsequent search attempts).[9] Be creative and unafraid with the search terms. As an example, in searching for information on the United Nations Charter, the researcher will find and use other search terms like: [charter], ["United Nations Charter"], [international], ["international organization"], ["international agreement"], ["formal statement"], or [constitution].
- *Consider how the subject might be catalogued.* Before searching, consider how a website might use the word or phrase and try to use those words. Websites are indexed according to subjects and keywords. Therefore thinking carefully about the words they might use will help achieve better results. In our case, the "United Nations Charter" might also be catalogued as "the Charter of the United Nations" and searching for the latter might produce different results.
- *Use Search Indexes and Directories.* For broad searches on a discipline, use Search Indexes (also called directories) on the internet. An index in a book also provides lists of search terms or phrases. Consider a Web Index/Directory like Best of the Web (BOTW) from the Open Directory Project (now DMOZ) that lists broad subject areas and associated dedicated websites. BOTW includes *Political Science* and *International Relations* subjects in the index and links to major websites in the disciplines.

4.B: PRIMARY SOURCE ON GLOBAL GOVERNANCE

Charter of the United Nations (excerpt, 1945)[10]

WE THE PEOPLES OF THE UNITED NATIONS DETERMINED

to save succeeding generations from the scourge of war, which twice in our lifetime has brought untold sorrow to mankind, and

to reaffirm faith in fundamental human rights, in the dignity and worth of the human person, in the equal rights of men and women and of nations large and small, and to establish conditions under which justice and respect for the obligations arising from treaties and other sources of international law can be maintained, and

to promote social progress and better standards of life in larger freedom,

AND FOR THESE ENDS

to practice tolerance and live together in peace with one another as good neighbours, and

to unite our strength to maintain international peace and security, and

to ensure, by the acceptance of principles and the institution of methods, that armed force shall not be used, save in the common interest, and

to employ international machinery for the promotion of the economic and social advancement of all peoples,

HAVE RESOLVED TO COMBINE OUR EFFORTS
TO ACCOMPLISH THESE AIMS

Accordingly, our respective Governments, through representatives assembled in the city of San Francisco, who have exhibited their full powers found to be in good and due form, have agreed to the present Charter of the United Nations and do hereby establish an international organization to be known as the United Nations.

CHAPTER I: PURPOSES AND PRINCIPLES

Article 1

The Purposes of the United Nations are:

1. To maintain international peace and security, and to that end: to take effective collective measures for the prevention and removal of threats to the peace, and for the suppression of acts of aggression or other breaches of the peace, and to bring about by peaceful means, and in conformity with the principles of justice and international law, adjustment or settlement of international disputes or situations which might lead to a breach of the peace;
2. To develop friendly relations among nations based on respect for the principle of equal rights and self-determination of peoples, and to take other appropriate measures to strengthen universal peace;
3. To achieve international co-operation in solving international problems of an economic, social, cultural, or humanitarian character, and in promoting and encouraging respect for human rights and for fundamental freedoms for all without distinction as to race, sex, language, or religion; and

4. To be a centre for harmonizing the actions of nations in the attainment of these common ends . . .

4.C: THE UNITED NATIONS AND GLOBAL GOVERNANCE

The *UN Charter* provides an important starting point for learners new to global politics because it helps identify important concepts, relationships, dynamics, and institutional forces in global political behavior. In order to make effective use of the question *what?* or *what is?*, learners should identify the main questions to ask and answer in order to fully understand the significance of a subject under study, as represented in the following list. The rest of the section delves into such questions with guidance for learners on how to go about searching for answers.

- *What is a charter?* When assessing or studying any primary document, it is crucial to have a good understanding of *what it is*, that is, the history of its usage and why it is important, especially the political relationships and other dynamics that it signifies. A speech, like that assessed in chapter 3, is different than a charter, for instance, in the reason for and method of its production, in its rationale and purpose, and in its political and social meaning and influence.
- *What historical events occurred to incentivize people to negotiate the UN Charter and who was involved in such negotiations?* Every document is created in a particular historical context and understanding the context is crucial for analyzing the reasons for its existence and considering its application to other circumstances.
- *What do the historical context, authors, and influence of the UN Charter reveal about international negotiations, diplomacy, or global governance problems and solutions?* This question reveals the social dynamics that are of primary concern in this chapter. A charter or other document will matter little if it is not created, upheld, and adhered to by the people who made it, and it will also mean little if its influence is not felt by the actors and issues it intends to affect.

What? Definition

International agreements, also called instruments, signify actions, policies, tactics, or shared visions and ideals between two or more parties. Global actors who sign agreements are usually state governments but can include nongovernmental actors as well. Some agreements are *bilateral* meaning they are written and signed by two state parties, and others are *multilateral*, signed by three or more parties. Such agreements are governed by and deposited with states or international organizations (IOs); the UN is depositary of hundreds of multilateral agreements.[11] The form and function of international agreements are themselves regulated by a treaty, the *Vienna Convention on the Law of Treaties* (1969).[12] Written international agreements are of many types: *Charter, Treaty, Convention, Covenant, Declaration, Resolution*, or *Memorandum of Understanding*.[13] Take some time to learn more about the different kinds of agreements at the international level (consult, for example, the UN Treaty Collection at treaties.un.org or find a secondary source like those listed in the endnotes or recommended reading list at the end of this chapter), and form answers to the following questions:

- When would governments want to use a *charter* versus a *declaration* as an international agreement and why?
- What does it mean to be a *state party* to an international agreement, like the *UN Charter*?

In considering the *UN Charter*, comparing dictionary entries of the term *charter* can be insightful (like the *Oxford English Dictionary*, *Cambridge*, or the *Merriam-Webster* online dictionary, using tactics as covered in chapter 2). All these definitions refer to "a formal statement" or a "constitution" that protects people's rights.[14] The *Cambridge Dictionary* provides different definitions for the United States (US) versus the United Kingdom (UK) usages that reveal differences in history and meaning: the US definition focuses on government action in providing charters that list citizen rights, whereas the UK definition focuses on the people themselves as being part of the creation of the list of rights and even demanding those rights of government.[15]

Each of the noun definition entries specifically mentions the *Charter of the United Nations*, which may indicate, at the very least, the ubiquitous nature and influence of the UN. After perusing the different noun, verb, and adjective definitions, a learner might decide that there are multiple definitions that could apply to the *UN Charter* but that a working definition is a *formal instrument establishing the United Nations and calling all state parties to collective action and collaboration to protect human rights everywhere in the world.* However, such working definitions prompt more questions to investigate:

- *Whose rights does the UN Charter guarantee and what rights does it guarantee?*

The *UN Charter* mentions "fundamental human rights" several times but does not give an exhaustive list (because its main purpose is to create the UN itself). Finding the list of human rights will take more research and entails reading other human rights treaties, including the "international bill of rights" and the nine core human rights treaties with their optional protocols. Start with the Universal Declaration of Human Rights (UDHR) (1948) and take some time to educate yourself on your human rights (then consult chapter 13 of this book for further discussion of human rights).[16]

The *UN Charter* also mentions the "sovereign equality of all its Members" indicating that states have rights, closely associated with one of the organs of the UN established in the *UN Charter*, the International Court of Justice. *Sovereignty* is an important concept in international relations that underpins the way that states interact with each other—it means that states have the right to act or make decisions without the interference of others. Yet, challenges to state sovereignty often arise in cases of human rights violations, genocide, war crimes, and crimes against humanity. The issue of state rights versus individual human rights is contentious and could be a fruitful line of inquiry.

- *What does it mean to be a party to a treaty in international law? Are all states parties to the UN Charter, and what if some states are not parties?*

As of 2020, there are 193 member states of the UN who are party to the *UN Charter*, meaning that the state agrees to follow the rules or commitments of the agreement. There are several options for a state to become a party to an international agreement. For instance, treaty ratification means that a country's parliament must agree to the treaty. Typically, without ratification a state government is not held accountable to an international agreement. Peruse the UN website to learn more about international law at treaties.un.org.[17]

What? Historical Context and Influential Actors

Understanding the historical context of a primary source document or situation under study, like the creation of the *UN Charter*, allows for much deeper insight into why people thought the document was important to negotiate and write at the time, and why we should continue to read and study it as an important aspect of global politics. Historical context questions about authors or other influential actors help develop critical thinking skills that reveal important relationships and dynamics that otherwise might go unnoticed. In the case of the *UN Charter*, the first or second glance would reveal that the *UN Charter* was negotiated, signed, and ratified by influential states at the end of World War II, but to talk about a state as an entity in international relations (as in, the US negotiated to create the *UN Charter*) is to belie or gloss over the actual groups and individuals who make up a state and who cause it to function or who actually conduct the negotiations. Begin your search by attempting an answer to the following question by searching for the *UN Charter* history on UN webpages.[18]

- Who negotiated the UN Charter, what were their ideologies, and how did they influence the final product?

All the people who were involved in prior conferences on international negotiations (like the Paris Peace Conference of 1919, for instance), the creation of international organizations that preceded the UN (like the League of Nations), and negotiations for the *UN Charter* itself, had their own ideologies, cultural influences, and idiosyncratic differences, even as they represented their states and negotiated with each other on shared goals. The conversations that created the main structure and ideas of the *UN Charter* were restricted to leaders and representatives from four major states, sometimes called *great powers,* and at the time labeled "the big four" who met at Dumbarton Oaks, a mansion in Washington DC before the San Francisco Conference where the *UN Charter* was signed. Leaders of states, like US President Franklin D. Roosevelt (FDR), Soviet Premier Joseph Stalin, UK Prime Minister Winston Churchill, Chinese Minister of Foreign Affairs Soong Tzu-wen, among others, impacted the negotiations and the ideas that would be included in the *UN Charter*. FDR and Churchill, for instance, created a precursor in the *Atlantic Charter* (1941), covered in chapter 5, that solidified ideals of state collaboration and considerations of protecting human rights that would be included a few years later in the *UN Charter*.[19] Underpinning national leadership, various state diplomats had an impact on the ideas that went into the *UN Charter*, people like US Secretary of State Edward Stettinius and Foreign Secretary of the UK Anthony Eden, among others.

The UN structure and function was based on that of the experience and ideals of the League of Nations and even the Concert of Europe, two *collective security* organization attempts that had come before it and for which influential people, like US President Woodrow Wilson in supporting the League of Nations, had negotiated and fought.[20] Attempts at *collective security* strive to unite states to commit to addressing shared threats together rather than *passing the buck,* that is, waiting for someone else to deal with a problem. The culminating event for the UN was when the *UN Charter* was signed at a conference in San Francisco on June 26, 1945,[21] but that only represented the apex of months, years, and even centuries of negotiations and discussions about how to facilitate international collaboration between government leaders to avoid war, to ensure human rights protection of all peoples, and to facilitate work on collective action problems.

International Conferences and Conference Diplomacy

International agreements are often signed during international conferences (also called a *peace conference*, *summit*, or *congress*) such as the one that finalized the *UN Charter*. The practice of holding international conferences, *conference diplomacy*, historically occurred between leaders and/or representatives of two groups who sought diplomatic ways of negotiating with each other on an item or issue, usually negotiating the end of conflicts or negotiating prevention of conflicts before they occur.[22] International conferences may also be called *summits*, and the negotiations called *summit diplomacy*, when the highest officials of a government meet with each other rather than their representatives. Below is a list of some historically significant peace conferences. Take some time to learn about these other, similar kinds of conferences—doing so helps in assessing the conference under study in which the *UN Charter* was signed, the San Francisco Conference, and provides comparative data.[23] Along with the information provided on their historical significance, especially in terms of international relations and global politics, find out for yourself who met at these conferences, how long they lasted, and what was decided and between whom.

- *The Congress of Westphalia* (December 1644 to October 1648): This conference finalized several peace treaties, often called the Peace of Westphalia, notably ending the Thirty Years' War in Europe. The conference negotiations and treaties were one of the first instances of articulating the concept of *state sovereignty* and the idea of a *nation-state*.[24]
- *The Congress of Vienna* (September 1814 to June 1815): This conference represented the final decisions and celebrations that ended the Napoleonic Wars in which delegates allocated political control of territory as well as established rules and institutions that would facilitate cooperation in opposing aggressor states in the future (e.g., the Concert of Europe that represented *great power politics*) and was influential in setting ideas and rules about international conference diplomacy thenceforth.[25]
- *The Paris Peace Conference* (January 1919 to January 1920): The Paris Peace Conference concluded negotiations on World War I, the deadliest international war up to that point in history, and finalized the Treaty of Versailles, wherein US president Woodrow Wilson supported creating the League of Nations as a *collective security* organization that would have more permanence and breadth than the vague diplomacy of the Concert of Europe.[26]

Notably, the preparatory work leading up to an international conference, and any agreements signed, takes months or years of negotiation between some or all of the parties (which may have resulted from previous agreement/s at conferences or meetings that apply to the new conference and agreement/s). Further, the conferences reviewed above were all negotiated between *great powers*, that is, *hegemons* or powerful states in the international system who were able and willing to send delegates, and who had influence and power over others.[27] Conferences include people representing governments labeled with the following nomenclature: *ambassadors, statesmen, representatives, plenipotentiaries, delegates, emissaries,* or other.

- Take a moment to look up the different definitions for labels of state representatives (find definitions using dictionaries and consider the different functions assigned to the different labels).
- When is it appropriate to use one versus another of these labels and why.

For example, a *plenipotentiary* is a person who has the full powers of their government so that they can take actions or make agreements for their state on their own, without having to discuss with anyone. A *delegate*, on the other hand, is assigned to represent a state government's position in a negotiation but not to make commitments or approve actions unless approved by higher authorities.

The San Francisco Conference

Several important conferences and international agreements occurred in the years preceding the San Francisco Conference that were crucial to its occurrence and to the negotiations written into the *UN Charter*. Take the time to learn more about the conferences (they are listed below for easy identification), agreements made (or not made) at each conference, and why they were important to the San Francisco Conference and the creation of the *UN Charter*. Utilize the skills reviewed in Section 2.B and Section 4.B on using library resources, journal articles, dictionaries, encyclopedias, and reliable internet sources to create overviews (like those provided in the section above) for each conference/agreement and make note of the important decisions that would have affected or been included in the *UN Charter* agreement.

- Paris Peace Conference (January 1919–January 1920); *Treaty of Versailles* and *Covenant of the League of Nations* (June 28, 1919)
- The Atlantic Conference; the *Atlantic Charter* (August 1941)
- The *Declaration of the United Nations* (January 1, 1942)
- Moscow Conference (1943); *Moscow Declaration* (signed October 30, 1943)
- Teheran Conference (December 1943)

- Dumbarton Oaks Conference (August–October 1944)
- Yalta Conference (February 1945)
- Potsdam Conference (July–August 1945)

The San Francisco Conference was hosted by four countries and their secretaries of state/foreign affairs ministers: the US, China, the Union of Soviet Socialist Republics (USSR), and the UK. The delegates of the "big four" countries (or what FDR himself called "the four policemen") decided on a location after having had several meetings in Washington DC (at Dumbarton Oaks) in 1944 (the US showed its influence and power over these negotiations in several ways, including by hosting the conferences on US territory), and invited 46 other countries. Not all countries were invited to the San Francisco Conference—a determining factor was whether the country's leader had signed the *Declaration of United Nations* that affirmed the *Atlantic Charter* (reviewed in chapter 5). Spending time understanding why the *Declaration of United Nations* was important, and unearthing more of the details reviewed here related to the Dumbarton Oaks and San Francisco Conference and its negotiations, will reveal a lot about the UN's origins and even reveal some of the challenges that the UN struggles with to this day.[28]

What? Other Concepts, Dynamics, and Relationships

The initial phrases in the *UN Charter* include reference to a variety of additional global political concepts, dynamics, and relationships that are important to define and learn more about. Many of them are political science concepts about which scholars and practitioners excessively theorize, study, discuss, and opine (in order to join the conversation, you need to master the language, definitions, and history). Consider the following items you may have identified in the first few phrases of the *UN Charter*: *war, human rights, justice, treaties, international law, social progress, standards of life, freedom*, among others.

War

As an example, let us consider the phenomenon of *war* that the *UN Charter* raises in the first phrase: "We the peoples of the United Nations determined to save succeeding generations from the scourge of *war*" (emphasis added). There are many questions related to war that international relations scholars and practitioners have long discussed. Consider the classics: *The Art of War* by Sun Tzu written in the fifth century BC, or *The Law of War and Peace* by Hugo Grotius from 1625 on just war theory, or *On War* by Carl Von Clausewitz about the means and ends of warfare, published in 1830.

Thousands of books have been written on World War I and World War II alone, attempts at identifying why the wars occurred, military battles and tactics, and on the implications and impacts for succeeding generations. As a practice or concept in which humans engage, *war* may seem quite obvious, but upon closer examination, understanding why wars occur and analyzing what that means for human life and livelihoods become rather murky (for a deeper dive into analyzing why humans go to war with one another, see chapter 10). As you read each bullet point below, take a moment to think about the questions and attempt to answer them with more than one answer, finding evidence to back up your answer, and then move on to compare your answer with the text. It will become clear that the answers to why *wars* occur are not so obvious:

- *What is war and when does war occur?* Scholars and practitioners use multiple terms in warfare: *conflict, armed conflict, fight,* or *battle,* to name a few. When do we label something a *battle* versus *armed conflict* versus *war*?

Some scholars and organizations have created *working definitions* to help them label and analyze war, for instance, the Uppsala Data Conflict Database defines war as "a state-based conflict or dyad which reaches at least 1000 battle-related deaths in a specific calendar year."[29] To experts, these phenomena look somewhat different (hence the constant arguments over definitions) because they illustrate different kinds of violent relationships between people. Notice that the Uppsala definition focuses on the number of deaths in a given year due to warfare.

- *Why does war occur?*

Von Clausewitz, a famous Prussian general who fought in the Napoleonic Wars and who is widely read for his treatise *On War* (1830), focused on the aims and ends of warfare in his definition, arguing that warfare was about destroying one's enemy in order to gain territory or some other benefit. Famously, he wrote, "War is a mere continuation of policy by other means."[30] The *UN Charter* calls state governments to work together to avoid war, the main premise of a *collective security* organization, but why are governments sometimes unable to diplomatically solve their problems and turn to warfare instead? (Review chapter 10 in this volume for a lengthier discussion.)

- *Who fights wars?* Does war occur between states in the same way that we talk about it, as in, the US and the USSR fought a Cold War with each other?

Political scientists use the qualifier *dyad* to refer to wars between two armed actors, at least one of which is a state government, as in, "Since the end of World War II, 627 dyads have been active in 286 conflicts in 158 locations."[31] Can war be defined when any group of people with weapons and the ability to fight engages in violence with any other group? Political scientists call such groups *non-state actors* that do not have the "monopoly on the legitimate use of force."[32] The ambiguous term of a state or dyad or actor hides the reality that humans fight wars with each other and die when they fight in wars.

The *UN Charter* almost immediately addresses *war* by reminding readers that the main impetus for creating the charter was overcoming World War I and World War II and preventing future wars. The focus and concern about warfare may be lost on readers today who have not directly experienced war, but those who have done so grasp the importance, pain, sorrow, and hell that is portrayed in the phrase "scourge of war." Robert McNamara, on reminiscing about his life and work as Secretary of Defense during the Vietnam War said, "I think the human race needs to think more about killing, about conflict. Is that what we want in the twenty-first century?"[33] And specifically on Truman's use of the nuclear bomb in Japan, McNamara said, "The human race prior to that time and today has not really grappled with what are, I'll call it 'the rules of war,'" an amazing statement considering the extensive literature on peace and warfare, or the multiple international peace treaties (some reviewed above) that were negotiated to end and prevent wars. But McNamara's point is poignant, that humans kill each other to achieve their aims, and grappling with what that means might actually result in changed behavior.[34] The *UN Charter* represents an attempt to think more deeply about war and to create rules and regulations between states that would keep humans from fighting with and killing each other.

4.D: RECOMMENDED READINGS ON THE UNITED NATIONS

Fasulo, Linda. *An Insider's Guide to the UN*. 3rd ed. New Haven: Yale University Press, 2015.

Hanhimäki, Jussi M. *The United Nations: A Very Short Introduction*. 2nd ed. New York; Oxford: Oxford University Press, 2008, 2015.

Jolly, Richard, Louis Emmerij, and Thomas G. Weiss. *UN Ideas that Changed the World*. Bloomington, IN: Indiana University Press, 2009.

Meisler, Stanley. *United Nations: A History*. New York: Grove Press. 1995, Reprinted 2011.

Weiss, Thomas G. *What's Wrong with the United Nations and How to Fix It*. 2nd ed. Cambridge: Polity Press, 2012.

NOTES

1. E.g., Margaret P. Karns, Karen A Mingst, and Kendall W Stiles, *International Organizations: The Politics and Processes of Global Governance*, 3rd ed. (Boulder, CO: Lynne Rienner Publishers, 2015); Thomas G. Weiss, *Thinking About Global Governance: Why People and Ideas Matter* (Hoboken: Taylor & Francis, 2012); Thomas G. Weiss and Ramesh Thakur, *Global Governance and the UN: An Unfinished Journey*, United Nations Intellectual History Project (Bloomington: Indiana University Press, 2010).

2. Excellent overviews of the United Nations include Jussi Hanhimäki, *The United Nations: A Very Short Introduction*, 2nd ed. Very Short Introductions (New York; Oxford: Oxford University Press, 2008, 2015), 199; Karen A. Mingst, Margaret P. Karns, and Alynna J. Lyon, *The United Nations in the 21st Century: Dilemmas in World Politic*, 5th ed. (New York: Routledge, 2018).

3. E.g., Bertrand G. Ramcharan, *Preventive Diplomacy at the UN*. United Nations Intellectual History Project Series (Bloomington, IN: Indiana University Press, 2008).

4. Your library most likely provides you with an online public access catalog and may also provide links to other OPACs. In 2019 the largest OPAC is found at Worldcat.org, a combined catalog of hundreds of libraries, allowing users to search particular areas and libraries for books and resources from around the world.

5. E.g., a search of [define charter] on July 18, 2019 revealed 418,000,000 results, and a second search on March 4, 2020 revealed 731,000,000 results.

6. An internet search for a term does not occur in real time. In the July 18, 2019, search for the term *charter* mentioned in f.n. 5 above, the search engine had already indexed the 418,000,000 websites according to its algorithm, so it only took a few moments (0.75 seconds according to Google) for the search to provide results. The *algorithm* is the calculation pre-specified to the search engine to help it determine which results to prioritize based on the websites that it has already indexed by keyword, subject, or title (or other criteria) in its search index. Each search engine uses hundreds of ranking factors to rank websites in an attempt to provide you with a list of the most reliable sources on the subject you are searching. Knowing the basics of how a search engine is ranking pages and prioritizing them on the list that comes up in your search will help you determine the validity of the source. Ranking factors include how often the webpage is linked by other webpages, professional indexing of the website, and the quality of the content.

7. Boolean operators have to be capitalized to work; search your library or the internet to find out more about how Boolean operators work.

8. E.g., Google Search Help. "How to Search on Google" accessed March 3, 2020 https://support.google.com/websearch/answer/134479?hl=en.

9. Find associated keywords in some search engines, like swisscows.com. For example, a search on swisscows.com on July 18, 2019, using the phrase ["United Nations Charter"] came up with keywords: international, signed, Francisco, conference, and others. The new terms can help to expand the search and support understanding the historical context (for instance, the *UN Charter* was signed at a conference in San Francisco which is why San Francisco comes up in the associated key world list on swisscows.com).

10. United Nations, *Charter of the United Nations* (charter, October 24, 1945, 1 UNTS XVI), accessed August 29, 2019 (all rights reserved, reproduced with permission of the Licensor, the United Nations), https://www.un.org/en/sections/un-charter/un-charter-full-text/.

11. The UN Treaty Collection website reports being depositary to more than 560 as of March 4, 2020. See United Nations Treaty Collection https://treaties.un.org/. A comprehensive list of UN treaties up to the most recent edition may be found in Edmund Jan Osmańczyk, *Encyclopedia of the United Nations and International Agreements* Volumes 1–4 (New York: Routledge, 2003). States and IOs are depositaries of treaties (but IOs have increasingly taken on the role); for the difference between depositary duties and registration duties in international law, see Arancha Hinojal-Oyarbide and Annebeth Rosenboom, "Managing the Process of Treaty Formation—Depositaries and Registration," in *The Oxford Guide to Treaties,* edited by Duncan B. Hollis (Oxford: Oxford University Press, 2013), 248–76. Other IOs that serve as depositaries of treaties include, inter alia, the International Labour Organization (ILO) and the World Trade Organization (WTO).

12. United Nations, "Vienna Convention on the Law of Treaties" (United Nations, 1969).

13. Handbooks or overviews of international law are excellent sources for understanding different international agreements. E.g., Anthony Aust, *Handbook of International Law*, 11th ed. (Cambridge, UK: Cambridge University Press, 2017).

14. Cambridge Online Dictionary, "Charter" accessed March 4, 2020, https://dictionary.cambridge.org/us/dictionary/english/charter; Merriam-Webster Online Dictionary, "Charter" accessed March 4, 2020 https://www.merriam-webster.com/dictionary/charter.

15. Micheline Ishay, *The Human Rights Reader: Major Political Essays, Speeches, and Documents from Ancient Times to the Present*, 2nd ed. (New York; London: Routledge, 2012).

16. For a list of Human Rights Treaties and links to the full texts, see OHCHR, "Human Rights Instruments" accessed March 4, 2020, https://www.ohchr.org/EN/ProfessionalInterest/Pages/CoreInstruments.aspx. See also United Nations High Commissioner for Human Rights, *The Core International Human Rights Treaties.* (New York: United Nations, 2014).

17. E.g., Duncan B. Hollis, ed. *The Oxford Guide to Treaties* (Oxford: Oxford University Press, 2012), 248–76. United Nations Treaty Collection, "Glossary" accessed March 4, 2020 https://treaties.un.org/Pages/Overview.aspx?path=overview/glossary/page1_en.xml.

18. The UN expounds on its history in many of its webpages. Limiting a search to those pages using the shortcut [site:www.un.org United Nations Charter] will produce a results list with only those webpages on that website devoted to the *UN Charter.*

19. E.g., Mingst, Karns, and Lyon, *United Nations in the 21st Century*, 24–25; Townsend Hoopes and Douglas Brinkley, *FDR and the Creation of the U.N.* (New Haven: Yale University Press, 2000); Stephen C. Schlesinger, *Act of Creation: The Founding of the United Nations: A Story of Superpowers, Secret Agents, Wartime Allies and Enemies, and Their Quest for a Peaceful World* (Boulder, CO: Westview, 2005).

20. E.g., Hoopes and Brinkley, *FDR and the Creation of the U.N.*, 1–11; Susan Pedersen, *The Guardians: The League of Nations and the Crisis of Empire* (New York: Oxford University Press, 2018).

21. United Nations, "Introductory Note" accessed July 8, 2019, https://www.un.org/en/charter-united-nations/.

22. Johan Kaufmann, *Conference Diplomacy: An Introductory Analysis* (Leiden: A.W. Sijthoff, 1968).

23. For an overview of the theories of world order after war, including a review of the 1815, 1919, and 1945 conferences discussed in this section, see John G. Ikenberry, *After Victory: Institutions, Strategic Restraint, and the Rebuilding of Order after Major Wars*, New ed. (Princeton Studies in International History and Politics. Princeton: Princeton University Press, 2019).

24. E.g., Olaf Asbach and Schröder Peter, *The Ashgate Research Companion to the Thirty Years' War* (Ashgate Research Companion. London: Routledge, 2016); Derek Croxton and Anuschka Tischer, *The Peace of Westphalia: A Historical Dictionary* (Westport, CT: Greenwood Press, 2002).

25. On the Congress of Vienna, see Brian E. Vick, *The Congress of Vienna: Power and Politics after Napoleon* (Cambridge, MA: Harvard University Press, 2014). On global governance and the lasting effects of the Congress of Vienna and the Concert of Europe, see, e.g., Jennifer Mitzen, *Power in Concert: The Nineteenth-Century Origins of Global Governance* (Chicago: University of Chicago Press, 2014).

26. On the League of Nations, see, e.g., Ruth B. Henig, *The League of Nations. Makers of the Modern World* (London: Haus Publishing, 2018).

27. John. J. Mearsheimer, *The Tragedy of Great Power Politics*, 1st ed. (New York: WW Norton, 2002).

28. Stanley Meisler, *United Nations: The First Fifty Years*, 4th ed. (New York: Atlantic Monthly Press, 2007).

29. Uppsala Universitet. Uppsala Conflict Database. https://ucdp.uu.se/.

30. Carl von. Clausewitz, *On War*. The Project Gutenburg. Produced by Charles Keller and David Widger. Original publication 1832. Last updated October 19, 2019, https://www.gutenberg.org/files/1946/1946-h/1946-h.htm.

31. Uppsala Conflict Database, "Dyads," accessed July 1, 2019, https://ucdp.uu.se/; Quotation from Therésa Pettersson, Stina Högbladh, and Magnus Öberg. "Organized Violence, 1989-2018 and Peace Agreements," *Journal of Peace Research* 56, no. 4 (June 2019): 589–603.

32. Morris, Errol. *The Fog of War: Eleven Lessons from the Life of Robert S. McNamara* (Culver City, CA: Columbia TriStar Home Entertainment, 2004).

33. Quotation in the documentary: Errol Morris, *The Fog of War: Eleven Lessons from the Life of Robert S. McNamara* (Culver City, CA: Columbia TriStar Home Entertainment, 2004).

34. Morris, *The Fog of War*.

Chapter 5

Where?

Assessing Geographic Location and Influence

The question *where?* asks us to focus on geographic location as a way to investigate the perspectives, motivations, and interests of the actors involved and how that geographic location impacts processes and outcomes in a given situation. The question helps us understand *geopolitics*, or the relationship between geography, on the one hand, and political decisions and economic outcomes, on the other. The *where?* question goes beyond geographic location, helping clarify matters of power and inequality related to the spatial and power positions of global actors relative to each other.

The *Atlantic Charter*, the primary document reviewed in this chapter, was a statement made by the leaders of two countries, President Franklin D. Roosevelt (FDR) of the United States (US) and Prime Minister Winston Churchill of the United Kingdom (UK), that would eventually unite their countries and forty-five others as allies in World War II (WWII) against Nazi Germany and its allies. Further, the *Atlantic Charter* paved the way for the negotiations to create the United Nations, as discussed in chapter 4. The two leaders were concerned with what would come after WWII ended, and with who would lead the world in creating a new postwar world order. Understanding this document means delving into the politics of the WWII context and requires special attention to geography and geopolitics.

Section 5.A reviews some new techniques for studying and ensuring that new knowledge stays in long-term memory: handwritten note-taking, and consistent study sessions. Section 5.B then includes the primary source for this chapter, the *Atlantic Charter* (1941) and Section 5.C reviews the main questions to ask of this charter focusing on the question of *where?* as the starting point of the inquiry and analyzing its geopolitical significance. Finally, Section 5.D provides recommended readings for those interested in learning more about geopolitics and about WWII and the *Atlantic Charter*.

5.A: HANDWRITTEN, GENERATIVE NOTE-TAKING, AND CONSISTENT STUDY METHODS

One of the best ways to learn a new subject matter is to take handwritten (also called *longhand*) notes with a pen and paper, and not type on a computer because writing notes helps learners understand the material better and retain the information longer.[1] Further, g*enerative* note-taking, in which learners summarize information rather than transcribe verbatim, allows the mind to creatively connect the new information with other ideas and to integrate into long-term memory.[2] While handwriting notes with pen on paper appears to be the best technique for learning and memory functioning, learners might also use a stylus on a computer or iPad.

The *Cornell Method of Notetaking* suggests that note-takers (whether taking notes on a lecture or reading materials) break up the note page into three sections that allow the learner to take short notes, generate questions about the notes, and summarize the notes. The note-taking column on the right-hand side of the paper allows learners to summarize information in short sentences or keywords. The cue column to the left of the note-taking column is a space to create questions to help recall notes later or create questions about how the information relates to other ideas and concepts. Finally, the summary column at the bottom of the page is to summarize main ideas directly after taking notes in order to facilitate memory retention.[3]

Figure 5.1 provides an example of notes taken using the Cornell Method based on a lecture by the *Khan Academy* about the beginning of WWII (information that helps build knowledge for reading the primary document in Section 5.B).[4] Consider how each of the sections of the notes deals with the new information gleaned from the lecture.

Consistent Study Methods

The point of learning new information is to apply what is learned, both now and later in life, to our own life experiences, helping all of us respond in appropriate and powerful ways to complex problems, and to create a world that we would like to live in. We have all experienced cramming for a test and taking the test, only to completely forget the information on that test a few days later (not to mention months or years later), but the point of learning is not to cram, memorize in the short term, and then forget. Given the importance of storing what we learn in long-term, not short-term memory, practice good memory storage tools and techniques like those outlined below.

- *Study consistently*. Studying every day for a short amount of time allows for memory retention. Avoid cramming learning into one or two study sessions;

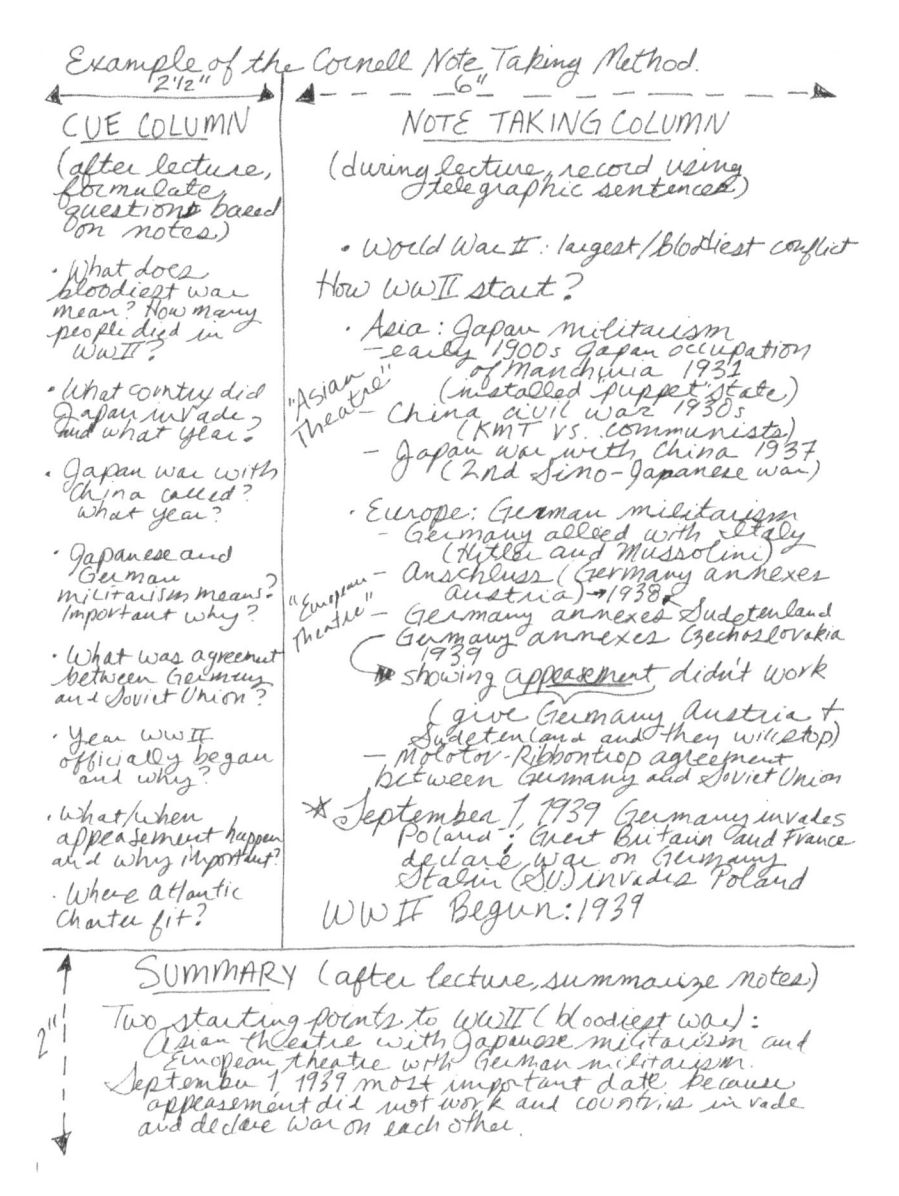

Figure 5.1 Example of the Cornell Note-taking Method.

- *Short study sessions.* Studying in short bursts with breaks in between gives the mind a rest and allows for healthier and longer memory retention (see chapter 6 for a description of the Pomodoro study method that suggests 25-minute study sessions with breaks);
- *Review and revisit learned information.* Consistently revisit notes, but not just to re-read. Rather, review the questions and try to recall information

previously learned (for example review the cue questions derived during the *Cornell Method of Notetaking*, but cover up the notes section and try to recall the information and answer the questions). Returning to notes over several days or weeks and training the mind to recall the information will help move the information into long-term memory;
- *Use flash cards or memory cues.* Recalling keywords, phrases, and events, along with explanations and definitions, is an important practice in the *recall method.* Do not just re-read the text or notes because re-reading gives learners an *"illusion of competence,"* that is, they think they know the information when they actually don't.[5]

5.B: PRIMARY SOURCE ON INTERNATIONAL AGREEMENTS

Atlantic Charter: Declaration of Principles issued by the President of the United States and the Prime Minister of the United Kingdom (1941)[6]

August 14, 1941. The President of the United States of America and the Prime Minister, Mr. Churchill, representing His Majesty's Government in the United Kingdom, being met together, deem it right to make known certain common principles in the national policies of their respective countries on which they base their hopes for a better future for the world.

First, their countries seek no aggrandizement, territorial or other;

Second, they desire to see no territorial changes that do not accord with the freely expressed wishes of the peoples concerned;

Third, they respect the right of all peoples to choose the form of government under which they will live; and they wish to see sovereign rights and self-government restored to those who have been forcibly deprived of them;

Fourth, they will endeavor, with due respect for their existing obligations, to further the enjoyment by all States, great or small, victor or vanquished, of access, on equal terms, to the trade and to the raw materials of the world which are needed for their economic prosperity;

Fifth, they desire to bring about the fullest collaboration between all nations in the economic field with the object of securing, for all, improved labor standards, economic advancement and social security;

Sixth, after the final destruction of the Nazi tyranny, they hope to see established a peace which will afford to all nations the means of dwelling in safety within their own boundaries, and which will afford assurance that all the men in all lands may live out their lives in freedom from fear and want;

Seventh, such a peace should enable all men to traverse the high seas and oceans without hindrance;

Eighth, they believe that all of the nations of the world, for realistic as well as spiritual reasons must come to the abandonment of the use of force. Since no future peace can be maintained if land, sea or air armaments continue to be employed by nations which threaten, or may threaten, aggression outside of their frontiers, they believe, pending the establishment of a wider and permanent system of general security, that the disarmament of such nations is essential. They will likewise aid and encourage all other practicable measure which will lighten for peace-loving peoples the crushing burden of armaments.

Franklin D. Roosevelt
Winston S. Churchill

5.C: GEOPOLITICS AND INTERNATIONAL AGREEMENTS

The first and most basic *where?* questions relate to geographic location. *Where* in the world is that place? Or, *where* did that event occur? Deeper *where?* questions in global political conversations ask about the political and economic significance of geographic positions and relationships. Bullet points in this section represent questions that a learner might ask concerning location and geographical influence. Try to answer the questions as you read them and then continue on to compare your answers with the text.

Geographic Origin

Questioning *where* in the world the people who sign the *Atlantic Charter* are from (or *which territory* and *which people* they represent in signing the agreement) helps illuminate the WWII context of the charter. FDR was the President of the United States (US), and Churchill the Prime Minister of the United Kingdom (UK) and as such acted as the highest authority for their governments, being able to sign agreements on behalf of their governments and people, while still being accountable to their respective parliaments.[7] Even though the US had not yet formally entered the war at the time of the signing, the US and UK leaders represented a group of states later called the Allies or Allied Powers, which were fighting against Nazi Germany and its allies, called the Axis Powers.

- What geographical territories and people who live in those territories were represented by those who signed and negotiated the *Atlantic Charter*?

In signing the *Atlantic Charter* declaration, FDR and Churchill indicated that US and UK citizens supported democratic principles around the world, and the document represented one of the steps in connecting the values, governments, and people of the countries in wartime efforts to defeat Nazi Germany. Though the *Atlantic Charter* did not have the force of law, its impact was powerful and felt around the world—for example, Nelson Mandela recalls the impact of the charter in South African politics in his autobiography when he wrote that it "reaffirmed faith in the dignity of each human being and propagated a host of democratic principles . . . inspired by the *Atlantic Charter* and the fight of the Allies against tyranny and oppression, the ANC created its own charter, called African Claims . . . ."[8]

The US and the UK represent geographic territories and people groups whose interests and values were influential in the document. Despite differences in history and culture, both countries spoke the same language and shared similar government structures based on ideals of democratic engagement and debate, and were therefore more likely to support each other in the war. But leaders of states also have to comply with historical domestic concerns and limitations. For instance, in foreign policy two overarching terms are used to indicate the general willingness of a government and its peoples to engage with other states, that of *isolationism* or *activism*. The former indicates a penchant to stay out of the affairs of other states and to focus on one's own country's problems and betterment (connected with economic policy, this is called *protectionism* or *mercantilism*); the latter tendency is to be engaged and involved in world matters with the idea that what happens outside a state's borders also affects what happens inside (another term is that of *liberal internationalism*).

At the time of the *Atlantic Charter*, the US followed an *isolationist* policy that had been supported by the American people and Congress for decades, to varying degrees, and the US, with the exception of some support for the UK and *allies* in the war, had remained neutral in WWII. The war started on September 1, 1939, almost three years before FDR and Churchill signed the *Atlantic Charter* in August 1941, and the US did not become involved until December 1941 when, based on Japan's attach of Pearl Harbor and FDR's subsequent leadership, the American people supported entering the war.

Geographic Position and Strategy

Many international agreements, such as those ending wars, are named after the places where they are negotiated and signed, which has significance for the power relationships that the locations imply. In this instance, FDR and Churchill met in Placentia Bay, Newfoundland, on a boat, the U.S.S.

Augusta, near the Atlantic Ocean, to agree on and sign the *Atlantic Charter*. Consider why the meeting took place in Placentia Bay. Newfoundland was a colony of the UK in the 1940s. (Indeed, the UK had many colonies all over the world based on its centuries of colonial and imperial expansion.) While the US was limited in what it could do to support the WWII effort once it started in September 1939 (because of isolationist policy and reticence on the part of the US Congress), FDR nevertheless negotiated several agreements to support the UK. The US supplied military equipment in exchange for control over UK land and resources: for example, the *Destroyers for Bases Agreement* in September 1940 gave the US ninety-nine-year leases on British colonial areas, including in Newfoundland and the Caribbean, and the *U.S. Lend Lease Act* in March 1941. Thus, the location in which the *Atlantic Charter* was signed indicates the geographic power and influence of the US and the UK, especially as relates to colonial history and holdings.

- Consider the *Atlantic Charter* again based on the new information about the location of Newfoundland: Does this new information change your thinking about the significance of the meeting place for the *Atlantic Charter*?

Actors in the global system seek access to the most strategic positions in the world in order to utilize them for their own benefit, whether it is strategic locations for naval, air, or military bases, or control over territories with important resources or markets. Returning to the question of why the charter was signed in Placentia Bay and why it was named the *Atlantic Charter*, consider a map of the world screenshot in Figure 5.2 (or look up a map of your own), find Newfoundland, and assess its geographic location.[9] Consider its proximity to the US and the UK and its geopolitical position (more in the geopolitics section below).

- Was Newfoundland a neutral meeting place for the leaders of the US and the UK? Why or why not?

The meeting took place between a United States Naval Cruiser, the U.S.S. *Augusta* and the United Kingdom warship the H.M.S. *Prince of Wales*, as they were anchored in Placentia Bay off the coast of Newfoundland. This is significant in terms of who had the most influence and power in the situation when the two leaders met. Though they met in a bay, they were on naval boats, in the case of the US, called a presidential flagship when used to carry the president as the commander in chief of the US. Consider that the laws of the flagship of the country apply on boats in the water, and in this case, the boat was itself considered US territory, even while it sat in open water. This new information might indicate that one country has more power and influence in this situation.

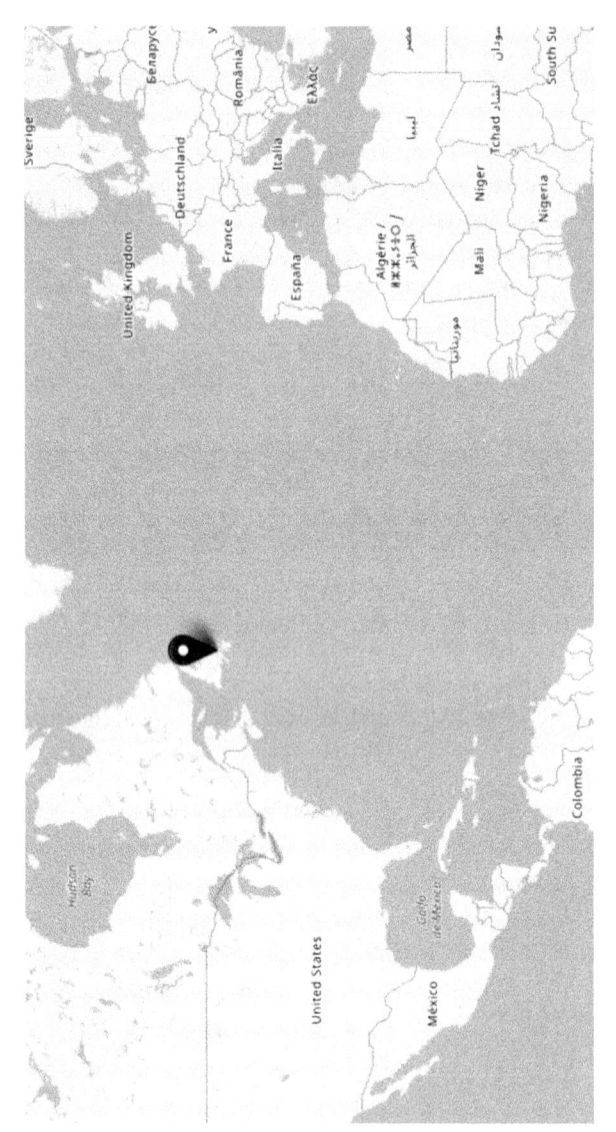

Figure 5.2 Geographical Location of Placentia Bay, Newfoundland.

Geopolitics

Geopolitics is the study of how geography and political/economic interests intersect, with special investigation into why political decisions would be made based on geographic characteristics as this common definition for *geopolitics* stipulates: "Politics, especially international relations, as influenced by geographical factors."[10] The role of geographical factors in political decision-making is considered often in international relations (IR) scholarship, especially through the use of the analytical heuristic of the *balance of power*, and gained notoriety during the Cold War era where the US and the Union of Soviet Socialist Republics (USSR) vied for geographic *spheres of influence*.[11] Further, geopolitical considerations arise frequently in discussions of the scope and impacts of *globalization* (a term signifying the increased frequency, breadth, and depth of political, social, economic, cultural, and environmental interactions across national borders).[12] Arguments range between ideas that *geopolitics* is a concern of the past because *globalization* has reduced geographical barriers, making moot any political decisions based on geography, and those arguing that geography will always be a consideration in political decisions because proximity to resources and neighbors are perennial concerns.[13]

- What is the relevance of geography on the political decision about where to sign the *Atlantic Charter* and what was included in the charter?
- Does geography have a large or small influence on political decisions?

As the definition of geopolitics implies, the location of a country (and access to resources) in the world has huge implications for its ability to utilize power: both forceful and influential power, otherwise known as *hard* versus *soft* power.[14] Consider why some countries seem to have a lot of wealth, military might, and access to resources while others do not; that is, wealth and power are tied to geographic location.[15] The US and the UK represented two of the most powerful countries in the world at the time that they signed the *Atlantic Charter* but also had significant control and access to worldwide resources, giving these two countries and their leaders additional bargaining power and influence as they conspired to bring an end to the Battle of the Atlantic and WWII itself. The US began as thirteen British colonies that united under one federalist government and then expanded to control both coasts and an immense amount of resources and land mass that supported farming, mining, etc. The UK had a long history of imperialism and colonialism and, as a *hegemon* in the nineteenth century, was credited with imposing an imperial peace around the world, the *Pax Britannica*.

Reading the *Atlantic Charter* carefully for geopolitical implications provides insight into how geography affects political decisions. Consider the IR concept of *territorial integrity* invoked in the second phrase that the US and the UK "seek no aggrandizement, territorial or other." That phrase is meant to indicate that control of land does not change easily or frequently between governments, that state boundaries remain the same unless under extreme circumstances; that is, that governments should support the status quo in land distribution and maintain respect for government and territorial sovereignty.

The norm of *territorial integrity* is contentious, and as with all norms, states (among other actors and groups) challenge it from time to time (consider the end of Cold War and breakup of the USSR into fifteen autonomous states, or the creation of the state of Kosovo or South Sudan in recent years, or ongoing challenges to the territorial sovereignty of empires by indigenous groups around the world). Associated with WWII, the phrase condemns the behavior of Japan and Germany who both sought aggrandizement by expanding their control of territory: Japan invaded Manchuria in 1931, and Germany invaded Czechoslovakia beginning in 1938, and the impetus for the war, Germany invaded Poland in September of 1939. Thus, when the US and UK leaders state in the *Atlantic Charter* that they think a postwar world should be one in which countries do not seek aggrandizement, they have good reason based on the experience of WWII.

Based on the information above, try to answer the following:

- How does the *Atlantic Charter* statement about *territorial integrity* envision a different geopolitical order after the war, thereby changing the relationship between geography and political decisions in the postwar world?
- If states are precluded from expanding their borders to gain more land, access to resources, and power, what other tactics might they deploy in order to gain power?
- One issue not discussed above is the connection and contrast with the IR concept of *self-determination* and the history and practices of *colonialism*.

In the subsequent phrases of the *Atlantic Charter*, the text indicates that territorial changes and control of government would be allowed "in accord with the freely expressed wishes of the people concerned," but not otherwise. Such phrases were important near the end of the age of colonialism in which imperial powers were being pressured to release control of their colonies and cede power to local, self-governing entities.

- Take some time to look up the issues and concerns associated with *self-determination*.

A pressing issue between states and other groups is who has access to, and rights to use and profit from, the resources that the earth provides (and what kinds of resources, such as farmland, water, forests, coal, oil, precious metals, and agricultural products). How do states obtain and maintain access to such resources? The fourth phrase of the *Atlantic Charter* refers to inequality in access to resources when it says that the US and the UK "will endeavor . . . to further the enjoyment by all States . . . on equal terms, to trade and to the raw materials of the world." The phrase implies that not all states have access to raw materials on equal terms.[16]

Questions about resource access and equity:

- Consider what the phrase about resources meant for different countries in 1941 (especially the colonies that mostly supported and bolstered colonist country access to wealth and resources).
- In the globalized world in which we live today, which countries, people groups, companies, or other actors have more access to resources and why?
- How does access to resources, fairness in trading practices, or labor standards (like wage or health protections, some of the principles listed in the *Atlantic Charter*), affect people's lifestyles, living standards, or ability to survive and thrive today?

Climate and geography influence social, political, and economic positions, and by extension, development prospects. Thus, when considering why a country is *developing* or has a low-income, it is critical to assess history and geography. Consider that not many landlocked states become superpowers: being landlocked means no access to a coast and therefore dependence on neighbors to access shipped goods and markets (90 percent of all products are transported from one place to another by boat, meaning that access to a coast is crucial for engaging in the global political economy).[17] Further, geography influences security prospects, especially in terms of climate change. Natural protective features, such as oceans or mountains, can make a huge difference in the way that people are affected by hurricanes, tsunamis, tornadoes, or other natural disasters.

Positionality: The United States, the United Kingdom, and the Balance of Power

The question *where?* also urges us to ask about how actors are positioned relative to one another, not only in terms of geographic space but also in terms of power, interests, and influence (see also chapter 3 on social positioning). Understanding how the actors in a situation under study are related to one another is crucial to understanding the context of the situation.

- Of any situation, ask yourself: which actors have more power in the situation, and how are those actors molding the situation to ensure that their desires or interests are met? When people in positions of power (whether it be government leaders of countries, company CEOs or Boards) make decisions, geographical characteristics of the situation may be important and influential.

In the situation under study in this chapter, the countries that entered into warfare with each other did so in the end because of geographic impacts and implications. The US eventually entered the war, despite the population's penchant to isolationism, because the war came to US territory in the form of an attack on the Pearl Harbor naval base in Hawaii. For much of the war (from the 1930s to December 1941), the US was not in close territorial proximity and therefore the fighting, politics, and even the economic implications, did not impact the US as greatly as many European countries. In similar fashion, albeit several years earlier, the UK and France declared war on Germany in 1939 after it became obvious that Hitler and the Nazi party would not stop territorial expansion. Indeed, Neville Chamberlain as Prime Minister of the UK from 1937 to 1940 (along with the leaders of Italy and France) had attempted a policy of *appeasement* in the Munich Agreement with Nazi Germany, giving concessions by allowing Germany to annex Czechoslovakia with the hopes that it would satisfy any needs for further territorial aggrandizement—unfortunately it did not suffice.

By comparing the power position of the two countries and leaders who signed the *Atlantic Charter*, we begin to see how they were positioned in relation to each other, and what that meant about whose interests would be considered. The meeting between FDR and Churchill in which the *Atlantic Charter* was signed took place in Placentia Bay, Newfoundland on a US Naval Cruiser, the U.S.S. *Augusta*. This information alone can tell us something about the US and the UK in relation to each other. Consider that by the time of this meeting the UK had been fighting Nazi Germany for almost two years (since it joined France in declaring war in September 1939), and yet did not seem to be making headway, especially without open US support. Thus, even the meeting place in Newfoundland showed the relative influence of the US vis-à-vis the UK and the dependence of the latter on the former for substantial support during the ongoing war with Nazi Germany. The *Destroyer for Bases* and *Lend Lease Act* represented initial support, but Churchill knew that the UK would need more if they were to win the war.

- What do the US-UK agreements signify about the relationship between the two countries and the power differential? Note that IR theorists use the term *balance of power* to refer to power differentials between states, including access to resources, people, power *fungibility* (the ability to turn wealth into military power), military might, territory, etc. *Great Powers* in the international system are thusly named because of their outsized, or *hegemonic*, position in the global balance of power.[18]

Another consideration in the context of the *Atlantic Charter* is the relative influence of the two countries who met together to sign this document, who led the negotiations on ending the war, and who further led negotiations on creating the international organizations that would follow the war, for example, the United Nations (UN) and the Bretton Woods Institutions. Considering how the US showed leadership in creating post–WWII institutions allows us to consider *hegemonic* status in global politics and to attempt to differentiate state governments' relative power and influence.[19] Perhaps the most crucial elements of the *Atlantic Charter* are what it suggests about the postwar world order and the propositions of international collaboration to ensure peaceful interactions thenceforth, principles that became evident in the San Francisco as well as Bretton Woods Conferences that created several international organizations.[20] If the US was to become involved in WWII, it wanted to be a major player in how the war would end and what the world would look like after the war. FDR was leading the US from isolationism to a much more engaged, activist foreign policy and as such intended to guide states on the principles that would guide global decisions and discussions.

The US influence in setting up the postwar world order is evident in the location of the negotiations that occurred for the international organizations envisioned in the *Atlantic Charter*. Recall from chapter 4 that the countries invited to the deliberations on the creation of the UN at the San Francisco Conference were limited to the countries that signed the *Declaration of United Nations* (1942), a wartime treaty that demanded wartime effort allegiance against Nazi Germany and the Axis powers from those leaders and countries who signed, and reaffirmed the principles that had been deliberated and proclaimed in the *Atlantic Charter*. Find a copy of the *Declaration of United Nations* (available for public access on the UN website) and compare it to the *Atlantic Charter*—what are the similarities and differences?[21] The Bretton Woods Institutions, the World Bank, International Monetary Fund, and General Agreement on Trade and Tariffs were also negotiated on US soil, in Bretton Woods, New Hampshire.

- Based on the discussion in this chapter, what other political decisions can you identify related to the *Atlantic Charter* that were influenced by geography?
- Consider that the *Atlantic Charter* is most concerned with what the postwar world order will look like and consider the historical development after

WWII: the agreements that ended the war; the distribution and control of Germany's land, colonies, and city of Berlin between the US, the Soviet Union, and France; or the international organizations created at the Bretton Woods Conference. Did these elements of the postwar world order resemble the principles in the *Atlantic Charter*—why or why not?
- Investigate the International Organizations (IOs) referenced in this chapter (like the UN or Bretton Woods Institutions) and assess their histories and structure—which countries have more power and influence in IOs and why? (Analyze voting rules and patterns, special committees and councils, or monetary contributions of member states.)

5.D: RECOMMENDED READINGS ON GEOPOLITICS

Alfred Thayer Mahan, *The Influence of Sea Power Upon History, 1660-1783*. New York: Little, Brown, 1890.
Dicken, Peter. *Global Shift*. 6th ed. New York: Guilford, 2011.
Gray, Colin S. and Geoffrey Sloan, eds. *Geopolitics, Geography, and Strategy*. New York: Routledge, 1999.
Sachs, Jeffery. *The End of Poverty*. New York: Penguin, 2005.

NOTES

1. E.g., Kenneth A. Kiewra, "A Review of Note-Taking: The Encoding-Storage Paradigm and Beyond." *Educational Psychology Review* 1, no. 2 (June 1989): 147-72; Pam A. Mueller and Daniel M. Oppenheimer, "The Pen Is Mightier than the Keyboard: Advantages of Longhand Over Laptop Note Taking," *Psychological Science*, 25, no. 6 (April 2014): 1159-168. Further, Mueller and Oppenheimer review the "encoding hypothesis" and the "external-storage hypothesis" in the introduction to their research paper, two ideas that suggest that writing down ideas help a learner to keep the ideas in long-term memory, whereas simply reading does not have the same effect: Mueller and Oppenheimer, 1159.

2. Mueller and Oppenheimer, "The Pen is Mightier than the Keyboard," 1160.

3. Cornell University Learning Center, "The Cornell Note-Taking System," accessed June 7, 2019, http://lsc.cornell.edu/notes.html.

4. Cornell note-taking example in figure 5.1 produced by Roni Kay O'Dell while listening to lecture from Khan Academy available online: "Beginning of World War II," Khan Academy, accessed June 7, 2019, https://www.khanacademy.org/humanities/us-history/rise-to-world-power/us-wwii/v/beginning-of-world-war-ii.

5. Barbara Oakley, *A Mind for Numbers: How to Excel at Math and Science* (New York: Penguin Random House, 2014).

6. *The Atlantic Charter* (document signed between Franklin D. Roosevelt (president of the United States) and Winston S. Churchill (prime minister of the UK) on

August 14, 1941), The Avalon Project, Yale Law School (all rights reserved, reproduced based on fair use doctrine from Section 107 of US Copyright Law), https://avalon.law.yale.edu/wwii/atlantic.asp.

 7. Each state government has its own rules and regulations regarding the titles and responsibilities of its leaders, though there is conformity and complementarity between similar types of governments. A good starting point for learning about particular governments is to visit the government website to find what they say about the role of their leader. See also, e.g., Patrick H. O'Neil, Karl J. Fields, and Donald Share. *Essentials of Comparative Politics with Cases,* 6th AP ed. New York: W.W. Norton & Company, 2018.

 8. Nelson Mandela, *Long Walk to Freedom: The Autobiography of Nelson Mandela* (New York: Bay Books, 1994), 96.

 9. Open Street Map Foundation. openstreetmap.org. (2020). https://www.openstreetmap.org/search?query=placentia%20bay#map=3/39.90/-45.09 on (accessed October 13, 2020).

 10. *Oxford English Dictionary*. For a good overview of geopolitics for students who study global politics, see: Saul Bernard Cohen, *Geopolitics: The Geography of International Relations*, 3rd ed. (Lanham, MD: Rowman & Littlefield, 2015). For a variety of geopolitical theories and investigations in the post–Cold World era, see: Gearóid Ó. Tuathail, Simon Dalby, eds. *Rethinking Geopolitics* (London: Routledge, 1998).

 11. John Agnew, *Geopolitics: Re-visioning World Politics*, 2nd ed. (New York: Routledge, 2003); Alfred Thayer Mahan, *The Influence of Sea Power Upon History, 1660-1783*. (Little, Brown, 1890); N. J. Spykman, *America's strategy in world politics. The United States and the Balance of Power.* Yale University. Institute of International Studies. (New York: Harcourt, Brace, 1942, reprinted 2007); Colin S. Gray and Geoffrey Sloan, eds. *Geopolitics, Geography, and Strategy* (New York: Routledge, 1999).

 12. Manfred B. Steger, *Globalization: A Very Short Introduction* (Oxford: Oxford University Press, 2003).

 13. The argument that globalization is important is represented, inter alia, by such authors as Thomas Freidman, *The World Is Flat: A Brief History of the Twenty-First Century*, 1st ed. (New York: Farrar, Straus and Giroux, 2005). For the argument that geopolitics is important see, e.g., Robert D. Kaplan, *The Revenge of Geography: What the Map Tells Us about Coming Conflicts and the Battle against Fate*, 1st ed. (New York: Random House, 2012).

 14. Joseph Nye, *Soft Power: The Means to Success in World Politics* (Public Affairs, Perseus Books Group, 2004).

 15. Jared M. Diamond, *Guns, Germs, and Steel: The Fates of Human Societies*, 1st ed. (New York: W.W. Norton, 1997). Consider Jared Diamond's argument (simplified here) that temperate climates and access to domesticated animals and specific types of grain allowed people to develop greater societies that in turn resulted in power and wealth. *Guns, Germs, Steel.*

 16. Critical theorists argue that the extension of capitalism around the world has created such unequal access. Consider Immanuel Maurice Wallerstein, *The Modern World System. Vol. 1, Capitalist Agriculture and the Origins of the European*

World-Economy in the Sixteenth Century Vol. 1 (Studies in Social Discontinuity. New York: Academic Press, 1974).

17. Collier, Paul, *The Bottom Billion: Why the Poorest Countries Are Failing and What Can Be Done About It* (Oxford: Oxford University Press, 2007).

18. Richard Little, *The Balance of Power in International Relations: Metaphors, Myths, and Models* (Cambridge: Cambridge University Press, 2014).

19. William Easterly, *The White Man's Burden: Why the West's Efforts to Aid the Rest Have Done so Much Ill and so Little Good* (New York: Penguin Press, 2006); Diamond, *Guns, Germs, and Steel.*

20. Eric Helleiner, *Forgotten Foundations of Bretton Woods: International Development and the Making of the Postwar Order* (Ithaca, New York: Cornell University Press, 2016); Benn Steil, *The Battle of Bretton Woods: John Maynard Keynes, Harry Dexter White, and the Making of a New World Order* (Princeton: Princeton University Press, 2014).

21. United Nations, "The Declaration by United Nations" accessed March 6, 2020, https://www.unmultimedia.org/searchers/yearbook/page.jsp?volume=1946-47&page=36&searchType=advanced.

Chapter 6

Why?

How Things Work in Global Politics

Modern state governments have created specific foreign policy practices to facilitate engagement with each other. Chapter 4 reviewed how governments use *conference diplomacy* to negotiate global politics, especially to keep the peace, negotiate peace settlements at the end of conflicts, or create plans to ameliorate issue-specific collective security problems. Governments also negotiate through *bilateral* or *multilateral* engagements directly with each other rather than using a conference or international organization as an intermediary. This chapter covers foreign policy diplomatic practices and how such practices are codified in national and international laws. The orienting question for investigating the primary document included in this chapter is *how?* as in, *how does foreign policy work?* which requires combining many of the skills discussed already in answer to questions like *who?*, *what or what is?*, and *where?*.

Section 6.A of this chapter first reviews an important study technique that learners might use and master in order to become more efficient in their study habits: the Pomodoro Technique. Section 6.B then presents three primary documents to help understand how the foreign policy of *containment* was articulated: the "Long Telegram" and X-Article, both written by a twentieth-century foreign service officer, George Kennan, and an excerpt from President Truman's address to the United States (US) Congress on March 12, 1947. The "Long Telegram" is an example of one foreign policy practice, communication using a *diplomatic cable*—a secret, encrypted letter between state government officials—that influenced the formation of the US policy of *containment* implemented during the Cold War from the 1950s to the 1980s.

Finally, Section 6.C utilizes the question *how?* as an orienting question for the way a new learner might approach a subject like foreign policy, and Section 6.D provides a list of recommended readings on foreign policy and containment policy.

6.A: AVOIDING HARMFUL PROCRASTINATION

Avoiding harmful procrastination, especially when there is a looming deadline, is a key skill. Keep in mind that sometimes taking time to let ideas sink into the brain is a good thing as it improves creativity and allows the brain to rejuvenate, but sometimes it can be harmful to a learner's ability to tackle a task in a timely fashion.[1] Often, a seemingly daunting task will keep learners from addressing it because they perceive it to be time consuming, nerve-wracking, or difficult to start. One may avoid such tasks, either doing other tasks or shirking responsibilities altogether (binge-watching television, perhaps), procrastinating until it is too late. Learners are then unable to spend the time needed to produce good work, and thus procrastination becomes a vicious cycle.

The Pomodoro Technique of studying may help learners avoid harmful procrastination, an easy trap to which many people fall prey, including us (the authors). The creator of the Pomodoro Technique, Francesco Cirillo, was a university student who practiced particular study habits to help himself overcome procrastination and study more efficiently.[2] The technique involves using a timer (Cirillo's timer looked like a tomato, in Italian, pomodoro) to focus for 25-minute time periods or study sessions without any distractions, including short breaks in between sessions and a long break after four focused sessions. Learners have found that the Pomodoro Technique promotes efficiency in studying, supports long-term memory retention, and helps avoid procrastination.[3]

As the Pomodoro Technique teaches, the best way to overcome the procrastination problem is simply to sit down and start a task, not focusing on the finished product but rather just beginning to work, for a short amount of time, on something associated with the task. The short amount of time, 25 minutes suggested by the Pomodoro Technique, helps ease conscious and unconscious fear that the task will take too long or be too hard to complete. Beginning work on the task helps learners overcome the fear of the task and allows them to see that they have the ability to tackle it. Further, when the short amount of time is distraction-free (turn off email notifications, text messaging, phone alerts), learners are able to focus the brain in a way that helps it retain information and increase productivity.[4]

6.B: PRIMARY SOURCES ON CONTAINMENT POLICY

"The Long Telegram" by George Kennan (excerpt, 1947)[5]

Telegram[6]
SECRET
Moscow, February 22, 1946—9:00 p.m. [Received February 22—3:52 p.m.]
511. Answer to Dept's 284, Feb 3 [13] involves questions so intricate, so delicate, so strange to our form of thought, and so important to analysis of our international environment that I cannot compress answers into single brief message without yielding to what I feel would be dangerous degree of oversimplification. I hope, therefore, Dept will bear with me if I submit in answer to this question five parts, subjects of which will be roughly as follows:

(One)   Basic features of post-war Soviet outlook.
(Two)   Background of this outlook
(Three) Its projection in practical policy on official level.
(Four) Its projection on unofficial level.
(Five) Practical deductions from standpoint of US policy.

I apologize in advance for this burdening of telegraphic channel; but questions involved are of such urgent importance, particularly in view of recent events, that our answers to them, if they deserve attention at all, seem to me to deserve it at once. There follows

Part 1: Basic Features of Post War Soviet Outlook, as Put Forward by Official Propaganda Machine
Are as Follows:
(a) USSR still lives in antagonistic "capitalist encirclement" with which in the long run there can be no permanent peaceful coexistence. As stated by Stalin in 1927 to a delegation of American workers:

"In course of further development of international revolution there will emerge two centers of world significance: a socialist center, drawing to itself the countries which tend toward socialism, and a capitalist center, drawing to itself the countries that incline toward capitalism. Battle between these two centers for command of world economy will decide fate of capitalism and of communism in entire world." . . .

Part 2: Background of Outlook
Before examining ramifications of this party line in practice there are certain aspects of it to which I wish to draw attention.

First, it does not represent natural outlook of Russian people. Latter are, by and large, friendly to outside world, eager for experience of it, eager to measure against it talents they are conscious of possessing, eager above all to live in peace and enjoy fruits of their own labor. Party line only represents thesis which official propaganda machine puts forward with great skill and persistence to a public often remarkably resistant in the stronghold of its innermost thoughts. But party line is binding for outlook and conduct of people who make up apparatus of power—party, secret police and Government—and it is exclusively with these that we have to deal . . .

Part 5: [Practical Deductions from Standpoint of US Policy]

In summary, we have here a political force committed fanatically to the belief that with US there can be no permanent *modus vivendi* that it is desirable and necessary that the internal harmony of our society be disrupted, our traditional way of life be destroyed, the international authority of our state be broken, if Soviet power is to be secure. This political force has complete power of disposition over energies of one of world's greatest peoples and resources of world's richest national territory, and is borne along by deep and powerful currents of Russian nationalism. In addition, it has an elaborate and far flung apparatus for exertion of its influence in other countries, an apparatus of amazing flexibility and versatility, managed by people whose experience and skill in underground methods are presumably without parallel in history. Finally, it is seemingly inaccessible to considerations of reality in its basic reactions. For it, the vast fund of objective fact about human society is not, as with us, the measure against which outlook is constantly being tested and re-formed, but a grab bag from which individual items are selected arbitrarily and tendenciously to bolster an outlook already preconceived. This is admittedly not a pleasant picture. Problem of how to cope with this force in [is] undoubtedly greatest task our diplomacy has ever faced and probably greatest it will ever have to face. It should be point of departure from which our political general staff work at present juncture should proceed. It should be approached with same thoroughness and care as solution of major strategic problem in war, and if necessary, with no smaller outlay in planning effort. I cannot attempt to suggest all answers here. But I would like to record my conviction that problem is within our power to solve—and that without recourse to any general military conflict. And in support of this conviction there are certain observations of a more encouraging nature I should like to make:

(One) Soviet power, unlike that of Hitlerite Germany, is neither schematic nor adventunstic. It does not work by fixed plans. It does not take unnecessary risks. Impervious to logic of reason, and it is highly sensitive to logic of force. For this reason it can easily withdraw—and usually does when strong resistance is encountered at any point. Thus, if the adversary has sufficient force and makes clear his readiness to use it, he rarely has to do so. If situations are properly handled there need be no prestige-engaging showdowns . . .

(Four) All Soviet propaganda beyond Soviet security sphere is basically negative and destructive. It should therefore be relatively easy to combat it by any intelligent and really constructive program . . .

"The Sources of Soviet Conduct" (a.k.a., "The X-Article") *Foreign Affairs* by George Kennan (excerpt, 1947)[7]

> The political personality of Soviet power as we know it today is the product of ideology and circumstances: ideology inherited by the present Soviet leaders from the movement in which they had their political origin, and circumstances of the power which they now have exercised for nearly three decades in Russia. There can be few tasks of psychological analysis more difficult than to try to trace the interaction of these two forces and the relative role of each in the determination of official Soviet conduct. Yet the attempt must be made if that conduct is to be understood and effectively countered. . . . Thus the decision will really fall in large measure on this country itself. The issue of Soviet-American relations is in essence a test of the overall worth of the United States as a nation among nations. To avoid destruction the United States need only measure up to its own best traditions and prove itself worthy of preservation as a great nation. Surely, there was never a fairer test of national quality than this. In the light of these circumstances, the thoughtful observer of Russian-American relations will find no cause for complaint in the Kremlin's challenge to American society. He will rather experience a certain gratitude to a Providence which, by providing the American people with this implacable challenge, has made their entire security as a nation dependent on their pulling themselves together and accepting the responsibilities of moral and political leadership that history plainly intended them to bear.

Address to Joint Session of Congress by Harry S. Truman, 33rd President of the United States (excerpt, March 12, 1947)[8]

> Mr. President, Mr. Speaker, Members of the Congress of the United States:
> The gravity of the situation which confronts the world today necessitates my appearance before a joint session of the Congress. The foreign policy and the national security of this country are involved. . . . One of the primary objectives of the foreign policy of the United States is the creation of conditions in which we and other nations will be able to work out a way of life free from coercion. This was a fundamental issue in the war with Germany and Japan. Our victory was won over countries which sought to impose their will, and their way of life, upon other nations. To ensure the peaceful development of nations, free from coercion, the United States has taken a leading part in establishing the United Nations. The United Nations is designed to make possible lasting freedom and independence for all its members. We shall not realize our objectives, however, unless we are willing to help free peoples to maintain their free institutions and their national integrity against aggressive movements that seek to impose upon them totalitarian regimes. This is no more than a frank recognition that totalitarian regimes imposed on free peoples, by direct or indirect aggression,

undermine the foundations of international peace and hence the security of the United States. . . . I believe that it must be the policy of the United States to support free peoples who are resisting attempted subjugation by armed minorities or by outside pressures. . . . I therefore ask the Congress to provide authority for assistance to Greece and Turkey in the amount of $400,000,000. . . . In addition to funds, I ask the Congress to authorize the detail of American civilian and military personnel to Greece and Turkey, at the request of those countries, to assist in the tasks of reconstruction. . . .

6.C: DIPLOMACY AND US FOREIGN POLICY

The creation and implementation of foreign policy is complex and difficult to determine because, while each state has a constitution or statutory laws that outline the basics of foreign policy, the practices and nuances of idiosyncratic human communication and deliberation can be difficult to follow and study. Further, states behave in ways that are different from, and even contradict, formal policies. Understanding the difference between *official* and *unofficial* foreign policy practice is important to keep in mind in considering foreign policy interactions.[9]

The question *how?* expands our understanding of a situation under study beyond definition and description to get at explanation. *How?* questions may be followed by adjectives or adverbs, and may delve into calculations and numerical values, for example, *how dangerous is . . .? how much is . . .? how many are included in . . .? how likely is it that . . .?* Questions about *how?* as in *how does this work?* are more easily approached with the advantage of prior research and knowledge, and therefore a learner will want to understand the basics (answers to *what?* or *where?* questions, for example, as covered in the previous chapters). The following section integrates basic information into the discussion to provide learners with an example of using the question *how?* as the primary question for investigation.

Throughout the rest of Section 6.C, bullet points with questions indicate a new topic worthy of examination in understanding how foreign policy works. Before reading each section that follows a bulleted question, try to find answers based on the learning, study habits, and research skills developed in the previous chapters.

- What is *foreign policy* and how is US foreign policy created? The primary documents in this chapter are showing how the US foreign policy of *containment* was first discussed, but is that the path for *all* US foreign policymaking?

In essence, *foreign policy* refers to the objectives that a government holds in relation to its position in the world and its engagement with other countries, and the strategies that a government uses to achieve those objectives.[10] The term itself is not complex, but understanding the theories, processes, and practice or implementation of foreign policy is difficult because it varies so substantially across situations and persons responsible. Foreign policy is inherently a social practice that is guided by human rules and norms, but idiosyncratically, and therefore evades simple definition and description. Foreign policy ideals and practices are often couched in terms of the *national interest* or *national security*, terms that are themselves bewildering, not least because they have many inconsistent definitions. The main idea associated with the *national interest* is that states, and the people who make decisions for governments (often called diplomats or statesmen), make decisions based on a concern with ensuring the continued existence and safety of the state's population and borders/territory.

National and International Statutory and Customary Law

Formal foreign policy and international interactions are regulated and described by statutory and customary international law.[11] Through the United Nations (UN), states have made efforts to regulate policies and interactions related to their diplomats in the form of *positive* or *statutory international law* (i.e., laws written down and codified in documents, such as in treaties deposited with the UN—review chapter 4 concerning treaty law). Further, state interactions are based on *customary international law* (i.e., norms of behavior solidified over extensive repetition and acceptance). In order to facilitate foreign policy states send *diplomats* to live in and work in other states and set up *diplomatic missions*, that is, the group of people sent to a *receiving* state to support the *sending* state's foreign policy and interactions with the receiving state.[12] Take some time to find out more about the specifics of international laws and consider thirteen such treaties deposited with the UN on regulating diplomatic relations.[13] Two international treaties bulleted below regulate interactions between states and their diplomats, all of which suggest the need for the codified laws to support "the promotion of friendly relations among nations."[14]

- *Vienna Convention on Diplomatic Relations* (1961):[15] This treaty outlines the definitions and framework for setting up diplomatic missions and covers how diplomats representing a sending state are expected to behave and be treated by the receiving state.
- *Vienna Convention on Consular Relations* (1963):[16] This treaty defines and records the framework for how consuls and consulates work, that is, the

part of a diplomatic mission sent to a country to facilitate their citizens' travel and stay in the receiving state, and facilitate other discussion over trade relations, etc.

Formal US Foreign Policy Structures

The first primary document reprinted in Section 6.B represents one of the ways that foreign policy is discussed, communicated, and created—through a *telegram* (or what is often called a *state cable*) between government officials, and reveals both formal and informal policymaking practices. George Kennan wrote the "Long Telegram" in his capacity as a temporary US ambassador (called a *chargé d'affaires*) to the Union of Soviet Socialist Republics (USSR). The telegram was delivered to government officers at the US State Department and was a response to a query and as part of a conversation about what foreign policy the US should pursue with the USSR.

- What is the difference between *formal* and *informal* foreign policy in this and other cases and how is US foreign policy conducted and implemented after a decision is made to pursue a particular policy?

To understand why Kennan's telegram would be significant in foreign policymaking, consider the formal mechanisms of foreign policymaking as outlined in the US Constitution: the president is given a broad mandate in Article II to engage in treaty negotiations with other countries and appoint high-level officials to represent the US (such as the secretary of state) to other governments; the US Congress (Legislative Branch) is given enumerated powers in Article I, Section 8 that provide specific instances of power in foreign policy, such as the ability to regulate trade or declare war; further, the US Congress has the ability to hold the Executive accountable for foreign policy through a process called "advice and consent" as well as through legislation that specifically addresses or creates foreign policy; finally, the Judiciary has the ability to interpret laws and policies, though the Supreme Court has not made many decisions or statements related to foreign policy over the years, leaving it to be decided between the Legislature and the Executive.[17] Foreign policy is then implemented through what the US calls the State Department and the secretary of state (other countries call these the Foreign Affairs Ministry and minister of foreign affairs or some derivation). Finally, states set up *diplomatic missions* made up of *consulates* and *embassies* in other countries to facilitate the ease of foreign affairs communication conducted through diplomats.

- How do the three branches of the US government and other government departments or agencies influence US foreign policy? [18]

Other formal mechanisms for guiding US foreign policymaking include statutory laws promulgated by the US Congress, presidential executive orders, and intelligence reports produced by government or even nongovernmental entities. While the US president has much leeway in guiding and directly US foreign policy, various governmental departments and agencies have been created over the years to support the president in considerations of policy on national security, such as committees that meet at the president's request to give advice on national security like the National Security Council (created by the National Security Act in 1947) and the National Intelligence Council (created in 1979), or individual advisor positions as in the national security advisor and the director of national intelligence. The following list gives examples of some of the most important documents that had a major effect on US foreign policymaking in the twentieth century.

- *National Security Act* (NSA—July 26, 1947):[19] This Act drastically changed and bolstered US foreign policy structures "to provide for the establishment of integrated policies and procedures for the departments, agencies, and functions of the Government relating to the national security"—notably, the NSA created the National Security Council (NSC) and the Central Intelligence Agency (CIA).[20]
- *National Security Council Paper 68* (NSC-68) (April 7, 1950):[21] The NSC produces reports at the request of the US president on various national security issues. Early on in its history, the NSC produced a report called NSC-68 on the US relationship to the USSR and it suggested possible foreign policies to pursue. NSC-68 reflected the views of some people in the US government that the best way to *contain* the threat represented by the USSR was to build up military power to ensure adequate response in case it was necessary. The idea of *containment* as a military deterrent went against Kennan's ideas of *containment* as ideological. Find NSC-68 online and compare its message with that of Kennan's telegram—in what ways are the two documents similar or different?
- *Gulf of Tonkin Resolution* (August 7, 1964):[22] This joint resolution, bathed in controversy, was directly linked to the United States' implementation of the foreign policy of containment. Passed by the US House and Senate, it gave the president power to wage war: "the United States is, therefore, prepared, *as the President determines*, to take all necessary steps, including the use of armed force, to assist any member or protocol state of the

Southeast Asia Collective Defense Treaty requesting assistance in defense of its freedom" (emphasis added). During the 1960s the US sent military advisors and naval vessels, including a destroyer ship, the U.S.S. *Maddox*, to Vietnam as an attempt to bolster the South Korean leaders against communist control, and in August 1964 the resolution was supported by Congress because of false reports that the U.S.S. *Maddox* had been attacked by North Vietnamese fighters.

- *War Powers Resolution* (passed as the War Powers Act in the Senate) (November 7, 1973):[23] This resolution/act was passed (over a veto from President Nixon) to reclaim the war-declaration power of the Senate as outlined in the US Constitution, even though most presidents since its passing have ignored it or declared it unconstitutional.

Despite efforts to regulate foreign policy in constitutions, statutory laws, and intelligence reports, such sources only provide the form of foreign policy, whereas its articulation, practice, and implementation is much more complex, and sometimes even appears to contradict such regulatory provisions. The bullets and descriptions below outline some of the important positions in US government that make or affect foreign policymaking and implementation, and gives specifics on the particular people and their actions in creating the policy of *containment* in the 1940s–1950s. Consider the following and expand on what is explained here using your own research capabilities:

- *Executive (President and Administration):* The US president is mainly responsible for foreign policy and has the most influence and leeway in foreign policy compared to domestic policy. President Truman was heavily influential in creating the policy of containment, but also influenced by many people around him in the forms of committees and advisors. In the end, Truman set the course for the United States following a militaristic rather than ideological version of containment.
- *State Department (Secretary of State and Foreign Service):* The State Department is made up of a plethora of positions, from the secretary of state to ambassadors and foreign service officers working in a multitude of positions in diplomatic missions worldwide. The main responsibility of the State Department is to implement the president's foreign policy. Kennan was a foreign service officer and his authoritative voice during the 1940s impacted the way that the State Department and other foreign policy committees and persons in the US government thought about the USSR.
- *Department of Defense (Chief of Joint Chiefs of Staff):* The secretary of defense plans and implements military policy and tactics in pursuit and support of the president's foreign policy, which may include wartime strategy

and tactics. The Joint Chiefs of Staff is a committee of the heads of all departments of the military that meet to advise the president on important military and national security matters. Various people in these capacities advised presidents to increase military force and might during the Cold War based on their understanding of containment policy, leading to costly proxy wars, like the Korean and Vietnam wars, both in lives lost and in money spent (for instance, Robert McNamara acted as the Secretary of Defense during the Vietnam War and encouraged increases in troops and military spending).

As is evident in the short descriptions above, foreign policy decisions and implementation depends not only on formal processes but also on the idiosyncratic ideas and influence of people in particular positions at any given time. Take more time to find out more about the policy of containment and the individuals responsible for its inception and implementation before you move on to the next section that gives a sense of how foreign policy is made and implemented in practice.

US Foreign Policy in Practice

In order to more fully appreciate US foreign policymaking and the significance of Kennan's Long Telegram it is especially important to consider how foreign policy is made and conducted in practice, and the limits of understanding foreign policy simply by knowing or following the rules. Foreign policy is articulated, created, and implemented in an iterative process both between and within governments and their diplomats and leaders. But in practice, foreign policy takes on multiple forms and models, and one way of creating a specific foreign policy is almost never like the next. Consider that while constitutions, in this case the US Constitution, delimit the main functions of actors who might be involved in foreign policy, they may not directly specify everyone who is involved, their positions or influence, or the practices of foreign policymaking and implementation developed over time. For instance, the US Constitution does not specify that policy could be articulated and formed based on telegrams (or in contemporary practice, Twitter statements), and yet it is clear that such modes of communication can have an indelible impact on the creation and implementation of foreign policy and the practice of foreign affairs.

One early practice of diplomacy between and within state governments was in the form of letters, and later telegrams (also called *cables*), carefully written, sealed, or encrypted communications to convey important information to other diplomats or leaders. In the early years of telegram communication, telegrams were sent by wire, or cables, laid down on the ocean floor. Later, in the 1970s, cables began to be communicated electronically but maintained the same rules for format.[24] Much like new technologies today, the telegram had a huge impact on the efficiency and speed of diplomatic communications, reducing communication from weeks and months to minutes. New technologies can have a huge impact on and change the way government officials conduct diplomacy.

- Who wrote the "Long Telegram," and who was its audience?

In the case of the primary document in this chapter, it is important to immediately learn more about the author of the telegram, George F. Kennan. Kennan was incredibly influential in American foreign policy from the 1920s to the 1960s, particularly in inspiring discussions that led to the US foreign policy of *containment*. Kennan was a foreign service officer (FSO), holding several posts in the foreign service, also called the *diplomatic corps* because of their charge to assist the US president in negotiations and diplomacy with other countries. He served as an FSO in several capacities: as chair of the 1940s Policy Priorities Committee, and as *chargé d'affaires* and later as US ambassador to the USSR. Further, Kennan helped open the first US embassy in the USSR in 1933, thereby gaining experience with the government, culture, and people.

- How might Kennan's experiences and positions have molded his perspective about US foreign policy toward the USSR?
- How might his experience have made him seem more reliable to his counterparts in the foreign service who would have read the "Long Telegram" when it was delivered in 1946?

The audience of a written work is often overlooked but is crucial to our ability to analyze a situation under study, particularly because people will write a piece with an audience in mind (refer to chapter 3 concerning asking *who?* questions of a situation). In this case, Kennan had received a question from the US State Department about Soviet foreign policy and written a telegram, also called a diplomatic cable, in response. A diplomatic cable, even to the present day, includes special acronyms and insignia on the cable itself that indicate its audience, that is, who holds the credentials to read the cable and to whom it should be disseminated. President Truman was in office when Kennan's cable was sent on February 22, 1946, having taken over for President Roosevelt who died the previous year on April 12, 1945. Consider how difficult it would be to take over for a president upon their death, particularly FDR who was dearly beloved by the American people and who was serving his fourth term as President. President Truman and his administration had been trying to articulate and implement foreign policy toward the USSR in a similar fashion as FDR had done, but new people and voices had more influence in Truman's administration and Kennan's telegram became influential for that reason.

- Take a moment to go back to the full telegram and find the instances where Kennan talks about these two groups: Soviet leaders and Soviet citizens. What does he say about them? Are his statements simply speculation or does he provide evidence for his statements? How might interpretation play into his conclusions? Would someone else have come to different conclusions?

In the telegram, Kennan wrote about the USSR leadership and postulated on their attitudes and beliefs as relates to foreign policy. He further wrote about USSR citizens and their attitudes and beliefs, which he indicates were different from the Soviet leadership. Notice that Kennan is harsh on Soviet leadership in representing their view of the world, that is, stating that the leadership needs to create an international enemy or threat in order to validate internal leadership, and that the threat of capitalism and the West have now replaced the Nazi threat. Notice also that Kennan is not as critical of the USSR citizens when he says that the Soviet leadership policy "does not represent natural outlook of Russian people." Whatever his intent, Kennan's portrayal of the USSR's leadership influenced the way that US citizens and leaders thought about them and interpreted their actions as only being influenced by a "logic of force."

- How influential was Kennan's "Long Telegram"? Now that you have learned a great deal about foreign policy communication and how foreign policy is conducted, take the time to try to answer this question for yourself and find out more about telegrams and diplomatic cables as used in the US government.

The 1947 exchanges within the US government as shown with Kennan's "Long Telegram" had to do with foreign policy in the aftermath of World War II, and specifically how to engage with the USSR, and reveals the informal aspects of foreign policymaking. Foreign policymakers are also often influenced by what they read in magazines, academic journals, research reports, and news sources. Consider the second document in Section 6.B is an excerpt from what was labeled the X-Article and was published in *Foreign Affairs* magazine—a magazine that includes pieces by academics and policymakers on foreign issues.

Kennan's ideas on the USSR and on the practical solutions on how to engage with and relate to the USSR were influential because of his dogged attempts to make his voice heard, first through the "Long Telegram" in sending a lengthy (and therefore expensive) telegram to State Department officials, and then making his ideas publicly known through subsequent publications.[25] After Kennan sent the "Long Telegram" he published an article on the same subject, attributed in publication anonymously to a Mr. X, in the widely read *Foreign Affairs* magazine, in order to expand on his original statements and to make his ideas more widely known since the "Long Telegram" was still classified and thus only seen by government officials. The X-Article was articulated quite differently than the "Long Telegram" (each for a different audience, but Kennan also reveals a change in his thinking about the USSR, or as some have argued, wrote the article too quickly and therefore did not articulate his ideas coherently).[26] Kennan submitted the article anonymously because he was part of the foreign service and did not want to speak for the Truman administration. Although the article was printed as written by Mr. X, people in foreign service in the US government recognized Kennan as the author and it incentivized people to think and talk about the ideas of the need for containment of the USSR.

- Review the X-Article excerpt in Section 6.B carefully (or better yet, find the complete version online or through the library), and notice where the tone differs from the "Long Telegram." Notice also the use of the word "contain" that will come up later in foreign policy. Consider how influential the X-Article might have been among foreign policy makers in DC.

Truman's Presidential Doctrine

The third document in Section 6.B shows how a *presidential doctrine* is articulated. A *presidential doctrine* indicates a particular president's foreign policy, including beliefs, objectives, and sometimes strategy. The development of the policy of *containment* in the Truman administration was an attempt by a new president, President Truman, to figure out how to relate to, interpret, and negotiate with the Soviet Union in the wake of President Roosevelt's death. The thinking and ideas about Soviet leadership represented in Kennan's telegram and article played a large part in Truman's articulation of what became known as the Truman Doctrine in a speech given to the Congress on March 12, 1947. Once US presidents decide on a particular foreign policy, they seek a way to communicate it to Congress and to the world in what are known as Presidential Addresses to Congress.

6.D: RECOMMENDED READINGS ON FOREIGN POLICY AND DIPLOMACY

Dorman, Shawn, ed. *Inside a U.S. Embassy: Diplomacy at Work.* 3rd ed. New York: FS Books/ American Foreign Service Association, 2011.

Gaddis, John Lewis. *George F. Kennan: An American Life.* New York: Penguin Books, 2011.

Gaddis, John Lewis. *The Cold War: A New History.* New York: Penguin Press, 2005.

Hastedt, Glenn P. *American Foreign Policy: Past, Present, Future.* 7th ed. Upper Saddle River, NJ: Pearson/Prentice Hall, 2009.

Kennan, George F. *American Diplomacy.* 60th Anniversary expanded ed. Chicago: University of Chicago Press, 2012.

Kissinger, Henry A. 1994. *Diplomacy.* New York: Simon & Schuster.

Zinn, Howard. *A Peoples' History of the United States.* New York: Harper Collins, 1980.

NOTES

1. Barbara Oakley, *A Mind for Numbers: How to Excel at Math and Science* (New York: Penguin Random House, 2014) (and free companion Coursera Course: *Learning How to Learn*).

2. Francesco Cirillo. *The Pomodoro Technique: The Life-Changing Time-Management System* (London: Virgin Books, 2018); See also, Oakley, *A Mind for Numbers.*

3. There are several online sources dedicated to supporting learners in using the Pomodoro Technique and the idea has been built into business practices and consulting as well, some of which require subscriptions and others are free. For example, see Cirillo's Consulting firm: https://francescocirillo.com/.

4. Oakley, *A Mind for Numbers.*

5. George Kennan, "Long Telegram" (February 22, 1946), History and Public Policy Program Digital Archive, National Archives and Records Administration, Department of State Records (Record Group 59), Central Decimal File, 1945-1949, 861.00/2-2246; reprinted in US Department of State, ed., Foreign Relations of the United States, 1946, Volume VI, Eastern Europe; The Soviet Union (Washington, DC: United States Government Printing Office, 1969), 696–709 (reproduced based on fair use doctrine from Section 107 of US Copyright Law), http://digitalarchive.wilsoncenter.org/document/116178.

6. As you read this telegram you will note that there are many grammatical errors or words missing (such as pronouns or conjunctions)—telegrams were meant to be short and concise documents because of the difficulty in transmission and the cost associated, and thus, grammatical rules were typically ignored. There are also misspelled words, such as "adventunstic" for "adventurous," or when "After Al" for "After All," showing that in foreign policy writings it is not always possible to

be perfect. See discussion later on the length of this particular telegram which was against the norm at the time.

7. George Kennan, "The Sources of Soviet Conduct" (a.k.a., "The X-Article") *Foreign Affairs* (July 1947) (all rights reserved, reproduced based on fair use doctrine from Section 107 of US Copyright Law).

8. Harry S. Truman, "Address Before a Joint Session of Congress" (Speech, Washington D.C., March 12, 1947), The Avalon Project, Yale Law School (all rights reserved, reproduced based on fair use doctrine from Section 107 of US Copyright Law), https://avalon.law.yale.edu/20th_century/trudoc.asp.

9. Many excellent introductions to foreign policy cover the main theories and practices. E.g., Glenn Hastedt, *American Foreign Policy: Past, Present, Future*, 7th ed. (Upper Saddle River, NJ: Pearson/Prentice Hall, 2009); Henry A. Kissinger, *Diplomacy* (New York: Simon & Schuster, 1994); George F. Kennan, American Diplomacy 60th Anniversary Expanded ed. (Chicago: University of Chicago Press, 2012).

10. "Diplomatic Dictionary" National Museum of American Diplomacy, accessed July 17, 2019, https://diplomacy.state.gov/discover-diplomacy/diplomatic-diction ary/. Check this website for a similar definition to foreign policy along with many other helpful definitions for concepts related to or describing foreign policy in practice.

11. E.g., Benedetto Conforti and Angelo Labella, *An Introduction to International Law* (Leiden, The Netherlands: BRILL, 2012).

12. Shawn Dorman, ed., *Inside a U.S. Embassy: Diplomacy at Work*, 3rd ed. (New York: FS Books/American Foreign Service Association, 2011).

13. United Nations Treaty Collection "Chapter III: Privileges and Immunities, Diplomatic and Consular Relations, Etc.," accessed March 10, 2020, https://treatie s.un.org/pages/ViewDetails.aspx?src=TREATY&mtdsg_no=III-1&chapter=3&cl ang=_en.

14. United Nations Treaty Collection, "Chapter III: Convention on the Privileges and Immunities, Diplomatic and Consular Relations, etc.; 6. Vienna Convention on Consular Relations," accessed March 9, 2020, https://treaties.un.org/pages/ViewD etails.aspx?src=TREATY&mtdsg_no=III-6&chapter=3. See the preambles of each of the documents listed such as phrase two of the Vienna Convention on Consular Relations.

15. United Nations Treaty Collection, "Chapter III."

16. United Nations Treaty Collection, "Chapter III."

17. United States Constitution, "The Constitution of the United States of America," accessed March 8, 2020 https://www.archives.gov/founding-docs/consti tution-transcript.

18. Some excellent "think tanks" and research organizations have compiled overview documents to help people understand the US Constitution and what it says about Foreign Policy. Consider the following: *Foreign Policy Association*, "How Foreign Policy is Made," accessed on July 15, 2019, https://fpa.org/features/index.cfm?act =feature&announcement_id=45&show_sidebar=0; Jonathan Masters, "U.S. Foreign Policy Powers: Congress and the President" *Council on Foreign Relations*, accessed

July 15, 2019, https://www.cfr.org/backgrounder/us-foreign-policy-powers-congress-and-president.

Toni Johnson, "Congress and U.S. Foreign Policy," *Council on Foreign Relations*, accessed July 15, 2019, https://www.cfr.org/backgrounder/congress-and-us-foreign-policy.

19. The NSA 1947 is public law and can be found online: Office of the Director of National Intelligence. National Security Act of 1947, accessed March 10, 2020, https://www.dni.gov/index.php/ic-legal-reference-book/national-security-act-of-1947.

20. For a discussion of the creation and early years of the NSC, including its flexibility, see, e.g., Robert Cutler, "The Development of the National Security Council," *Foreign Affairs Magazine,* 34, no. 3 (April 1956): 441–58.

21. National Security Council. "National Security Council Report, NSC 68, 'United States Objectives and Programs for National Security,'" April 14, 1950, History and Public Policy Program Digital Archive, US National Archives. http://digitalarchive.wilsoncenter.org/document/116191.

22. Avalon Project, Documents in Law, History and Diplomacy, Yale University. "The Tonkin Gulf Incident: 1964," Last modified 2008. Source: Department of State Bulletin, August 24, 1964. https://avalon.law.yale.edu/20th_century/tonkin-g.asp.

23. Avalon Project, Documents in Law, History and Diplomacy, Yale University, "War Powers Resolution," accessed March 12, 2020, https://avalon.law.yale.edu/20th_century/warpower.asp.

24. Joshua Keating, "Why Do Diplomats Still Send Cables?" *Foreign Policy* (November 30, 2010), https://foreignpolicy.com/2010/11/30/why-do-diplomats-still-send-cables/.

25. Consider that Kennan's telegram was 5,200 words (as a side note, you may have found reliable sources that indicate the telegram was 8,000 words—that oft-cited "fact" is actually a mistaken estimation by Kennan himself in his memoirs about the length—researchers have used that number ever since without verifying it!) Story related in Gaddis interview, halfway through the interview: Council on Foreign Relations, "The Lasting Legacy of George F. Kennan," Interview of John Lewis Gaddis conducted by Richard N. Haass on Monday, June 4, 2012, accessed August 26, 2019, https://www.cfr.org/event/lasting-legacy-george-f-kennan-0.

26. John Lewis Gaddis, *George F. Kennan: An American* Life (New York: Penguin Books, 2011); See also John Lewis Gaddis, *The Cold War* (New York: Penguin Books, 2005); Council on Foreign Relations, "The Lasting Legacy of George F. Kennan."

Chapter 7

When?

Outlining Chronology

The question *when?* introduces another dimension for describing, understanding, analyzing, and thinking critically about global politics. In the first instance, the question is an historical one, asking us to think about the location of a given text in time. More deeply, though, the question asks us to think about the whole context and content of the text and how the context, as well as the concepts, and ideas in the text itself, relates in time to other contexts, concepts, and ideas. Thinking about historical context while reading any type of document is essential for deciphering its meaning and significance.

This chapter uses the question *when?* to situate primary source material in an historical, global political context. Robert S. McNamara, whose foreword to the 1978 *World Development Report* (WDR) appears in Section 7.B, served as US Secretary of Defense under Presidents Kennedy and Johnson, and played a major role in the Vietnam War, before joining the World Bank in 1968 where he served as president until 1981. The 1978 WDR was the first such report published by the World Bank—an *intergovernmental organization* or IGO—roughly marking a historical pivot in the World Bank's lending strategies away from project-based development lending toward deeper and more comprehensive development programming.

Section 7.A discusses logical reasoning and presents logical fallacies of which learners should be wary. Section 7.B then provides the primary document for this chapter, the 1978 WDR. While reading the document, consider whether the text itself reveals anything about the context and time period in which it was written, and mark those places for later analysis. A discussion of international development in historical context follows in Section 7.C and a list of references is provided in Section 7.D for those who would like to understand more about development and global political economy.

7.A: LOGICAL REASONING, FALLACIES, AND TIMELINES

Learning and research require one to understand and interpret facts about the world. It is easy to misinterpret facts, and even experts make mistakes or common errors in logical reasoning, that is, *logical fallacies*. There are hundreds of logical fallacies, some more common than others, a few of which are highlighted here: familiarize yourself with these and with as many others as possible.[1] Good command of logical fallacies will help learners to avoid them and become more logical thinkers, speakers, and writers. Further, taking the time to assess the logic of global political actors, for example, in their speeches or writings, is a powerful critical thinking tool. Logical fallacies create a partial foundation for thinking critically about the ideas and information we receive from others. Along these lines, some professions like speechwriting, lobbying, fundraising, public relations, marketing, and advertising deploy logical fallacies as tools of the trade, using them deliberately to craft persuasive arguments—being able to identify logical fallacies as you encounter them in your daily life will keep you from being duped or taken advantage of.

Four logical fallacies that we, the authors, encounter often in discussions of global politics are:[2]

1. *Hasty generalizations*: This fallacy involves making broad or general claims based on a small number of observations. For example, making the claim that "all countries developed based on a straightforward commitment to capitalism and democracy" based on observations only about the United Kingdom is a hasty generalization because it is based on a small sample size (only one country).
2. *Authority fallacy*: People try to make their argument more persuasive by associating it with an authority figure or someone who is famous. For example, if someone supported their claim that "neoliberal reform promotes economic growth" by arguing that "Ronald Reagan adopted neoliberal reform because it promotes economic growth," they are offering no logical reasons to support the argument, and instead are trying to tie the argument to a prominent authority figure in order to make it seem more legitimate.
3. *Ad hominem fallacy*: The ad hominem fallacy involves attacking the person making an argument rather than the argument itself. For example, a suggestion that it is not possible to take Subcomandante Marcos' writings or ideas seriously because he wears a ski mask when speaking publicly is an ad hominem fallacy.[3]
4. *Post hoc ergo propter hoc*: The *post hoc* fallacy involves assuming that the order of events in time indicates causality when it does not (i.e., if *B*

occurred after *A*, then *A* caused *B* when in fact, *B* is caused by something else). The *post hoc* fallacy cautions us not to confuse correlation for causation. Arguing, for example, that "economic growth in Uganda took off in the 1990s after neoliberal reforms were introduced" would indicate a post hoc fallacy because, while growth did occur chronologically after the reforms, research suggests that Ugandan growth in the 1990s owed more to rising coffee prices (Uganda's major export) than to neoliberal reform.[4]

Other common fallacies in global politics include the *either-or* fallacy, *slippery slope* fallacy, *bandwagon* fallacy, *strawman* fallacy, *red herring* fallacy, and *appeal to emotion* fallacy.

Creating Timelines to Contextualize Subject Matter

One excellent study technique is to create timelines to visually orient the subject matter in its historical context. The timeline should note dates, titles, and names for key events, international conferences and agreements, and even important and influential ideologies (these are discussed in Section 7.C below in the context of McNamara's 1978 WDR introduction). Create a space above or below the timeline to add notes about the nature of the event and why it was important. Start a timeline early on in the study of a new event and add to the timeline and revise as you continue to learn more about the subject and its historical context. If you prefer to create a digital timeline, most software packages include such abilities, such as Microsoft Word or PowerPoint "SmartArt" tab with timeline templates—a timeline example based on this chapter's analysis of the historical context of the WDR is included in figure 7.1, created using Microsoft Word SmartArt. What is missing from

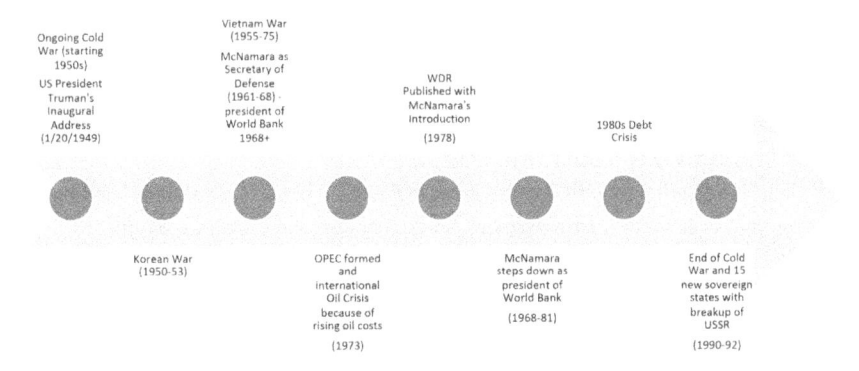

Figure 7.1 Timeline: History of Development in the Post–World War II Period.

the timeline that you think is important for understanding McNamara's statement? Add your ideas to the timeline.

7.B: PRIMARY SOURCE ON DEVELOPMENT

"Foreword" to the 1978 *World Development Report* by Robert McNamara (excerpt, 1978)[5]

The *World Development Report*, 1978, along with its statistical annex, is the first of what we expect will be a series of annual reports providing a comprehensive assessment of the global development issues. This first report deals with a number of fundamental problems confronting the developing countries, and explores their relationship to the underlying trends in the international economy. Since it is not possible to address every major question in this initial volume, the analysis will be extended to other aspects of development in subsequent years.

The past quarter century has been a period of unprecedented change and progress in the developing world. And yet despite this impressive record, some 800 million individuals continue to be trapped in what I have termed absolute poverty: a condition of life so characterized by malnutrition, illiteracy, disease, squalid surroundings, high infant mortality, and low life expectancy as to be beneath any reasonable definition of human decency.

Absolute poverty on so massive a scale is already a cruel anachronism. But unless economic growth in the developing countries can be substantially accelerated, the now inevitable increases in population will mean that the numbers of the absolute poor will remain unacceptably high even at the end of the century.

The twin objectives of development, then, are to accelerate economic growth and to reduce poverty.

Greater progress toward these goals will require an immense effort by the developing countries; an effort that must be matched by a more realistic level of support from the industrialized nations. It is a fact that the international economy is growing more interdependent.

That evolution can and should benefit developing and developed countries alike, but if it is to do so there must be adjustments in the global patterns of trade to reflect shifts in comparative advantage.

These adjustments will not be easy, but the alternative to a more rational economic framework can only mean, in the end, greater penalties for all.

In the meantime, whatever the uncertainties of the future, governments have to act. They are faced with the necessity of daily decisions. And hence the quality of the information, and the range of available choices on which those decisions will have to be made become critically important.

That is why we have undertaken this analysis. The World Bank, with its broad-based membership, its long experience, and its daily involvement with the development problems of its members is in a unique position to analyze the interrelationships between the principal components of the development process. To the extent that these are more clearly understood, the institution itself, and all of its member governments individually, will be able to cooperate more effectively in accelerating economic growth, and reducing the intolerable deprivations of massive poverty. . . .

7.C: GLOBAL POVERTY AND DEVELOPMENT

In almost any field of study, including global politics, learners and researchers assess historical dates and time periods so as to situate inquiries and research, and understand actors' motivations and actions. Global politics, as an interdisciplinary field of study, includes conversations about all countries, regions, cultures, and people of the world, and therefore draws on timelines and chronologies that are multiple and complicated. For example, disciplines like physics establish timelines that start at the beginning of the universe itself and find ways into global political conversations when thinking about resource extraction, the environment, and sustainability. Additionally, global politics draws on a variety of social sciences that utilize different timelines, some starting with the evolution of *Homo sapiens*, others beginning several centuries before the Common Era (CE),[6] and still others that ground their inquiries in the modern period beginning in (roughly) the sixteenth century.

It is a good idea for learners developing expertise in global politics to start accumulating and organizing crucial dates, events, historical periods, and other markers that will reveal deeper meaning in a situation under study. As learners develop a sense of history in relation to global politics, it becomes easier to connect knowledge about people and places around the world, and to ask increasingly sophisticated questions about historical context, even becoming more adept at checking their own biases and assumptions. A word of caution before we proceed: it is important to consider a document or situation under study in its own context, and to try to avoid over-interpreting the situation from the vantage point of our own historical period. While in some cases hindsight allows for more pointed critiques of historical mistakes and misjudgments, doing so carelessly can have the opposite effect, confusing and distorting interpretations of the subject matter.

Timelines and Chronologies in Global Politics

People who study global politics often use similar historical reference points when discussing global history and placing a document like McNamara's WDR introduction in context. Scholars identify important events, processes, or other kinds of dynamics broadly viewed as marking significant changes in the global system, for example, war, colonialism, financial crisis, ideological shifts, or landmark international conferences, treaties, or pieces of legislation. In order to understand McNamara's introduction more fully, consider the historical context in which it was written and how McNamara may have been influenced by and interpreted worldwide or local events based on his life experience.

The following questions help orient the discussion below and provide good starting points for independent research:

- *When* in global history is McNamara writing (what was happening in the world during the 1970s?) and how might that time period impact his ideas or interpretations of world events (consider, for example, how McNamara thinks about poverty or the economy)?
- Are there any global events that occurred before 1978 that might be useful in understanding McNamara's statement and what is useful about them?
- Are there any global events that occurred after 1978 that might help situate his statement within a useful chronology and even show the impact of his writing?

War

Historians and international relations scholars alike identify major wars—especially World War I (1914–1919), World War II (1938–1945), and the Cold War (1945–1991, including *proxy* wars like the US wars in Korea and Vietnam)—to mark time over the course of the twentieth century. Other wars, like the American Revolution (1765–1783), the French Revolution (1789–1799), or the revolutions in Europe (1848), mark time in prior centuries.[7] Wars create disruptions in how countries, corporations, communities, and other actors relate to one another on the global stage. The world becomes divided into enemies and allies, alliances and treaties are forged and broken, and open violence generates massive casualties and disrupts work, production, trade, travel, and migration.[8] During and at the end of wars, emergent and powerful countries form new global relationships (such as the 1941 *Atlantic Charter* discussed in chapter 5), write new rules and laws (for example, the *1915 Treaty* between the United States and Haiti in chapter 8), and create new institutions (such as the United Nations reviewed in chapter 4, established in 1945).

Consider the major ongoing war at the time of the writing of McNamara's forward: the Cold War.[9] The World Bank published its first *World Development Report* in 1978, at a time when the Cold War was at its height as an ongoing ideological (and physical) conflict between the world's two superpowers (the United States and the Soviet Union), operating in what IR scholars term a *bipolar* international system (as opposed to a *multipolar* or *unipolar* international system—the terms indicate the number of *hegemonic* powers that have influence and power and hold each other accountable or keep each other in check, possibly resulting in or avoiding international wars—what type of system do you think we currently live in?). Indeed, McNamara began his term as World Bank president in 1968 when the outcome of the Cold War was still uncertain.

- Take some time to read about the Cold War and the main ideological divides between the US and the USSR. Review President Truman's inaugural address covered in chapter 1; the address outlined the conflict between democracy and communism and supported a new way of thinking about development and international poverty. Indeed, Truman gave his speech in part to encourage the US Congress to devote aid to development, a practice that continued and resulted in US support of the World Bank in subsequent years.
- Do you think McNamara's seemingly urgent call to support growth and poverty reduction in the developing world is motivated by Cold War concerns? Why or why not?
- Have you researched the *who?* question yet? Recall from the introduction of this chapter what job/s McNamara had before becoming World Bank president. How would his previous jobs and experience have influenced his perspective and policies as World Bank president, especially in thinking about the relevance of the Cold War?

The World Bank, founded during the 1944 Bretton Woods Conference as the International Bank for Reconstruction and Development (IBRD), was originally intended to provide financing for post–World War II reconstruction in Europe, yet McNamara's presidency changed its primary focus to worldwide poverty reduction.[10] Over the course of his tenure at the World Bank, McNamara oversaw massive increases in World Bank fundraising and lending to developing countries, partially because of Cold War politics. From the 1950s to the 1980s the World Bank supported development projects and loans to countries in Latin America, Africa and the Middle East, Asia, and Oceania, consistently expanding its membership as well as influence throughout the world. However, because of the Cold War *bipolar* international structure, the Soviet Union and its satellite countries did not become members of the World Bank until after the Soviet Union dissolved in 1990–1992.[11]

Thinking about historical contexts leads us to ask, then, whether World Bank lending may have played a political role in the Cold War. Did World Bank lending help reinforce the power of the US relative to the USSR? Scholars argue that World Bank and International Monetary Fund (IMF) lending during the Cold War worked to prevent developing countries from turning to communism and allying with the USSR, by providing loans and other supports for capitalist growth and poverty reduction in low-income countries. Could this be why McNamara's tone seems so urgent in the excerpt above, given that 1978 was a peak of hostilities between the US and USSR? (Recall the practice of *containment* as a policy discussed in chapter 6 and consider how the US and the USSR contained each other by supporting development around the world.)

Imperialism, Colonialism, and Independence

Imperialism, *colonialism*, and *national independence* are dynamics that strongly influence thinking about development and poverty (see also Shiva's discussion of development in chapter 2, Section 2.B). Imperial conquest, colonial rule and occupation, struggles for independence and self-determination, and winning political independence are central events and dynamics in the histories of most peoples, communities, countries, and regions around the world, and thus important when answering the question *when?*

- Take a moment to look up the definition of colonialism and find those areas of the world that were former colonies, determine which imperial powers ruled in which territories and regions at which times in history, and also identify those territories around the world that remain colonies today.[12]

McNamara's introduction focuses mainly on problems of economic stagnation and poverty across the developing world. Yet, many of the countries to which McNamara implicitly refers did not achieve national political independence until the 1960s and 1970s (most countries in Sub-Saharan Africa, for example), which impacts their development status, including the levels of absolute poverty (among other things, colonialism means that foreign peoples have power over the colonial economy and government, and are thus able to impact many aspects of the economy and the state that are important for thinking about development).

The impact of *colonialism* thus raises some important *when?*-related questions:

- How were developing countries' experiences with imperialism, colonization, and/or independence related to (or how do such experiences contribute to) the slow growth and poverty that McNamara mentions?
- Does the history of colonialism continue to impact the economies of former colonies after they declare independence? (Search and find out more about *neocolonialism*.)

- How might McNamara's call for the industrialized powers (many of them former empires) to match the efforts of developing countries relate to the history and influence of colonialism (both as a boon for the imperial powers and as a detriment to those colonized)?

Colonialism and the colonization process proved intrusive, disruptive, oppressive, coercive, and extremely violent for most people who experienced it. Colonialism quite literally transformed entire societies of people, including bringing about changes in cultures (languages, religions, customs, and traditions), law, government and politics, economic systems, and social and ecological practices and behaviors.[13] Struggles for national independence involved massive mobilizations of people who were called to fight for their freedom, often in extremely bloody and deadly conflicts that counted massive casualties. In the wake of independence movements, new societies were created yet again, many of them assemblages of colonial, pre-colonial, and post-colonial ideas, policies, and practices. Colonialism and independence also impact the balance of power in the international system, as well as the circuits of wealth, goods, and services that anchor the global economy. Indeed, transitions from *unipolarity* to *multipolarity* in the international system can involve the breakup of empires and the division of overseas imperial territories and colonies into smaller pieces (e.g., dissolution of former territories occurred in parts of the Ottoman and British empires after World War I, and in the Soviet Union after the Cold War).[14]

Historian Harry Magdoff discusses two different forms of imperialism since the late fifteenth century: imperialism *with colonies* and imperialism *without colonies* (the latter is also sometimes referred to as *neocolonialism* or *neoimperialism*).[15] While many global political conversations today rightly center on European and US colonial practices since the birth of capitalism in 1492 and their consequences, it is important to keep in mind that colonization is an old practice that dates to ancient times.

- Take some time to research the following empires, each of which ensured its dominion over foreign peoples and territories using colonization, in addition to a host of other approaches and tactics (such as trade, debt, and war):
  - Roman Empire (roughly 27 BCE–476 CE, spreading from contemporary North Africa to the United Kingdom)
  - Chinese Empire and Dynasties (roughly 2100 BCE–1912, spreading across contemporary China; consider also China's contemporary colonial control of Tibet, Taiwan, and Hong Kong).
  - Aztec Empire (roughly 1100–1521 CE when the Spanish conquistadors conquered Tenochtitlan and began Spanish colonial control)
- What impact did each of these imperial systems have on the world at the time?

- What impact do these historical empires still have today in the form of cultural influence, continued relationships, or transformed economic and political systems?

Even for countries that gained independence before the twentieth century (e.g., most Latin American countries became independent in the nineteenth century), historical colonization is important for thinking about contemporary poverty and slow growth. Scholars argue that former empires retained control over Latin American economies long after political independence, using tools like debt, trade, and foreign aid to ensure continued imperial wealth and dominance at the expense of local people and the local economy (see the US-Haiti Treaty of 1915 in chapter 8 for more discussion).[16] In the 1980s, shortly after McNamara's forward was written, the World Bank would preside with the IMF over the *lost decade* in Latin America, a period critics of the World Bank and IMF argue is evidence of neocolonialism.[17]

Economic and Financial Crisis

Economic crises have a huge impact on global social dynamics of all kinds. As with other major events, economic crisis is frequently disruptive and difficult, not only for individual communities and countries but sometimes for whole regions or the entire world economy. Economic crises generate unemployment, poverty, hunger, and sometimes also political and social instability, and environmental degradation. New laws, rules, programs, and institutions are also often formed in the wake of economic and financial crises.[18] The most frequently referenced *global* economic crises in contemporary global political conversations are (arguably) the Great Depression (1929–1936) and the Great Recession (2008–2014), both of which had substantial and long-lasting impacts for almost every country, community, and person on earth (they also impacted nonhuman species in significant ways).[19]

- Based on your own research, which economic crises are significant in the twentieth century?
- Are there any that may have influenced McNamara's considerations of the global economic system and economic growth? Why?

Coming back to McNamara's statement, it is useful to consider how turbulence in the global economy during the 1970s impacted his thinking. The 1970s is generally considered a period of global economic stagnation (the global economy slowed down and created fewer jobs). The US and other countries reliant on oil imports experienced a period of *stagflation* in the 1970s marked by both slow growth and high inflation (inflation is a rise in the overall level of prices). The slow-moving economic effects of stagflation were made worse by the 1973 oil price crisis, in which the Organization for Oil Exporting Countries (OPEC) raised oil prices quickly in response to the 1973 Arab-Israeli War.[20] The economic crisis was further aggravated by another oil price crisis in response to the 1978 Iranian Revolution. While for oil-exporting countries the 1970s oil crises generated windfall profits, for most countries, growth required oil imports, which became increasingly expensive. Rising oil prices had an especially devastating effect in least developed countries where even small increases in prices can have a large impact. Even further, rising oil prices put upward pressure on prices in other markets, meaning that inflation ate away at standards of living across the developing world (and in industrialized nations too).

- Do you think that several years of slow global growth and rising prices may be factoring into McNamara's statement? Why or why not?

Economic Frameworks and Ideological Shifts

McNamara notes in his introduction that "the alternative to a *more rational economic framework* can only mean, in the end, greater penalties for all" (emphasis added). In contrast to the events and dynamics we have discussed so far, ideological shifts in global political history are more difficult to precisely date. That said, global political conversations often reference periods in which certain kinds of ideas and ideologies are *hegemonic*, that is, dominant and influential in the thinking of policymakers, public officials, scholars, pundits, and the general public.[21] Empires have a propensity to export their ideologies to their colonies and dependents, and ideological preferences spread geographically through globalization processes (e.g., ideas and practices in economy, culture, society, and politics).[22]

As we consider the 1970s, it is important to reflect on which economic frameworks were *hegemonic* at this time, or widely accepted, and by whom. During the Cold War the USSR generally favored *communism* and the US favored *capitalism*. However, by the 1970s, the USSR's economy was stagnating, along with many other economies around the world. This was seen by some as evidence of the specific failure of central economic planning (supported by the economic framework of communism) to provide for the general welfare in the USSR. By extension, the 1970s economic crises more generally cast doubt upon economic policy approaches in which the government had a heavy hand, possibly contributing to McNamara's call for a new economic framework.[23] Since the Great Depression, even the most powerful capitalist countries (like the United States and the United Kingdom) had embraced a more *interventionist* economic policy sometimes referred to as *Keynesianism*, in which the state managed and regulated markets with an eye toward avoiding crisis, mitigating economic inequality, and stimulating employment (following a policy framework called *managed* capitalism—see the excerpt from Keynes in chapter 2). As the 1970s unfolded the *Keynesian* ideological perspective waned in popularity, giving way to a more *free-market* approach that favored more unfettered markets and less government management and regulation (called *neoliberalism*, see excerpt from Friedman in chapter 2).

- Take some time to learn more about the economic ideologies, frameworks, and concepts discussed in this section including communism, capitalism, Keynesianism, and neoliberalism. How are they represented in McNamara's statement or how might one or all of them be influential in development thinking of the 1970s and today?

Defining Concepts in Historical Context: Poverty

Understanding McNamara's statement in the foreword to the 1978 *WDR* in historical global political context requires one to leverage the skills and knowledge of global politics discussed in previous chapters, including defining key concepts like *poverty*. McNamara specifically discusses *absolute poverty* in paragraph two of his introduction: "a condition of life so characterized by malnutrition, illiteracy, disease, squalid surroundings, high infant mortality, and low life expectancy as to be beneath any reasonable definition of human decency." He estimates at that time that some 800 million people around the world lived in conditions of absolute poverty.[24]

Poverty is characterized by deprivation and a low standard of living, as *destitution* or *indigence*. Poverty can be *absolute* (as with McNamara's definition), meaning that it refers to the bare minimum requirements for survival, and in McNamara's case, "human decency." Poverty can also be *relative*, meaning that it refers to the conditions in which some people live relative to others in their society. One could be absolutely poor but not relatively poor if they live in a society in which everyone more or less struggles equally to survive. One could be relatively poor but not absolutely poor if they are surviving fairly well but live among people who enjoy a much higher standard of living (relative poverty thus relates to *inequality*). One can be both absolutely and relatively poor if they struggle to survive and they live in a society in which some members are much better off than they are.[25]

Beyond such generalities, poverty is defined and measured and discussed in different ways in global political conversations. Global debates about poverty often seem complex because of differences in understanding of what poverty means, and what it *should* mean, across scholars, politicians, activists, IGOs, and people and communities in poverty around the world.[26] Historically, the era starting after World War II marks a change in thinking about poverty, a shift toward considering poverty a social malady (rather than an individual or cultural one) that requires redress by governments, international organizations, nonprofits, and other actors via a process that we call *development*.[27] Moreover, in the decades since World War II, global thinking about what *poverty* is has changed considerably within international organizations like the World Bank, IMF, and United Nations Development Programme, over time moving away from solely income- and wealth-based definitions to ones that also include other measures of well-being such as health, education, and political rights.[28] Changing ideas about what poverty means corresponded to significant changes in development programming in these organizations over time, and in equally significant changes in the national policies of countries around the world to whom they provide assistance and advice.[29]

Hasty Generalizations in the History of Global Development

As with any discipline, some conversations about international development among scholars, pundits, and politicians deploy sweeping generalizations about historical development experiences around the world that are important to recognize and interpret. In response, some critics orient their work toward showing that such generalizations are not accurate, often by pointing to conflicting evidence or evidence that points to a different, less general conclusion. To give an example, in their book *Reclaiming Development*, Chang and Grabel discuss a series of "myths" about development that they frame, more or less, as *hasty generalizations*, one of the logical fallacies discussed in Section 7.A. They argue that development myths, based in misinterpretations of historical evidence, perpetuate a set of development policies called the Washington Consensus. Washington Consensus policies were formulated in the 1970s and 1980s while McNamara was at the World Bank, and were implemented broadly across the global South via *structural adjustment programs* in the wake of the 1980s debt crisis (more than forty developing country governments defaulted on their sovereign debts over the course of the decade, beginning with Mexico in 1982). Such policies are thusly named because they were motivated and directed by the US, the most powerful member country in the IMF and World Bank, with the headquarters of these organizations located in the US capitol, Washington DC. Unfortunately, while these policies seemed to work well for the US, they did not often work well for the countries implementing them.[30]

Combating the generalization that Washington Consensus policies are beneficial for every country, Chang and Grabel describe myth number one as "today's wealthy countries achieved success through a steadfast commitment to the free market."[31] Chang and Grabel investigate whether this is an accurate, general statement about how today's rich countries became rich by conducting research into historical development policies and outcomes. They ultimately find the claim to be fallacious, arguing that the historical record shows that today's rich countries—for example, the US and the UK—intervened heavily in the economy in the nineteenth and twentieth centuries to support trade and industrial development.[32] In this way, the scholars leveraged historical facts from two particular country cases to dispel an overly general claim about how the world works, illustrating how isolating errors in logical reasoning can propel critical thinking and original research.

Experts consistently apply critical thinking and logical reasoning skills in analyzing any document, whether primary or secondary sources, and practicing such skills will help learners better interpret global politics. For instance, there are several other primary sources in this book that speak in one way or another to matters of global poverty and development: Truman's 1946 inaugural speech (chapter 1), Marx and Engels and Shiva excerpts (chapter 2), the 1915 US-Haiti Treaty (chapter 8), excerpts from Nobel Peace Prize Laureates King and Maathai (chapter 11), and three primary sources on industrialization and the environment in the nineteenth century (chapter 12).

- As you read any document (whether primary sources like those included in the B sections of each of the chapters in this book, or a secondary source, like Chang and Grabel's book discussed above) consider whether or not the author/s makes any broad generalizations in their statements, and if they do, analyze those statements, find the evidence, and apply careful interpretation to the facts, assessing why the author is making generalizations or other logical fallacies.

7.D: RECOMMENDED READINGS ON DEVELOPMENT

Chang, Ha-Joon and Ilene Grabel, eds. *Reclaiming Development: An Alternative Economic Policy Manual.* New York; London: Zed Books, 2004.

Escobar, Arturo. *Encountering Development: The Making and Unmaking of the Third World.* Princeton, NJ: Princeton University Press, 1995.

Lenin, Vladimir Il'ich. *Imperialism: The Highest Stage of Capitalism.* Great Ideas. London: Penguin, 2010, originally published 1917.

Magdoff, Harry. *Imperialism without Colonies.* New York: Monthly Review Press, 2003.

Sen, Amartya. *Development as Freedom.* New York: Anchor Books, Division of Random House, 1999.

Stiglitz, Joseph. *Globalization and Its Discontents.* New York: W.W. Norton, 2002.

Stokke, Olav. *The UN and Development: From Aid to Cooperation.* Bloomington, IN: Indiana University Press, 2009.

NOTES

1. For a good overview of fallacies see, e.g., Irving M. Copi, Carl Cohen, and Victor Rodych, eds. *Introduction to Logic*. 15th ed. (New York, NY: Routledge, 2019); Frances Howard-Snyder, Daniel Howard-Snyder, and Ryan Wasserman, "Chapter 4: Informal Fallacies" in *The Power of Logic*. 6th ed. (New York: McGraw-Hill Higher Education, 2019). Introduction to logic texts, of which there are many available in online open access, include discussions of the main ideas of logical analyses and some include chapters dedicated to fallacies as discussed here.

2. This list of four fallacies is inspired by the following publicly available handout on fallacies from the Writing Center at UNC Chapel Hill that helps learners understand more about logical fallacies: UNC Chapel Hill, "Fallacies," accessed March 6, 2020 https://writingcenter.unc.edu/tips-and-tools/fallacies/; See also: Patrick J. Hurley, *A Concise Introduction to Logic*. 13th ed. (Boston, MA: Cengage Learning, 2018); Andrea Lunsford and John Ruszkiewicz, *Everything's an Argument* (Boston: Bedford Books, 1998).

3. Rafael Sebastián Guillén Vicente, also known as Subcomandante Marcos and Delegate Zero, is a leader of Mexico's Zapatista National Liberation Army (ELZN), a revolutionary group that fights for the rights of indigenous peoples and the poor against the Mexican government, and speaks powerfully against neoliberalism, globalization, imperialism, and industrialism.

4. E.g., Sam Hickey, *The Government of Chronic Poverty: From the Politics of Exclusion to the Politics of Citizenship?* (Abingdon: Routledge, 2011), 82.

5. World Bank, "Forward by Robert S. McNamara," *World Development Report 1978*. Washington, D.C. © World Bank, 1978 (all rights reserved, reproduced based on fair use doctrine from Section 107 of US Copyright Law) https://openknowledge.worldbank.org/handle/10986/5961 License: CC BY 3.0 IGO.

6. Scholars use the Common Era (CE) and Before the Common Era (BCE) to denote times before and after the year zero. CE and BCE are contemporary terms used in place of the more dated references of the Judeo-Christian calendar that you may be familiar with, that is, the calendar that uses the English phrase "Before Christ" (BC) to reference what occurred before the year designated as 0, and the Latin phrase Anno Domini (AD), meaning "in the year of our lord," to reference anything occurring after the year designated as 0. The version that uses CE and BCE is a secular version designed to be inclusive of people from all faith traditions, as well as people who do not practice any faith at all.

7. For a discussion of the various ways to define war, see chapter 5, Section 5.C.

8. Chapter 5 discusses how the *Atlantic Charter* was an attempt by the United States and the United Kingdom to form an alliance against Nazi Germany and its allies during World War II.

9. John Lewis Gaddis, *The Cold War: A New History* (New York: Penguin Press, 2005).

10. Introductions to the World Bank can be helpful for new learners to become familiar with the history and tenets. E.g., World Bank, *Getting to Know the World Bank: A Guide for Young People* (World Bank E-Library. Washington, DC, 2005);

Katherine Marshall, *The World Bank: From Reconstruction to Development to Equity*, Global Institutions Series (London; New York: Routledge, 2017). There are also many critiques of the World Bank that are useful for a new learner to examine, e.g., on critiques of its human rights legacy, Galit A. Sarfaty, *Values in Translation: Human Rights and the Culture of the World Bank*, Stanford Studies in Human Rights (Stanford, CA: Stanford University Press 2012); for general critiques about the negative impact of the Bretton Woods Institutions, see, e.g., Ngaire Woods, *The Globalizers: The IMF, the World Bank, and Their Borrowers* (Cornell Studies in Money, Ithaca, NY: Cornell University Press, 2014).

11. Fifteen Soviet satellite countries declared their independence from the USSR around this time and began transitioning toward more capitalist economic systems; they had been colonies, more or less, with communist economies under Soviet rule.

12. A few suggestions for getting started on reading about colonialism include Fanon, Frantz. *Black Skin, White Masks*, Translated by Charles Lam Markmann, Evergreen Black Cat Book (New York: Grove Press, 1967); Frantz Fanon, *The Wretched of the Earth*, Translated by Constance Farrington (New York: Grove Press, 1965); Lenin, *Imperialism*.

13. Two informative fictional examples of how the colonial process affected African cultures and religions can be found in Chinua Achebe, *Things Fall Apart* (Greenwich, CT: Fawcett, 1959); Josph Conrad, *Heart of Darkness*, the Project Gutenburg. Produced by Judith Boss and David Widger, Original Publication 1899, Last updated March 2, 2018 https://www.gutenberg.org/files/219/219-h/219-h.htm.

14. E.g., Leften Stavros Stavrianos, *Global Rift: The Third World Comes of Age* (New York: Morrow, 1981).

15. Harry Magdoff, *Imperialism without Colonies* (New York: Monthly Review Press, 2003).

16. E.g.: Lenin, *Imperialism*; Arturo Escobar, *Encountering Development: The Making and Unmaking of the Third World* (Princeton, NJ: Princeton University Press, 1995); Anne McClintock, *Imperial Leather* (New York: Routledge, 1995).

17. For more information on the "lost decade" and the World Bank's and IMF's *structural adjustment programs*, see, e.g., Noreena Hertz, *The Debt Threat* (New York: Harper Collins, 2004); Joseph Stiglitz, *Globalization and Its Discontents* (New York: W.W. Norton, 2002); Chang and Grabel, *Reclaiming Development*; Narcis Serra and Joseph Stiglitz, *The Washington Consensus Reconsidered* (London: Oxford, 2008).

18. A poignant example is the New Deal law developed in the United States after the Great Depression. See, e.g., Eric Rauchway, *The Great Depression & the New Deal: A Very Short Introduction* (Oxford: Oxford University Press, 2008).

19. For the Great Depression, see Rauchway, *The Great Depression*. For an overview of the Great Recession and discussion of lessons learned (and not learned) see Tamim A. Bayoumi, *Unfinished Business: The Unexplored Causes of the Financial Crisis and the Lessons Yet to Be Learned* (New Haven: Yale University Press, 2017).

20. Dag Harald Claes and Giuliano Garavini, eds. *Handbook of OPEC and the Global Energy Order: Past, Present, and Future Challenges* (Routledge International

Handbooks. Abingdon, Oxon: Routledge, 2020); Karen R. Merrill, *The Oil Crisis of 1973-1974: A Brief History with Documents*, the Bedford Series in History and Culture (Boston: Bedford/St. Martin's, 2007).

21. For an extensive overview of global ideologies and influences see, e.g., Alan Cassels, *Ideology and International Relations in the Modern World* (The New International History Series. London: Routledge, 1996). On development ideology see, e.g., Devin Joshi and Roni Kay O'Dell, "Global Governance and Development Ideology: The United Nations and the World Bank on the Left-Right Spectrum," *Global Governance* 19, no. 2 (April–June 2013): 249–75.

22. This agreement is arguably rather widespread, among critics and proponents alike. See, e.g., Benjamin Barber, *Jihad versus McWorld* (New York: Times Books, 1995); Francis Fukuyama, *The End of History and the Last Man* (New York: Free Press, 1992); McClintock, *Imperial Leather*; Deepak Lal, "In Defense of Empires," From the Henry Wendt Lecture at the American Enterprise Institute, October 2002.

23. At the same time, developing countries had been calling for a new economic framework from the 1960s to the 1970s in opposition to the negative impacts of global capitalism, and they created a voting block and new UN agency called the UN Conference on Trade and Development (UNCTAD) to support the idea for a New International Economic Order (NIEO) led by Raul Prebisch. See, e.g., Matias Margulis, ed. *The Global Political Economy of Raúl Prebisch*, Ripe Series in Global Political Economy (Abingdon, Oxon: Routledge, 2017); Ian Taylor and Karen Smith, *United Nations Conference on Trade and Development (UNCTAD)*, Global Institutions (London: Routledge, 2007).

24. 2018 estimates continue to suggest roughly 800 million people living in absolute poverty; however, the proportion of the population has changed as well as the way that the poverty level is estimated. Check the World Bank's website for more information: https://www.worldbank.org/en/topic/measuringpoverty; See also on measuring poverty: Shaohua Chen and Martin Ravallion, "Absolute Poverty Measures for the Developing World, 1981-2004," Proceedings of the National Academy of Sciences of the USA, 104, no. 43 (October 2007): 16757–62. https://www.pnas.org/content/104/43/16757.full?tab=author-info.

25. To begin learning more about poverty, see, e.g., Daryl Collins, Jonathan Morduch, Stuart Rutherford, and Orlanda Ruthven, *Portfolios of the Poor: How the World's Poor Live on $2 a Day* (Princeton: Princeton University Press, 2009).

26. Sasha Breger Bush, "Poverty," In *The Encyclopedia of Political Thought*, edited by Michael T. Gibbons, Wiley Online Library, September 15, 2014, https://onlinelibrary.wiley.com/doi/book/10.1002/9781118474396; Joshi and O'Dell, "Global Governance and Development Ideology."

27. Escobar, *Encountering Development.*

28. E.g., Amartya Sen, *Development as Freedom* (New York: Alfred A. Knopf, 1999); United Nations Development Program, *Human Development Report* (New York: United Nations, 1990).

29. E.g., Woods, *The Globalizers.*

30. See, e.g., William Russell Easterly, *The White Man's Burden: Why the West's Efforts to Aid the Rest Have Done so Much Ill and so Little Good* (Oxford: Oxford University Press, 2006); Stiglitz, *Globalization and its Discontents*; Woods, *The Globalizers*.

31. Chang and Grabel, *Reclaiming Development*.

32. Chang and Grabel, *Reclaiming Development*, 10–13.

Chapter 8

What's the Point?

Isolating Main Ideas

The analytical and critical questions discussed in previous chapters—*who? what? where? when? why?/how?*—are usefully complemented by another foundational question to pose when considering and trying to understand any global political event or text: *What is the main idea?* The *main idea* is the author's central topic, the focal point around which their statement or argument is constructed. By contrast, the author's *thesis statement* briefly relates the author's perspective on and/or argument about the main idea. Section 8.A of this chapter discusses approaches and practices useful for identifying main ideas and creating a thesis statement around a main idea.

The primary document included in Section 8.B, the *1915 Treaty* between the United States (US) and Haiti, provides a rich, context-specific historical framework for developing knowledge and understanding of the *international system*—the principles and structures that guide the dynamic and often turbulent relationships among states and other actors at the global level. Section 8.C then works with learners on identifying main ideas in a text by applying the tools of Section 8.A to the *1915 Treaty*. Finally, Section 8.D provides a list of additional recommended readings on the international system and the *1915 Treaty* in particular.

8.A: IDENTIFYING MAIN IDEAS AND THESIS STATEMENTS

The people who wrote global political documents, like the *1915 Treaty*, knew what they were doing, had a vision for what they wanted to say and what they were researching, and tried to convey the information clearly and concisely. However, as a reader, especially one coming from a different time period and context, the *main idea* might not be as accessible and obvious as it would have been to the authors themselves or even to people in their own time period and context. And thus, this section provides tools learners may use to isolate an author's main idea in nonfiction texts, and further assists learners in developing their own arguments about main ideas by constructing *thesis statements*.

It is often the case that a text includes several main ideas. Further, the main idea of a text, like the *1915 Treaty*, may be somewhat obscured by its formal presentation and organizational structure, or by the language itself (older documents, for instance, utilize formal or archaic English, or variants on the English dialect, that may be difficult to understand). It is also sometimes the case that the main idea is deliberately obscured, or otherwise manipulated, for political reasons, as the authors try to present their goals and actions in as favorable a light as possible. The approaches listed below assist learners in identifying one or several main ideas; keep in mind that it may take more than one approach to adequately identify main ideas.

Identifying the Main Idea in a Text

The *organization of a text* provides clues about the author's main idea. Text organization varies greatly between different types of work—for instance, a peer-reviewed journal article versus a history book. Readers must use their critical thinking skills to decipher the intent, focus, and significance of a text.

When reading a new text, try the following suggestions to identify main ideas based on the organizational schemes and clues in the text:

- *Titles and subtitles*: The title of a text sometimes includes ideas and concepts that relate to the author's main idea. If you are lucky, the main idea *is* the title. The subtitle of a text (if there is one) can also be helpful. Sometimes authors choose to make the title jazzier to appeal to a wider readership, with the subtitle clearly describing the nature and content of the text.
- *Abstract*: Authors of an academic journal article, a conference proceeding, or a working paper will typically include an abstract. Abstracts are short overviews that summarize the content of the work, including the main idea, the argument or thesis statement, and the findings and conclusions.
- *Table of contents, headings, and subheadings*: Within a given text, authors organize their main points and ideas using the table of contents, headings, and subheadings. Examining these elements of a text, even before reading the text, may give readers a sense of what is coming and allow them to follow along with ease. Typically, headings tell the reader about the main idea in that section with subheadings identifying supporting ideas and topics.

- *Prefaces, preambles, and introductions*: A text's *front matter* is often used by authors as a space to discuss their work and ideas in the broadest possible terms (just like the introductory chapter of this book). Authors may discuss their inspiration, the origins of their project, how their thinking evolved over time, relevant current events, and other pieces of context that orient the reader to the main idea. In scholarly research papers organized in the standard academic way, the author's main idea *and* their thesis statement are often found in the first or second paragraph in the introductory section.
- *The body of the text*: Reading and analyzing the body of the text *after* carefully reading and thinking about titles, headings, abstracts, and introductions allows learners to understand the main part of the text within its organizational scheme and thereby place the main ideas and subtopics in context.
- *Word repetition*: Words repeated often in a text can sometimes (though not always) give clues about the major focus of the work. Identifying repetitive words and key concepts either in or associated with a text can be helpful in interpretation. While transitional words do not carry the main ideas and may be ignored (for instance, definite articles like *the*, or conjunctions, like *and*) being attentive to the specific, repetitive language of global politics in the text will provide clues to main ideas. Repetition indicates that the term or concept is important to the author, even if it takes the reader a lot of thinking and investigating to determine if and how repeated terms are related to or represent the main idea.

Practicing the active reading skills outlined above helps learners identify main ideas and understand why a text is important and worth reading. Further, taking purposeful notes while reading may make identifying the main idea more efficient. Yet, sometimes the main idea of a text is not readily apparent, even after assessing the text's organization. In such scenarios it is a good idea to conduct some research on the text or topic, by, for example, finding a commentary on the work (e.g., reviews, summaries, critiques, or responses). Such commentaries may be useful in thinking about the author's main idea even if interpretations of the work may diverge—it is good practice to find at least three such commentaries so as to gather a spectrum of interpretations and reconcile their respective thoughts about the main idea. Find such commentaries on the internet, in the stacks or reference section of the library, or by consulting with a librarian (see chapters 2–4 for suggestions on how and where to search for such resources).

Identifying Thesis Statements in a Text

A thesis statement is conveyed in a concise sentence (or two) that appears in the first or second paragraph of the introduction to an essay or article, and clearly relates to the author's main argument(s). Authors use thesis statements to keep their writing consistent and on point, returning and referring throughout their work to their main thesis statement (for example, by defining key terms related to the thesis statement, by providing context and historical background, and by offering evidence and data to support the thesis statement). Identifying a thesis statement early on when reading a new work helps learners comprehend what they are reading and allows them to make continuous connections between the author's points and the main argument.

A good thesis statement has the following characteristics:

- Clearly conveys the author's argument about the main idea in one or two concise sentences;
- Can be descriptive, critical, or prescriptive (Descriptive: About what *is*. Critical: About what's *wrong*. Prescriptive: About what *should be*);
- Is typically preceded by an introductory statement intended to grab the reader's attention; and
- Is typically followed by an *organizational* statement that outlines the structure of the essay or book to follow, with reference to the thesis statement.

8.B: PRIMARY SOURCE ON THE INTERNATIONAL SYSTEM

Treaty between the United States and Haiti: Finances, Economic Development and Tranquility of Haiti (1915)[1]

Signed at Port-au-Prince, September 16, 1915
Ratification Advised by the Senate, February 16, 1916
Ratified by the President, March 20, 1916
Ratified by Haiti, September 17, 1915
Ratifications Exchanged at Washington, May 3, 1916
Proclaimed, May 3, 1916

By the president of the United States of America.

A proclamation
  Whereas a Treaty between the United States of America and the Republic of Haiti having for its objects the strengthening of the amity existing between the two countries, the remedying of the present condition of the revenues and finances of Haiti, the maintenance of the tranquility of that Republic, and the carrying out of plans for its economic development and prosperity, was concluded and signed by their respective Plenipotentiaries at Port-au-Prince, on the

sixteenth day of September, one thousand nine hundred and fifteen, the original of which Treaty, being in the English and French languages, is word for word as follows:

Treaty between the United States and the Republic of Haiti
Preamble

The United States and the Republic of Haiti desiring to confirm and strengthen the amity existing between them by the most cordial cooperation measures for their common advantage;

And the Republic of Haiti desiring to remedy the present condition of its revenues and finances, to maintain the tranquility of the Republic, to carry out plans for the economic development and prosperity of the Republic and its people;

And the United States being in full sympathy with all of these aims and objects and desiring to contribute in all proper ways to their accomplishment;

The United States and the Republic of Haiti have resolved to conclude a Convention with these objects in view, and have appointed for that purpose, Plenipotentiaries,

The President of the United States, Robert Beale Davis, Junior, Chargé d'Affaires of the United States;

And the President of the Republic of Haiti, Louis Borno, Secretary of State for Foreign Affairs and Public Instruction, who, having exhibited to each other their respective powers, which are seen to be full in good and true form, have agreed as follows:—

Article I

The Government of the United States will, by its good offices, aid the Haitian Government in the proper and efficient development of its agricultural, mineral and commercial resources and in the establishment of the finances of Haiti on a firm and solid basis.

Article II

The President of Haiti shall appoint, upon nomination by the President of the United States, a Financial Adviser, who shall be an officer attached to the Ministry of Finance, to give effect to whose proposals and labors the Minister shall lend sufficient aid. The Financial Adviser shall devise an adequate system of public accounting, aid in increasing the revenues and adjusting them to expenses, inquire into the validity of the debts of the Republic, enlighten both governments with reference to all eventual debts, recommend improved methods for collecting and applying the revenues, and make such other recommendations to the Minister of Finance as may be deemed necessary for the welfare and prosperity of Haiti.

Article III

The Government of the Republic of Haiti will provide by law or appropriate decrees for the payment of all customs duties to the General Receiver, and will extend to the Receivership, and to the Financial Adviser, all needful aid and full protection in the execution of the powers conferred and duties imposed herein; and the United States on its part will extend like aid and protection.

Article IV
Upon the appointment of the Financial Adviser, the Government of Haiti, in cooperation with the Financial Adviser, shall collate, classify, arrange and make full statement of all the debts of the Republic, the amounts, character, maturity and conditions thereof, and the interest accruing and the sinking fund requisite to their final discharge.

Article V
All sums collected and received by the General Receiver shall be applied, first, to the payment of the salaries and allowances of the General Receiver, his assistants and employees and expenses of the Receivership, including the salary and expenses of the Financial Adviser, which salaries will be determined by previous agreement; second, to the interest and sinking fund of the public debt of the Republic of Haiti; and, third, to the maintenance of the constabulary referred to in Article X, and then the remainder to the Haitian Government for purposes of current expenses.

Article VI
The expenses of the Receivership, including salaries and allowances of the General Receiver, his assistants and employees, and the salary and expenses of the Financial Adviser, shall not exceed five per centum of the collections and receipts from customs duties, unless by agreement of the two Governments.

Article VII
The General Receiver shall make monthly reports of all collections, receipts and disbursements to the appropriate officer of the Republic of Haiti and to the Department of State of the United States, which reports shall be open to inspection and certification at all times by the appropriate authorities of each of the said Governments.

Article VIII
The Republic of Haiti shall not increase its public debt except by previous agreement with the President of the United States, and shall not contract any debt or assume any financial obligation unless the ordinary revenues of the Republic available for that purpose, after defraying the expenses of the Government, shall be adequate to pay the interest and provide a sinking fund for the final discharge of such debt.

Article IX
The Republic of Haiti will not without a previous agreement with the President of the United States, modify the customs duties in a manner to reduce the

revenues therefrom; and in order that the revenues of the Republic may be adequate to meet the public debt and the expenses of the Government, to preserve the tranquility and to promote material prosperity, the Republic of Haiti will cooperate with the Financial Adviser in his recommendations for improvement in the methods of collecting and disbursing the revenues and for new sources of needed income.

Article X
The Haitian Government obligates itself, for the preservation of domestic peace, the security of individual rights and full observance of the provisions of this treaty, to create without delay an efficient constabulary, urban and rural, composed of native Haitians. This constabulary shall be organized and officered by Americans, appointed by the President of Haiti, upon nomination by the President of the United States. The Haitian Government shall clothe these officers with the proper and necessary authority and uphold them in the performance of their functions. These officers will be replaced by Haitians as they, by examination, conducted under direction of a board to be selected by the senior American officer of this constabulary and in the presence of a representative of the Haitian Government, are found to be qualified to assume such duties. The constabulary herein provided for, shall, under the direction of the Haitian Government, have supervision and control of arms and ammunition, military supplies, and traffic therein, throughout the country. The high contracting parties agree that the stipulations to this Article are necessary to prevent factional strife and disturbances.

Article XI
The Government of Haiti agrees not to surrender any of the territory of the Republic of Haiti by sale, lease, or otherwise, or jurisdiction over such territory, to any foreign government or power, nor to enter into any treaty or contract with any foreign powers that will impair or tend to impair the independence of Haiti.

Article XII
The Haitian Government agrees to execute with the United States a protocol for the settlement, by arbitration or otherwise, of all pending pecuniary claims of foreign corporations, companies, citizens or subjects against Haiti.

Article XIII
The Republic of Haiti, being desirous to further the development of its natural resources, agrees to undertake and execute such measures as in the opinion of the high contracting parties may be necessary for the sanitation and public improvement of the Republic, under the supervision and direction of an engineer or engineers, to be appointed by the President of Haiti upon nomination by the President of the United States, and authorized for that purpose by the Government of Haiti.

Article XIV
The high contracting parties shall have authority to take such steps as may be necessary to insure the complete attainment of any of the objects comprehended in this treaty, and, should the necessity occur, the United States will lend an efficient aid for the preservation of Haitian Independence and the maintenance of a government adequate for the protection of life, property and individual liberty.

Article XV
The present treaty shall be approved and ratified by the high contract parties in conformity with their respective laws, and the ratifications thereof shall be exchanged in the City of Washington as soon as may be possible.

Article XVI
The present treaty shall remain in full force and virtue for the term of ten years, to be counted from the day of exchange of ratifications, and further for another term of ten years if, for specific reasons presented by either of the high contracting parties, the purpose of this treaty has not been fully accomplished.

In faith whereof, the respective Plenipotentiaries, have signed the present Convention in duplicate, in the English and French languages, and have thereunto affixed their seals.

Done at Port-au-Prince, Haiti, the 16th day of September in the year of our Lord one thousand nine hundred and fifteen.

8.C: SOVEREIGNTY, SUBJUGATION, AND THE INTERNATIONAL SYSTEM

The *1915 Treaty* between the US and Haiti is salient in conversations about diverse global issues including matters of US *foreign policy, national security, World War I (WWI), imperialism, globalization, development, global finance*, and the structure and dynamics of the *international system*. The *1915 Treaty* does not have a thesis statement, at least not in the way we typically use thesis statements in argumentative essays or editorials, but it does have main ideas. It also contains normative or argumentative elements, for example, in its judgments of the quality of Haiti's government and the benefits of US intervention, even if such judgments are not formulated as an argument or formal thesis statement.

Main Ideas in the *1915 Treaty*

In thinking about how to identify main ideas and interpret the *1915 Treaty* (or any text) it is important to consider the "intention of the parties" and the "spirit of the treaty," which require a good understanding of the political and

What's the Point? 137

historical context as well as the ability to ask critical questions.[2] For example, critical questions and comments that focus on the *appearance* of the *1915 Treaty* (at first glance, the treaty appears as helpful and well-intentioned) relative to the *reality* of the treaty (historical knowledge and political context reveal the *1915 Treaty* as rooted in ulterior motives, even by the most charitable reading) are excellent fodder for discussion and critical thinking. The discussion below investigates the main idea of the treaty by selectively deploying some of the tools discussed in Section 8.A of this chapter. Learners will encounter bulleted questions alongside the discussion points below, each of which is a great starting place for independent research and analysis.

- What clues about main ideas might be gleaned by carefully assessing the *title and subtitles* of the *1915 Treaty*?

The title, "Treaty with Haiti" and "Treaty between the United States and Haiti" indicate that this is a *bilateral treaty* (between two state governments, also called parties to the treaty). At this point, learning crucial information about treaties and treaty law is important for a learner so that they understand what it is they are assessing and how to assess it. A treaty is a written agreement between state governments that indicates commitments they have made to each other.[3] Bilateral treaties are negotiated between two state governments, often without a negotiator or international organization to mediate, and may contain elements that are beneficial to one party at the expense of the other. The subtitle references "finances," "economic development," and "tranquility" in Haiti indicating that the US and Haiti have negotiated on how the two countries will engage in economic relations with each other.

- The *1915 Treaty* does not include an *abstract*, although short introductory descriptions and preambles in the treaty can be utilized in place of an abstract (using skills learned in chapter 2 and chapter 4 by consulting dictionaries or encyclopedias). What do such *short descriptions* and *preambles* reveal about the main ideas of the treaty?

The *1915 Treaty* does contain a few lines at the beginning that act like an abstract, entitled "A proclamation." Similar ideas are reiterated in the *preamble* to the treaty, a second introductory section of the text that elaborates a bit further on the preceding short description. While the title makes the treaty sound like a well-intended and helpful agreement, the short introduction and preamble indicate that there may be subtext worth exploring. The treaty aims to "strengthen the amity" of the two nations (*amity* means friendship), suggesting that the US and Haiti were perhaps not on friendly terms in 1915. It also says that Haiti's finances need "remedying," implying that something is wrong with them at the time the treaty was being negotiated. In trying to navigate and understand *subtext*, external commentaries are helpful. In this case, ones that discuss the treaty's historical and political context may be especially useful.[4] Such commentaries and overviews provide insight into more complex main ideas and global phenomena associated with the treaty, for example colonization, political instability, and US imperialism. One source describes the outcome of the treaty bluntly as follows: "The United States gained complete control over Haitian finances, and the right to intervene in Haiti whenever the U.S. Government deemed necessary."[5]

- What do the *headings* and *subheadings* of the *1915 Treaty* indicate about its main ideas?

While typical books (like this one) or journal articles will use headings as signposts that indicate what is included in each section, making clear how the author is building their argument, treaties are written to be much more concise and each part of the treaty easily accessible and citable. Thus, the headings and subheadings are organizational rather than substantive. If a lawyer wanted to cite that the US had agreed to give Haiti aid, they might cite Article I of the treaty. Yet, the headings and subheadings, especially those providing information about the ratification status of parties to the treaty, can be insightful in that these indicate the willingness of both parties to enter into the treaty and commit to its strictures.

- What does the *body of the text* reveal about the main ideas?

The body provides the substance of the *1915 Treaty*, indicating what the parties to the treaty are committing their governments and people to do, and it allows learners to ask deeper questions about the reasons for and history surrounding the treaty, starting with an analysis of *sovereignty*. Consider Articles I–III that outline one of the requirements of the treaty, that of creating a position of Financial Advisor for Haiti. The US is presented as the powerful government, making all the decisions and giving all the advice, while Haiti is represented as capitulating to the will and desires of the US, giving whatever resources and support are required. Consider that the US nominated the financial advisor, and notice the amount of power the financial advisor is given in Article II:

> The Financial Adviser shall devise an adequate system of public accounting, aid in increasing the revenues and adjusting them to expenses, inquire into the validity of the debts of the Republic, enlighten both governments with reference to all eventual debts, recommend improved methods for collecting and applying the revenues, and make such other recommendations to the Minister of Finance as may be deemed necessary for the welfare and prosperity of Haiti.

- At this point, what do you think is the main idea of the *1915 Treaty*? Are there multiple main ideas?

Haiti, the United States, and the International System

The disciplinary context within which a text is considered and analyzed influences the main ideas a reader might identify as significant. As mentioned in previous chapters, accumulating expert vocabulary and knowledge of key concepts is an important task for learners in global politics. Concepts that describe international interactions act as *heuristic devices*, that is, tools that allow learners to more efficiently and effectively think about and analyze an event or issue in global politics. For students of global politics, the *1915 Treaty* between the US and Haiti raises critical questions about the *international system*, along with other related and overlapping dynamics, such as *hegemony*, *anarchy*, *polarity*, *sovereignty*, *interdependence*, *zero-sum* and *positive-sum games*, and dynamics of *cooperation, competition, conflict*, and *subjugation*. Before moving on to the discussion below, take a moment to reflect on these concepts and reflect on whether they describe any of the main ideas or dynamics that stood out to you when reading the *1915 Treaty*. See Textbox 8.1 for a discussion of key concepts helpful for thinking about the international system.

TEXTBOX 8.1: THE INTERNATIONAL SYSTEM AND OTHER KEY CONCEPTS

The list of key concepts below provides learners with a starting point for understanding a global text or issue by giving short definitions, resources for further reference, and questions one might ask to isolate main ideas in any situation under study.

International System: It refers to the structures, rules, norms, institutions, and dynamics that shape and constrain state interactions and relationships with one another over time. Some international relations scholars distinguish between the *international structure* and the *international system*.

- What are the important features and characteristics of the international system? How is it structured?
- How do states behave in the international system? In what ways does the structure of the system impact the behavior of states operating in it?
- How has the international system changed over time? In response to what kinds of forces and dynamics?
- Is the international system durable or fragile? Is it prone to war or peace? Under what conditions?

- Is it more useful to postulate a *global* system, in which nation-states and the international system are merely parts of a broader global system? How and why and with what effects do states interact with non-state actors in the global system?

Sovereignty: To say the states that populate the international system are *sovereign* is to attest to the following attributes: "Having superior or supreme rank or power," "paramount," "principal," "greatest."[1] Traditional arguments hold that the international system is a community of *sovereign* states that navigate the international arena with regard to their own *interests*. In the international system states have the *sovereign right* to rule the territory within their borders as they see fit and they operate relatively independently, cooperating or competing or warring with one another when their interests dictate.[2]

- How is state sovereignty assured in the international system (through what international organizations, laws, rules, and/or norms)?
- In what contexts is state sovereignty violated? Are there rules or norms that govern such interventions? (Consider the theories and practices around humanitarian intervention and responsibility to protect in cases of genocide, war crimes, and crimes against humanity, but consider also that state sovereignty is often violated in the international system for reasons *not* prescribed by such laws, rules, and norms, raising questions about the legitimacy of such interventions.)
- What is the historical practice of sovereignty in state interactions?

Anarchy, polarity, balance of power, great powers, and *hegemony*: An *anarchic* international system is one that does not have a supranational authority telling states how to behave and interact. There is no hierarchical power that can force states to behave in certain ways. *Anarchy* does not necessarily mean chaos, however, since states will follow certain norms and rules, often allowing for consistent and ordered interactions. Sometimes powerful states compel less powerful states to comply with particular norms or rules by using force, the threat of force or other coercive means (such as granting or withholding foreign aid). *Great power* states are those that have relatively more power and influence in the international system (because they have more land and resources, bigger population, greater military capacity, etc.). *Polarity* in the international system refers to the number of *great powers*, and the *balance of power* refers to how state powers compare with each other. When there is one *great power* or *hegemonic* state, the international system is called *unipolar*, when there are two *great powers* it is a *bipolar* structure, and when there are multiple *great powers* that are relatively evenly pitted against one another it is called a *multipolar* system.

- Who or what governs and controls the international system? Is it really *anarchic*, that is, is there no supranational authority guiding state behavior?
- Where do *superpowers* and *empires* fit into the international system? Where do they fit into international organizations like the United Nations (UN) and the World Trade Organization (WTO)?
- What is the current structure of the international system? Is it unipolar, bipolar, or multipolar?
- How or when does the structure of the international system change over time?

Cooperation, reputation, and *competition*: States interact with each other in multiple ways to achieve national or shared goals and they pay attention to what other states think of their actions, that is, they are concerned with their *reputation* (reputation is an important dimension of a state's *soft power*). States may *cooperate* by, for example, signing international agreements and committing to particular actions. States may also *compete* with each other to try to gain more access to resources or produce more goods than others.

- How do states engage in cooperation and collaboration with each other, even in an anarchic international system?
- Why, and under what conditions, do states compete? When does competition lead to conflict and war?
- Do states worry about how much power other states have? How do they deal with such concerns?
- What happens to smaller and weaker states in systems where wealth, power, and capability are distributed unequally? Do strong states push weaker states around?

Zero-sum and positive-sum games: Some international relations theorists have tried to model state behavior to show what the outcomes of state interaction might look like given specific conditions in certain scenarios. *Zero-sum games* model state behavior that is motived by the idea that a win for one actor is a loss for another. *Positive-sum games* model state behavior that is motived by the idea that it is possible to agree on policies and actions that will benefit all actors.

- Do the rules and norms of the international system allow for states to achieve their interests simultaneously?
- Can states all achieve their interests if they cooperate to achieve shared goals?
- When states gain power, does it have to be at the expense of other states?

State power and the *national interest*: *State power* can be measured or assessed by considering territory, national income, access to resources, ability to use resources, population, influence with other states, etc. Each state makes decisions based on their *national interest*, that is, the concern with maintaining and gaining power and assuring continued existence (although definitions and theories of what *national interest* means vary widely between theorists and politicians).

- How is state power measured and how is power compared between states?
- Is there such a thing as the *national interest*?
- Whose interests are represented when the state acts in the international arena?
- Should states care about the interests of other states and the people who live in them?

Recommended Readings on the International System and Related Concepts

Jackson, Robert H. *Quasi-States: Sovereignty, International Relations and the Third World.* Cambridge UK: Cambridge University Press, 1990.

Kratochwil, Fredrich. *The Puzzles of Politics: Inquiries into the Genesis and Transformation of International Relations.* New York: Routledge, 2011.

Biersteker, Thomas and Cynthia Weber. *State Sovereignty as a Social Construct.* Cambridge, UK: Cambridge University Press, 1996.

Porter, Robert Odawi. *Sovereignty, Colonialism and the Indigenous Nations: A Reader.* Durham, NC: Carolina University Press, 2005.

Stavrianos, Leften Stavros. *Global Rift: The Third World Comes of Age.* New York: William Morrow and Associates, 1981.

Weber, Max. "Politics as a Vocation." Speech, Munich, Germany, January 28, 1919.

[1] Oxford English Dictionary. "Sovereign, *n.* and *adj.*" Oxford, UK: OUP, 2019 (online edition).

[2] E.g., Thomas Hobbes, *Leviathan*, A. D Lindsay, Everyman's Library, Philosophy and Theology (London: J.M. Dent, 1928, originally published 1651); Max Weber, "Politics as a Vocation" (Speech, Munich, Germany, January 28, 1919).

*Interpreting Main Ideas from the 1915
Treaty in Global Political Context*

The key concepts in Textbox 8.1 represent intellectual pathways along which learners may interpret and assess global political issues, texts, and events. They also represent different ways that international relations (IR) scholars interpret and analyze how states relate to each other. Thinking about the *1915 Treaty* through the lenses provided by these concepts permits learners to refine their understandings of the main ideas presented therein. The discussion below interprets the treaty via the *international system* and *sovereignty*. Following the discussion, try to integrate the remaining concepts from Textbox 8.1, including *zero-sum games*, *positive-sum games*, and the *national interest*, into your thinking about the meaning of the treaty.

The International System. Notice that the treaty is between two state governments: the United States of America and the Republic of Haiti. This nomenclature reveals the way that humans think about, talk about, and engage in global or international affairs by suggesting that "the United States of America" is something that exists and makes decisions, when, in fact, it is really just an abstraction representing the interactions of people at multiple levels, especially government officials making decisions for and representing groups of people within a territory. Thus, talking about countries doing something is a heuristic device meant to allow learners to more easily grasp what happens between government officials and groups of people they represent. Similarly, IR scholars refer to the *international system*, meaning that they are assessing how governments (nation-states) act and interact, what decisions they make, and how they generally operate at the supranational level (that is, beyond the limits of the national government or domestic policy considerations). A distinction between global and international is useful: while the *global* system includes many different actors (such as corporations, transnational communities, or international organizations), the *international* system—which literally means *between nations*—describes the structures, rules, norms, institutions, and dynamics that shape and constrain state relationships with one another over time.

The modern international system originates in the early colonial period—formally institutionalized at the Peace of Westphalia in 1648 ending the Thirty Years' War in Europe—and established modern definitions of the *nation-state* and at least a pretense of *state sovereignty* through practices like *state-building*. The establishment of overseas trading posts and colonies is a dimension of *state-building*, or the purposeful development of the power, wealth, and capabilities of a state. Beginning in the sixteenth century, the colonization process merged control of territory by fledgling European states, on the one hand, with growing levels of political, social, and economic control, on the other, arguably the defining feature of the modern nation-state. The connection between colonization and state-building is important and may provide an interpretive clue as you think about the *1915 Treaty*. As Max Weber controversially argues, the modern state retains a territorial "monopoly" on "violence and taxation."[6] In the context of the definition of a modern state, then, consider that Haiti ceded its control of the military, police, tax collection, and government spending to the US in the *1915 Treaty*—was Haiti a modern state in Weber's sense of the term, and was it able to practice state sovereignty?

- How might the *1915 Treaty* reflect competition among *great powers* during a transitional period in the international system? What does the treaty suggest about the nature of relationships between great powers and lesser powers in the international system?

The *1915 Treaty* was negotiated in the midst of WWI, revealing how states interacted with one another. The period of British hegemony in the international system, from roughly 1800 to 1914 (otherwise known as the *long nineteenth century* or *pax Britannica*), unraveled in the lead up to and during WWI, pushing the international system from a unipolar structure to a multipolar one. In the years preceding World War I, new state powers (Germany, France, and the US) had arisen on the international stage to challenge British hegemony, and to a lesser extent also challenge the power of the older Ottoman Empire. According to some historians, the competition between Britain and emerging great powers was one of the causes of WWI.[7] The treaty also raises key questions about the plight of *lesser* powers, those smaller, impoverished, and weaker states that comprise the vast majority of nation-states in the system that generally operate within constraints imposed by relatively stronger states.

State Sovereignty. The *1915 Treaty* is an example of how state interactions challenge state *sovereignty*. Section by section, the treaty transfers the powers of the Haitian government—its power over debt repayment, customs duties, general financial management, the terms of exchange for the country's land, its natural resources, and its military and police—to the US.[8] Supreme control over territory and resources is a defining characteristic of state sovereignty. What does it mean for one state to hand powers over to another state? IR scholars disagree on the substance of the concept of sovereignty, for instance, on how, why, to what extent, for how long, and in which contexts might a state's *interests* be brought into alignment with more cosmopolitan values and goals or norms.[9] Thinkers with *realist* perspectives in IR, and also some variants on *liberalism*, postulate a sovereign-state international system in which all states are somewhat equal, not in terms of wealth and power but rather in terms of political status and right.

In IR, versions of *liberalism*, *English School*, *constructivism*, *Marxism*, and a variety of *indigenous* political traditions, state *sovereignty* as a feature of the international system is not assumed and is actively questioned. Scholars ask whether states are really autonomous and independent, whether all states really have the freedom and power to advocate for their own interests, or whether some states have power to assert their sovereignty while other states struggle. Some of the more radical variants on such perspectives suggest that sovereignty is a luxury enjoyed by the richest and most powerful states in the international system while weaker and poorer states become dangerously dependent on and *subjugated* to powerful states' interests, with strong states often intervening in the sovereign affairs of weaker ones in imperial fashion. For such theorists, the myth of sovereignty works to grow and legitimize the power of strong states, with sovereignty variously invoked and ignored as their interests dictate.

It is also important to consider the role of non-state actors and how they enable and constrain state wealth, power, and capability. Contemporary conversations about economic globalization, for example, highlight the growing power of global capital (e.g., multinational corporations, and other global investors) in the post–WWII period to influence and evade state regulations.[10] Critical commentators in the earlier period of globalization that ended with WWI also questioned the influence of big business on the conduct of nation-states in the international arena, as the *1915 Treaty* perhaps suggests. To the extent that smaller and weaker powers in the international system are perceived to be subjugated to the interests of great powers and global financial elites, conversations about sovereignty often invoke dynamics of *neocolonialism* (or *neoimperialism*).

Thesis Statements about the *1915 Treaty* and the International System

The *1915 Treaty* between the US and Haiti provides a powerful example of how the international system works at the specific time and place in question. The previous chapters offer a variety of analytical and critical questions to use to start turning the treaty into a *case study*. A case study is a well-developed example that analyzes a given phenomenon or dynamic with detail and nuance and extensive attention to context. As noted at the outset of this chapter, the questions from previous chapters—*who? what? where? why? when? how?*—are tools that help build knowledge about context from the ground up. For example, is it significant that the treaty was negotiated during WWI? What was Germany's relationship to Haiti in 1915? Does Haiti have a historical relationship with the US? If so, is it friendly? Where is Haiti geographically located? Is Haiti equal in power to the US? Why does Haiti seem to owe so much money to other countries? Having developed knowledge about the context, it is possible to start thinking more deeply about how the terms and concepts about the international system discussed above relate to the *1915 Treaty*, and to start formulating arguments about how the international system works based on this particular case.

Arguments about global politics, when they are written in a scholarly way in an academic essay or article, are typically framed and stated initially with a *thesis statement*. Let's take the following prompt: "Based on your reading of the *1915 Treaty* between the US and Haiti, how would you describe the international system?" Here are several examples of thesis statements we, the authors, constructed on the basis of our reading of the treaty, its context, and our knowledge of key ideas about the international system. Take some time to read through them, think about them, ask questions about them, and criticize them. Are they all concise and clear? Are they well-written? Do they contain logical fallacies? Do you think all of them could be supported with evidence from the treaty? Could they be supported using evidence from your research on background and context, do you agree with any of them? Do you disagree with any of them? Why or why not?

- The *1915 Treaty* between Haiti and the US illustrates that the international system is populated by states with unequal levels of wealth, power, and capability.
- The *1915 Treaty* between the US and Haiti demonstrates that the international system is a zero-sum game. It supports Thucydides' maxim about the international system as a place where the "strong do what they can, and the weak suffer what they must."[11]
- The *1915 Treaty* between the US and Haiti shows that the international system is a place where all states can achieve their mutual interests through cooperation and collaboration.
- The *1915 Treaty* between the US and Haiti reveals that the international system is not always anarchic. It shows how powerful states use their power to facilitate stability and cooperation during times of conflict.
- The *1915 Treaty* between the US and Haiti is a great example of how the myth of sovereignty works to support neocolonial relationships in the international system.

8.D: RECOMMENDED READINGS ON US-HAITI RELATIONSHIP AND DEBT

Bauduy, Jennifer. "The 1915 Invasion of Haiti: Examining a Treaty of Occupation." *Social Education* 79, no. 5 (October 2015), 244–49.

Douglas, Paul H. "The American Occupation of Haiti I." *Political Science Quarterly* 42, no. 2 (June 1927): 228–58.
George, Susan. *A Fate Worse than Debt*. New York: Grove Press, 1990.
Gibbs, William E. "James Weldon Johnson: A Black Perspective on 'Big Stick' Diplomacy." *Diplomatic History* 8, no. 4 (Fall 1984): 329–47.
Hertz, Noreena. *The Debt Threat*. New York: Harper Collins, 2004.
Office of the Historian. "US Invasion and Occupation of Haiti, 1915-1934." Washington, DC: US Department of State. Last updated 2016. Accessed August 15, 2019. https://history.state.gov/milestones/1914-1920/haiti.

NOTES

1. United States and Haiti, "Treaty between the United States and Haiti," signed at Port-au-Prince September 16, 1915. Presented by Mr. Pomerene, ordered to be printed in 1922. Washington DC: Government Printing Office, accessed July 23, 2020 (all rights reserved, reproduced based on fair use doctrine from Section 107 of US Copyright Law) https://www.loc.gov/law/help/us-treaties/bevans/b-ht-ust000008-0660.pdf.

2. Richard K, Gardiner, *Treaty Interpretation* (The Oxford International Law Library. Oxford: Oxford University Press, 2008), 6.

3. E.g., the following text on treaty law: Anthony Aust, *Handbook of International Law*, 11th ed. (Cambridge, UK: Cambridge University Press, 2017). Treaties are largely governed by customary international law as outlined in the 1969 Vienna Convention on the Law of Treaties.

4. For example: Office of the Historian. "US Invasion and Occupation of Haiti, 1915-1934." Washington, DC: US Department of State (2019). https://history.state.gov/milestones/1914-1920/haiti (accessed August 15, 2019); William Gibbs, "James Weldon Johnson: A Black Perspective on "Big Stick" Diplomacy," *Diplomatic History* 8, no. 4 (Fall 1984): 329–47. Jennifer Bauduy, "The 1915 Invasion of Haiti: Examining a Treaty of Occupation," *Social Education* 79, no. 5 (October 2015): 244–49; Paul H. Douglas, "The American Occupation of Haiti I," *Political Science Quarterly* 42, no. 2 (June 1927): 228–58.

5. Office of the Historian, "US Invasion of Haiti."

6. Max Weber, "Politics as a Vocation," Speech, Munich, Germany, January 28, 1919.

7. For a discussion of imperial competition in the lead up to World War I see, e.g., Lenin, Vladimir Il'ich, *Imperialism: The Highest Stage of Capitalism* (Great Ideas, London: Penguin, 2010, originally published 1917).

8. See these sources, e.g., for conversations about sovereignty as a concept and social construct: Fredrich Kratochwil, *The Puzzles of Politics: Inquiries into the Genesis and Transformation of International Relations* (New York: Routledge, 2011); Thomas Biersteker and Cynthia Weber, *State Sovereignty as a Social Construct* (Cambridge, UK: Cambridge University Press, 1996); Robert H. Jackson, *Quasi-States: Sovereignty, International Relations and the Third World* (Cambridge UK:

Cambridge University Press, 1990); Robert Odawi Porter, *Sovereignty, Colonialism and the Indigenous Nations: A Reader* (Durham, NC: Carolina University Press, 2005).

9. Alan Bloomfield and Shirley V. Scott, *Norm Antipreneurs and the Politics of Resistance to Global Normative Change* (London: Routledge, 2017). In this volume, the authors call attention to the exclusion of non-state actors from debates about norms, and also engage the politics of non-Western countries and actors in this context.

10. E.g., Kenichi Ohmae, *The Borderless World in the Interlinked Economy* (New York: Harper Business, 1990); Paul Hirst and Grahame Thomson, and Simon Bromley, *Globalization in* Question, 3rd ed. (New York: Polity, 2009); John B. Goodman and Louis W. Pauly, "The Obsolescence of Capital Controls? Economic Management in an Age of Global Markets," *World Politics* 46, no. 1 (October 1993): 50–82; Eric Helleiner, *States and the Reemergence of Global Finance* (Ithaca, NY: Cornell University Press, 1994).

11. Thucydides. *History of the Peloponnesian War.* Translated by Benjamin Jowett (Amherst, NY: Prometheus Books, 1998).

Chapter 9

Making Connections

Applying Knowledge across Global Political Contexts

Many of the ideas, dynamics, patterns, events, and relationships visible in one part of the global political arena have partial (and sometimes perverse) reflections in others. When *applying* knowledge from one context to another, learners call on existing knowledge of global politics and analytical skills to cultivate deeper insights. To apply knowledge from one context to another is to leverage knowledge of global politics to understand new and different situations. This chapter deals with a foundational analytical question that lies at the heart of efforts to apply knowledge across contexts: *Why/how is this relevant?* As policymakers, politicians, activists, and scholars it is crucial to think about how theory applies to practice, how research findings apply to policy and activism, and how events in one place apply to those in another.

Section 9.A reviews the important study skill of recall, as opposed to rereading, as a way to store information more effectively in long-term memory. Then, Section 9.B includes an excerpt from Eugene Debs' Canton Ohio Speech (1918) on social class and war, and Section 9.C uses the excerpt to show how knowledge from one global politics situation and issue (in this case World War I (WWI) of 1914–1917) can provide insight into another situation and issue (the Iran-Iraq War of 1980–1988). Further Section 9.C covers techniques for applying knowledge to new contexts in an organized way, including the use of key concepts to structure and systematize the application. In the example, an analysis of the way Debs discusses *inequality*, and the issues of *inequality* that became evident in WWI, is used as a way to discuss and apply knowledge to understand and interpret the Iran-Iraq War context. Finally, Section 9.D provides a list of recommended readings on application skills as well as understanding reactions to war and inequality.

9.A: RECALL AND RETRIEVAL RATHER THAN RE-READING

Learners of a new subject sometimes fall into the trap of studying by re-reading the material rather than putting the new knowledge to memory, a mistake that then threatens their capacity to apply knowledge to new circumstances or situations. The issue is that re-reading promotes false confidence, a sense that one has mastered knowledge when they have not or when they are only vaguely familiar with the material.[1] Mastering a subject matter requires that learners be able to recall relevant knowledge when needed so as to use it readily and apply it to new situations and contexts. Learning strategies that require learners to recall—that is, that facilitate *retrieval practice*—are important for ensuring that the information is not merely superficially gained for only a short time. The brain's neural pathways grow stronger, and memory thus more extensive and reliable, when "the memory is retrieved and the learning is practiced."[2] The list below provides a starting point for learners to think about how to practice recalling and retrieving information after first learning it, but this is just a short list—dedicated learners consistently find ways to recall information so as not to lose it.

Strategies to Practice Recall and Retrieval:

- *Use flashcards* rather than re-reading text to commit knowledge to memory: on one side include a key concept, hint about history, important person's name, or other, and on the other side include more detailed information that should be recalled.
- *Write short summaries and reviews after reading* the important information in the text *without* looking at the text or notes. See how much you can remember, then review the text or notes to see what you missed. Write reviews several times over days, weeks, or months to practice recalling the information and test whether you have actually incorporated the information into long-term memory.
- *Create visual representations of the material.* Humans are visual creatures and connecting pictures, symbols, and other visual representations to the information can help recall and remember better. Associate a concept with a mental picture that helps tie it with other mental pictures and concepts.
- *Create games* that make recalling newly learned information more fun and enjoyable. Learners could create new question and answer cards for the boardgame Trivial Pursuit, challenge themselves to recall three newly learned pieces of information during each commercial break in a favorite television show, or play boardgames like Risk, Battleship, or Life in which newly learned facts and ideas about society, economy, war, or geopolitics can "come to life" and be part of the discussion while playing the game.

9.B: PRIMARY SOURCE ON WAR

The Canton, Ohio Speech by Eugene V. Debs (excerpt, 1918)[3]

Comrades, friends and fellow-workers, for this very cordial greeting, this very hearty reception, I thank you all with the fullest appreciation of your interest in and your devotion to the cause for which I am to speak to you this afternoon.

To speak for labor; to plead the cause of the men and women and children who toil; to serve the working class, has always been to me a high privilege; a duty of love.

I have just returned from a visit over yonder, where three of our most loyal comrades are paying the penalty for their devotion to the cause of the working class. They have come to realize, as many of us have, that it is extremely dangerous to exercise the constitutional right of free speech in a country fighting to make democracy safe in the world. . . .

Let us come down the line a little farther. You remember that, at the close of Theodore Roosevelt's second term as President, he went over to Africa to make war on some of his ancestors. You remember that, at the close of his expedition, he visited the capitals of Europe; and that he was wined and dined, dignified and glorified by all the Kaisers and Czars and Emperors of the Old World. He visited Potsdam while the Kaiser was there; and, according to the accounts published in the American newspapers, he and the Kaiser were soon on the most familiar terms. They were hilariously intimate with each other, and slapped each other on the back. After Roosevelt had reviewed the Kaiser's troops, according to the same accounts, he became enthusiastic over the Kaiser's legions and said: "If I had that kind of an army, I could conquer the world." He knew the Kaiser then just as well as he knows him now. He knew that he was the Kaiser, the Beast of Berlin. And yet, he permitted himself to be entertained by that Beast of Berlin; had his feet under the mahogany of the Beast of Berlin; was cheek by jowl with the Beast of Berlin. And, while Roosevelt was being entertained royally by the German Kaiser, that same Kaiser was putting the leaders of the Socialist Party in jail for fighting the Kaiser and the Junkers of Germany. Roosevelt was the guest of honor in the white house of the Kaiser, while the Socialists were in the jails of the Kaiser for fighting the Kaiser. Who then was fighting for democracy? Roosevelt? Roosevelt, who was honored by the Kaiser, or the Socialists who were in jail by order of the Kaiser?

"Birds of a feather flock together."

When the newspapers reported that Kaiser Wilhelm and ex-President Theodore recognized each other at sight, were perfectly intimate with each other at the first touch, they made the admission that is fatal to the claim of Theodore Roosevelt, that he is the friend of the common people and the champion of democracy; they admitted that they were kith and kin; that they were very much alike; that their ideas and ideals were about the same. If Theodore Roosevelt is the great champion of democracy—the arch foe of autocracy, what business had he as the guest of honor of the Prussian Kaiser? And when he met the Kaiser, and did honor to the Kaiser, under the terms imputed to him, wasn't it pretty strong proof that he himself was a Kaiser at heart? Now, after being the guest of Emperor Wilhelm, the Beast of Berlin, he comes back to this country, and wants you to send ten million men over there to kill the Kaiser; to murder his former friend and pal. Rather queer, isn't it? And yet, he is the patriot, and we are the traitors. I challenge you to find a Socialist anywhere on the face of the earth who was ever the guest of the Beast of Berlin, except as an inmate of his prison. . . .

They tell us that we live in a great free republic; that our institutions are democratic; that we are a free and self-governing people. This is too much, even for a joke. But it is not a subject for levity; it is an exceedingly serious matter.

To whom do the Wall Street Junkers in our country marry their daughters? After they have wrung their countless millions from your sweat, your agony and your life's blood, in a time of war as in a time of peace, they invest these untold millions in the purchase of titles of broken-down aristocrats, such as princes, dukes, counts and other parasites and no-accounts. Would they be satisfied to wed their daughters to honest workingmen? To real democrats? Oh, no! They scour the markets of Europe for vampires who are titled and nothing else. And they swap their millions for the titles, so that matrimony with them becomes literally a matter of money.

These are the gentry who are today wrapped up in the American flag, who shout their claim from the housetops that they are the only patriots, and who have their magnifying glasses in hand, scanning the country for evidence of disloyalty, eager to apply the brand of treason to the men who dare to even whisper their opposition to Junker rule in the United Sates. No wonder Sam Johnson declared that "patriotism is the last refuge of the scoundrel." He must have had this Wall Street gentry in mind, or at least their prototypes, for in every age it has been the tyrant, the oppressor and the exploiter who has wrapped himself in the cloak of patriotism, or religion, or both to deceive and overawe the people. . . .

Every solitary one of these aristocratic conspirators and would-be murderers claims to be an arch-patriot; every one of them insists that the war is being waged to make the world safe for democracy. What humbug! What rot! What false pretense! These autocrats, these tyrants, these red-handed robbers and murderers, the "patriots," while the men who have the courage to stand face to face with them, speak the truth, and fight for their exploited victims—they are the disloyalists and traitors. If this be true, I want to take my place side by side with the traitors in this fight. . . .

Wars throughout history have been waged for conquest and plunder. In the Middle Ages when the feudal lords who inhabited the castles whose towers may still be seen along the Rhine concluded to enlarge their domains, to increase their power, their prestige and their wealth they declared war upon one another. But they themselves did not go to war any more than the modern feudal lords, the barons of Wall Street go to war. The feudal barons of the Middle Ages, the economic predecessors of the capitalists of our day, declared all wars. And their miserable serfs fought all the battles. The poor, ignorant serfs had been taught to revere their masters; to believe that when their masters declared war upon one another, it was their patriotic duty to fall upon one another and to cut one another's throats for the profit and glory of the lords and barons who held them in contempt. And that is war in a nutshell. The master class has always declared the wars; the subject class has always fought the battles. The master class has had all to gain and nothing to lose, while the subject class has had nothing to gain and all to lose—especially their lives.

They have always taught and trained you to believe it to be your patriotic duty to go to war and to have yourselves slaughtered at their command. But in all the history of the world you, the people, have never had a voice in declaring war, and strange as it certainly appears, no war by any nation in any age has ever been declared by the people.

And here let me emphasize the fact—and it cannot be repeated too often—that the working class who fight all the battles, the working class who make the supreme sacrifices, the working class who freely shed their blood and furnish the corpses, have never yet had a voice in either declaring war or making peace. It is the ruling class that invariably does both. They alone declare war and they alone make peace.

Yours not to reason why;
Yours but to do and die.

That is their motto and we object on the part of the awakening workers of this nation.

If war is right let it be declared by the people. You who have your lives to lose, you certainly above all others have the right to decide the momentous issue of war or peace.

9.C: INEQUALITY AND WORKING-CLASS POLITICS DURING WORLD WAR I

The tools and approaches developed in previous chapters are useful in thinking about how to apply knowledge about new global politics contexts or situations. Each previous chapter presents an analytical angle from which learners might productively *apply* Debs' speech to other contexts in a systematic and organized way: using key concepts, focusing on the individual actors, placing the text in historical context, or asking deeper questions such as *how does this work?* or *what is the main idea?* This section provides an overview of how to use the tools from previous chapters to perform a more complex analysis of a text in order to apply the knowledge to different situations by offering ideas and questions that a learner might fruitfully research in consideration of Debs' speech. The main question(s) are bullet points below and followed by ideas for answers and further questions—before continuing reading, it is a good idea for learners to stop at each bullet point to see if they can find the answers for themselves and then compare their answers to what is provided. Remember that there are many fine ways to answer a question or interpret new information, meaning that the answers provided are not the only correct or important ones.

- Does Debs use any conceptual language in the speech that is important or useful? Have you encountered any of his ideas before? In what contexts?

Some of the language that Debs marshals in his speech echoes the language used by Marx and Engels, and Lee (excerpts in chapters 2 and 3, respectively), namely ideas about *social class* (the *working class* and *capitalists*), and the notion of *exploitation*. Further, Debs focuses on a variety of injustices that befell WWI laborers at the hands of powerful and wealthy elites—similar to how Marx and Engels discuss capitalist exploitation of laborers in the context of nineteenth-century European industrialization, and to how Lee discusses how capitalists exploit farmers in the context of late-twentieth-century globalization. A central idea of Debs' speech, then, echoed in the writings of other thinkers, is that certain actors command more wealth and power than others, and that discrepancies in wealth and power in the global system contribute to exploitation and injustice. In other words, Debs is generally talking about *inequality* and its consequences. Ideas and concepts that *echo* in this way, across different times, places, and voices, are worth thinking about critically and at length. The application of knowledge of the issues and history surrounding Debs' speech, especially oriented around the key concept of inequality, is explored in further depth later in this section.

- Who is Eugene Debs? What actors does Debs discuss in the speech?

Doing a bit of research on *who?* reveals other potential avenues for application. Debs was an activist, labor leader and union organizer, and a leader of the Socialist Party of America during the late nineteenth and early twentieth centuries (he ran for President and lost five times).[4] The speech included in Section 9.B landed Debs in prison (he was found in violation of the 1917 Espionage Act and sentenced to 10 years in prison; he ran for President for the fifth time in 1920 from prison in Atlanta, Georgia, and won 3.4 percent of the vote). The US Supreme Court ultimately decided *Debs v United States* in 1919, finding unanimously that his attempts to disrupt the military draft were mutinous and treasonous. Do the political controversies and political animus surrounding Debs' speech and trial remind you of other famous episodes in global politics or other instances in which political prisoners strongly influenced the political debates of their day? (Some very influential voices in global political history were imprisoned for their ideas, including Socrates, Martin Luther King, Jr., Nelson Mandela, and Aung San Suu Kyi).

• How does Debs' speech analyze power relationships between individuals and the states they represent?

The ability to apply knowledge to new contexts is bolstered by thinking systematically about actors, institutions, groups, and communities, and their positions, perspectives, and interests. Debs' speech considers many actors, from workers and soldiers to capitalists and Wall Street titans, from US President Theodore Roosevelt to the German Kaiser Wilhelm. Much of the speech is dedicated to criticism of capitalists' and political leaders' behavior, especially their treatment of the working class, in the lead up to and during WWI. Consider the relationship that Debs criticizes, between US President Theodore Roosevelt and the German Kaiser Wilhelm. How does his criticism of Roosevelt's relationship with Wilhelm connect to his criticism of Wall Street Junkers, who "scour" Europe looking for suitable partners in marriage for their children?

In radical political traditions like *Marxism*, a school of thought that strongly influenced Debs' ideas and political activism, the state is viewed as a *superstructure*, a political apparatus that built on top of deeper, underlying class divisions and inequalities in ownership of the means of production. Thus, Debs views Roosevelt and the Wall Street Junkers together as a piece, both functionaries in a socio-economic system in which working people are systematically subjected to the interests of the wealthy and powerful. In this vein, Debs views US foreign policy under Roosevelt as *imperial* in nature, facilitating the domination of foreign lands and foreign peoples by wealthy and powerful Americans on Wall Street and in Washington.

As evidence for why Debs might have applied the critique of imperialism to the US, consider the *Roosevelt Corollary* to the *Monroe Doctrine*, a key piece of US foreign policy that provides important background for understanding Debs' critiques of Roosevelt, that was announced in President Roosevelt's 1904 *State of the Union* speech. In the speech, Roosevelt argued that it was the duty of the United States to interfere in the affairs of other states in the Western Hemisphere in order to promote reasonable efficiency and decency in political matters. . . . Chronic wrongdoing, or an impotence which results in a general loosening of the ties of civilized society, may in America, as elsewhere, ultimately require intervention by some civilized nation, and in the Western Hemisphere the adherence of the United States to the Monroe Doctrine may force the United States, however reluctantly, in flagrant cases of such wrongdoing or impotence, to the exercise of an international police power.[5]

It is the elite, capitalist, imperial policy orientation that partly connects Roosevelt and Kaiser Wilhelm, for as Debs notes in reference to these two leaders, "Birds of a feather flock together." Recall also that the US was at war with Germany and the Kaiser in 1918 when Debs gave his speech. Do you think it was controversial for Debs to so closely compare the US president with the leader of Germany, against whom the US was actively fighting?

- *What* kind of political action does Debs' speech represent? *What* issues did he raise in his speech that ran contrary to the established government narrative about the war?

Debs gave his speech as the keynote address to the annual Socialist Party Convention in Canton, Ohio, and was then arrested for the content of the speech (especially its antiwar rhetoric). Debs' speech can thus be viewed as an act of civil disobedience, or the deliberate violation of an unjust law.[6] The Espionage Act under which Debs was charged only became law a year before he gave the speech. He was indicted "for allegedly attempting to cause insubordination and refusal of duty in the US military. He was also accused of attempted obstruction of recruitment and enlistment."[7]

Debs' speech is a *counterhegemonic* narrative about WWI, an alternate story that opposes or undermines the generally accepted or mainstream story that is told about an event or issue.[8] Debs not only casts into doubt the common understanding of WWI as a "war for democracy" but even goes so far as to discourage the American public from supporting the war, especially people who are called up to serve via the *military draft*. Debs notes in his speech, "They have always taught and trained you to believe it to be your patriotic duty to go to war and to have yourselves slaughtered at their command," implying that it is *not* a patriotic duty for Americans to support or fight in the war.

Debs' speech also challenges the reasons for war and argues that the real motivations of elites to enter the war are different from the ones they state publicly. For instance, US President Woodrow Wilson made the following argument to Congress on April 2, 1917 to garner support and approval for US entry in WWI:

Our motive will not be revenge or the victorious assertion of the physical might of the nation, but only the vindication of right, of human right, of which we are only a single champion. . . . Our object now, as then, is to vindicate the principles of peace and justice in the life of the world as against selfish and autocratic power and to set up amongst the really free and self-governed peoples of the world such a concert of purpose and of action as will henceforth ensure the observance of those principles.[9]

Wilson's statement indicates that the war is about promoting freedom, justice, and peace, about protecting others from "selfish" tyrants. Debs offers a markedly different interpretation in his speech, one that reflects his understandings of *capitalism*, *power*, and *inequality*: "Every solitary one of these aristocratic conspirators and would-be murderers claims to be an arch-patriot; every one of them insists that the war is being waged to make the world safe for democracy. What humbug! What rot! What false pretense! . . . Wars throughout history have been waged for conquest and plunder." Note the important connection between Debs' critiques here of the reasons for WWI, and his critiques of Roosevelt and Kaiser Wilhelm discussed above: Debs perceives that political leaders are motivated in their foreign policy endeavors by desires for wealth and power, in peacetime and wartime alike. (See chapter 10 for further discussion of the various rationales leaders use for going to war.)

- *Where* did Debs deliver his speech and *what* is the significance of that locale? What does a politician's choice of venue indicate about their interests, goals, and perspectives?

Consider the locations politicians frequently choose when they give speeches (both local and global). Recall the importance of location in relation to the choice of Newfoundland as the site of the meeting between FDR and Churchill discussed in chapter 5. Debs delivered his speech in Ohio in the US, a part of the Midwest some call the *Rustbelt*. Is the location significant in thinking about Socialist Party politics, presidential politics, or the politics of the military draft? Consider the importance of Ohio elections to presidential bids and the number of US presidents who were from Ohio (especially in the nineteenth century).

Consider also the locale in the context of the larger influence of war. In the late eighteenth and early nineteenth centuries Ohio was a mining and manufacturing powerhouse, producing coal, locomotives, and other industrial staples to fuel the US economy, with this industrial capacity shifting to support the war effort by 1914. For example, Jeffery Manufacturing, a producer of coal locomotives in Columbus, Ohio, during this period, famously organized Jeffery's Artillery and Jeffery's Battery, groups of soldiers, many of whom were company employees, to support the war effort.[10] Additionally, Ohio was the site of extensive labor unrest and labor organizing by mine and factory workers during the nineteenth and early twentieth centuries, including massive strikes by coal miners and railroad workers in the 1870s through the 1890s, and the site of a major steel strike at the end of the war in 1919. As a labor activist, Debs was an active participant in and organizer of strikes and other forms of labor protest by workers across the US for much of his career, revealing a connection between choice of place and the content of his speech. Ohio also contributed a disproportionate number of soldiers to the war, as volunteers and draftees. By the end of the war, 263,000 Ohioans contributed to US military forces, roughly 5.3 percent of the US' total military manpower.[11]

- *What is the main idea of Debs speech?* Is this an antiwar speech? Is it about social class and inequality and exploitation? About social solidarity and justice? Is it a good example of a stump speech for a hopeful presidential candidate?

Remember that the main idea is given not only in the speech itself but also by context clues. Depending on the context in which learners are thinking and analyzing, any and all of these main ideas may be appropriate. Take, for example, Debs' use of the word *comrade*, a term used among socialists all over the world that indicates a common political stance and solidarity with one another, and his statement, "I speak for labor." These textual clues, combined with background information on Debs' life and career, make a case for thinking about *labor solidarity* as a main idea. Indeed, Debs' speech can be interpreted as an attempt to draw workers closer to one another on the basis of their common class position in the interests of opposing capitalism, imperialism, and war. Of course, Debs' insistence on calling out major political figures of the day for their perceived lies and crimes is similar to the manner in which modern-day politicians point to the failures and mistakes of their political competitors. In this respect, the speech is also quite clearly intended to score political points with potential voters and supporters. In the discussion below, the speech is interpreted in light of yet another main idea, as a class-based critique of inequality during wartime.

After learning as much as possible about the basic background of a situation, as represented by the bullets and discussion above on Debs' speech, the next thing to do in coming up with a way to apply the new knowledge is to decide on one heuristic device. The discussion above reviewed possible options: using key concepts in analysis, focusing on the individual actors, placing the text in historical context, or asking deeper questions such as *what is the main idea?* The next section shows how to use key concepts as a way to focus and assess a situation and apply the knowledge of that situation to other contexts or situations.

Applying Knowledge of Inequality from One Context to Another

This section now takes the knowledge of the historical context and information gleaned by studying Debs' speech and shows how one might apply it to a different context to help illuminate meaning and expand understanding in the new context. The application technique might follow many routes, but we suggest the following, as outlined further below:

1. Narrow down the key concepts, ideas, or historical realities that will be applied to the new context and define them, both in and out of the contexts under study.
2. Identify appropriate new contexts on which to conduct the application (it might not be appropriate or beneficial to apply knowledge between some contexts and thus having a good rationale for the application is necessary).
3. Conduct research on the new context so as to fully understand it (learning the same sort of information as done above by asking *who? what? when? where?* and *why?/how?*).
4. Finally, compare the two contexts and make assertions about how the first context can help us understand and interpret the new context through the use of key concepts chosen.

Narrow Down and Define Concepts: Inequality in Debs Speech and Context

When presented with an opportunity to apply a given speech or letter or treaty to other contexts, it is tempting to talk and write about *all* the possible applications. While such brainstorming is important, it results in a rather superficial analysis that teaches very little about global politics. It is important to focus in on one or two features of Debs' speech and develop the application with more attention to nuance and detail. Narrower applications that probe the speech and global politics deeply, and provide evidence and discussion, are more useful as a heuristic (i.e., a framework for understanding the situation better), more challenging, and demonstrate higher order analytical skills.

To start, several chapters in this volume covered the importance of identifying and understanding *key concepts*—ideas that represent significant dynamics, relationships, and features of the global system—in global politics as a way to understand a situation or text more deeply. Chapters 2, 4, 8, and 11 specifically reviewed the importance of identifying, defining, and then utilizing key concepts like a pair of tinted glasses through which the world looks different depending on which tint is being used. Debs discusses the concept of *inequality* in his speech, a concept that can be usefully applied elsewhere.

The selection of one heuristic device over others to be used in an analysis and application reveals the perspectives and interests of the person choosing. For instance, the choice of *inequality* as a heuristic in the example below reflects our (the authors') positions, perspectives, interests, and experiences with and knowledge of global politics. It also reflects our interpretations of the speech itself. We noticed that inequality is important to Debs (he spends a lot of time talking about it), and that his attention to this issue creates an opportunity for a more nuanced application. The more Debs talks about inequality, the more content we can use from this primary source when we think through our application (things that he mentions only briefly do not enable this sort of depth).

Identifying Appropriate New Contexts for Application

- To what other contexts could we apply Debs' ideas about inequality? And a better question specific to Debs' speech and historical setting: To what other *wartime* contexts can we apply Debs' ideas about inequality?

After you decide *what* to apply, another key question to ask when embarking on an application is about *which* other context/s you think Debs' discussion of inequality could be applied. In other words, you must keep refining your answer to the initial question about the relevance of this document, getting increasingly narrow and precise as you go. Consider, then, that Debs' discussion of inequality is situated squarely within a wartime context (WWI). Thinking about other wars, and how inequality appears and works in a different wartime context, would allow for the kind of narrow focus appropriate to apply Debs' ideas.

Yet again, performing a nuanced and useful application requires us to make hard choices. Which wartime context should we select to apply Debs' ideas about inequality? As the authors, we ultimately selected the Iran-Iraq War (1980–1988), largely because when we were reading Debs again as we wrote this book, we *recalled* some interesting political economy dynamics related to that conflict that paralleled some of Debs' comments. The necessity to recall and draw on existing knowledge of global politics and put it to use in a new context when you perform applications is one of the reasons that this skill set is of higher order.

Making Connections 161

Our choice of *what* to apply (Debs' ideas about *inequality*) and in which context to apply it (the *Iran-Iraq War*) provides structure for the work that comes next: the application requires us to talk about Debs' speech, his conceptions of inequality, and then how ideas about inequality help clarify some of the circumstances of the Iran-Iraq War.

- How, exactly, does Debs conceive of inequality? As Nobel Prize–winning economist Amartya Sen would ask, "Inequality of what?"[12]
- Where does Debs see inequalities play out in the world, as indicated in his speech?
- What are the consequences of inequalities and for whom?
- Finally, we come to an application question: How do our answers to the questions posed above inform our understanding of the Iran-Iraq War?

To start the application process, consider the definition and context of the concept of *inequality* revealed in Debs' speech. Global political conversations often reference the concept of *inequality*. But this concept—connoting in the most general way *unevenness* or *difference* that is socially consequential—is used in different ways and contexts. What kind of inequality is Debs' talking about? Who is unequal to whom? In what ways? With what consequences? Consider the second to last full paragraph from Debs' speech that discusses the "feudal barons" and the "poor, ignorant serfs" and notice how Debs points out the inequality between the two groups, ending with: "The master class has always declared the wars; the subject class has always fought the battles." What other parts of Debs' speech are significant for describing and explaining the kind of inequality he is talking about?

Debs' speech wraps together several different kinds of inequalities that we could generally call *inequalities in wealth and power*. The "feudal barons" of the Middle Ages he references owned and controlled land, and thus also had power over the serfs who needed to farm the land to survive. Similarly, according to Debs, WWI–era capitalists also had control over land and other resources giving them power over workers who need to sell their labor to survive (Marx, whose philosophy grounds Debs' ideas in this speech, calls these kinds of productive resources, the ones we use to make the things we need to survive, the *means of production*).

Central for Debs are several additional inequalities that extend from these fundamental inequalities in ownership and control of the means of production: the power to declare war, the power to profit from war, and the power to have others fight wars. Debs argues that these inequalities in wealth and power between workers and capitalists have the effect during WWI of making existing inequalities even worse: capitalists gain even more wealth and power owing to their wartime profiteering,[13] while the workers who fight the war often end up injured or dead. "Yours not to reason why; yours but to do and die," says Debs toward the end of the speech.

To sum up, then, Debs focuses on inequalities in wealth and power in capitalist systems, arguing that during wartime inequalities appear as differences in who declares and profits from wars, and who fights wars, and as differences in well-being and quality of life. His general inference, along with many other thinkers on this subject, is that inequality in one domain often results in inequality in another.[14]

Conduct Research on the New Context: Iran-Iraq War

It is important when speaking or writing about applications like this one to *not* over-generalize (see discussion of logical fallacies in chapter 7) and to include caveats in your discussion (that is, being honest about how much can be compared across different contexts and how much is context specific). In terms of Debs' speech, the historical and social context of WWI cannot be wholly compared to the historical and social context of the Iran-Iraq War, two wars that were fought in different places and times by different people whose cultures and histories varied, and who fought the war for context-specific reasons. What you *can* do, however, is probe Debs' WWI-era speech for ideas and insights that might shed light on a new context, in our case, the Iran-Iraq War.

The Iran-Iraq War (1980–1988) began when Iraq launched an incursion into Iran in September 1980. Important questions arise that require independent research from learners in order to perform this application well: Why did Iraq invade Iran? Why did Iraq choose this particular time to start its offensive? How did Iran respond? Critical for applying Debs' ideas to this context are additional questions about inequalities in wealth and power, wartime profiteering, and who declared and fought this war (these questions relate to the elements of inequality that we highlighted in the discussion above). Who declared this war? Who fought in this war? Were the soldiers *workers* or *capitalists*? Who suffered and died in this war? How did they die? Who profited from this war? How much? What countries are the profiteers from? How did they earn their profits?

Begin the Application by Comparing the Contexts and Explaining the New Context: Iran-Iraq War as an Example of Inequality

Finally, the application process allows the learner to understand and interpret a new context based on the knowledge gleaned from the first context under study. Consider Debs' central insight on inequality: that inequality in one domain leads to inequality in another. More specifically, Debs asserts that when the rich wage war, it is the poor who die. Inequalities in wealth and resources spawn inequalities in power, specifically the power to declare and profit from war while others, in weaker and poorer and more vulnerable social positions, do the fighting, bleeding, sacrificing, and dying. While many details, both large and small, are significantly different across the two wartime contexts under study here, this particular insight of Debs from the WWI period seems helpful for thinking critically about dynamics of the Iran-Iraq War, a war in which experts estimate that more than a million Iranians and Iraqis were killed and in which certain international businesses and foreign governments made a lot of money.[15]

Consider the following quotes from one source on the Iran-Iraq War listed in Section 9.D and see if you can make any inferences about or interpretations of inequality in this new context based on what you know from Debs' speech. These quotations, and the data they contain, represent a small bit of the research required to empirically support the application:

- "Mainly because of its duration, the war already ranks third among post-World War II wars . . . in battlefield victims, with some 300,000-500,000 casualties."[16]
- "Total Iranian arms imports since August 1980 have been higher than $10 billion, while Iraq has imported more than $30 billion worth. About one-third of the purchases have been from private dealers, with the rest coming from governments or government-controlled arms producing companies."[17]
- "Private dealers obviously have nothing to gain from a peace between Iraq and Iran. Governments, on the other hand, would seem to have a stake in stopping the human suffering, eliminating the danger of escalation, and reopening the two countries to exports of civilian goods. Compared to the economic incentives of arms sales, however, the political interest in stopping the war is weak, and the emergence of new suppliers undermines it further. Neither the U.N. General Assembly nor the Security Council has produced concerted action to stop the flow of arms."[18]

At this point, our argument about how Debs' ideas about inequality might apply to thinking about the Iran-Iraq War is merely an assertion. So far, we have narrowed our focus, homed in upon a central idea of Debs' (inequality), and then explained and described our interpretation of Debs using evidence from the speech (we used direct quotes from this primary source for our evidence). To transform our assertions and hunches into a well-evidenced argument about how Debs' ideas apply to the Iran-Iraq War, we need evidence and support for our claims, well beyond the facts related in the bullet points above. The research required on the Iran-Iraq War draws on many of the skills and practices developed thus far, including efficiently searching the internet and databases, using the library, using data and evidence, and practicing proper citation. In Section 9.D we provide an initial list of sources you might investigate.

- As you begin your research on the Iran-Iraq War, make special note about facts or statements that you think would resonate with Debs and why you think so.
- Constantly ask yourself what other kinds of information would be needed to applying the concept of inequality to the Iran-Iraq War and to begin making rigorous interpretations or arguments.

9.D: RECOMMENDED READINGS ON DEBS, INEQUALITY, AND THE IRAN-IRAQ WAR

Brzoska, Michael. "Profiteering on the Iran-Iraq war." *Bulletin of the Atomic Scientists* 43, no. 5 (1987): 42–45.

Engelbrecht, Helmuth Carol, and Frank Cleary Hanighen. *Merchants of Death: A Study of the International Armament Industry*. New York: Dodd, Mead and Co, 1934.

Hertz, Noreena. *The Debt Threat*. New York, Harper Collins, 2004.

Salvatore, Nick. *Eugene V. Debs: Citizen and Socialist*, 2nd ed. Urbana, IL, University of Illinois Press, 2007.

Sen, Amartya. *Inequality Reexamined*. Cambridge. Cambridge: Harvard University Press, 1992.

NOTES

1. David Glenn, "Close the Book. Recall. Write It Down," *The Chronicle of Higher Education* 55, no. 34, A1, May 01, 2009, https://www.chronicle.com/article/Close-the-Book-Recall-Write/31819.

2. Peter C. Brown, Henry L. Roediger III, and Mark A. McDaniel, *Make It Stick: The Science of Successful Learning* (Cambridge, MA: Belknap Press of Harvard University Press, 2014).

3. Eugene Debs, "The Canton, Ohio Antiwar Speech" Speech, Canton, OH, June 16, 1918, Marxist Internet Archive, Marxists.org (all rights reserved, reproduced based on fair use doctrine from Section 107 of US Copyright Law), https://www.marxists.org/archive/debs/works/1918/canton.htm. To hear the actor Mark Ruffalo perform parts of this speech, follow this link to the Voices of a People's History project: https://peopleshistory.us/watch/mark-ruffalo-reads-eugene-debs-voices-of-a-peoples-history-of-the-us/.

4. Nick Salvatore, *Eugene V. Debs: Citizen and Socialist*, 2nd ed. (Urbana, IL, University of Illinois Press, 2007).

5. Theodore Roosevelt, "Annual Message to Congress," Speech, Washington, DC, December 6, 1904, A National Initiative on American History, Civics, and Service, OurDocuments.gov. https://www.ourdocuments.gov/doc.php?flash=false&doc=56&page=transcript.

6. Henry David Thoreau, *On the Duty of Civil Disobedience* (Project Gutenberg. June 1, 1993, originally published 1849), http://www.gutenberg.org/ebooks/71.

7. "Debs v. United States." *Oyez Free Law Project, Cornell Legal Information Institute*. Accessed June 3, 2020. https://www.oyez.org/cases/1900-1940/249us211.

8. For the original discussion of hegemony and counter-hegemony: Antonio Gramsci, *Prison Notebooks* (New York: Colombia University Press, 2011).

9. Woodrow Wilson, "War Message to Congress." Speech, Washington, DC, April 2, 1917. https://wwi.lib.byu.edu/index.php/Wilson%27s_War_Message_to_Congress.

10. "General Henri Gouraud visiting Jeffrey Manufacturing Company," World War I in Ohio Collection, accessed July 23, 2020, https://www.ohiomemory.org/digital/collection/p16007coll51/id/11789.

11. "Ohio in World War I," the United States World War I Centennial Commission, accessed July 23, 2020, https://www.worldwar1centennial.org/index.php/ohio-in-ww1-home-page.html.

12. Amartya Sen, *Inequality Reexamined* (Cambridge: Harvard University Press, 1992).

13. A classic work on wartime profiteering during World War I is Engelbrecht, Helmuth Carol, and Frank Cleary Hanighen. *Merchants of Death: A Study of the International Armament Industry* (New York: Dodd, Mead and Co, 1934).

14. Sen, *Inequality Reexamined*.

15. Michael Brzoska, "Profiteering on the Iran-Iraq War," *Bulletin of the Atomic Scientists* 43, no. 5 (1987): 42–45. Brzoska estimates that battlefield victims amounted to 300,000–500,000 casualties.

16. Brzoska, "Profiteering on the Iran-Iraq War," 42

17. Brzoska, "Profiteering on the Iran-Iraq War," 42.

18. Brzoska, "Profiteering on the Iran-Iraq War."

Chapter 10

Breaking It Down
Categorizing and Analyzing Topics

A perennial question for those who study global politics and international relations is why countries go to war with each other. One way to investigate the answer is to use *analytical* tools to break down larger concepts, like war, into smaller pieces of information, and *classify* or *categorize elements* so as to understand the whole more clearly. The example presented in this chapter is that of World War II (WWII), a defining point in human history because of the massive destruction and death that occurred between 1939 and 1945.

Section 10.A provides an overview of specific tools learners might use to analyze information about global politics, those of *chunking* knowledge, and *interpreting political rhetoric and propaganda*. Three primary document excerpts (speeches) are included in Section 10.B from the leaders of Germany, the United Kingdom (UK), and the United States (US) at the point of their agreement to enter into WWII. The speeches reveal how leaders used propaganda and rhetoric to inspire their followers, and how they provided rationales for entering into the war. While the reasons in the speeches may be couched in rhetoric and justificatory language that was meant to convince their respective parliaments and populations that going to war was the right thing to do, we can use their speeches to assess and analyze the historical realities as well as the political expediencies that incentivize war between countries rather than settling disputes in other ways. Section 10.C provides guidance on how learners might analyze the speeches and Section 10.D then provides a recommended reading list on WWII and rhetoric/propaganda.

10.A: CHUNKING AND NAVIGATING PROPAGANDA

When practicing the skill of analysis, learners break a large concept or issue, like war, into smaller component parts so as to understand each of the parts as they relate to the whole. The practice of analyzing is especially important for understanding complex phenomena or ideas that cannot be grasped or understood all at once.

Chunking

Chunking is a study technique that helps learners memorize new information, and it also provides an example of how to conduct an analysis. In cognitive psychology chunking is "the process by which the mind divides large pieces of information into smaller units (chunks) that are easier to retain in short-term memory."[1] We practice the technique of chunking in our daily lives, separating numbers in social security numbers or phone numbers, for instance. Applying the practice while studying allows learners to more easily remember information and make "the mental leap that helps you unite bits of information together through meaning."[2]

Chunking Techniques for Analysis:

- *Start by trying to grasp the main topic as a whole.* Just like starting a puzzle before putting the pieces together (one might examine the picture on the box by making note of the colors, shapes, and borders of the picture), a learner should have a good understanding of the main topic or issue before breaking it down.
- *Create categories or "chunks" of information out of the main topic.* When studying a new topic, it is useful to create categories to organize new terms, concepts, dynamics, or relationships by grouping them together in a more accessible and memorable way. Going back to the puzzle analogy, one might lay out all the puzzle pieces face-up and group them together by size, shape, and color to make it easier to find the individual pieces and discern how they connect to the whole.
- *Memorize the categories, or chunks, of information* using mnemonic devices to remember how terms and concepts are grouped together, utilizing flash cards to challenge the memory, etc.

Section 10.C includes an example of how to conduct the chunking study method of analysis (by taking a main topic, *war* along with the question, *why do countries go to war with each other?*) and breaking it down into categories of reasonings and justifications given by leaders who make the decision to enter into war (based on the three primary documents in Section 10.B).

Interpreting Political Rhetoric and Propaganda

Understanding when and how language and facts are used by leaders in speeches and statements or other materials, whether as *rhetoric* or *propaganda*, is an important skill for those who study global politics. People consistently encounter rhetoric and propaganda in their everyday lives, whether when listening to a speech from leaders or engaging in a debate with a work colleague or family member. Studying *rhetoric* entails analyzing how language is used by a speaker in an effective manner and may sometimes be considered as an attempt at persuasion but often simply just as the art of using language well. Students of *propaganda* focus more intently on how speakers use specific language, facts, or evidence (often in a misleading way) so as to convince their audience to support a particular action or agenda.[3] Politicians, heads of companies, and motivational speakers, among other types of leaders, write and deliver speeches intended to persuade their audience of a particular course of action.

Political leaders, in particular, write and deliver speeches as a way to prove their *legitimacy* to their constituents or people and leaders from other countries.[4] For political leaders, *legitimacy* means that citizens approve of their goals and behaviors and support their policies. When leaders are perceived as illegitimate by their people, they risk losing reelection, or even the possibility of opposition to their power in the form of protest, social unrest, military coups, etc.[5] Further, when leaders are perceived as illegitimate by foreign peoples and governments, they may encounter foreign interference in their domestic politics, including (covert) financial and military assistance to the opposition, military invasion and/or occupation, regime change, and/or war.[6]

As a part of propaganda, errors in logical reasoning are often deployed purposefully as persuasive devices (see Section 7.A on logical fallacies). For example, a *hasty generalization* can make relatively localized or infrequent events seem commonplace and regular, thus legitimizing bold action on matters that are in reality only of relatively minor importance. Moreover, speakers sometimes distort, bend, or otherwise manipulate facts with their rhetoric in order to persuade others about the legitimacy of their goals and behaviors. Systematic distortions of fact and reality that are designed to influence public opinion are called *propaganda*. When used by governments, propaganda may appeal to a sense of *national identity* and *patriotism* among citizens of a country, both of which work to legitimize and support the established power structure. Corporate propaganda may appeal to a sense of shared identity and values among consumers or shareholders. Recognizing how leaders use rhetoric and propaganda opens the door to a variety of critical questions to ask when analyzing their communications (and may be applied to the analysis of the speeches included in Section 10.B).

Questions to use to identify rhetoric or propaganda:

- Are the main ideas in the speech supported by evidence and facts, or are they opinion or a particular interpretation of facts?
- Whose interests are served by the statements or overall argument of the speech?
- In what ways might the speech make the speaker seem more legitimate to their audience?
- Does the speech include any logical fallacies or other persuasive devices, like appeals to patriotism, nationalism, or emotion?

10.B: PRIMARY SOURCES ON RATIONALES FOR WAR

Address before the Reichstag leading to the Invasion of Poland by Adolph Hitler, Chancellor of the Reich (excerpt, September 1, 1939)[7]

For months we have been suffering under the torture of a problem which the Versailles Diktat created—a problem which has deteriorated until it becomes intolerable for us. Danzig was and is a German city. The Corridor was and is German. Both these territories owe their cultural development exclusively to the German people. Danzig was separated from us, the Corridor was annexed by Poland. As in other German territories of the East, all German minorities living there have been ill-treated in the most distressing manner. More than 1,000,000 people of German blood had in the years 1919-1920 to leave their homeland.... It is impossible to demand that an impossible position should be cleared up by peaceful revision and at the same time constantly reject peaceful revision. It is also impossible to say that he who undertakes to carry out these revisions for himself transgresses a law, since the Versailles Diktat is not law to us. A signature was forced out of us with pistols at our head and with the threat of hunger for millions of people. And then this document, with our signature, obtained by force, was proclaimed as a solemn law.... I am determined to solve (1) the Danzig question; (2) the question of the Corridor; and (3) to see to it that a change is made in the relationship between Germany and Poland that shall ensure a peaceful co-existence. In this I am resolved to continue to fight until either the present Polish government is willing to continue to bring about this change or until another Polish Government is ready to do so. I am resolved to remove from the German frontiers the element of uncertainty, the everlasting atmosphere of conditions resembling civil war. I will see to it that in the East there is, on the frontier, a peace precisely similar to that on our other frontiers.

In this I will take the necessary measures to see that they do not contradict the proposals I have already made known in the Reichstag itself to the rest of the world, that is to say, I will not war against women and children. I have ordered my air force to restrict itself to attacks on military objectives. If, however, the enemy thinks he can form that draw carte blanche on his side to fight by the other methods he will receive an answer that will deprive him of hearing and sight.

Blood, Toil, Tears, and Sweat Speech to the House of Commons by Winston Churchill, Prime Minister of the United Kingdom (excerpt, May 13, 1940)[8]

I beg to move,
That this House welcomes the formation of a Government representing the united and inflexible resolve of the nation to prosecute the war with Germany to a victorious conclusion.... We have before us an ordeal of the most grievous kind. We have before us many, many long months of struggle and of suffering. You ask, what is our policy? I can say: It is to wage war, by sea, land and air, with all our might and with all the strength that God can give us; to wage war against a monstrous tyranny, never surpassed in the dark, lamentable catalogue of human crime. That is our policy. You ask, what is our aim? I can answer in one word: It is victory, victory at all costs, victory in spite of all terror, victory, however long and hard the road may be; for without victory, there is no survival. Let that be realised; no survival for the British Empire, no survival for all that the British Empire has stood for, no survival for the urge and impulse of the ages, that mankind will move forward towards its goal. But I take up my task with buoyancy and hope. I feel sure that our cause will not be suffered to fail among men. At this time I feel entitled to claim the aid of all, and I say, "come then, let us go forward together with our united strength."

Address to a Joint Session of Congress Leading to a Declaration of War Against Japan by Franklin D. Roosevelt, President of the United States (excerpt, December 8, 1941)[9]

Mr. Vice President, and Mr. Speaker, and Members of the Senate and House of Representatives:
Yesterday, December 7, 1941—a date which will live in infamy—the United States of America was suddenly and deliberately attacked by naval and air forces of the Empire of Japan.
The United States was at peace with that Nation and, at the solicitation of Japan, was still in conversation with its Government and its Emperor looking toward the maintenance of peace in the Pacific. Indeed, one hour after Japanese air squadrons had commenced bombing in the American Island of Oahu, the Japanese Ambassador to the United States and his colleague delivered to our Secretary of State a formal reply to a recent American message. And while this

reply stated that it seemed useless to continue the existing diplomatic negotiations, it contained no threat or hint of war or of armed attack.

It will be recorded that the distance of Hawaii from Japan makes it obvious that the attack was deliberately planned many days or even weeks ago. During the intervening time the Japanese Government has deliberately sought to deceive the United States by false statements and expressions of hope for continued peace.

The attack yesterday on the Hawaiian Islands has caused severe damage to American naval and military forces. I regret to tell you that very many American lives have been lost. In addition American ships have been reported torpedoed on the high seas between San Francisco and Honolulu. . . . As Commander in Chief of the Army and Navy I have directed that all measures be taken for our defense.

But always will our whole Nation remember the character of the onslaught against us.

No matter how long it may take us to overcome this premeditated invasion, the American people in their righteous might will win through to absolute victory. I believe that I interpret the will of the Congress and of the people when I assert that we will not only defend ourselves to the uttermost but will make it very certain that this form of treachery shall never again endanger us.

Hostilities exist. There is no blinking at the fact that our people, our territory, and our interests are in grave danger.

With confidence in our armed forces—with the unbounding determination of our people—we will gain the inevitable triumph—so help us God.

I ask that the Congress declare that since the unprovoked and dastardly attack by Japan on Sunday, December 7, 1941, a state of war has existed between the United States and the Japanese Empire.

10.C: GOING TO WAR

Considered in the light of the death toll that wars take on society, it is difficult to comprehend why people would go to war with each other. The first section of the Bhagavad Gita on two soldiers' ruminations on the battlefield sums up the problem well: "I do not see that any good can come from killing our relations in battle."[10] Recall from chapter 4 in this text that the United Nations (UN) Charter outlines the main reasons for creating the UN as a collective security organization to "save succeeding generations from the scourge of war" and that war is not an easy concept to define. War might be defined and conceptualized as a conflict that occurs between two or more actors in the international system (most often, state governments and their militaries), and might be so named based on the number of battle deaths in a given year.[11] War may also be conceptually connected to other concepts such as *politics, diplomacy, the international system* and *balance of power, sovereignty, treaty negotiations, nationalism,* and *the nation-state,* or *patriotism* (review these concepts from previous chapters, especially Section 8.C, Textbox 8.1). In order to determine why states (and the people who lead them) would go to war with one another, the rest of this section shows how to break down the concept of war and reasons for going to war using the analytical process of *chunking*.

Background and Context

Using WWII as an example to help conceptualize *war* is useful for the analysis of the documents in Section 10.B, which requires some research.[12] As you continue reading through this section, take a moment to stop at each bullet point question and try to find the answer before you read on.

Step One in Chunking: Identify the main topic and its component parts—grasp the main topic as a whole:

- Who? Where? When? Identify the actors involved in WWII (i.e., the state governments and militaries who actually engage in warfare), where in the world this conflict was waged, and when in history it occurred.

States in the *international system* fought WWII primary over access to land, based in *nationalistic rhetoric and ideology,* as members of *alliances* of countries primarily from two regions of the world (Europe and Asia), eventually encompassing other states and colonies worldwide in the fighting. Although Germany and Japan annexed and captured territory throughout the 1930s (Germany annexed Austria, Sudetenland, and Czechoslovakia, and Japan invaded Manchuria), WWII didn't officially start until September 1, 1939, when Germany invaded Poland and the UK and France finally responded to Germany's territorial expansion by declaring war. Alliances formed as states sought to gain advantage in the *balance of power*: Germany allied with Italy and others as the Axis Powers, while the UK and France allied with the US and the Union of Soviet Socialist Republics (USSR) as the Allied Powers. The US entered the war on December 4, 1941, after the Japanese attacked the US naval base at Pearl Harbor in Hawaii. War officially ended when Germany and its allies surrendered in 1945 and *diplomatic* agreements were made by the Allied Powers at the Potsdam Conference of 1945 and *treaty negotiations* ended in 1947 in Paris.[13]

- Identify the number of people who died during WWII, both in battle deaths and civilian casualties.

The other mechanism for defining war is identifying the number of battle deaths that occurred in a particular period of time, that is, the number of people who died fighting in combat. It is difficult to identify how many people died in WWII, both in terms of combatants who were fighting the war and in terms of the number of civilians whose lives and livelihoods were affected by the war, yet a general consensus among statisticians and scholars puts the death toll somewhere between 60 and 75 million people, of which roughly 15 million are considered battle deaths.[14] Included in the numbers are 6–9 million people who were brutally murdered by the Nazi Regime in Germany during the Holocaust. The Holocaust was a genocide motived by racism and nationalism, led and incited by the leader of the Nazi Party, Adolph Hitler, and inflicted against the Jewish population as well as the Roma, disabled, elderly, and gay and lesbian population in Germany (as well as in territories controlled by Germany) beginning in 1933.[15]

Analyzing Reasons for Entry into World War II

Inductive reasoning involves examining facts and data from a situation under study and then using these *premises* to develop tentative *conclusions* about the situation under study as a whole. But even a simple concept like a country's rationale for war becomes incredibly complex once you begin assessing it in a deep and nuanced way. To understand the whole picture (the causes of WWII), we need to break the speeches down into their component parts.[16]

Step Two in Chunking: Create categories or chunks of information out of the main topic:

- Read the speeches from Section 10.B carefully and create categories or chunks of information out of the main topic.

Table 10.1 provides an example of how a learner might follow the analytical process of chunking by starting with the main topic, then breaking it down to smaller topics, and lastly synthesizing the smaller topics into groups of information that help comprehend and understand the whole. The left-hand column in Table 10.1 is a list of information derived from notes from reading the speeches on entry into WWII. The list in the middle column is an example of chunking: taking the first list in the left-hand column and breaking it down

Breaking It Down 175

Table 10.1 Chunking Rationales for World War II

Initial list (unchunked)	Chunked list (from left)	Analyzed list (connecting with larger picture)
From Hitler's speech	**Places**	**Rationales for going to war**
Hitler (Chancellor of the Reich)	Danzig	*Regaining Territory*
Versailles "Diktat"	The Corridor (Poland)	• Hitler's list of places mostly comprised of territory lost in Versailles Treaty at the end of World War I
Danzig	Germany	
The Corridor (Poland)	Austria	
Poland	Sudetenland	
Germany and German people	Bohemia	
National Socialist Party	Moravia	• Churchill and FDR list of places comprised of places where fighting is occurring—desire to keep borders as they are
Austria	Moravia	
Sudetenland	Italy	
Bohemia	Soviet Union	
Moravia	Norway	
Reichstag	Holland	*National Interest and Nationalism, Racism, and Ethnocentrism*
Reich	Mediterranean	
Claim of German Minority oppression in Poland	Island of Oahu, Hawaii	• Hitler call to regain territory lost as "German" and struggle so that "Germany shall live"
	American deaths	
Italy (as ally to Germany)	Malaya	
Molotov-Ribbentrop Pact (between Germany and the Soviet Union, August 1939)	Hong Kong	
	Guam	• Churchill seeking victory to ensure "survival of British Empire"
	Philippine Islands	
	Wake Island	
From Churchill's speech	Midway Island	• FDR call to fight to protect "our people, territory, and our interests"
Churchill (Prime Minister)	**Political units**	
House of Commons (UK Parliament)	Reichstag (German Parliament)	
	National Socialist Party (Germany)	*Protection of Minorities*
King of UK (His Majesty)	House of Commons (UK Parliament)	• Hitler claim that German people in Polish territories are being mistreated as minorities
New Administration formed	New Administration formed (UK)	
Call for bipartisanship (include all parties)	War Cabinet (UK)	
	Ministers appointed (UK)	
War Cabinet	Congress (US Parliament)	*Defense or Retaliation against Aggression*
Ministers appointed (UK)	Secretary of state (US)	
Norway	Japanese ambassador	• Hitler's claim that Versailles Diktat was signed by force and territories wrongfully taken from Germany
Holland	American Navy and Military	
Mediterranean	**People**	
Tyranny (fighting against)	German people	
British Empire	German minorities	
From FDR's speech	Women and children	• Churchill's claim that must fight against "tyranny" for "without victory, there is no survival"
FDR (President, Commander in Chief of Army and Navy)	Polish soldiers	
	Japanese squadrons	
Attack on Pearl Harbor (December 7, 1941)	Japanese emperor	
	Our people	• FDR's claim that Japan surprise attack and offensive that threatens "the very life and safety of our Nation"
Japan	Our whole nation	
Island of Oahu, Hawaii	**Government leaders**	
Surprise attack (bombing) despite diplomatic negotiations	Hitler (Chancellor of the Reich, Germany)	
	Franklin Delanor Roosevelt (President of the US)	*Morality of War or Just War Theory*
Secretary of State (US)	Churchill (Prime Minister of the UK)	• All three speeches refer to need to protect nationals of country, both within own territory or outside of
Japanese ambassador	King of UK (His Majesty)	
Attack on American Navy and military	**Historical Settings and Events**	
	Versailles Treaty (Diktat) (November 1918)	
American deaths	Claim of German minority oppression in Poland	• All three speeches refer in some way to defensive reasons for engaging in war actions
Malaya		
Hong Kong	Molotov-Ribbentrop Pact (between Germany and the Soviet Union, August 1939)	
Guam		
Philippine Islands		
Wake Island	Attack on Pearl Harbor (7 December 1941) and other territories	
Midway Island		
Surprise offensive (in Pacific)		

into more accessible parts using categories that seem helpful for figuring out what is important to study in more depth in order to understand the whole. Finally, the third list in the right-hand column of the table is an example of how to connect the chunks and analyze the information contained within the categories established in the middle column. Analyzing and understanding the chunks allows learners to develop a deeper perspective on the whole.

The first thing that might stand out in the speeches are the rationales each of the leaders give for entry into war. Each of the speeches was made to the countries' respective parliaments by the head of government as a way to convince the parliament that going to war was the only option. Consider the rationales below, mirrored in the right-hand column of table 10.1 where the chunked information is synthesized into meaningful parts that illuminate the picture of war as a whole.

Control of Territory

One clear reason why states go to war with one another is to gain control of territory and thereby access to resources. All the speeches in Section 10.B reference the issue of territory in some way. Hitler argues the need to regain territory taken from Germany after World War I (WWI); FDR references the attack on US territory and the necessity of defense; and Churchill calls for protecting the British Empire. To expand, Hitler's speech shows a desire for more territory, as in *territorial expansion*. Studying maps while reading Hitler's speech will help immensely in understanding what was at stake for Hitler and the German people in 1939.[17] Hitler delivered his speech in a special session to the German parliament (Reichstag) to announce plans to invade Poland and justify those plans to German lawmakers and to the world. During the 1930s Hitler and the Nazi Party acted aggressively to procure agreements with Poland, France, and the UK in an attempt to regain territory (such as the Sudetenland and Czechoslovakia), before invading Poland in 1939. But *appeasement*, the term applied to the practice of giving in to the demands of an opponent (here Germany) in the hope that they will be satisfied and cease their aggressive behavior, did not satisfy Hitler and the Nazi Party's desire for more territory.

- What was the Versailles Treaty and why would Hitler use it as a way to justify invading Poland?

Notice that Hitler refers immediately in his speech to the strictures of the Versailles Treaty that ended WWI. Hitler refers to the territories that he considered "German" but that the Versailles Treaty had named as independent, sovereign areas or states in the international system, as with Danzig (as a free city under the power of the League of Nations), the Polish corridor (an area separating the new German border from East Prussia that included Danzig), Austria, Sudetenland, Bohemia, and Moravia. The rationale for invading Poland and starting a war, in this case then, is to regain territory that had been previously lost/taken (the term for this is *revanchism*, derived from the French word for *revenge*).

Hitler's speech brings up many questions about the legality and morality of the Versailles Treaty, most notably the way it was negotiated by the major world powers after WWI (US, France, UK) with little input from others, that it broke up territories in problematic ways, and that it was imposed with force. Refer back to chapter 4 where we discussed the League of Nations and recall that the international organization was created by the Versailles Treaty and that the US Senate never ratified the treaty.

- Does your research thus far lead you to think that control over territory is so important to a state that they should risk lives in a war to gain that control? In what ways might the speeches by Hitler, FDR, and Churchill represent rhetoric rather than reality related to access to or defense of territory?

Historical Grievances, Self-Defense, or Protection of Minorities

The next rationale that stands out in all three of the speeches is a desire to protect or defend a nation and its people under threat. Hitler's speech argues that German minorities in the territories that had been created by the Versailles Treaty were mistreated, especially in Poland, and needed protection. Determining whether or not this statement was true is more difficult to assess than whether territories were redrawn by the Versailles Treaty. However, we can connect this point with the larger discussion that had been ongoing since the end of WWI about *self-determination* of peoples and whether colonialism was a problem and should be ended. Around the 1930s, but especially after WWII, groups of people around the world living in colonies called for decolonization and the ability to govern themselves. Hitler's suggestion, then, was associated with this movement for nations of people to unite under one government. There was also a mounting (and now perennial) question about how states should act or react when other states mistreat people in their territories (see chapter 13 for more discussion concerning human rights).

- Is defense, or the protection of minorities, a legitimate reason for countries to violate the *sovereignty* of other states or to wage war with them?

FDR's and Churchill's speeches represent a desire to defend territories, gain victory over an oppressive force (that is how Germany and Japan are presented in the speeches), and to protect people within their borders from possible threats to existence. Indeed, FDR references the devastating effects of the Japanese attacks: "I regret to tell you that very many American lives have been lost," using that as a rationale for entering WWII. Churchill less directly argues that the war must be fought against "a monstrous tyranny" that threatens the "British Empire." One gets the sense that Hitler is also seeking to defend "the German people."

- What was it that incentivized defensive behavior or acts of aggression on the part of all these states? How had the US been engaging with Japan up to this point? What was the UK's relationship with Germany before declaring war?

Studying the history and relationships of the states involved in WWII is crucial to understanding their leader's rationales and meanings. For instance, the attack on Pearl Harbor is associated with Japan's aggression and their justification for starting a war with the US. They had already invaded Manchuria against the condemnation of the League of Nations and were expanding southward, enlarging their territory, but the US had blocked their access to oil and they felt the need to retaliate. UK too, ostensibly entered the war for defensive reasons, though this is a bit less clear cut than in the US case. While Churchill's speech was given in May 1940, Britain had officially declared war on Germany in September 1939, after Germany invaded Poland. At that time, UK, France, and Poland were bound by the terms of the 1939 Anglo-Polish Agreement, which stipulated that both the UK and France would protect Poland and ensure its independence if they were attacked. The agreement arose out of a sense of international betrayal stemming from Britain's and France's refusal to assist Czechoslovakia when they were invaded by the Nazis the year prior in 1938. Under the leadership of Prime Minister Neville Chamberlain, the British had—up until 1939—pursued a policy of *appeasement* with Germany, and hoped that ceding Czechoslovakia to the Germans would satisfy Hitler's territorial ambitions. Shortly after Churchill's speech, the blitz of England began, a campaign of aerial bombardment of English cities, towns, and industries carried out by the Germans during 1940 and 1941.

National Interest and Nationalism

Another theme that runs through all the speeches is a sense of nationalism, a devotion to one's country and to its people. Yet, the terms *nationalism* and *patriotism* are often confused, and have historically produced both positive and negative outcomes. For instance, one definition of *patriotism* is "the feelings of affection and pride that people have for their country."[18] *Nationalism* more often than not is associated with affection, pride, and loyalty to a group of people who share similar characteristics, such as cultural, religious, shared history, ethnicity, or racial characteristics.[19] Note that the definitions create questions about what affection and pride mean as related to a country and group of people: Does *country* mean the people in it, the culture, or the territory, or some amalgam of these elements?

When Hitler stated in his speech that "Danzig was and is a German city," he was stating a nationalist sentiment about a hypothetical German people and history, one that upon closer study did not exist with such purity (think here also about how such statements might be part of German government *propaganda*). Consider how a sense or ideology of nationalism has the power to incentivize and inspire both positive and negative actions and behaviors. In the speech, Hitler uses the sense of German nationalism to justify invasion of another country, Poland, which ultimately sparked retaliation on the part of neighboring countries (the UK and France).

All three speakers utilize nationalist rhetoric to gain support from and cultivate legitimacy among the members of their respective parliaments. Hitler called on the Reichstag to support his plans: "it is essential that our people shall live, that Germany shall live." FDR and Churchill both cater to a sense of nationalism and protectionism. FDR says "the American people, in their righteous might will win through to absolute victory" while Churchill argued that it was necessary to win the war else there would be "no survival for the British Empire."

- Consider how the ideas of nationalism can so easily turn into racism, ethnocentrism, and general bigotry toward anyone perceived as different in the context of one's own culture and history.

Morality of War or Just War Theory

The three speeches all refer to moral tenets about war. Theorists have long attempted to define and delimit when governments and their militaries could lawfully go to war with one another and how they would act during war in a body of literature referred to as *just war theory*. One of the earliest works to which international relations scholars often refer is Thucydides' *History of the Peloponnesian War* describing and explaining the wars between the Greek cities of Athens and Sparta.[20] In a famous passage called the "Melian Dialogue" Thucydides records one of the delegations in a negotiation between Sparta and Melos as saying, "The strong do what they will and the weak suffer what they must." Yet this invocation never sat well with theorists in the Christian tradition who meant to be concerned with human welfare. The Christian doctrine of military engagement, begun by St. Augustine and St. Aquinas, suggests that there should be rules that delimit why people go to war with each other and how they should be treated. Such rules eventually became codified in international law, as in the Geneva Conventions.[21] The leaders of the three countries under study here all refer to the tenets in one way or another. Note, first, how Hitler justified invading Poland under the idea that German minorities were being mistreated and needed protection. Note how Roosevelt refers to the just cause of defending the American people and that the American people would respond with their "righteous might." Note too how Churchill rationalizes the war as a righteous battle against a "monstrous tyranny" guilty of the darkest "human crimes."

The Geneva Conventions and Humanitarian Law: While the speeches do not refer to the Geneva Conventions, they are important for understanding global politics and international relations, for the rules they inscribe and for the actors they recognize. We recommend finding the Conventions and reading them carefully, and learning about Henri Dunant and his experience in Solferino, Italy, during the Napoleonic Wars. Dunant was the impetus behind the formation of the Red Cross, a nongovernmental humanitarian organization, and the first 1864 version of the Geneva Convention to protect medical personnel during warfare. After reviewing the tenets and rules of just war theory and the Geneva Conventions on your own, return to the speeches and consider: in what ways did the US, Germany, or the UK follow or break the conventions' rules? The Geneva Conventions were updated in 1949 based on the experience of WWII—take a moment to consider how they were updated and whether they have encouraged states to engage in just war since then.

After breaking down a situation under study into chunks, like we have done with the speeches for entering WWII, identifying various rationales and historical elements necessary to the task, it is possible put them together to analyze the whole.

- What *did* cause WWII? Why *did* the US, the UK, or Germany go to war?

10.D: RECOMMENDED READINGS ON PROPAGANDA, RHETORIC, WAR, AND GENOCIDE

Interpreting Propaganda and Rhetoric

Gavin, William F. *Speechwright: An Insider's Take on Political Rhetoric*. East Lansing: Michigan State University Press, 2011.

Herman, Edward S., and Noam Chomsky. *Manufacturing Consent: The Political Economy of the Mass Media*. 1st ed. New York: Pantheon Books, 1988.

Jowett, Garth, and Victoria O'Donnell. *Propaganda & Persuasion*. 7th ed. Thousand Oaks, CA: SAGE Publications, 2019.

Kovach, Bill, and Tom Rosensteil. *Blur: How to Know What's True in the Age of Information Overload.* New York: Bloomsbury, 2010.

Martin, James. *Politics and Rhetoric: A Critical Introduction.* London: Routledge, 2013.

On War and Genocide

Clausewitz, Carl von. *On War.* The Project Gutenburg. Produced by Charles Keller and David Widger. Original publication 1832. Last updated October 19, 2019. https://www.gutenberg.org/files/1946/1946-h/1946-h.htm.

Fisher, David. *Morality and War: Can War be Just in the 21st Century?* New York: Oxford, 2011.

Keegan, John. *The Second World War.* New York: Penguin, 2016.

Snyder, Timothy. *Bloodlands: Europe between Hitler and Stalin.* London: Vintage, 2015.

Waltzer, Michael. *Just and Unjust Wars.* New York: Basic Books, 2015.

Weitz, Eric D. *A Century of Genocide: Utopias of Race and Nation.* Princeton, NJ: Princeton University Press, 2003.

Wiesenthal, Simon. *The Sunflower: On the Possibilities and Limits of Forgiveness.* New York: Schocken Books, 1997.

NOTES

1. American Psychological Association, "Chunking," APA Dictionary of Psychology, accessed July 24, 2020 https://dictionary.apa.org/chunking; Fernand Gobet, Peter C.R. Lane, Steve Croker, Peter C-H. Cheng, Gary Jones, Iain Oliver, and Julian M. Pine, "Chunking Mechanisms in Human Learning," *Trends in Cognitive Sciences* 5, no. 6 (2001): 236–43.

2. Oakley, Barbara, *A Mind for Numbers*: *How to Excel at Math and Science* (New York: Penguin Random House, TarcherParigree, 2014), 57.

3. Good overviews of rhetorical analysis include, e.g., Sam Leith, *Words Like Loaded Pistols: Rhetoric from Aristotle to Obama* (New York: Basic Books, a member of the Perseus Books Group, 2016); James Martin, *Politics and Rhetoric: A Critical Introduction* (London: Routledge, 2013). To learn more about propaganda see, e.g., Garth Jowett and Victoria O'Donnell, *Propaganda & Persuasion*, 7th ed. (Thousand Oaks, CA: SAGE Publications, 2019).

4. William F. Gavin, *Speechwright: An Insider's Take on Political Rhetoric* (East Lansing: Michigan State University Press, 2011); Bill Kovach and Tom Rosensteil, *Blur: How to Know What's True in the Age of Information Overload* (New York: Bloomsbury, 2010).

5. Examples of leadership being challenged because of lack of domestic legitimacy include the protests against the Vietnam War and eventually against President Nixon in the United States in the 1970s that, along with other challenges, culminated

in Nixon's resignation, or the Arab Spring in which long-time dictators were removed from power in Tunisia, Libya, and Egypt in 2011 in the wake of protests.

6. As examples of foreign interference using or into finances of another country, consider the political and economic influence that the United States had over Haiti through the *1915 Treaty* (reviewed in this text in chapter 9) or the increase of financial aid to Greece and Turkey requested by President Truman in 1949 as a way to counter domestic communist groups and the influence of the USSR (reviewed in this text in chapter 1).

7. Adolph Hitler, "Address Before the Reichstag," Speech, Berlin, Germany, September 1, 1939, The Avalon Project, Yale Law School (all rights reserved, reproduced based on fair use doctrine from Section 107 of US Copyright Law), https://avalon.law.yale.edu/wwii/gp2.asp.

8. Winston Churchill, "Blood, Toil, Tears and Sweat," Speech to the House of Commons, London, May 13, 1940, the International Churchill Society, WinstonChurchill.org. (all rights reserved, reproduced based on fair use doctrine from Section 107 of US Copyright Law), https://winstonchurchill.org/resources/speeches/1940-the-finest-hour/blood-toil-tears-and-sweat-2/.

9. Franklin Delano Roosevelt, "Joint Address to Congress Leading to a Declaration of War Against Japan," Speech, Washington D.C., December 8, 1941, Franklin D. Roosevelt Presidential Library and Museum, A National Initiative on American History, Civics, and Service, OurDocuments.gov. (all rights reserved, reproduced based on fair use doctrine from Section 107 of US Copyright Law), http://www.ourdocuments.gov/doc.php?doc=73&page=transcript.

10. Easwaran Eknath, trans, *The Bhagavad Gita*, 2nd ed. Classics of Indian Spirituality (Tomales, CA: Nilgiri Press, 1985, 2007), verse 31, 80.

11. UCDP Conflict Encyclopedia "War" Uppsala Conflict Data Program, Uppsala University, accessed July 24, 2020, www.ucdp.uu.se. Consider the Uppsala Conflict Database definition of war: "A state-based conflict or dyad which reaches at least 1000 battle-related deaths in a specific calendar year."

12. Many excellent sources and archives on World War II are available to the public and contain primary and secondary source documentation of the war. E.g., University of North Texas Digital Library, "World War Two Collections" accessed March 26, 2020, https://digital.library.unt.edu/explore/collections/WWII/; Southern Methodist University Libraries, "Historic Government Publications from World War II" accessed March 26, 2020, https://www.smu.edu/libraries/digitalcollections/hgp/; Library of Congress, "Guide to World War II Materials" accessed March 26, 2020, https://www.loc.gov/rr/program/bib/ww2/ww2bib.html?&loclr=reclnk.

13. For a good overview of World War II see Martin Gilbert, *The Second World War: A Complete History* (New York: Holt Paperbacks, 1989).

14. Martin Gilbert, *The Routledge Atlas of the Second World War*, 2nd ed. (Routledge Historical Atlases. London: Routledge, 2019).

15. Eric D. Weitz, "The Primacy of Race: Nazi Germany," *A Century of Genocide: Utopias of Race and Nation* (Princeton, NJ: Princeton University Press, 2003), 102–43.

16. Puzzle analogy inspired by Oakley, *A Mind for Numbers*, 57.

17. Google maps or online libraries often have easily accessible maps. A good book source is Gilbert, *The Routledge Atlas of the Second World War*.

18. Oxford English Dictionary, "Patriotism" Oxford English Dictionary, accessed July 29, 2019, https://www.lexico.com/en/definition/patriotism.

19. The Stanford Encyclopedia of Philosophy provides an excellent overview of the problems associated with studying nationalism and adds to the definition that it is not only about *affection* but also about *actions*. Nenad Miscevic, "Nationalism," Stanford Encyclopedia of Philosophy, last updated December 15, 2014, accessed July 24, 2020, https://plato.stanford.edu/entries/nationalism/#:~:text=The%20term%20%E2%80%9Cnationalism%E2%80%9D%20is%20generally,or%20sustain)%20self%2Ddetermination.

20. Thucydides, *History of the Peloponnesian War*, Translated by Benjamin Jowett (Amherst, NY: Prometheus Books, 1998).

21. Augustine, *The City of God*, Translated by Marcus Dods (New York: Modern Library, 1950).

Chapter 11

Compare and Contrast
Clarifying and Distinguishing Concepts and Ideas

Analyzing global politics often requires one to compare concepts and ideas from people who are thinking about similar issues. In terms of Bloom's Taxonomy, this chapter builds on remembering, understanding, and applying in order to perform an analysis that draws on higher-order skills. A major goal in performing a compare-contrast analysis is to gain conceptual clarity by considering the related ideas of two thinkers together. While identifying and parsing similarities is an important task, especially in tracing the historical lineage of important ideas over time, a nuanced comparison requires identification and analysis of discontinuities, differences, and disagreements. It is often the case that one can more easily understand what an idea or dynamic *is* by taking time to think about what it *is not*.

To provide learners with tools and suggestions for how to compare and contrast ideas across texts or situations, this chapter offers an example of how to begin an comparative analysis and start an essay (though it does not provide an example of what the final essay would look like). Section 11.A offers some writing tips and guidance on the writing process. Section 11.B provides an example of two primary documents that discuss the concept of *peace* from Dr. Martin Luther King Jr. and Dr. Wangari Maathai, both recipients of the Nobel Peace Prize. Section 11.C then integrates a variety of tools, practices, habits, and approaches to form a more complex comparative analysis, leveraging active and close reading skills, definitional tools, basic internet research using credible sources, T-charts, the basic questions (*who? what? where? why? when?/how?*), and main idea isolation to analyze the excerpts in Section 11.B.

11.A: BRAINSTORMING WITH MINDMAPS AND USING WRITING TIPS

The goal in this chapter is to encourage systematic and organized approaches to starting a project, especially one that requires writing and analysis. The skills build on the way that previous chapters and methods, like the method of *chunking* from chapter 10, encouraged memory and retention by supporting higher-order critical thinking skills. This section offers some tools for starting and working on projects. When starting a project, using mindmaps can help brainstorm ideas, as described below. Further, when engaging in a project, especially one that requires writing, such as an essay, use project management techniques as described below to create excellent work.

Mindmaps

A mindmap is a freeform exercise that helps learners brainstorm ideas, visually representing ideas in the way that the human mind actually thinks. The mind does not think in sentence structure, but more like a spider's web in the way that ideas, experiences, knowledge, and memory all connect to help interpret new information. Drawing a mindmap on a piece of paper or using one of the many excellent apps and online programs to create mindmaps presents the way that the brain works in visual format. Creating a mindmap at the beginning of a project, as in when defining key concepts or identifying main ideas, can help overcome procrastination, get the ideas flowing, and guide the project forward.

Making a mindmap involves the following steps:

- Start in the center of the paper or mindmap software with a bubble or square that includes one simple main idea.
- Create lines that connect to other bubbles or squares (use different shapes to reflect different kinds of ideas or hierarchies) with connected ideas, or sub-topics.
- Create lines (solid or dotted) to form more connections and to add other ideas (add quotes, references to other documents, or other useful connections).

See the example of a mindmap in Figure 11.1, Section 11.C.

Writing Tips

An organized and purposeful approach to analysis and writing is critical as learners develop expertise in global politics and refine analytical and communication skills. The process of analysis and writing is not one big task but rather a collection of smaller, interrelated pieces that build on one another. Developing a strategy to guide analysis and writing is a good idea for several reasons, including that one is more likely to develop clear and robust analyses of global political issues, and better able to manage time. The following discreet steps can, to some extent, be performed separately (which means a writer doesn't necessarily need to devote one large period of time to analysis, but rather can do a little bit today, a bit more tomorrow, and the rest later on when there is more time). In other words, the plan can serve as a guide for completing the analysis systematically and efficiently.

The following list delineates a scaffolded series of stages in the process of writing a comparative essay or argument. The process will help learners manage time and guide thinking for an analysis like that included in Section 11.C.

- *Active reading and note-taking*: It is important to focus your reading and note-taking. For instance, the primary sources in Section 11.B are rich and offer expansive knowledge and understanding about a multitude of issues. Reading the sources without a focus or purpose might mean that learners miss out on main ideas or become overwhelmed. The guidance in Section 11.C suggests using the conceptual lens of *peace* as a way to guide the reading. Using the concept of *peace* yields different takeaways than, for example, if they were considered through the lens of *social movements* or *democracy*. Thus, research on any text, document, book, or topic benefits from focusing on one key concept and actively reading and note-taking on that concept.
- *Research*: It is often necessary to conduct outside research in order to effectively compare thinkers and their ideas. Biographical and historical research clarifies the context in which ideas arise for specific thinkers, allowing for more detailed, precise, and nuanced comparisons. Scholarly research is useful for uncovering expert terminology, and for identifying and understanding key controversies about ideas among experts.
- *Defining key terms*: Any term that is central to the comparative analysis, and even some that are more tangential, require robust conceptual definitions.
- *Organizing notes and selecting dimensions for comparison*: Active reading and research typically result in copious notes that become unwieldy and difficult to manage but that, when organized, can help clarify thoughts. Mindmaps and T-charts, among other tools, are useful for summarizing and consolidating information to make notes manageable. When organizing notes, try creating a mind map from memory, using recall to retrieve information stored in the brain, only going back to notes if necessary. T-charts can offer further clarification to notes by helping summarize comparisons and contrasts and reveal main ideas to emphasize in the analysis. Note that it is important to be fair to the thinkers being analyzed, making sure one

concept is not over-emphasized or misinterpreted. Return to the original text to make sure your interpretations are as charitable as possible.
- *Take a break*: Rest is really important. Research indicates that taking a break can sometimes be a productive approach. Postponing work for a short time provides you with time to think, to make new connections, to clarify ideas or language. Indeed, the right kind of break can make you more creative.[1] Don't avoid the assignment until the last minute, rather, give your mind time to rest. Rest and daydreaming and other activities allow you to create and reinforce neural connections in your brain.
- *Just write, edit later*: Many learners or first-time writers aim for perfection when they write. We, the authors, humbly suggest that trying to write perfectly is a mistake. We encourage you to *just write*. To start, put away your readings, notes, mind maps, and T-charts; you have most of the information in your mind anyway. Next, reduce any distractions: put away your phone, disable your social media accounts. Finally, pull up a new Word document. To begin writing we also recommend something that may seem strange: cover or turn off your computer monitor, and just write. Not being able to see the letters and words you are writing might feel strange, but they will still be there—not being able to see them reduces your urge to try and edit and it allows you to be creative in writing your thoughts and ideas.
- *Edit extensively*, re-write, and add references, quotations, evidence, and other details.

When you have written as much as you can, save your work and take a break. When you return to your computer, your first draft will be waiting for you. Re-save the document as *draft 2* (so as to archive all of your drafts and have them all available should you need them later; though, if you are working in Google docs or a similar program, there are applications that will save your drafts for you so you may return to them, such as *draftback*). Get to work on organizing your paper, polishing up your evidence and quotes (making sure they are in quotation marks where appropriate and checking that you transcribed correctly), and editing for quality (evidence and support, organization, clarity), consistency, concision, word count, and spelling and grammar.

Interesting things happen when writing in this manner. For example, you may not have a thesis statement at the beginning of your first draft, but you may find that you have made your argument later in the paper. You may have written a line or two at the very end of that first draft that sums up your argument quite well. As you edit, you can move your thesis statement to the introduction and reorganize accordingly. Allowing your words to flow creatively as you write your first drafts saves you time and effort and frustration later on.

You may need to work on several drafts before the analysis shapes up in a way you are proud of. Professional writers never submit their first drafts because they are almost always terrible, including our first chapter drafts for this book. Expect at least two drafts or more and extensive editing before submitting your work.

11.B: PRIMARY SOURCES ON PEACE

A Time to Break Silence Speech by Martin Luther King, Jr. (excerpt, 1967)[2]

There is at the outset a very obvious and almost facile connection between the war in Vietnam and the struggle I, and others, have been waging in America. A few years ago there was a shining moment in that struggle. It seemed as if there was a real promise of hope for the poor—both black and white—through the poverty program. There were experiments, hopes, new beginnings. Then came the buildup in Vietnam, and I watched this program broken and eviscerated, as if it were some idle political plaything of a society gone mad on war, and I knew that America would never invest the necessary funds or energies in rehabilitation of its poor so long as adventures like Vietnam continued to draw men and skills and money like some demonic destructive suction tube. So, I was increasingly compelled to see the war as an enemy of the poor and to attack it as such.

Perhaps a more tragic recognition of reality took place when it became clear to me that the war was doing far more than devastating the hopes of the poor at home. It was sending their sons and their brothers and their husbands to fight and to die in extraordinarily high proportions relative to the rest of the population. We were taking the black young men who had been crippled by our society and sending them eight thousand miles away to guarantee liberties in Southeast Asia which they had not found in southwest Georgia and East Harlem. And so we have been repeatedly faced with the cruel irony of watching Negro and white boys on TV screens as they kill and die together for a nation that has been unable to seat them together in the same schools. And so we watch them in brutal solidarity burning the huts of a poor village, but we realize that they would hardly live on the same block in Chicago. I could not be silent in the face of such cruel manipulation of the poor. . . .

We are called to speak for the weak, for the voiceless, for the victims of our nation and for those it calls "enemy," for no document from human hands can make these humans any less our brothers. . . .

A true revolution of values will lay hand on the world order and say of war, "This way of settling differences is not just." This business of burning human beings with napalm, of filling our nation's homes with orphans and widows, of injecting poisonous drugs of hate into the veins of peoples normally humane, of sending men home from dark and bloody battlefields physically handicapped and psychologically deranged, cannot be reconciled with wisdom, justice, and love. A nation that continues year after year to spend more money on military defense than on programs of social uplift is approaching spiritual death.

Nobel Prize Acceptance Speech by Wangari Maathai (excerpt, 2004)[3]

As the first African woman to receive this prize, I accept it on behalf of the people of Kenya and Africa, and indeed the world. I am especially mindful of women and the girl child. I hope it will encourage them to raise their voices and take more space for leadership. I know the honour also gives a deep sense of pride to our men, both old and young. As a mother, I appreciate the inspiration this brings to the youth and urge them to use it to pursue their dreams.

Although this prize comes to me, it acknowledges the work of countless individuals and groups across the globe. They work quietly and often without recognition to protect the environment, promote democracy, defend human rights and ensure equality between women and men. By so doing, they plant seeds of peace. I know they, too, are proud today. To all who feel represented by this prize I say use it to advance your mission and meet the high expectations the world will place on us.

This honour is also for my family, friends, partners and supporters throughout the world. All of them helped shape the vision and sustain our work, which was often accomplished under hostile conditions. I am also grateful to the people of Kenya—who remained stubbornly hopeful that democracy could be realized and their environment managed sustainably. Because of this support, I am here today to accept this great honour.

I am immensely privileged to join my fellow African Peace laureates, Presidents Nelson Mandela and F.W. de Klerk, Archbishop Desmond Tutu, the late Chief Albert Luthuli, the late Anwar el-Sadat and the UN Secretary General, Kofi Annan.

I know that African people everywhere are encouraged by this news. My fellow Africans, as we embrace this recognition, let us use it to intensify our commitment to our people, to reduce conflicts and poverty and thereby improve their quality of life. Let us embrace democratic governance, protect human rights and protect our environment. I am confident that we shall rise to the occasion. I have always believed that solutions to most of our problems must come from us.

In this year's prize, the Norwegian Nobel Committee has placed the critical issue of environment and its linkage to democracy and peace before the world. For their visionary action, I am profoundly grateful. Recognizing that sustainable development, democracy and peace are indivisible is an idea whose time has come. Our work over the past 30 years has always appreciated and engaged these linkages.

My inspiration partly comes from my childhood experiences and observations of Nature in rural Kenya. It has been influenced and nurtured by the formal education I was privileged to receive in Kenya, the United States and Germany. As I was growing up, I witnessed forests being cleared and replaced by commercial plantations, which destroyed local biodiversity and the capacity of the forests to conserve water.

Excellencies, ladies and gentlemen,

In 1977, when we started the Green Belt Movement, I was partly responding to needs identified by rural women, namely lack of firewood, clean drinking water, balanced diets, shelter and income.

Throughout Africa, women are the primary caretakers, holding significant responsibility for tilling the land and feeding their families. As a result, they are often the first to become aware of environmental damage as resources become scarce and incapable of sustaining their families.

The women we worked with recounted that unlike in the past, they were unable to meet their basic needs. This was due to the degradation of their immediate environment as well as the introduction of commercial farming, which replaced the growing of household food crops. But international trade controlled the price of the exports from these small-scale farmers and a reasonable and just income could not be guaranteed. I came to understand that when the environment is destroyed, plundered or mismanaged, we undermine our quality of life and that of future generations.

Tree planting became a natural choice to address some of the initial basic needs identified by women. Also, tree planting is simple, attainable and guarantees quick, successful results within a reasonable amount time. This sustains interest and commitment.

So, together, we have planted over 30 million trees that provide fuel, food, shelter, and income to support their children's education and household needs. The activity also creates employment and improves soils and watersheds. Through their involvement, women gain some degree of power over their lives, especially their social and economic position and relevance in the family. This work continues.

Initially, the work was difficult because historically our people have been persuaded to believe that because they are poor, they lack not only capital, but also knowledge and skills to address their challenges. Instead they are conditioned to believe that solutions to their problems must come from "outside." Further, women did not realize that meeting their needs depended on their environment being healthy and well managed. They were also unaware that a degraded environment leads to a scramble for scarce resources and may culminate in poverty and even conflict. They were also unaware of the injustices of international economic arrangements.

In order to assist communities to understand these linkages, we developed a citizen education program, during which people identify their problems, the causes and possible solutions. They then make connections between their own personal actions and the problems they witness in the environment and in society. They learn that our world is confronted with a litany of woes: corruption, violence against women and children, disruption and breakdown of families, and disintegration of cultures and communities. They also identify the abuse of drugs and chemical substances, especially among young people. There are also devastating diseases that are defying cures or occurring in epidemic proportions. Of particular concern are HIV/AIDS, malaria and diseases associated with malnutrition.

On the environment front, they are exposed to many human activities that are devastating to the environment and societies. These include widespread destruction of ecosystems, especially through deforestation, climatic instability, and contamination in the soils and waters that all contribute to excruciating poverty. . . .

Although initially the Green Belt Movement's tree planting activities did not address issues of democracy and peace, it soon became clear that responsible governance of the environment was impossible without democratic space. Therefore, the tree became a symbol for the democratic struggle in Kenya. Citizens were mobilised to challenge widespread abuses of power, corruption and environmental mismanagement. In Nairobi's Uhuru Park, at Freedom Corner, and in many parts of the country, trees of peace were planted to demand the release of prisoners of conscience and a peaceful transition to democracy.

Through the Green Belt Movement, thousands of ordinary citizens were mobilized and empowered to take action and effect change. They learned to overcome fear and a sense of helplessness and moved to defend democratic rights.

In time, the tree also became a symbol for peace and conflict resolution, especially during ethnic conflicts in Kenya when the Green Belt Movement used peace trees to reconcile disputing communities. During the ongoing rewriting of the Kenyan constitution, similar trees of peace were planted in many parts of the country to promote a culture of peace. Using trees as a symbol of peace is in keeping with a widespread African tradition. For example, the elders of the Kikuyu carried a staff from the *thigi* tree that, when placed between two disputing sides, caused them to stop fighting and seek reconciliation. Many communities in Africa have these traditions. . . .

In the course of history, there comes a time when humanity is called to shift to a new level of consciousness, to reach a higher moral ground. A time when we have to shed our fear and give hope to each other.

That time is now. . .

The challenge is to restore the home of the tadpoles and give back to our children a world of beauty and wonder.

Thank you very much.

Compare and Contrast 193

11.C: MAKING PEACE

This section provides learners with an example of how to structure a comparative essay using the techniques as laid out in Section 11.A and comparing and contrasting the primary sources in Section 11.B on the key concept of *peace*. Considering the two primary sources in Section 11.B, and conducting a comparative analysis of them, draws on a variety of tools and techniques outlined at the beginning of the chapter. The example below was created by following the first six steps outlined in Section 11.B and gives an example of what a first draft of a comparative essay might look like. Note that first drafts of essays are always incredibly unrefined and need lots more work. Thinking does not really begin until one starts putting the thoughts into words, and a first draft reveals the main ideas and foundational steps but needs a lot of work and revision from there. However, it is helpful to see what a first draft might look like in order to get a sense of how to start and where to go from there.

Thus, in writing the initial draft of the example of a comparative essay shown in Textbox 11.1 we, the authors, systematically and methodically followed the stages outlined in Section 11.A. First, we read the primary source readings carefully and actively, taking notes along the way. As part of this first step, we created a mindmap, shown in Figure 11.1, to brainstorm key concepts and ideas from the primary documents that could be included in conducting a project that compared and contrasted between the two documents.

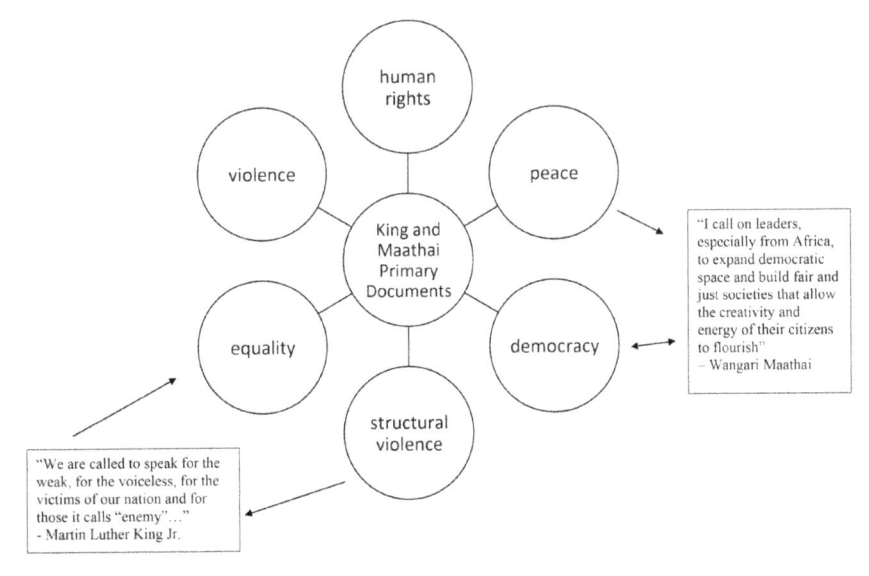

Figure 11.1 Mindmap of Main Ideas in King's and Maathai's Speeches.

Next, we did some research into King and Maathai, their lives and experiences and accomplishments and struggles. We also did some brief reading of some basic scholarly primers and articles from the field of *peace studies*, a sub-field in international relations. We did this research into scholarly work so that we could find and start using some of the language that peace scholars in the field use to talk about peace and violence. When we found this language, we defined the terms we did not know using multiple sources to do so.

We organized our notes into mind maps, which help to brainstorm, summarize, and visualize what is important to King and Maathai. Next, we consolidated these ideas into a T-chart, so that we could easily see those conceptual dimensions along which comparisons and contrasts were possible. One column of our chart was labeled "similarities" and the other was labeled "differences." At this stage we also considered these dimensions broadly in order to derive a few main ideas, those ideas that seemed most important to the authors in thinking about peace. Then we took a break to clear our heads. Last, we just wrote. We wrote what had emerged in our minds, having read and researched and organized our thoughts. The results appear in Textbox 11.1, our first written draft of this comparative analysis.

TEXTBOX 11.1: EXAMPLE OF THE FIRST DRAFT OF A COMPARATIVE ESSAY

Draft Title: Peace and Violence in the Writings of King and Maathai

King and Maathai both center on a holistic idea of peace that not only incorporates admonitions against direct and structural violence, but also requires society to dedicate itself to the task of building a *positive peace* by rectifying social, political, and ecological inequalities and injustices. King's ideas about violence and peace are situated within the *triple threat* of militarism, capitalism, and racism. In contrast, Maathai's ideas are formulated in reference to gender inequality, deprivation of political rights, and environmental destruction.

King and Maathai on Violence

For King, writing during the Vietnam war, the reality of physical violence loomed large (*direct violence*). He is thinking about American troops in Vietnam, and the Vietnamese people they are fighting. But, pointing to his conception of *structural violence*, he sees American and Vietnamese people as equals, both exploited and used by wealthier and more powerful actors pursing more power and profit. He perhaps echoes Marx and Engels

(1848), thinking about the global proletariat. King speaks of the threat posed by both capitalism and communism, as systems of unfreedom that pursue empire in foreign lands and treat ordinary people as disposable. King's concerns about imperialism are related to his discussion of poverty in the US (structural violence; also, everyday violence?), a stark expression of class inequality. King also discusses inequalities based in race, citing the denial of rights and freedoms to African Americans in the US, including African American soldiers fighting in Vietnam. He makes another link between inequality at home and war abroad with his comments about how funding the war is draining the coffers at home, and thereby depriving impoverished communities at home of resources and social supports.

Like King, Maathai also thinks about violence in a broad way. Her speech is not as focused on physical violence during wartime, but more on the violence of everyday life for women living in poverty in rural Kenya. Women and girls bear the brunt of the responsibility for food preparation, water and fuel collection, caregiving and farming, responsibilities that became more burdensome with environmental degradation over time. Like King, she focuses on poverty and inequality, linking such social ills to undemocratic and corrupt political and economic institutions (yet, her focus on the environment distinguishes her from King). Both think about violence in terms of class inequality.

While King focuses on inequalities based in race, Maathai delves more deeply into gender inequality and how these social inequalities deprive Kenyan women of political rights and voice, economic necessities, and natural resources.

King and Maathai on Peace

It is clear that for both thinkers, creating peace requires much more than merely ceasing violence (*negative peace*). Both call broadly upon society—domestic and international—to join together to work to overcome the social, political, economic, and ecological problems that lead to violence, experienced both during wartime and in everyday life. They are advocating for a negative *and* positive peace. Forging this kind of peace requires us to *act*, to change the world, to make the world better. It is no coincidence that both of these thinkers are social activists who led critically important social movements in their respective countries. Through their activism, they both show us not only what peace means, but also how to achieve peace.

While both King and Maathai clearly point to the importance of solidarity, community, courage, love, wisdom, democracy, and justice as tools for forging peace, Maathai's emphasis on solidarity and love and justice for

> the Earth sets her apart from King. It is as if Maathai sees the importance of peaceful human relations with other species on Earth to be as important as peaceful social relations among humans. In this regard, the import of historical context is clear, with Maathai writing in 2004 and King in 1967. In the 37 years that elapsed between these thinkers and social movements, the plight of Earth grew significantly more dire, with a disproportionately devastating impact on equatorial, agricultural communities in the global South. . . .

The draft in Textbox 11.1 provides clues into how a writer progresses through their work. There are many problems with the draft that writers would address in subsequent drafts. For instance, the draft is incomplete and malformed in important ways. It does not clearly define the terms, like *structural violence* and *positive peace*, rather, the terms are used in context. There are no quotes or evidence to back up the arguments, nor does the draft essay practice proper citation. The draft even shows parenthetical references to the writers, as questions and reminders to go back and insert terminology and definitions.

And yet, the draft is well organized and provides clues into how writing without editing (step 6) can provide an excellent way to form ideas and thoughts that will be clarified upon further reflection and editing. In the draft, there is something that looks like a thesis statement at the beginning, where it articulates the overall impression of the comparison. Then, the draft talks about King first and then Maathai on *violence*, followed by King first and then Maathai on *peace*. In each section the writing deploys compare-contrast language like *similarly* and *likewise* and *both*, and *by contrast* and *contrary to* and *distinct from*. It also weaves key terms across the draft, creating continuity in the conceptual framing. Summarizing and consolidating and organizing notes, by way of mind maps or T-charts or other devices, often results in a relatively more organized first draft because organizing notes is actually a process of organizing thoughts, and organizing thoughts can lead to more organized writing, which can encourage more effective reading and note-taking, in a kind of virtuous cycle.

Now, take some time to practice your writing and editing skills by assessing the draft: as a learner and writer, how would you edit and refine the draft and turn it into something more polished and complete? What do you think of the argument? What ideas do you have for this comparison? Would you have used different language? Different elements of the primary sources? What kinds of quotes from the primary sources could we have used to help bolster our argument? Re-write the draft or come up with your own comparative essay based on the steps outlined in Section 11.A.

11.D: RECOMMENDED READINGS ON PEACE AND LEARNING

On Peace

Fahey, Joseph J. and Richard Armstrong, eds. *A Peace Reader: Essential Readings on War, Justice, Non-violence, and World Order.* New York: Paulist Press, 1992.

Maathai, Wangari. *The Green Belt Movement: Sharing the Approach and the Experience.* New York: Lantern Books, 2003.

Richmond, Oliver. *Peace: A Very Short Introduction.* Oxford: Oxford University Press, 2014.

Shiva, Vandana. *The Violence of the Green Revolution.* New York: Zed Books, 1989.

Washington, James M., ed. *A Testament of Hope*: *The Essential Writings and Speeches of Dr. Martin Luther King, Jr.* San Francisco: Harper Collins, 1986.

On Learning

Clegg, Brian. *Instant Time Management.* London: Kogan Page, 1999.

Weston, Anthony. *A Rulebook for Arguments.* 4th ed. Hackett Publishing, 2008.

White, Katherine. *Strategies for Analysis: Analyzing Information for Classroom, Homework and Test Success.* New York: Rosen Publishing Group, 2006.

Wong, Linda. *Essential Study Skills.* 6th ed. Boston: Houghton Mifflin, 2009.

Zinsser, William. *On Writing Well: The Classic Guide to Writing Nonfiction*, reprint ed. New York: Harper Perennial, 2016.

NOTES

1. Adam Grant, "Why I Taught Myself to Procrastinate" *New York Times,* January 16, 2016, https://www.nytimes.com/2016/01/17/opinion/sunday/why-i-taught-myself-to-procrastinate.html.

2. Martin Luther King Jr., "A Time to Break Silence," Speech, New York City, April 4, 1967, In *A Testament of Hope*, Edited by James M. Washington (San Francisco: Harper Collins, 1986) (all rights reserved, reproduced based on fair use doctrine from Section 107 of US Copyright Law).

3. Wangari Maathai, "Nobel Lecture." Speech, Oslo, Norway, December 10, 2004. The Nobel Foundation, Nobel Media AB 2020 (all rights reserved; reproduced with permission of the Licensor, The Nobel Foundation). https://www.nobelprize.org/prizes/peace/2004/maathai/26050-wangari-maathai-nobel-lecture-2004/.

Chapter 12

Tying the Pieces Together

Synthesizing Information about Global Politics

Synthesizing information and knowledge requires learners to make links and connections between ideas, concepts, facts, events, dynamics, and/or relationships in order to combine knowledge and understandings of global politics together to form a whole. To synthesize is to rethink, reorganize, and reconceptualize so as to bring new information or knowledge to light. A synthesis is a meaningful set of connections. Finally, synthesizing information allows for the introduction of a new concept or idea that helps describe and explain the links between a collection of phenomena that initially appear disconnected or even random.[1]

As an advanced set of analytical skills, effectively synthesizing global politics information requires learners to draw deeply upon existing knowledge of and expertise in global politics. This chapter focuses on a fundamental skill of synthesis: the capability to take several sources of information and organize or combine them in a new way—in this case, the primary documents in Section 12.B include an excerpt from the 1845 British Inclosure Act, an 1855 letter to the editor of the *London Times* from the British scientist Michael Faraday, and an 1860 editorial in *The New York Times*. Section 12.C provides learners with an outline of how to conduct a synthesis, and an example in which the primary sources from section 12.B are analyzed using the concept of *collective action problems* and the heuristic of the *Tragedy of the Commons*. Finally, Section 12.D provides learners with recommended readings.

12.A: GOAL SETTING, ADAPTATION, AND SELF-REFLECTION

Learning effectively requires one to set, plan, and strategize about how to meet goals, to self-reflect on learning accomplishments and achieving goals, and to make small changes if necessary.

Goal Setting and Adaptation

Setting goals is critical for a learner's success, both in learning and in life, because it allows for purposeful, strategic, and critical thinking about learning behaviors and outcomes. Learning involves "deliberate practice" that "takes place outside one's comfort zone" and "involves well-defined, specific goals."[2] Whatever the goal—whether to master a new skill, for example, or understand a global politics issue or event—successfully achieving that goal requires one to first formulate the goal so as to have a sense of the desired change or outcome. It is wise to brainstorm multiple strategies for completing goals. Depending on the effectiveness of your first strategy, you might use it again (if it worked) or put it aside (if it failed). Developing effective learning strategies is a trial and error endeavor, and different people may develop different effective strategies for achieving the same goal. Keep track of goals and strategies and make notes about the ways in which the strategies helped or hindered achievement of the goals.

The trial and error process of setting goals, developing strategies, implementing strategies, and then reflecting on the results can seem like a complex endeavor. Sometimes it is. But sometimes making small changes or adapting study habits can make a big difference. For example, as a learner, if you *hit a wall* studying, lose your focus, and can't seem to recall or grasp any of the material, a simple change in scenery may help. Changing the *physical* study environment allows the brain to retain and recall information more effectively, combat boredom and refresh the mind, and improve productivity. Another small but important change might be to avoid *distractions*, especially electronic distractions (turn off the cell phone and put it in another room, log out of messaging apps, etc.).[3]

Finally, one of the most effective and deceptively simple changes to improve study habits is to improve time management. Make a calendar in which to record goal achievement dates, steps necessary (with deadlines) in order to achieve the goal, planned study and reading sessions, and other activities (like healthy physical and mental activities or work and family obligations). Organizing one's time on a calendar will help with time management, as can making a more detailed daily or weekly schedule in which one deliberately dedicates time to specific tasks.

Self-reflection

Practicing self-reflection is an excellent way to articulate goals, refine goals, set deadlines, and strategize on how to achieve goals, and modify strategies or study habits based on your experience. Self-reflection allows learners to be aware of their thoughts and thought processes—*metacognition*—and learners who (critically) self-reflect on their own learning habits are more likely to learn on their own and improve their learning and performance over time.[4]

Self-reflection Practices:

- Keep a journal or record of learning and study habits. Answer the questions:
  - What am I doing to learn and am I learning what I want to learn?
  - Which specific tactics and practices am I using and how successful are these tactics and practices? (Am I learning the material? How do I feel after implementing each tactic or practice?)
  - How long are my study sessions and how often do I study? Am I spending enough time or too much time studying?
  - Where do I study and how is the environment affecting me? (What improvements in the air or sound quality, smell, or people around me might help me study better?)
  - What are the results of my study efforts? (Have I achieved my learning goals or personal development goals? If not, how can I improve my study habits so as to achieve those goals?)

12.B: PRIMARY SOURCES ON COLLECTIVE GOODS

The British Inclosure Act (excerpt, 1845)[5]

1845 CHAPTER 118 8 and 9 Vict

An Act to facilitate the Inclosure and Improvement of Commons and Lands held in common, the Exchange of Lands, and the Division of intermixed Lands; to provide Remedies for defective or incomplete Executions, and for the Non-execution of the Powers of general and local Inclosure Acts; and to provide for the Revival of such Powers in certain cases [8th August 1845]. . . .

Descriptions of land subject to be inclosed under this Act.

All such lands as are herein-after mentioned, (that is to say,) all lands subject to any rights of common whatsoever, and whether such rights may be exercised or enjoyed at all times, or may be exercised or enjoyed only during limited times, seasons, or periods, or be subject to any suspension or restriction whatsoever in respect of the time of the enjoyment thereof; all gated and stinted pastures in which the property of the soil or of some part thereof is in the owners of the cattle gates or other gates or stints, or any of them; and also all gated and stinted pastures in which no part of the property of the soil is in the owners of the cattle gates or other gates or stints, or any of them; all land held, occupied, or used in common, either at all times or during any time or season, or periodically, and either for all purposes or for any limited purpose, and whether the separate parcels of the several owners of the soil shall or shall not be known by metes or bounds or otherwise distinguishable; all land in which the property or right of or to the vesture or herbage, or any part thereof, during the whole or any part of the year, or the property or right of or to the wood or underwood growing and to grow thereon, is separated from the property of the soil; and all lot meadows and other lands the occupation or enjoyment of the separate lots or parcels of which is subject to interchange among the respective owners in any known course of rotation or otherwise, shall be land subject to be inclosed under this Act. . . .

Letter from Michael Faraday to the *London Times* (1855)[6]

Sir,

I traversed this day by steam-boat the space between London and Hangerford Bridges between half-past one and two o'clock; it was low water, and I think the tide must have been near the turn. The appearance and the smell of the water forced themselves at once on my attention. The whole of the river was an opaque pale brown fluid. In order to test the degree of opacity, I tore up some white cards into pieces, moistened them so as to make them sink easily below the surface, and then dropped some of these pieces into the water at every pier the boat came to; before they had sunk an inch below the surface they were indistinguishable, though the sun shone brightly at the time; and when the pieces fell edgeways the lower part was hidden from sight before the upper part was under water. This happened at St. Paul's Wharf, Blackfriars Bridge, Temple Wharf, Southwark Bridge, and Hungerford; and I have no doubt would have occurred further up and down the river. Near the bridges the feculence rolled up in clouds so dense that they were visible at the surface, even in water of this kind.

The smell was very bad, and common to the whole of the water; it was the same as that which now comes up from the gully-holes in the streets; the whole river was for the time a real sewer. Having just returned from out of the country air, I was, perhaps, more affected by it than others; but I do not think I could have gone on to Lambeth or Chelsea, and I was glad to enter the streets for an atmosphere which, except near the sink-holes, I found much sweeter than that on the river.

I have thought it a duty to record these facts, that they may be brought to the attention of those who exercise power or have responsibility in relation to the condition of our river; there's nothing figurative in the words I have employed, or any approach to exaggeration; they are the simple truth. If there be sufficient authority to remove a putrescent pond from the neighbourhood of a few simple dwellings, surely the river which flows for so many miles through London ought not to be allowed to become a fermenting sewer. The condition in which I saw the Thames may perhaps be considered as exceptional, but it ought to be an impossible state, instead of which I fear it is rapidly becoming the general condition. If we neglect this subject, we cannot expect to do so with impunity; nor ought we to be surprised if, ere many years are over, a hot season give us sad proof of the folly of our carelessness.

I am, Sir,

Your obedient servant,

M. FARADAY.

Royal Institution, July 7

"Dearth of Food—A Startling View" editorial from *The New York Times* (1860)[7]

We published yesterday a remarkable letter from Liebig, the great German chemist, addressed to Mechi, the famous English farmer, upon that most momentous of all sublunary themes, the production of corn. He shows that the corn-producing power of the civilized, cultivated countries of the globe, is rapidly becoming exhausted; that it is owing to guano that the decline has not been more rapid and more marked; but that the existing supply of guano, if it continues to be consumed at its present rate, will not last more than twenty-five or thirty-five years at the utmost. He predicts accordingly, that unless war, or pestilence, or famine, or emigration *en masse*, largely diminishes the population of the older countries, they will find themselves, at no very distant day, if the existing system of cultivation be pursued, in actual want of bread, and the Malthusian theory will thus receive an early and certainly unlooked-for exemplification.

These conclusions, thus massed together, are so startling that, even when they come from an eminent scientific man, one finds some difficulty in accepting them. But a very cursory inspection of what is actually occurring within our own knowledge, both here and in Europe, places their general correctness beyond doubt. For many years before the repeal of the Corn laws, in 1847, England was only enabled to keep up the supply of wheat for her own population by the existence of high protective duties, and consequently a high price of bread and low standard of living on the part of the masses. As soon as the duties were removed, the farmers were unable to produce it at the natural market price, and had to give way before the competition of Russia and the United States, and betake themselves to cattle-raising and green crops. With these they are thriving, as perhaps they never throve before, but the annual yield of home-grown wheat has been enormously diminished, and English bread is now mainly the product of the Eastern Steppes and Western prairies, purchased with British manufactures.

It is, however, notorious that the same exhaustion is now showing itself in the lands which have been longest under cultivation here, and corn is ceasing to be a profitable product through all the Eastern states. In New-England, and New-York, and Virginia, the yield per acre is rapidly diminishing; and as the process of exhaustion goes on, we seek our bread further and further west. In Germany and Eastern Europe, the same decline in fertility is also to be witnessed, the cause being everywhere the same—the continued extraction from the soil of the leements of productiveness, without the smallest attempt at their restoration. Owing to the abundance of land with which we have so far been blessed, our farmers have rarely taken the trouble to manure their fields. They found them virgin soil; they get all they can out of them, and when they are exhausted, abandon them. In Europe, and especially in England, stern necessity has compelled the cultivator to take some pains to restore to the soil some portion of the vitality of which his crops each year deprive it. The ordinary farm-yard manure was long relied on for this purpose; but even that at last ceased to produce the required effect. Guano then made its appearance; but according to Liebig the supply of guano cannot last much longer, and this once exhausted, some means must be devised of supplying its place, or the people of the civilized world will soon find themselves face to face with a deficiency of bread—a crisis which, if it did not cause absolute famine, would certainly entail a descent to a much lower standard of living, and corresponding moral degradation.

The formula on which all this gloomy foreboding is based is a very simple one. To render and keep soil productive, the elements which are withdrawn in the harvests must be restored. The ordinary barnyard manures, where they are used, partially suffice for this purpose; but only partially. They leave every year a deficiency, and this deficiency, multiplied by fifty or one hundred, gives in its final result total barrenness. Guano would supply the need, if the supply were inexhaustible. As it is not so, Liebig insists that we must fall back on the sewerage of towns. These great consumers of food, which modern civilization is creating and developing on such an enormous scale, must be made to keep up the fertility of the surrounding country by discharging their sewerage over the fields, instead of filling the harbors and choking the rivers with it, and allowing it to run to waste. The mechanical and engineering difficulties of such an enterprise are no doubt great, but not too great for modern science to overcome, if the farmers were once made sensible of the consequences of perseverance in the existing mode of cultivation.

The political aspects of this question are by no means the least interesting and important. The growth and prosperity of a nation are now, and will always continue to be, largely dependent on its power of feeding itself. When that power once leaves it, its greatness is no longer in its own hands. Rome was invincible as long as her bread was the product of Italian farms. When she began to draw her supplies from Sicily and Africa, she was already on the downward path, and she involved her granaries in the same ruin as she suffered herself.

12.C: COLLECTIVE ACTION PROBLEMS AND THE ENVIRONMENT

Different kinds of synthesizing devices may be used to combine disparate pieces of information into a whole that is meaningful for global politics. The precise device deployed depends not only on the information and context at hand but also on how much practice one has in synthesizing information, and how broad and deep is one's existing knowledge of global politics. It is unlikely that a single synthesizing device will be able to address every element of every excerpt or situation. As with other analytical skills discussed in previous chapters, synthesizing information from excerpts requires brainstorming ideas and strategies and making hard decisions about how to narrow the analytical focus (for example, refer to chapter 9). Bloom's seminal book concerning synthesis suggests three possible products or outcomes of a synthesizing practice: "a unique communication" intended to inform or educate, "a plan or proposed set of operations" that result in an outcome, or "a set of abstract relations" that bind disparate knowledge together.[8] It is the third synthesizing practice, that is, connecting knowledge drawn from several sources and contexts by using a set of related (abstract) concepts and ideas, on which this section focuses. Consider the following quote in which Bloom describes the process:

> In the third sub-category, one may view the product of synthesis as primarily a set of abstract relations. The set of relations may be derived from an analysis of certain observed phenomena, in which case they may be considered possible relations, or hypotheses to be tested; or they may be derived from an analysis of relations among propositions or other symbolic representations, in which case they may be considered necessary relations, or deductions.

Consider the following possible synthesizing techniques and the questions one might ask and research if used to synthesize, for instance, the primary documents in Section 12.B:

- *Timeframe*: the historical time period in which the excerpts were written can serve as a synthesizing device, involving analysis of all three texts in light of the dynamics, cultures, politics, scientific knowledge, etc., of their time periods. For example, all three were written in the mid-nineteenth century during the industrial revolution which would account for the delayed but urgent response to environmental damage.
- *Geography*: The synthesis could focus on the geographic locale and local landscape, respective access to resources, or geopolitical significance of specific dynamics or events. For instance, all three primary documents originate from the West, specifically from United Kingdom (UK) and the United States (US). These two countries have traditionally had expansive access to resources and technologies for turning those resources into industrialized products. Both countries were further blessed with arable farmland and a temperate climate conducive to production of staple cereal crops (like wheat), and early industrial development in each relied extensively on increasing agricultural production.
- *Written format*: The format in which ideas are presented can provide information for synthesis. The three primary documents in Section 12.B were initially created in paper form to be distributed in order to raise awareness and call for action around environmental goods like land/soil and water.
- *Implicit Assumptions*: The synthesizing device could be a focus on the implicit assumptions seemingly made by the authors. As one example, all of the primary documents in Section 12.B take a similar stance on the relationship between humanity and nature, assuming that humanity justifiably dominates the natural world via land ownership and resource use (including pollution), among other modes of domination.
- *Central processes or dynamics*: The synthesizing device could focus on crucial processes and dynamics, for example, processes of urbanization or depeasantization, dynamics of early industrialization, or processes of environmental degradation.
- *Single conceptual framework*: A conceptual framework or use of key concepts provide a way to link the three excerpts together, for example, deploying *power*, *inequality*, or *capitalism* as conceptual lenses through which to consider the significance of and relationships between the primary sources.

As the focus narrows according to the specific synthesizing device selected, it is important to be aware of one's personal perspective (based on interests and positions, cultural milieu and education, among other factors) because it impacts and affects the way the synthesis is conducted and the final interpretation or message provided. Further, keep in mind the historical and political context in which one is learning or conducting an analysis and synthesis compared to the context of the situation under study (which may be very different and therefore account for widely varying interpretations).

Synthesis Using a Concept: Collective Action Problems

Using a concept as a synthesizing device requires an excellent grasp of that concept and the associated tools and techniques of analysis and application that go along with it, including how the concept has been applied before by other thinkers and scholars. The following provides an overview of the concept of *collective action problems* and then guides learners through the process of using it as a synthesizing device for the three excerpts in this chapter.

Identify the Main Concept or Problem

The first step in synthesis using a key concept is to define and identify the components of the concept chosen, recording information in detailed notes while conducting the necessary research. Consider the basic contours of the *collective action problem*: working together for the *collective*, or common, good sometimes makes everyone better off.[9] But there are many reasons—or *disincentives*—that may discourage individuals from collaborating to achieve the collective good.[10] Indeed, most collective action problems involve ethical and moral considerations and situations where individuals must sacrifice; that is, they bear a cost or a risk, in order to contribute to the common good.[11] For example, maybe the common good is beneficial in the long term but requires short-term sacrifices (the tradeoff is mismatched in time) and inspires the question: *Why sacrifice today for some distant benefit?* Maybe the common good is more beneficial to some than to others, and more costly for some than for others (costs and payouts are unequally distributed and/or disproportionate). People may ask: *Why should I shoulder such a large burden for something that only benefits me a little bit?* Maybe members of the collective do not trust one another to make the necessary sacrifice, and this uncertainty encourages them to *defect* rather than to cooperate: *Why should I sacrifice if my neighbor is just going to* free ride *on my efforts?*[12]

The basic, if oversimplified, model of a collective action problem to which international relations scholars often refer is called the *Prisoner's Dilemma*.[13] As an analogy, it involves two criminals who have been arrested for a crime, and who are being questioned separately by investigators. The prisoners cannot communicate with each other and must make a decision about how much they will reveal about the crime based on limited knowledge of what the other prisoner will do. Therefore, they may reveal information that gives them a suboptimal outcome: one prisoner may reveal that they committed the crime while the other stays silent, meaning they both might have to serve time in prison whereas if they both remained silent they could possibly be freed. Applied to global politics, the idea is that countries and their leaders are consistently required to make important and life-changing (or life-threatening) decisions based on limited or incomplete knowledge and thereby produce suboptimal results for their country and people and for the world.

Identify the Context of a Concept

After identifying the definitions and associated elements of a concept, the next step is to understand the context, in this case, when and where do *collective action problems* arise? Does the problem differ from place to place, and over time? In a *collective action problem*, the common good at issue can and does vary from context to context. Collective action problems exist at most *levels of analysis*, from households all the way up to the global level (if alien life is ever discovered in the universe, we will probably see galactic or universal collective action problems too). Indeed, international organizations were created largely to support state governments in collaborating and coordinating to address collective action problems; recall from chapter 4 that the United Nations (UN) was created as a collective security organization to assist states in collaborating to address state aggressive behavior and other existential threats.

For example, achieving *world peace* is a collective action problem. Peace would be good for everyone, eliminating violence, bloodshed, and suffering. But peace requires countries to sacrifice, to trust one another, and to put down their weapons.[14] A contemporary example involves worldwide and country-specific attempts at nuclear non-proliferation and nuclear disarmament. In the former, six countries negotiated with Iran to try to encourage Iran to limit its nuclear capacity and technology which resulted in the *Joint Comprehensive Plan of Action* (JCPA). In order to sign the agreement Iran had to trust that the US (or perhaps more to the point, Israel) would not attack them in the future, especially with the use of nuclear weapons. Unfortunately for Iran and the goal of nuclear non-proliferation, as of the time of this writing the US backed out of the JCPA under the Trump administration, putting a halt on the monitoring agreements.

Achieving world peace through nuclear disarmament, as the *Strategic Arms Limitation Treaty I and II* (SALT) and the *Strategic Arms Reduction Treaty* (START) attempted to do between the US and the Union of Soviet Socialist Republics (USSR) and later Russia, would require country agreement and monitoring, as well as major arms manufacturers to cease their businesses, resulting in lost profits and revenues for corporations and governments alike. It might be pretty cheap for, say, Haiti to sign an agreement that requires them to stop manufacturing weapons for export abroad, but for Russia to sign such an agreement, they would have to give up an industry that represents about 20 percent of global arms sales and a significant portion of Russian employment and Gross Domestic Product (GDP).[15] The example shows the moral dilemma states face when making such decisions: why would Russia, for example, give up their arms manufacturing capability if they suspect that Germany, another major global arms supplier, will not?

Investigate Other Instances of Concept Application or Synthesis with Relevant Context

For the next step in conducting a synthesis using a concept, it is critical to think about when and where and how the concept has been used in the past to synthesize information (by scholars, practitioners, or others). In this case, the classic environmental example of a collective action problem is called the *Tragedy of the Commons* (biologist Garett Hardin coined the term in the 1960s).[16] Based on an analysis of eighteenth-century England, Hardin told a story about farmers and sheep, by way of analogy, paraphrased as follows: Imagine we're in medieval England, and most people in rural areas farm for a living. Many of them raise sheep for wool and meat. They graze their sheep on common pasture, lands that are open and available for anyone to use whenever they wish. Each individual farmer, wanting enough meat and wool to support their families (reasonable enough, no?), brings as many sheep as possible to graze on the commons. Other farmers do the same. The population of sheep and people continue to grow, and more and more farmers bring more and more sheep down to graze.[17]

Eventually, all the grass is eaten, and the soil is depleted, the consequence of constant grazing by too many sheep. The commons are so degraded that none of the farmers can use the pasture to graze. The sheep have nothing to eat. The sheep, hungrier by the minute, are quickly slaughtered for one last batch of meat. There are no more sheep. The farmers now have no wool and no meat. They suffer. The moral of the story? In the absence of intervention, individuals looking out for their own interests will degrade and destroy common resources.

Hardin argues that there are two basic political mechanisms available to help solve the tragedy. First, the market-based route: divide the common lands into smaller parcels that are owned and managed privately by individuals. This way, each farmer uses only their own land to graze their own sheep. If they fail to care for the land, they suffer alone. If they care for it well, they prosper. Second, the government management route: Keep the common pasture common but appoint or elect a manager to govern grazing on the common pasture. The manager would set up a schedule for each farmer and regulate the number of sheep that can graze, thus ensuring that there is enough land for others to graze their sheep and that the commons is not degraded over time. Of course, there are other ways to solve this problem, beyond those Hardin discusses. Can you think of any? How else could a bunch of shepherds grazing their herd on common land ensure that all people, sheep, and the land itself are taken care of well? In other words, how else could we preserve the commons?

Before moving on to the next section in which concepts of *collective action problems* and specifically *the tragedy of the commons* is used to show how to perform a synthesis on the primary documents in this chapter, it is a good idea to think critically about how the *tragedy of the commons* story portrays *human nature* so as to interpret the impact and reason for the synthesis.[18] Hardin's argument has been subjected to scrutiny over the years, with many arguing that his story is really just a (self-serving) myth that provides little evidence to support the claim that resources held in common will necessarily be misused and abused.[19] Also important for critical reflection is the historical and political context of Hardin's original article—it was written during a time of global panic over population growth, echoing similar panic by Thomas Malthus in the late eighteenth century.[20]

Critics of Hardin's and Malthus' arguments about the fears of overpopulation focus in part on the global politics of race, gender, class, and imperialism, and provide important perspectives on Hardin's assumptions about humans (especially people in poverty) and the implications of his argument for marginalized and oppressed communities around the world. (Hardin's broader argument presented the *tragedy of the commons* as an analogy for what he saw happening in countries in the global South at the time of his writing in 1968.) As Raj Patel puts it in his criticism of Malthus' concerns about population growth outstripping the global resource base (in this case, the food supply): "Through this logic the poor were reduced to three basic organs: growling stomachs, clenched fists and insatiable genitalia."[21] This kind of context is of major importance for learners because it usefully complicates seemingly simple concepts and encourages nuanced and careful applications that take into account the ethical and historical baggage such concepts often trail with them.

Performing a Synthesis of the Excerpts Using the Collective Action Problem Concept

The following steps are useful for completing a synthesis of the primary sources in Section 12.B using the concept of *collection action problems*. As with previous chapters, whenever you come across a bullet point with a question, take time to try to answer it yourself and then read on to compare your work with what is provided in the text.

- First, consider how each of the excerpts refers to *common good/s* and whether it references a problem like the *collective action problem* described above. Which common goods does each of the excerpts discuss?

The first excerpt, from the *1845 British Inclosure Act* (hereafter *1845 Act*), is a historical example of one of various possible political resolutions for tragedies of the commons, that is, land privatization. The *1845 Act* uses the language related to the concept of *collective action problems*, the *common good*, but means it in a historically specific way: in the first sentence, "Commons and Lands held in common, the Exchange Lands, and the Division of intermixed Lands" references how land was managed in nineteenth century British law. The excerpt continues to refer to the *common good* of land: "all gated and stinted pastures," and "soil" is referenced several times. It appears, then, that the Inclosure Act is itself a referent point for the *collective action problem* described above, especially when considering Hardin's analysis. In addition to the *1845 Act*, the British Parliament passed a long series of Inclosure (another spelling of the term is enclosure) Acts from the seventeenth to the nineteenth century.

The second excerpt, Michael Faraday's 1855 letter to the editor of the *London Times,* speaks to the degradation of a different kind of *common good*, in this case, the Thames River. Significantly, most people did not have easy access to clean running water in the nineteenth century—this means they had to find a river in which to bathe, draw water for drinking and cooking, and clean their clothes. How would the conditions of the Thames affect people who relied on the water for drinking and cleaning needs? How would the condition of the Thames affect sailors? Would the conditions affect people in the countryside?

Similarly, the third excerpt, the 1860 editorial from *The New York Times*, speaks simultaneously to degradation of land (soil quality), and rivers and oceans (contaminated by sewage). Notice the use of the term *guano*—in the context of the nineteenth century, *guano* was fertilizer. Some important questions that learners might consider researching are as follows: What is guano and where did it come from? Who harvested it and who transported it? What affect did guano production have, according to the letter, on land, river, and ocean conditions?

- *Who* is using the common goods and for what purpose?

Such a determination allows for identification of who has access and who is being deprived of the *common good* in question, and helps bring to light matters of interests and power. We might identify who benefits (*cui bono?*) and who doesn't, either because they are identified in the text or through additional research. For example, the first excerpt identifies land held in common and is specifically referencing *commons* according to British law in the nineteenth century. A reader might not be able to tell from the text *who* owns the land, but they can get a sense of it, especially with some more research about the particular *1845 Act* which was part of a series of inclosure acts meant to parcel the land into smaller lots that were individually owned and no longer subject to land regulation as *commons*. Who benefited and who suffered from the inclosure acts? Do you think they were a good idea?

- Third, determine rules and regulations (or norms) referenced in the excerpt about the *common good/s* identified. Do rules, regulations, or norms exist that protect the common good; in what ways do they protect? Is there a lack of protection of the common good?

The answer to these questions is quite noticeable in all three texts, for all three texts appear to be addressing the fact that there are no rules, regulations, or norms surrounding the use of the common goods identified, and because of the lack of rules, regulations, and norms, the common goods are being overused, misused, depleted, or destroyed in some way. Note the ways the common goods are being misused and what the authors suggest as ways to fix the problems that arise (of course, the first document, the *1845 Act*, is itself a solution to an identified problem).[22]

- Finally, use the information gleaned in the textual analysis and answers to questions in the sets above to come up with an interpretation, argument, or theory that synthesizes the main ideas of the primary documents under study. What kind of synthesized argument can be made here? How, exactly, does the concept of *collective action problem* help join the excerpts together?

As an initial answer, for instance, one could make an argument that the three excerpts all speak to and illuminate the important set of *collective action problems* associated with common use of land and river resources, revealing a series of tragedies of the commons. One could also make an argument that the three excerpts show how lack of rules, regulations, and norms around the collective use of land and river resources may result in the degradation of those resources. In order to back up one's arguments refer to quotes, examples, data, and details from the excerpts. Arguments work to synthesize information from the primary sources into a new and original whole. What other arguments are possible here? How might different arguments emerge by using different synthesizing techniques like those described in the beginning of this section?

12.D RECOMMENDED READINGS ON COLLECTIVE ACTION PROBLEMS AND THE ENVIRONMENT

Cohen, Youssef. *Radicals, Reformers, Reactionaries: The Prisoner's Dilemma and the Collapse of Democracy in Latin America.* Chicago: University of Chicago Press, 1994.

Hardin, Garrett. "The Tragedy of the Commons." *Science* 162, no. 3859 (December 13, 1968): 1243–48.
Olson, Mancur. *The Logic of Collective Action*. Cambridge, MA: Harvard University Press, 1965.
Ostrom, Elinor. *Governing the Commons: The Evolution of Institutions for Collective Action. The Political Economy of Institutions and Decisions*. Cambridge: Cambridge University Press, 1990, reprinted 2015.
Sasser, Jade. S. *On Infertile Ground: Population Control and Women's Rights in the Era of Climate Change*. New York: NYU Press, 2018.
United Nations. *The Rio Declaration on Environment and Development*. Geneva: United Nations.

NOTES

1. Bloom's original taxonomy differs from Anderson. We agree with Anderson's update but think that *synthesis* should be kept as a category separated from *create* because synthesis is the act of pulling together and adding new knowledge. Consider this quote from Bloom: "However, it should be emphasized that [synthesis] is not completely free creative expression since generally the student is expected to work within the limits set by particular problems, materials, or some theoretical and methodological framework." Benjamin Bloom, *Taxonomy of Educational Objectives: The Classification of Educational Goals, Handbook I: Cognitive Domain* (New York: Longmans, Green, 1956), 162.

2. Anders Ericsson and Robert Pool, *Peak: Secrets from the New Science of Expertise*, 1st Mariner Books ed. (Boston: Mariner Books/Houghton Mifflin Harcourt, 2017), 99.

3. Student performance on exams, for example, is negatively correlated with students' physical proximity to their cell phones, according to recent research. E.g., Jeffery H. Kuzenkoff, "The Impact of Mobile Phone Usage on Student Learning," *Communication Education* 62, no. 3 (February 2013): 233–52.

4. Barry J. Zimmerman, "Becoming a Self-Regulated Learner: An Overview," *Theory into Practice* 41, no. 2 (2002): 64–72. Zimmerman's review of the scholarly literature notes, "Interestingly, simply asking students to self-record some aspect of their learning, such as the completion of assignments, often led to 'spontaneous' improvements in functioning. . . . These effects, termed reactivity in the scientific literature, implied that students' metacognitive (i.e., self) awareness of particular aspects of their functioning could enhance their self-control" (65).

5. United Kingdom, "Inclosure Act 1845," legislation.gov.uk, accessed July 24, 2020 (all rights reserved, reproduced based on fair use doctrine from Section 107 of US Copyright Law), https://www.legislation.gov.uk/ukpga/Vict/8-9/118.

6. Michael Faraday, "The State of the Thames," *Times* (July 9, 1855), 8 (all rights reserved, reproduced based on fair use doctrine from Section 107 of US Copyright Law).

7. "Dearth of Food-A Startling View," *New York Times*, January 5, 1860. Digital Archive Accessed June 3, 2020 (all rights reserved, reproduced based on fair use

doctrine from Section 107 of US Copyright Law), https://www.nytimes.com/1860/01/05/archives/dearth-of-fooda-startling-view.html.

8. Bloom, *Taxonomy of Educational Objectives*, 163–64.

9. E.g., Russell Hardin, *Collective Action. Resources for the Future* (Baltimore: Published for Resources for the Future by the Johns Hopkins University Press, 1982); Jeffery Fields, ed. *State Behavior and the Nuclear Nonproliferation Regime* (Athens, GA: University of Georgia, 2014); Marcello Basili, Franzini, Mauricio, and Vercelli, Alesandro, eds. *Environment, Inequality and Collective Action* (London: Routledge, 2006).

10. An important example is the problem of human impact on global warming and environmental degradation: people and countries support continued industrialization practices that destroy the environment but are unable to collaborate on agreeing what to do to stop the effects. Rachel Carsen, *Silent Spring* (Boston: Houghton Mifflin Company, 1962).

11. E.g., Dylan Kissane and Alexandru Volacu, eds. *Modern Dilemmas: Understanding Collective Action in the 21st Century* (Stuttgart, Germany: Ibidem-Verlag, 2015); Mancur Olson, *The Logic of Collective Action* (Cambridge, MA: Harvard University Press, 1965).

12. A *free rider* is someone who lets *other* people sacrifice for the common good, enjoying the benefits of the collective effort without paying any of the costs.

13. Martin Peterson, ed. *The Prisoner's Dilemma* (Cambridge: Cambridge University Press, 2015).

14. Immanuel Kant, for example, argued that a true and lasting peace could only be obtained if countries maintained their armies. Immanuel Kant, *Perpetual Peace*, Project Gutenburg, Produced by Turgut Dincer, Ramon Pajares Box, https://www.gutenberg.org/files/50922/50922-h/50922-h.htm.

15. Leonid Bershidsky, "Trump Is Winning, Putin's Losing in Global Arms Trade," *Bloomberg*, March 12, 2019, https://www.bloomberg.com/opinion/articles/2019-03-12/u-s-is-no-1-in-arms-sales-as-russia-loses-market-share.

16. Garrett Hardin, "The Tragedy of the Commons," *Science* 162, no. 3859 (December 13, 1968): 1243–48.

17. Hardin, "The Tragedy of the Commons."

18. A good source for beginning to think about human nature is Glenn Tinder, *Political Thinking: The Perennial Questions*, 6th ed. (New York: Longman Classics Series, 2004).

19. E.g., David Bollier, *Think Like a Commoner: A Short Introduction to the Life of the Commons* (Gabrioloa Island, British Colombia: New Society Publishers, 2014).

20. For example, Paul Ehrlich published a book in 1968 that had people worried that the population would exceed the earth's ability to sustain it: Paul R. Ehrlich, *The Population Bomb* (A Sierra Club-Ballantine Book. New York: Ballantine Books, 1968). Thomas Malthus had the same concerns two centuries earlier: Thomas Malthus, *An Essay on the Principle of Population as It Affects the Future Improvement of Society* (London: John J. Johnson in St. Paul's Churchyard, 1798). See also, Robert L. Heilbroner, *The Worldly Philosophers*, 7th ed. (London: Penguin, 2000), 75–104.

21. Raj Patel, *Stuffed and Starved* (Hoboken, NJ: Melville House, 2007).

22. In the Marxist tradition, the *myth* of the commons is engaged directly, with many scholars arguing that the major goal of enclosure was not to preserve common resources but rather to encourage peasants to move out of the countryside into the cities where they could work in factories (depeasantization), and also making way for agricultural mechanization (industrialization) in rural areas. See, e.g., Karl Marx, *Das Kapital, A Critique of Political Economy, Volume I* (Chicago: H. Regnery, 1959).

Chapter 13

Determining Value
Evaluation and Assessment

A dominant topic in international relations (IR) scholarship and foreign policy is that of human rights. Human rights come up frequently in IR discussions as an international *regime*, a set of rules and standards of behavior that states follow in the way they treat human beings within their territories.[1] The *human rights regime* is both philosophical and practical. It is philosophical in that it is built on theories about what it means to be human (and how humans should be treated). It is practical in that human rights are *codified*, or written formally, in international law, defined and delimited in many bilateral and multilateral documents, conventions, and treaties that hold state governments accountable for following the rules and standards of behavior set down in them. The human rights regime is also *hegemonic* in that it has dominated IR discussions since World War II (WWII) on how to protect and provide for human beings.

Section 13.A reviews one final technique that learners of global politics may find useful as they gain knowledge and expertise in global politics, that of becoming their own teacher and upending the student-teacher dichotomy. Section 13.C provides learners with an example of how to conduct the higher order skill of evaluation by evaluating the human rights regime utilizing the Universal Declaration of Human Rights (UDHR) that is included in Section 13.B. The UDHR, included in its entirety, was an attempt to make human rights binding in international law in the twentieth century and, more than six decades later, remains the foundational document that lists rationales and the set of rights that constitute how humans should be treated and how state governments should protect, provide, and not deprive humans of their human rights.[2] Finally, Section 13.D provides suggestions for further reading on the subject of human rights.

13.A: BE A TEACHER!

When you are learning a new topic, being a teacher, and not only a student, allows you to practice using—and ultimately master—knowledge and skills. As reviewed in the introductory chapter, the philosophical foundation of this book, *learner-centered teaching* (LCT), argues that learning and teaching is a dynamic dialogue between teacher-students and student-teachers. LCT is not just an ethical position; acting like a teacher is also a highly effective learning and studying habit. When a learner tries to teach someone else, they develop a stronger command of the material and are also able to better communicate what they have learned to others. This is true even if teaching oneself by talking out loud when studying and trying to explain concepts and ideas.

Teachers who use learner-centered teaching pedagogy engage almost every technique and habit of mind discussed in this book, from remembering and describing to analyzing, synthesizing, and evaluating. Teachers constantly recall information and knowledge and apply it to different contexts, developing multiple ways of explaining the same concept or dynamic, so as to answer questions and clarify meaning. Stepping into the role of teacher by attempting to teach the material to others in a study group, for example, quickly reveals which parts of the material one does *not* know well and which parts are difficult to communicate. Thus, take this suggestion as a challenge and use the tools and techniques you have learned in this book to practice being a teacher yourself.

13.B: PRIMARY SOURCE ON HUMAN RIGHTS

Universal Declaration of Human Rights, United Nations (1948)[3]

> Whereas recognition of the inherent dignity and of the equal and inalienable rights of all members of the human family is the foundation of freedom, justice and peace in the world,
>
> Whereas disregard and contempt for human rights have resulted in barbarous acts which have outraged the conscience of mankind, and the advent of a world in which human beings shall enjoy freedom of speech and belief and freedom from fear and want has been proclaimed as the highest aspiration of the common people,
>
> Whereas it is essential, if man is not to be compelled to have recourse, as a last resort, to rebellion against tyranny and oppression, that human rights should be protected by the rule of law,
>
> Whereas it is essential to promote the development of friendly relations between nations,

Whereas the peoples of the United Nations have in the Charter reaffirmed their faith in fundamental human rights, in the dignity and worth of the human person and in the equal rights of men and women and have determined to promote social progress and better standards of life in larger freedom,

Whereas Member States have pledged themselves to achieve, in co-operation with the United Nations, the promotion of universal respect for and observance of human rights and fundamental freedoms,

Whereas a common understanding of these rights and freedoms is of the greatest importance for the full realization of this pledge,

Now, Therefore THE GENERAL ASSEMBLY proclaims THIS UNIVERSAL DECLARATION OF HUMAN RIGHTS as a common standard of achievement for all peoples and all nations, to the end that every individual and every organ of society, keeping this Declaration constantly in mind, shall strive by teaching and education to promote respect for these rights and freedoms and by progressive measures, national and international, to secure their universal and effective recognition and observance, both among the peoples of Member States themselves and among the peoples of territories under their jurisdiction.

Article 1. All human beings are born free and equal in dignity and rights. They are endowed with reason and conscience and should act towards one another in a spirit of brotherhood.

Article 2. Everyone is entitled to all the rights and freedoms set forth in this Declaration, without distinction of any kind, such as race, colour, sex, language, religion, political or other opinion, national or social origin, property, birth or other status. Furthermore, no distinction shall be made on the basis of the political, jurisdictional or international status of the country or territory to which a person belongs, whether it be independent, trust, non-self-governing or under any other limitation of sovereignty.

Article 3. Everyone has the right to life, liberty and security of person.

Article 4. No one shall be held in slavery or servitude; slavery and the slave trade shall be prohibited in all their forms.

Article 5. No one shall be subjected to torture or to cruel, inhuman or degrading treatment or punishment.

Article 6. Everyone has the right to recognition everywhere as a person before the law.

Article 7. All are equal before the law and are entitled without any discrimination to equal protection of the law. All are entitled to equal protection against any discrimination in violation of this Declaration and against any incitement to such discrimination.

Article 8. Everyone has the right to an effective remedy by the competent national tribunals for acts violating the fundamental rights granted him by the constitution or by law.

Article 9. No one shall be subjected to arbitrary arrest, detention or exile.

Article 10. Everyone is entitled in full equality to a fair and public hearing by an independent and impartial tribunal, in the determination of his rights and obligations and of any criminal charge against him.

Article 11. (1) Everyone charged with a penal offence has the right to be presumed innocent until proved guilty according to law in a public trial at which he has had all the guarantees necessary for his defence. (2) No one shall be held guilty of any penal offence on account of any act or omission which did not constitute a penal offence, under national or international law, at the time when it was committed. Nor shall a heavier penalty be imposed than the one that was applicable at the time the penal offence was committed.

Article 12. No one shall be subjected to arbitrary interference with his privacy, family, home or correspondence, nor to attacks upon his honour and reputation. Everyone has the right to the protection of the law against such interference or attacks.

Article 13. (1) Everyone has the right to freedom of movement and residence within the borders of each state. (2) Everyone has the right to leave any country, including his own, and to return to his country.

Article 14. (1) Everyone has the right to seek and to enjoy in other countries asylum from persecution. (2) This right may not be invoked in the case of prosecutions genuinely arising from non-political crimes or from acts contrary to the purposes and principles of the United Nations.

Article 15. (1) Everyone has the right to a nationality. (2) No one shall be arbitrarily deprived of his nationality nor denied the right to change his nationality.

Article 16. (1) Men and women of full age, without any limitation due to race, nationality or religion, have the right to marry and to found a family. They are entitled to equal rights as to marriage, during marriage and at its dissolution. (2) Marriage shall be entered into only with the free and full consent of the intending spouses. (3) The family is the natural and fundamental group unit of society and is entitled to protection by society and the State.

Article 17. (1) Everyone has the right to own property alone as well as in association with others. (2) No one shall be arbitrarily deprived of his property.

Article 18. Everyone has the right to freedom of thought, conscience and religion; this right includes freedom to change his religion or belief, and freedom, either alone or in community with others and in public or private, to manifest his religion or belief in teaching, practice, worship and observance.

Article 19. Everyone has the right to freedom of opinion and expression; this right includes freedom to hold opinions without interference and to seek, receive and impart information and ideas through any media and regardless of frontiers.

Article 20. (1) Everyone has the right to freedom of peaceful assembly and association. (2) No one may be compelled to belong to an association.

Article 21. (1) Everyone has the right to take part in the government of his country, directly or through freely chosen representatives. (2) Everyone has the right of equal access to public service in his country. (3) The will of the people shall be the basis of the authority of government; this will shall be expressed in periodic and genuine elections which shall be by universal and equal suffrage and shall be held by secret vote or by equivalent free voting procedures.

Article 22. Everyone, as a member of society, has the right to social security and is entitled to realization, through national effort and international co-operation and in accordance with the organization and resources of each State, of the economic, social and cultural rights indispensable for his dignity and the free development of his personality.

Article 23. (1) Everyone has the right to work, to free choice of employment, to just and favourable conditions of work and to protection against unemployment. (2) Everyone, without any discrimination, has the right to equal pay for equal work. (3) Everyone who works has the right to just and favourable remuneration ensuring for himself and his family an existence worthy of human dignity, and supplemented, if necessary, by other means of social protection. (4) Everyone has the right to form and to join trade unions for the protection of his interests.

Article 24. Everyone has the right to rest and leisure, including reasonable limitation of working hours and periodic holidays with pay.

Article 25. (1) Everyone has the right to a standard of living adequate for the health and well-being of himself and of his family, including food, clothing, housing and medical care and necessary social services, and the right to security in the event of unemployment, sickness, disability, widowhood, old age or other lack of livelihood in circumstances beyond his control. (2) Motherhood and childhood are entitled to special care and assistance. All children, whether born in or out of wedlock, shall enjoy the same social protection.

Article 26. (1) Everyone has the right to education. Education shall be free, at least in the elementary and fundamental stages. Elementary education shall be compulsory. Technical and professional education shall be made generally available and higher education shall be equally accessible to all on the basis of merit. (2) Education shall be directed to the full development of the human personality and to the strengthening of respect for human rights and fundamental freedoms. It shall promote understanding, tolerance and friendship among all nations, racial or religious groups, and shall further the activities of the United Nations for the maintenance of peace. (3) Parents have a prior right to choose the kind of education that shall be given to their children.

Article 27. (1) Everyone has the right freely to participate in the cultural life of the community, to enjoy the arts and to share in scientific advancement and its benefits. (2) Everyone has the right to the protection of the moral and material interests resulting from any scientific, literary or artistic production of which he is the author.

Article 28. Everyone is entitled to a social and international order in which the rights and freedoms set forth in this Declaration can be fully realized.

Article 29. (1) Everyone has duties to the community in which alone the free and full development of his personality is possible. (2) In the exercise of his rights and freedoms, everyone shall be subject only to such limitations as are determined by law solely for the purpose of securing due recognition and respect for the rights and freedoms of others and of meeting the just requirements of morality, public order and the general welfare in a democratic society. (3) These rights and freedoms may in no case be exercised contrary to the purposes and principles of the United Nations.

Article 30. Nothing in this Declaration may be interpreted as implying for any State, group or person any right to engage in any activity or to perform any act aimed at the destruction of any of the rights and freedoms set forth herein.

13.C: THE INTERNATIONAL HUMAN RIGHTS REGIME

This chapter discusses how to evaluate a topic, regime, policy, institution, program, and/or outcome in global politics, determining its value (importance, usefulness, and worth) based on internal logic and/or external performance standards. The skill of *evaluation* is a higher-order one, not only because it requires an excellent grasp of the topic at hand in order to make a determination of value but also because evaluating requires one to make judgments about what standards to apply and how to logically (and consciously and critically) analyze those judgments from multiple perspectives, with close attention to the assumptions entailed in making them. The evaluation below is different from how one might practice evaluation on a day-to-day basis based on egocentric[4] evaluation standards (when ordering coffee or choosing a movie to watch, for example). Rather, the evaluation is based on internal logic or external performance standards from multiple perspectives.

Evaluating builds off the foundational skills of remembering, understanding, applying, analyzing, and synthesizing. It is essential that learners practice evaluation skills with advanced knowledge of answers to the basic questions about a situation under study. Without building that knowledge first, any evaluation will likely be fraught with errors and miscalculations. Before moving on to evaluate the human rights regime, challenge the knowledge and skills you have developed thus far in your studies and answer the following questions.

Basic Knowledge Necessary for Evaluating Human Rights:

- *Who* is the author/s of the UDHR, *who* is the UDHR's audience, and *who* has been involved in protecting and implementing the UDHR?
  - The document included many perspectives and voices and was authored by a group of people in the UDHR Drafting Committee appointed by the UN Commission on Human Rights. To start research on this question, then, consider the following people who were influential in writing the text and find out about their backgrounds, philosophies, education, cultural values, etc.: René Cassin, P.C. Chang, Eleanor Roosevelt, Charles Malik, and John Humphrey, among others.
- *What* key concepts or political dynamics and relationships are revealed in the UDHR and important in the human rights regime?
  - The following key concepts, derived from a close reading of the UDHR and commentaries, are worth investigating further: *human rights, inalienable, dignity, freedom, justice, peace, tyranny, rule of law*, and *fundamental freedoms*.
- *When* and *where* did human rights emerge and what historical precedents or contextual situations shaped the way the UDHR was written?
  - Start with a review of WWII and the Holocaust (the atrocities committed were the inspiration for creating the UDHR) and then consider historical precedents, like the writings of Plato and Aristotle on justice, Hammurabi's Code, Kautilya's writings, the *Magna Carta* (1215), the *English Bill of Rights* (1689), the *United States Declaration of Independence* (1776), or the *French Declaration of the Rights of Man and Citizen* (1789).
- *Application, Analysis, Synthesis.*
  - How does the human rights regime provide information or ways of assessing other global politics issues or events?
  - What are the component parts of the human rights regime (what institutions, treaties, international agreements, advocacy groups, etc., make up the whole and what are the disparate functions and influence of each)?
  - How do the component parts of the human rights regime combine to form a whole and in what ways are human rights protected, provided, and not deprived around the world? Alternately, in what ways are human rights deprived or ignored?

In addition to gathering basic knowledge and understanding of the UDHR and human rights regime, as outlined in the questions above, it is essential to identify the main ideas in the UDHR, analyze those ideas by breaking them up and identifying and assessing the components, or various parts, of the human rights regime (for a review of identifying main ideas and applying analytical tools, see chapters 8–11). In the case of the human rights regime, the UN did not cease its efforts to protect the rights of individual humans with the UDHR. Indeed, when the UDHR was signed, the UN General Assembly (UNGA) charged the Human Rights Commission to continue its work to create more binding documents that would become part of international law, thereby better holding states accountable. Over the subsequent decades, the UNGA approved eighteen human rights documents, each with their own particular supporters, written to address specific injustices experienced by human beings in specific communities, countries, and regions.

- The eighteen international documents are called the "core instruments" of human rights. Who wrote or sponsored each convention? Why were they sponsored? Was something occurring in the world at the time that would incentivize the writing and passing of each convention? How many states have signed and ratified each of the conventions?[5]

Evaluating Human Rights based on Internal Logic or External Criteria

Evaluation provides an opportunity for learners to decide for themselves what they think about a situation under study and to justify their position based on the evidence and individual interpretation of that evidence. There are a multitude of logical reasons, standards, and criteria one might use to evaluate in any context. The most important part of evaluating is being open and honest about one's criteria, and constantly questioning one's own assumptions, perspectives and biases, while being considerate of, and even empathetic of, other points of view (empathizing does not necessarily mean agreement). Evaluation can be done by assessing the internal logic or using external criteria, as listed below and conducted in the following section. The list represents different categories of evaluative criteria that one could apply to thinking about human rights but is not an exhaustive list.

- Evaluating Internal Logic
  - Context Clues and Assumptions
  - Internal Logic and Consistency
  - Internal Contradictions or Errors
- Evaluating Using External Performance Standards or Criteria
  - Means versus Ends Rationality
  - Efficiency and Effectiveness

Evaluating Internal Logic

One method of evaluating is to assess the internal logic of a concept, argument, or situation under study. When evaluating *internal logic* one assesses the main assumptions or whether or not the concept or item under study has internal inconsistencies or errors in logical reasoning.[6] In what follows in this section, whenever you come to a bulleted question, take some time to try to find the answers yourself and then compare your answers with the information provided below.

Context Clues and Assumptions

- What context clues (historical or otherwise) or assumptions does the UDHR rely on in order to describe and enumerate human rights?

The historical period in which a document is created is important to study, for it provides the context and underlying reasons for its creation. World War II was the impetus for creating the *UN Charter* and the UDHR. Consider what major events occurred in the 1940s that may have incited people to begin talking about what it means for humans to have rights and how humans should be treated. For example, how the Holocaust, a German state and Nazi-Party-supported genocide against the Jewish and Roma populations, incited discussions about human rights. Further, Eleanor Roosevelt, the US representative appointed as chair of the UDHR drafting committee that negotiated the language of the UDHR, had a huge impact on its logic and influence.

Human rights did not emerge in the middle of the twentieth century fully formed as an international declaration. The philosophical and practical foundations for human rights had been working themselves out in human history for thousands of years.[7] The ideas of justice found in the writings of early philosophers (e.g., Plato and Aristotle), the concerns about what it mean to be a good monarch found in Confucius' writings, or the injunctions found in ancient law codes (like Hammarabi's code from modern-day Middle East, or Kautilya from modern-day India), or the philosophies of the Enlightenment period that focus on individualism and humanist ideas, all bear the markings of foundations for human rights.[8] Further, humans created laws and philosophized about what it meant to be human (and how other humans should be treated) based on the events that occurred in human history, especially in the aftermath of wars or conflict.[9]

In developing a deeper understanding of the context and underlying assumptions of the UDHR and human rights regime, consider the first phrase: "recognition of the inherent dignity and of the equal and inalienable rights of all members of the human family is the foundation of freedom."

The statement is based on an assumption, or an interpretation, of freedom that might conflict with other assumptions or interpretations. Note that Enlightenment philosophies were influential to the UDHR. One philosophy is the notion of *individual* versus *collective freedom*. The authors of the UDHR chose to prioritize individuals as the *unit of analysis* rather than the community, thus influencing the phrase above about the foundations of freedom as necessitating the protection of individuals. Other philosophies, such as Confucianism, prioritize the community as the unit of analysis and critique the notion that freedom should be based on the primacy of the individual. How might the UDHR have been written differently had the *community* been viewed as the primary social unit rather than the *individual*?

Internal Logic and Consistency

- What are the internal logics and arguments utilized in order to create and enumerate a list of human rights?

Taken as a whole, *human rights* is an expansive and deeply philosophical concept that eludes simple definition. Most definitions of human rights, like that in the *Oxford English Dictionary*, are tautological and simply repeat the language contained in the term itself: a right is a right. Most definitions also say that human rights are rights that belong to a (every) person, but what does *belonging* to a person mean? Further complicating matters, and indicating that we are dealing with expert terminology or *jargon*, the definition from the UN Office of the High Commissioner for Human Rights says they are "interrelated, interdependent and indivisible"[10] and the *Stanford Encyclopedia of Philosophy* says that "human rights are international norms that help to protect all people everywhere from severe political, legal, and social abuses."[11]

Human rights furthermore rely on a thick theoretical foundation for definition. For instance, Jack Donnelly's introduction to human rights struggles with the problem of definition: "Human rights—*droits de l'homme, derechos humanos, Menschenrechte*, "the rights of man"—are literally the rights that one has because one is human. What does it mean to have a right?"[12] After reviewing the ideas of human nature and social construction of rights, Donnelly points out that "human rights are not just abstract values" but rather "the minimum set of goods, services, opportunities, and protections that are widely recognized today as essential prerequisites for a life of dignity."[13] Finally, the word *inalienable* is often used as an adjective to human rights to indicate that human rights cannot be taken away from humans, that is, that there is no argument that any entity (like another human or a state government) can make that justifies taking the human right away.[14]

The following bulleted questions and subsequent discussions provide an overview of the foundations and conceptual issues in thinking about the definition of human rights and how human rights are protected and provided in the world. Consider the questions in order to evaluate the internal logic of human rights arguments.[15]

- *Enlightenment*: What philosophers, philosophies, and ideologies affected and continue to influence the way humans think about and implement human rights?
- Do philosophies of *individualism* and *humanism* on which the human rights regime is based contradict other ways of protecting humans?

The term *enlightenment* refers to the period of extensive development of philosophical and scientific knowledge and writing that took place in Europe from the seventeenth to nineteenth centuries—such philosophies continue to impact human rights theory and practice. *Individualism*, for instance, is the idea that each human deserves respect and acknowledgment on the basis of their humanity. Further, *humanism* is the notion that humans have the ability to be good and create good in the world. Finally, Enlightenment notions include the idea that humans engage in *rationality*, that humans can utilize their reasoning capacities to understand their place in the world and improve their condition.[16] Because of where and who wrote the UDHR (mostly people with a Western education and Western/enlightenment cultural values), human rights are all based on such philosophies, as opposed to others that might support community over the individual, for example.

- *Ethics, natural law*, and *natural rights*: On what basis do thinkers argue for human rights?

Some scholars suggest that ethics, as the study of practical reasoning about what it means to be good and just, may be considered a foundation for human rights in normative theory.[17] Further, natural law argues that standards of right and wrong are founded in nature, rather than in society, and this argument provides a normative foundation for human rights as we know them.[18] Natural law holds that there are standards and rules that are self-evident to everyone, everywhere, across time and space, and belong to all people and societies, though whether natural law results in natural rights is debatable.

- *Cultural relativism* versus *universalism*: Are human rights universally applicable or bound to specific moments in time and space?

Cultural relativism suggests that cultures judge people's actions and behaviors using different moral and ethical standards, and sometimes those differing cultural standards disagree with one another. Therefore, what is right in one culture is not right in another, and it is difficult to agree about universal values or rights. *Universalism* is the notion that some rights or claims made by human beings apply to all human beings everywhere no matter their culture, geography, ethnicity, or time period.[19]

- What is the difference between *positive* and *negative* rights, and how are such rights implemented?

Finally, in considering how to implement human rights the discussion of rights *from* something (freedom from interference, for example, as a *negative* right) versus rights *to* something (right to goods or services or agency, for example, as a *positive* right) comes into play when considering internal consistency. For instance, the idea that a civil right is a *negative* right (that government should not interfere in the lives of citizens) versus social rights as *positive* (the government has responsibility to provide food, clothing, shelter to those who are not able to procure such goods) might call into question the relevance or efficacy of human rights to protect human beings from abuse or limitations.[20]

The discussion above shows the importance of considering how the internal logic provides a certain way of thinking about human rights that needs to be assessed in order to understand and assign it value. In the next section, questions about internal inconsistencies and errors in logic provide a further way for a learner to determine the value of human rights.

Internal Contradictions or Errors

- Are there any internal contradictions in the human rights regime, that is, two or more beliefs or ideas that are inconsistent with one another?
- Does each of the enumerated human rights build on and support the others or is there evidence of contradictions between one human right and another?
- Are there any *logical fallacies* in the UDHR preamble in how human rights are described and enumerated?
- On what basis would one conclude that *all* people have rights, especially in the face of evidence that they do not, in fact, all have rights?

The UDHR preamble provides basic statements and rationales for the list of human rights that follow and gives clues about its internal logic and even inconsistencies. For instance, several statements suggest that human rights are *inalienable*, that is, if you are a human, your rights cannot be taken away for any reason or by any authoritative or non-authoritative actor: "All human beings are born free and equal in dignity and rights. . . . Everyone is entitled to all the rights and freedoms set forth in this Declaration" (Articles 1 and 2). However, we know that people all over the world routinely have their rights violated (just look at any recent report from Amnesty International or Human Rights Watch).

To explain the contradiction between possessing a right versus enjoying a right some human rights scholars have discussed what they call the *possession paradox*. While humans have the right (that is, the claim to something that must be provided or not deprived by someone), society prevents some people from enjoying those rights because of laws, statutes, societal norms and practices, or outright deprivation. A good example is in Article 3: "Everyone has the right to life, liberty . . ." and yet, societies through the ages have practiced norms or implemented laws that allow for depriving a person's life depending on their actions (convicted criminal offenses leading to arrest and detention or the death penalty) or even for community benefit (sacrificing the one for the many).[21] What do you make of this apparent internal contradiction?

Notice also that some of the enumerated rights require additional support, making it difficult, if not impossible, for a person to be able to access or enjoy the right without support. For instance, civil rights and political rights assume a government that actually has the ability to provide and implement them; the "right to take part in government . . . through freely chosen representatives. . . . The will of the people shall be . . . expressed in periodic and genuine elections" (Article 21) assumes that a state government has democratic rules and laws that support republican (i.e., representative) regimes, that the state government has the financing to provide citizens with voting booths, etc. Further, social, economic, and cultural rights require additional support: "everyone has the right to a standard of living adequate for the health and well-being of himself" (Article 25.1), but if a person cannot find a job (or has a disability that precludes access to most work), how does the person reach that standard of living? In societies with well-developed welfare systems, states may provide healthcare and a minimum income, but what about people who live under governments without such resources or systems in place?

Finally, as you continue analyzing the human rights as enumerated in the articles of the UDHR you might ask whether the rights themselves contradict one another in that one right might limit the enjoyment of another right.

Evaluating Using External Performance Standards or Criteria

Most of the evaluating one might do involves assessing the value of a concept, situation, institution, policy, program, or outcome based on outside criteria. Such criteria can be derived from multiple places, including theories, logical assessment, or cultural perspective and experience. It is important to keep in mind that evaluative criteria, no matter which ones are selected, reflect particular sets of values, norms, priorities, and beliefs. To evaluate is to *judge*, and as such it is critical to be self-aware and self-reflective. Further, when evaluating using external criteria it is common practice to justify and provide a rationale for the criteria selected, and to also anticipate and try to address (even if only partially) the likely critiques of the evaluative scheme.

Means versus Ends

A common method of evaluation using external criteria is to assess the means (the processes, practices, tools, and techniques used to achieve a goal) in relation to the ends (the stated goals and objectives to be achieved).

- What are the ends sought in creating and enumerating human rights in the UDHR?
- What specific mechanisms do the UDHR and the human rights regime suggest in order to achieve these ends? And do the means specified contradict the ends sought?

In this case, it is important to spend some time determining what the means and ends are, as identified in the UDHR and the human rights regime more broadly. Are human rights the ends desired? Or is the list of human rights enumerated in the UDHR a *means* to an end, a tool that can be used to promote "freedom, justice and peace in the world" as the first phrase in the preamble implies? If human rights are a *means* to achieving freedom, justice, and peace, it might be a good idea to consider the philosophical origins of and definitions for *freedom, justice*, and *peace*, and challenge those assumptions about our collective goals as a species, perhaps drawing on the work of thinkers working outside of the enlightenment tradition. Or one might assess the decades of practice in the human rights regime and look at contemporary human experience: in what ways have human rights led to, or deterred from, a world that is free, just, and peaceful? In other words, has this tool that we call human rights helped us reach our goals? The answer to this question will be nuanced and require additional assumptions and criteria; it will also require a lot of work in assessing the history and practice of human rights implementation.[22]

If we consider human rights as the *ends* themselves, rather than *means*, it might be worthwhile to consider the UDHR as an international legal document (along with the subsequently codified human rights legal documents). That the authors of the UDHR chose to write an international document and then build on it with conventions that had more legal accountability structures suggests a particular *means* for achieving the human rights enumerated in the UDHR: international law. International law is voluntary—that is, state governments voluntarily sign and ratify documents, conventions, and treaties and agree to be bound by the rules therein—and there is no supranational authority that holds states accountable for action through a binding authority structure (a situation termed *anarchy* in IR, see chapter 8, Textbox 8.1). Rather, states are often held accountable by reputation, and other states try to *shame* and *blame* states to get them to follow their commitments.

State governments might also use more forceful ways to induce other state governments to follow suit and protect human rights: governments might use military or monetary aid as a pressure tool (either withholding, as in sanctions, or providing for good behavior); they might engage in military intervention (whether supported by the international community through the UN or in some sort of coalition); or they might pressure a government to act through international juridical units, like the International Criminal Court (ICC). Thus, it is important to ask whether the *means* of human rights (international law) is effective in achieving the *ends*, and if there are any other alternative means that would better ensure human rights access and enjoyment.

Efficiency and Effectiveness:

- Are human rights effective in ensuring that humans live lives worthy of dignity?
- Is the human rights regime effective in achieving human rights protections and provisions?

If human rights are considered as the *ends* to be achieved, and international law to be the *means* by which we achieve the ends, then it is possible to evaluate based on whether or not state governments have signed and ratified international human rights treaties. When governments sign and ratify (or approve) a treaty, this represents at least a minimal commitment to the principles espoused and behavioral changes required in it. The UN (as well as other *organizations* like Amnesty International or Human Rights Watch, sometimes called *watchdog organizations*) compiles signature/ratification statuses. Consider Figure 13.1, a map that shows the current ratification status of countries on eighteen human rights documents, reported on by the UN Office of the Higher Commissioner for Human Rights (see the website: https://indicators.ohchr.org/).[23]

Notice the difference in signature and ratification status for different countries. Take a moment to do some research on specific conventions, such as the *Convention on the Rights of the Child* (CRC) and find which countries have and have not signed and/or ratified and consider the following questions in relation to whether or not the human rights regime is effective in protecting humans.

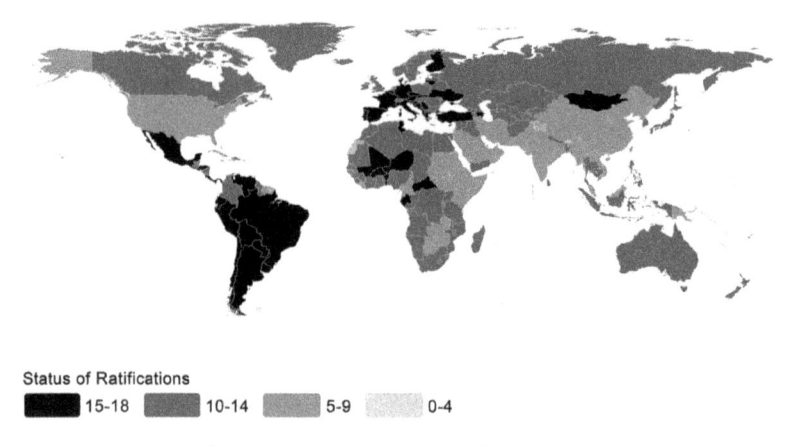

Figure 13.1 Map of Human Rights Treaty Ratification. Office of the United Nations High Commissioner for Human Rights.

- For example, as of August 30, 2019, the US is the only country in the world (of those that are recognized by the UN) to have not ratified the CRC. Why would the US Senate not agree to ratify the CRC, especially when literally every other country has done so?
- What are the implications when almost every country of the world is a state party to a human rights document like the CRC?
- What are the implications when every country of the world except the most powerful (in terms of military strength and also possibly influence) is a state party to a human rights document? (Consider what happened to the League of Nations when the US Senate refused to ratify the *Treaty of Versailles* and did not become a party—see chapter 4.)
- Consider also some of the other human rights treaties that states could sign and ratify, like the *Convention on the Rights of Migrant Workers and their Families* (ICRMW). What are the implications when only 54 out of 193 states (as of August 29, 2019) are state parties to a ICRMW?

In both cases of analyzing treaty compliance above (of the CRC and ICRMW) one might identify positive and negative aspects of effectiveness (do treaties produce the desired human rights end or result?) and efficiency (do treaties produce the desired end or result in the most competent or effective way?). *Effectiveness* is a multidimensional and contested idea. We do not all agree on what constitutes an effective means to achieve a desired end. In the human rights context, does effective mean quick, cheap, comprehensive, or universal? Would the treaty system be effective if just one person was able to enjoy and exercise their human rights? How many people would need to enjoy and exercise their human rights for the treaty system to be considered effective?

Even when a government becomes a state party to a document like the UDHR it can submit what are called *reservations*, indicating that they do not agree with some parts of the treaty (and therefore do not agree to comply with said parts). Further, while the treaty bodies conduct research and follow-up on state implementation, the major way that states are held accountable is through reputation and shaming/blaming states to follow suit. Based on understandings of international law and politics (including the importance of state sovereignty to the international system), one might pragmatically decide that human rights, as implemented and achieved in an efficient and effective manner, are the best way to protect human beings from maltreatment, especially maltreatment by governments. In contrast, one might also decide that the current system of human rights international law is just a ruse, a *rhetorical tool* for states to use in order to achieve their own national objectives. Making that call is what evaluation is all about, after carefully assessing the information based on a particular set of criteria.

- What other criteria or standards, ones that aren't used in the discussion above, could be important in evaluating the human rights regime?
- What other criteria or standards have you seen others apply to evaluate global political topics, regimes, ideas, concepts, programs, policies, institutions, or outcomes?
- Do you agree with the standards and criteria you identified in answer to the two questions above? Why or why not?
- Recall, for example, that in chapter 9 Eugene Debs evaluates several US policies and programs during the WWI period. Which criteria did Debs use?
- In chapter 11 Martin Luther King, Jr., evaluates US policy during the Vietnam War era. Which criteria does he use? What do you think and feel about these evaluations?

13.D: RECOMMENDED READINGS ON HUMAN RIGHTS

Donnelly, Jack. *Human Rights in Theory and Practice*. 3rd ed. Ithaca, NY: Cornell University Press, 2013.

Hopgood, Stephen. *Keepers of the Flame: Understanding Amnesty International*. Ithaca, NY: Cornell University Press, 2006.

Ishay, Micheline R. *The History of Human Rights: From Ancient Times to the Globalization Era*. Berkeley and Los Angeles, CA: University of California Press, 2004.

Lauren, Paul Gordon. *The Evolution of International Human Rights: Visions Seen*. 3rd ed. Philadelphia, PA: University of Pennsylvania Press, 2011.

Mertus, Julie. *Bait and Switch: Human Rights and U.S. Foreign Policy.* New York and London: Routledge, 2004.

Morsink, Johannes. *The Declaration of Human Rights: Origin, Drafting, and Intent.* Philadelphia: University of Pennsylvania Press, 1999.

NOTES

1. Robert O. Keohane, *After Hegemony: Cooperation and Discord in the World Political Economy* (Princeton: Princeton University Press, 1984). On multiple human rights regimes that function concurrently in the international system see Jack Donnelly, *Human Rights in Theory and Practice*, 3rd ed. (New York: Cornell University Press), 161–96.

2. Donnelly uses the language of protecting, providing, and not depriving. Donnelly, *Human Rights in Theory and Practice.*

3. United Nations, "Universal Declaration of Human Rights," Dec. 8, 1948. G.A. Res. 217A (III), U.N. Doc. A/810 at 71 (1948) accessed July 24, 2020 (all rights reserved, reproduced based on fair use doctrine from Section 107 of US Copyright Law), https://www.un.org/en/universal-declaration-human-rights/.

4. Benjamin Bloom, *Taxonomy of Educational Objectives: The Classification of Educational Goals Handbook I: Cognitive Domain* (New York: Longmans, Green, 1956), 185.

5. Core instruments listed on the UN Website: United Nations, "The Core International Human Rights Instruments and their monitoring bodies," Office of the High Commissioner for Human Rights, accessed August 3, 2019, https://www.ohchr.org/EN/ProfessionalInterest/Pages/CoreInstruments.aspx. The United Nations lists the states that have signed and ratified treaties in several places. Two good places to consider are the UN Office of the High Commissioner for Human Rights that provide updates the signature and ratification: https://indicators.ohchr.org/. Consider also the information from nongovernmental organizations or research institutions that report on human rights progress, such as in the University of Minnesota Human Rights Library: "Ratification of International Human Rights Treaties by Country," *University of Minnesota Human Rights Library*, accessed July 24, 2020, http://hrlibrary.umn.edu/research/ratification-index.html.

6. Anderson and Krathwohl name the element of evaluating internal inconsistencies as "checking." Lorin W. Anderson and David R. Krathwohl, *A Taxonomy for Learning, Teaching, and Assessing*, Abridged ed. (Boston, MA: Bacon, 2001), 83.

7. Micheline Ishay makes a strong case for the historical foundations of human rights in her two books on the topic: Micheline R. Ishay, *The History of Human Rights: From Ancient Times to the Globalization Era* (Berkeley and Los Angeles, CA: University of California Press, 2004); Micheline R. Ishay, *The Human Rights Reader: Major Political Essays, Speeches, and Documents from Ancient Times to the Present*, 2nd ed. (New York: London: Routledge, 2012).

8. See, e.g., Ishay, *The History of Human Rights*; Lauren, *The Evolution of Human Rights.*

9. Ishay, *The History of Human Rights*.

10. United Nations Office of the High Commissioner for Human Rights (UN Human Rights), "What are Human Rights," *UN Human Rights*, accessed August 12, 2019, https://www.ohchr.org/en/issues/pages/whatarehumanrights.aspx.

11. James Nickel, "Human Rights," *Stanford Encyclopedia of Philosophy*, accessed July 24, 2020, https://plato.stanford.edu/entries/rights-human/.

12. Donnelly, *Human Rights in Theory and Practice*, 7.

13. Donnelly, *Human Rights in Theory and Practice*, 17.

14. As Donnelly notes, "Human rights also are *inalienable* rights: one cannot stop being human" (emphasis in original). Donnelly, *Human Rights in Theory and Practice*, 10.

15. For excellent overviews of human rights that include in depth discussion of the above and more see Seyom Brown, *Human Rights in World Politics* (New York: Longman, 2000). Donnelly, *Human Rights in Theory and Practice*; Ishay, *The History of Human Rights*.

16. Ishay, *The History of Human Rights*, 63–116. Note, though, that while Enlightenment ideals may have inspired some of the human rights thinking, they were not exclusively relied upon: Johannes Morsink, *The Declaration of Human Rights: Origin, Drafting, and Intent* (Philadelphia: University of Pennsylvania Press, 1999), 320.

17. For instance, Ishay notes in her historical review of human rights that while "there are no universal ethics . . . the survivors [of World War II] were determined as never before to resurrect a lasting universal ethics." Ishay, *The History of Human Rights*, 16; further, Mertus discusses the varying ethical traditions as a basis for human rights: ethical universalism versus ethical particularism: Mertus, *Bait and Switch*, 7–8.

18. Morsink, for example, shows how often the concept of "natural law" came up in discussions during the drafting of the UDHR: Morsink, *The Declaration of Human Rights*.

19. Donnelly provides a good overview of cultural relativism versus universalism. Donnelly, *Human Rights in Theory and Practice*, 93–105.

20. E.g., on negative and positive rights as normative theory: Leif Wenar, "Rights," *Stanford Encyclopedia of Philosophy*, accessed August 1, 2019, https://plato.stanford.edu/entries/rights/; see Donnely, *Human Rights in Theory and Practice*, 42, for further discussion as relates to human rights.

21. Stephen Hopgood, *Keepers of the Flame: Understanding Amnesty International* (Ithaca, NY: Cornell University Press, 2006).

22. To start: Lauren, *The Evolution of International Human Rights*.

23. United Nations Office of the High Commissioner for Human Rights (UNOHCR), "Ratification of 18 International Human Rights Treaties Map," UNOHCR Data and map on website, Definition and meta-data: http://www.ohchr.org/Documents/Issues/HRIndicators/MetadataRatificationStatus.pdf. Source: DatabaseoftheUnitedNationsOfficeofLegalAffairs(OLA) https://treaties.un.org, accessed August April 10, 2020, https://indicators.ohchr.org/.

Conclusion

Creating and Negotiating the Future

Chapters 9–13 layered higher-order thinking skills, tools, and techniques used regularly by global politics scholars and practitioners on top of the basic and foundational skills and practices discussed in chapters 1–8. This last chapter engages the ultimate thinking exercise: *Creating*! Creating something new requires a solid foundation in the ideas, concepts, and facts relevant to the subject, in historical and social context, and in what has been said and done related to the subject in the past (i.e., previous analyses conducted by others). Anderson et al. are worth quoting here on their definition of *create*:[1]

> Unlike *Create*, the other categories involve working with a given set of elements that are part of a given whole; that is, they are part of a larger structure the student is trying to understand. In *Create*, on the other hand, the student must draw upon elements from many sources and put them together into a novel structure or pattern relative to his or her own prior knowledge. *Create* results in a new product, that is, something that can be observed and that is more than the student's beginning materials. A task that requires *Create* is likely to require aspects of each of the earlier cognitive process categories to some extent, but not necessarily in the order in which they are listed in the Taxonomy Table. (emphasis in the original)[2]

Consider this book itself. There are many textbooks in global politics and international relations that are useful for learning about global politics—why write another one? The main reason is that we, the authors of this book, saw something *missing* from other books about global politics, that is, an emphasis on encouraging learners to take responsibility for their own learning. For our specific purposes, we wanted a book that we could use in our courses that would provide the foundations for our students to know how to pursue learning for themselves in the context of learning about global politics. However, we also wanted to write a book that could be utilized by anyone outside the context of a classroom. Thus, we took what we knew about global politics, synthesized it with the information on learner-centered teaching and critical pedagogy, added our own perspectives and experiences, and *created* this textbook. This chapter is intended to help you think about ways you can also create new information, products, and ideas.

PROBLEM-POSING EDUCATION, RESEARCH, AND WRITING

This is a *problem-posing* book that not only posed questions to learners throughout the chapters but also recommended making questions for oneself and challenging oneself to critically think about the world. Building off of that, the *create* category of higher-order thinking requires one to pose problems in a deep and sophisticated way in a process that takes time to develop: "In problem-posing education, people develop their power to perceive critically *the way they exist* in the world *with which* and *in which* they find themselves: they come to see the world not as a static reality, but as a reality in process, in transformation" (emphasis in original).[3] Taking responsibility for one's own learning requires trust: you must trust yourself and that you have something to add to the conversation. We, the authors, trust that you do. As instructors in higher education, one of the most valuable and unexpected benefits of our transition from the banking model of teaching to LCT is that it requires us to trust and have faith in our students.[4] Not even once have we been disappointed with the outcome: Our students—including *you*—are capable of tremendous things.

One of the steps in the *creative* process is that of *generating:* "*Generating* involves representing the problem and arriving at alternatives or hypotheses that meet certain criteria" (emphasis in original).[5] Once a problem is posed, the next step is to *represent* that problem, identifying associated elements of that problem, a process that, in itself, is cumbersome and takes extensive time and research. Then it is possible to begin *generating* solutions to the problem. The generative stage can benefit greatly from mindmaps or other tools that help brainstorm and visualize ideas (consider using a small whiteboard or word document to brainstorm solutions to problems by writing down thoughts and ideas). It is often the case during this phase of a creative project that new ideas pop into one's head at strange times, for the brain often develops new connections when resting or thinking about something else (keep a small notebook with you so as to jot ideas down if they inconveniently pop into your brain while at the grocery store or stopped at a red light). Solutions to the problem can be thought of as the *argument* or *hypothesis*: *generating* ideas in response to problems posed allows a learner to consider all the elements of a problem and think of ways it may be addressed or solved, not just based on what other people have done or said (although it is important to know what has gone before) but also based on one's own perspective and experiences.

Learning, Researching, and Writing as Creative, Generative Experiences

Everyone is able to *create* by offering a different perspective based on their individual, unique experiences in life—experiences that are worthy of respect and recognition—and by *creating* new projects or products to reveal new ways to address problems. Such projects and projects can include written works (like essays, op-eds, books), oral works (like podcasts, radio broadcasts, speeches), or art works (paintings, drawings, sculptures). With anything that you write or produce, whether for an instructor, for your job, or for your own enjoyment, *include your own voice, your own perspective, and your own experience*. Doing the work of building the foundation, amassing knowledge, and understanding what others have done before are necessary, difficult, and time-consuming tasks, but they are essential for *creating* new and innovative answers and solutions. But building that knowledge and *then* using your own life experience to add new ideas, or interpret and evaluate in new ways, permits you to *create* something new that is worth other peoples' time and attention.

Focus on the Process, not the Product

Whatever you create, whether an essay, a podcast, or a new work of art, it requires a focus on process, not outcome. In any project, focusing on the tasks at hand and avoiding worrying about the final product is freeing and invigorating and allows *creators* the space needed for exciting innovation and new ideas. Focusing on the process helps avoid procrastination and other problems associated with being overwhelmed. To be sure, setting goals, and creating deadlines and bench markers are important so as to finish the project in an appropriate amount of time, but being overly concerned with small details about the final product may inhibit successfully completing a project and stifle creativity.

Managing a project means having a general sense of what the outcome needs to be and breaking it down into smaller manageable chunks in order to help you get there. Thus, along with enjoying and focusing on the process, also learn to utilize *project management* as you begin working on a project, and throughout the project, keep the final goal in mind and plan accordingly. Plan so that you can give yourself enough time to be creative and avoid cramming new information into your brain. The process of breaking down a large project into smaller parts, and then sequencing those parts in order to finish the project, is called *project management*. Just as shown in chapter 10 with *chunking*, a practice that helps you remember and learn more information and organize analyses, so too with large projects breaking down the component parts and giving oneself assignments, devoting significant time to each of the assignments so as to finish in a timely manner, and pulling them all together in the end are key parts of the process of *creating*.

No one can think, learn, and create in a vacuum. In order to be creative ourselves, we need to be inspired by what others have done and are doing, and thus we need to read and learn from all kinds of media. It is important to immerse oneself in the ideas, observations, experiences, and language *of other people* in order to develop new ideas, make new connections, and create new work. As with a vegetable garden, one's brain needs to be seeded and fertilized, tended and cultivated, so that it is tempted to think new thoughts, even weird thoughts. Read and read broadly: do not limit yourself only to those materials that you think are relevant. Rather, select materials that are also tangential to your topic, or that even initially seem unrelated. Humans can find inspiration in all kinds of places, and find ways to associate meaningful and relevant insights, parallels, and connections that spring from reviewing materials that don't obviously fit with a chosen topic.

When starting and working on a project it is important to work on it consistently: get down your thoughts and ideas immediately and continuously as you go through the process of research, reading, and studying. Do not wait until the last minute to record your thoughts for whatever kind of project you are working on. Use some of the tools and tactics reviewed in the A sections of the chapters of this text, such as writing annotated bibliographies, creating T-charts, taking notes using the Cornell method, practicing efficient study sessions using the Pomodoro method, reviewing notes and asking questions of the notes, and posing problems and generating answers to those problems. The act of writing or working on a project (articulating ideas out loud, drawing, or painting something new) is an act of thinking. On writing: people do not have the thoughts and words perfectly formed in their minds before they start writing; it is through the process of writing that those thoughts and words are formed, and that leads to the crucially important part of creating a final product: revision. Writing and revision are the processes that allow you to say what you mean and mean what you say.

Revising and Drafting: First Drafts Don't Look Like Final Drafts

Revising what one has created (whether written, oral, artwork, etc.) is one of the most difficult practices to learn but is absolutely necessary for creating a better final product. The creative process is not a simple transcription of ideas (in your mind) to paper (or computer) or to audio or canvas. In other words, one only begins to think well once the work has begun, and the first version is usually very messy—and so are the second and third and fourth versions. No project is perfect on the first, or even third, attempt. Revise your work constantly and in multiple iterations, whether writing or working on some other generative product. For writing, revision does not mean changing one or two words in a sentence or merely adding or deleting a sentence or punctuation mark. Sometimes revision means changing the whole way your work is organized, or re-writing and re-working an entire section so that it almost does not resemble the first attempt, or revising the wording of a paragraph significantly, or even changing your main argument. In order to find the words, phrases, and sentence structures to convey your meaning you have to search for them in your mind, and in the work of others, and that takes time and effort. Allow yourself to have a terrible first draft of your project that looks almost nothing like the final draft, for it is in the process of revision that you truly realize and understand what you want to say.

One of the major obstacles to effective revision is the simple fact that it is often emotionally difficult to destroy something you have created; with revision, you must *kill your darlings*, so to speak. Try it. Go write a sentence and then delete the whole sentence. How does it feel? Now write the sentence in a different way. Is it better or worse? Now delete that. Now write the sentence again in a different way. The process of revising is a process of constantly searching for the right word/s to use to express yourself in the most creative, clear, and articulate way possible, a process that is only possible by repeatedly negating and erasing your own ideas and words. But, again, that process requires intense revision and emotional fortitude in order to express what you mean. (To overcome the anxiety associated with revision, consider archiving prior drafts to reduce the emotional toll of deleting your own creations.)

Consider this book. As we, the authors, wrote the chapters, each of us produced a first draft of half of the chapters, then edited each other's drafts and gave each other comments and suggestions (sometimes suggesting immense changes to the initial drafts of the text); we then went back through and revised/edited the next draft based on feedback, then shared those again with each other for further revisions/edits; after revising each draft again a few more times (including extensive discussion about phrasing, organization, etc.), we then sent the chapter drafts to our publisher to obtain *peer review* from experts in the field who do not know us and who were kind enough to review the drafts and give us feedback on how to revise/edit; we then revised and edited based on their feedback, going through several revisions; we also beta-tested the book with our students and received feedback from them to help with the editing; we then did several more rounds of iterative editing ourselves; we then worked with a copyeditor to ensure grammatical clarity and proper format.

Writing this book was a long and difficult, yet satisfying, process! We had been thinking about ideas for this text for at least five years, and once we started writing, the writing/revising process took about two years. We posed a problem to ourselves and then, finally and with much trial and error and revision and frustration, found a solution presented to you in the format of this book. We encourage you to do the same and be creative! Use what you have learned about global politics to do good in the world in some form, generating new ideas and solutions to global problems.

THE FUTURE OF GLOBAL POLITICS

Because the global political system is dynamic and complex, the global political landscape is constantly changing. Being capable and agile in thinking about the world thus requires that we hone our critical thinking skills, adapt our thinking to changing realities, and forge creative solutions to new problems as we encounter them. In an ever-changing global context, independent, critical, and creative thinking and scholarship are of primary importance. The process of studying and researching, brainstorming ideas, and creating new knowledge and ideas and solutions, whether in written form or some other medium, allows one to adapt one's mind to change in the global system more generally. In other words, creating a final product and going through the revision process to get to something wonderful requires flexibility in thinking and the capability to adapt one's thinking to changing conditions and constraints, in dialogue with one another. This is also what is required of learners navigating the future of global politics.

The global political arena is full of examples of thinkers who adapted and revised their thinking in response to changing external realities and new experiences in dialogue with others. International economist Paul Krugman, for example, used to think about the global economy along *neoclassical* economic lines and tended to recommend neoliberal economic policies associate with contemporary *globalization*. Much of Krugman's early scholarship, based in formal modeling techniques standard to the neoclassical tradition, took for granted that markets are typically efficient, and that mainstream economic approaches were generally the correct lens through which to view the world. But as time progressed, Krugman's understandings of neoclassical economics, and its assumptions and failures, changed significantly, such that by the time of the 2007–2010 Great Recession he penned the following lines in a now-famous op-ed for the *New York Times*: "Few economists saw our current crisis coming, but this predictive failure was the least of the field's problems. More important was the profession's blindness to the very possibility of catastrophic failures in a market economy."[6] Similar kinds of blindness and inflexibility are already apparent within the cascading crises the world is facing as this book goes to print, associated with the coronavirus pandemic of 2020 and the COVID-19 disease.

Over time, then, Krugman, and others who observe and adapt their knowledge and ideas to the world around them, think deeply and sometimes change their minds about beliefs once held dear. Consider, for example, Saul of Tarsus who participated in persecuting Christians in ancient Rome but who ultimately changed his mind about Christianity, becoming one of its most ardent supporters and proselytizers in the Roman Empire (he is known to us now as Saint Paul, an apostle of Christ). The great Indian prince Siddhartha gave up his throne and his riches to live an ascetic life of poverty as the Buddha. The author George Orwell began his career in the British civil service, supporting the British colonial administration in Burma, only to change his mind later in life, becoming a vocal opponent of the British Empire. Major political figures from around the world provide more examples of substantially revising perspectives over time and adapting to new global realities, for instance, UK Prime Minister Margaret Thatcher, Emperor Constantine of Rome, and former Soviet President Mikhail Gorbachev.

As shown in the examples above, and throughout this book, problem-solving is part of our everyday lives and we urge you to think about how to use experiences from your lives to help you with higher-order thinking skills of applying, analyzing, and evaluating global politics issues and events. Even difficult interactions in intercultural communication help us understand global interactions. Our own life experiences help us decipher global politics and develop important insights about world problems. Our life experiences are like keys that allow us to open closed doors and find unexpected problems and solutions. In closing, then, consider the words of Canadian author Malcom Gladwell and take the learner-centered challenge to build your own knowledge and generate your own solutions to the world's problems: "I feel I change my mind all the time. And I sort of feel that's your responsibility as a person, as a human being—to constantly be updating your positions on as many things as possible. And if you don't contradict yourself on a regular basis, then you're not *thinking*. . . . If you create a system where you make it impossible, politically, for people to change [their] mind, then you're in trouble."[7]

RECOMMENDED READINGS ON CREATIVITY

Haidt, Jonathan. *The Righteous Mind: Why Good People are Divided by Politics and Religion.* New York: Vintage Books, 2012.

Messner, Kate. *Real Revision: Authors' Strategies to Share with Student Writers.* Portland, ME: Stenhouse Publishers, 2011.

Zinsser, William. *On Writing Well: An Informal Guide to Writing Nonfiction.* New York: Harper Perennial, 1994.

NOTES

1. In considering *create* as a category in which students add their own perspectives and ideas, we diverge from Lorin W. Anderson, and David R. Krathwohl, *A Taxonomy for Learning, Teaching, and Assessing*, abridged ed. (Boston, MA: Bacon, 2001). First, Anderson and Krathwohl took out Bloom's category of synthesis and made evaluate the penultimate category, with *create* as the ultimate category that includes both synthesis and producing something that is unique or original. We have followed their outline, with the exception that we kept *synthesis* as a separate category and consider *create* as something that adds uniqueness. Thus, we make the distinction between work that not only synthesizes but also adds one's own perspective or comes up with what might be labeled as having "originality and uniqueness" (85). Anderson and Krathwohl argue that what is unique or original is decided by the instructor: "educators must define what is original and unique" (85), and surely instructors have their expertise in the subject area and can provide feedback from a vast array of knowledge of the foundational material to guide students when their ideas might not be completely new. Yet, we also suggest that students have individual experience and expertise of their own that instructors should support and trust, and we consider Freire's injunction important here: "Dialogue further requires an intense faith in human kind, faith in their power to make and remake, to create and re-create, faith in their vocation to be more fully human . . . faith in people is an *a priori* requirement for dialogue" (emphasis in original, 71): Freire, Paulo. *Pedagogy of the Oppressed.* Translated by Myra Bergman Ramos (London: Penguin Press, 1996).

2. Anderson and Krathwohl, *A Taxonomy for Learning, Teaching, and Assessing*, 85.

3. Freire, *Pedagogy of the Oppressed*, 64.

4. Singham, Mano. "Away from the Authoritarian Classroom," *Change: The Magazine of Higher Learning* 37, no. 3 (May/June 2005): 50–57. Singham addresses faculty and administrator marked lack of trust of students in higher education, focusing on the structure and content of the syllabus.

5. Anderson and Krathwohl, *A Taxonomy for Learning, Teaching, and Assessing*, 86.

6. Paul Krugman, "How Did Economists Get It so Wrong?" *New York Times*, September 6, 2009.

7. Maria Popova, "Malcom Gladwell on Criticism, Tolerance, and Changing Your Mind," *BrainPickings*, June 24, 2014. https://www.brainpickings.org/2014/06/24/malcolm-gladwell-nypl-interview/.

Bibliography

Aaronson, Susan Ariel. *Taking Trade to the Streets: The Lost History of Public Efforts to Shape Globalization.* Ann Arbor: University of Michigan Press, 2014.

Achebe, Chinua. *Things Fall Apart.* Greenwich, CT: Fawcett, 1959.

Agnew, John. *Geopolitics: Re-visioning World Politics.* 2nd ed. New York: Routledge, 2003.

Akram-Lodhi, Haroon. *Hungry for Change.* Halifax: Fernwood, 2013.

Anderson, Lorin W., and David R. Krathwohl. *A Taxonomy for Learning, Teaching, and Assessing.* Abridged ed. Boston, MA: Bacon, 2001.

Aquinas, Thomas. *Summa Theologica.* Complete English edition in five volumes. Westminster, MD: Christian Classics, 1981.

Art, Robert J., and Robert Jervis, eds. *International Politics: Enduring Concepts and Contemporary Issues.* New York: Longman (Division of Pearson), 2017.

Asbach, Olaf, and Peter Schröder. *The Ashgate Research Companion to the Thirty Years' War.* London: Routledge, 2016.

Atlantic Charter, The. Document signed between Franklin D. Roosevelt (President of US) and Winston S. Churchill (Prime Minister of UK) on August 14, 1941. *The Avalon Project, Yale Law School.* https://avalon.law.yale.edu/wwii/atlantic.asp

Augustine. *The City of God.* Translated by Marcus Dods. New York: Modern Library, 1950.

Aust, Anthony. *Handbook of International Law.* 11th ed. Cambridge, UK: Cambridge University Press, 2017.

Avalon Project, Documents in Law, History and Diplomacy, Yale University. "The Tonkin Gulf Incident: 1964." Last modified 2008. Source: Department of State Bulletin, August 24, 1964 https://avalon.law.yale.edu/20th_century/tonkin-g.asp.

Avalon Project, Documents in Law, History and Diplomacy, Yale University. "War Powers Resolution." Last modified 2008 https://avalon.law.yale.edu/20th_century/warpower.asp.

Baglione, Lisa A. *Writing a Research Paper in Political Science: A Practical Guide to Inquiry, Structure, and Methods.* 4th ed. Thousand Oaks, CA: CQ Press, an Imprint of SAGE Publications, 2020.

Barber, Benjamin. *Jihad versus McWorld.* New York: Times Books, 1995.

Barkley, Elizabeth F. *Student Engagement Techniques: A Handbook for College Faculty.* San Francisco: Jossey-Bass, 2015.

Barr, Robert B., and John Tagg. "From Teaching to Learning-A New Paradigm for Undergraduate Education." *Change* 27, no. 6 (November/December 1995): 12–25.

Basili, Marcello, Franzini, Mauricio, and Alesandro Vercelli, eds. *Environment, Inequality and Collective Action.* London: Routledge, 2006.

Bauduy, Jennifer. "The 1915 Invasion of Haiti: Examining a Treaty of Occupation." *Social Education* 79, no. 5 (October 2015), 244–249.

Baylis, John, Steve Smith, and Patricia Owens. *The Globalization of World Politics: An Introduction to International Relations.* Oxford: Oxford University Press, 2017.

Bayoumi, Tamim A. *Unfinished Business: The Unexplored Causes of the Financial Crisis and the Lessons Yet to Be Learned.* New Haven: Yale University Press, 2017.

Bello, Walden. *The Food Wars.* London: Verso, 2009.

Benassi, Victor A., Catherine E. Overson, and Christopher M. Hakala, eds. *Applying Science of Learning in Education: Infusing Psychological Science into the Curriculum.* Division 2, American Psychological Association, 2014. http://teachpsych.org/ebooks/asle2014/index.php.

Bershidsky, Leonid. "Trump Is Winning, Putin's Losing in Global Arms Trade." *Bloomberg,* March 12, 2019. https://www.bloomberg.com/opinion/articles/2019-03-12/u-s-is-no-1-in-arms-sales-as-russia-loses-market-share.

Bhagwati, Jagdish N. *In Defense of Globalization.* London: Oxford, 2007.

Bhagwati, Jagdish N., and Mathias Hirsch. *The Uruguay Round and Beyond: Essays in Honor of Arthur Dunkel. Studies in International Economics.* Ann Arbor: University of Michigan Press, 2001.

Biersteker, Thomas, and Cynthia Weber. *State Sovereignty as a Social Construct.* Cambridge, UK: Cambridge University Press, 1996.

Blakemore, Sarah-Jayne. *The Learning Brain: Lessons for Education.* New York: Blackwell, 2005.

Bloom, Benjamin. *Taxonomy of Educational Objectives: The Classification of Educational Goals, Handbook I: Cognitive Domain.* New York: Longmans, Green, 1956.

Bloomfield, Alan, and Shirley V. Scott. *Norm Antipreneurs and the Politics of Resistance to Global Normative Change.* London: Routledge, 2017.

Bollier, David. *Think Like a Commoner: A Short Introduction to the Life of the Commons.* Gabrioloa Island, BC: New Society Publishers, 2014.

Bova, Russell. *How the World Works: A Brief Survey of International Relations.* Pearson: New York, 2011.

Breger Bush, Sasha. "Poverty." In *The Encyclopedia of Political Thought,* edited by Michael T. Gibbons. Wiley Online Library, 15 September 2014. https://onlinelibrary.wiley.com/doi/book/10.1002/9781118474396.

Breger Bush, Sasha and Roni Kay M. O'Dell. "Teaching About Poverty and Inequality: Critical Pedagogy and Personal Experience in the Learner-Centred Classroom." *International Journal of Pluralism and Economics Education* 9, no. 1–2 (June 2018): 81–105.

Brookfield, Stephen D. *Becoming a Critically Reflective Teacher*. 2nd ed. San Francisco: Jossey-Bass, 2017.
Brown, Peter C., Henry L. Roediger III, and Mark A. McDaniel. *Make it Stick: The Science of Successful Learning*. Cambridge, MA: Belknap Press of Harvard University Press, 2014.
Brown, Seyom. *Human Rights in World Politics*. New York: Longman, 2000.
Brzoska, Michael. "Profiteering on the Iran-Iraq War." *Bulletin of the Atomic Scientists* 43, no. 5 (1987): 42–45.
Burchill, Scott, and Andrew Linklater. *Theories of International Relations*. 5th ed. Hampshire, UK: Palgrave Macmillan, 2015.
Burns, Tom, and Sandra Sinfield. *Essential Study Skills: The Complete Guide to Success at University*. 4th ed. London: Sage, 2016.
Cameron, Maxwell A., and Brian W. Tomlin. *The Making of NAFTA: How the Deal Was Done*. Ithaca, NY: Cornell University Press, 2000.
Campbell, Karlyn Kohrs, and Kathleen Hall Jamieson. *Presidents Creating the Presidency: Deeds Done in Words*. Chicago: University of Chicago Press, 2013.
Campbell, Patricia J, Aran MacKinnon, and Christy R Stevens. *An Introduction to Global Studies*. Somerset: Wiley, 2010.
"Capitalism, n.2." *Oxford English Dictionary (OED) Online*. Accessed June 1, 2019. https://www-oed-com.aurarialibrary.idm.oclc.org/view/Entry/27454?rskey=982XHj&result=2
Carey, Benedict. *How We Learn: The Surprising Truth About When, Where, and Why It Happens*. New York: Random House, 2015.
Carsen, Rachel. *Silent Spring*. Boston: Houghton Mifflin Company, 1962.
Carlsen, Laura. "WTO Kills Farmers: In Memory of Lee Kyung Hae." Last modified September 16, 2003. http://www.countercurrents.org/glo-carlsen160903.htm.
Cassels, Alan. *Ideology and International Relations in the Modern World*. The New International History Series. London: Routledge, 1996.
Chang, Ha-Joon and Ilene Grabel, eds. *Reclaiming Development: An Alternative Economic Policy Manual*. New York; London: Zed Books, 2004.
Chen, Shaohua and Martin Ravallion. "Absolute Poverty Measures for the Developing World, 1981-2004." *Proceedings of the National Academy of Sciences of the USA*, 104, no. 43 (October 2007): 16757–16762. https://www.pnas.org/content/104/43/16757.full?tab=author-info.
Herman, Edward S., and Noam Chomsky. *Manufacturing Consent: The Political Economy of the Mass Media*. 1st ed. New York: Pantheon Books, 1988.
Churchill, Winston. "Blood, Toil, Tears and Sweat." Speech to the House of Commons, London, May 13, 1940. The International Churchill Society, WinstonChurchill.org. https://winstonchurchill.org/resources/speeches/1940-the-finest-hour/blood-toil-tears-and-sweat-2/.
Cirillo, Francesco. *The Pomodoro Technique: The Life-Changing Time-Management System*. London: Virgin Books, 2018.
Claes, Dag Harald, and Giuliano Garavini, eds. *Handbook of OPEC and the Global Energy Order: Past, Present, and Future Challenges*. Routledge International Handbooks. Abingdon, Oxon: Routledge, 2020.

Clausewitz, Carl von. *On War*. The Project Gutenburg. Produced by Charles Keller and David Widger. Original publication 1832. Last updated October 19, 2019. https://www.gutenberg.org/files/1946/1946-h/1946-h.htm.

Clegg, Brian. *Instant Time Management*. London: Kogan Page, 1999.

Cohen, Saul Bernard. *Geopolitics: The Geography of International Relations*. 3rd ed. Lanham, MD: Rowman & Littlefield, 2015.

Cohen, Youssef. *Radicals, Reformers, Reactionaries: The Prisoner's Dilemma and the Collapse of Democracy in Latin America*. Chicago: University of Chicago Press, 1994.

Collier, Paul. *The Bottom Billion: Why the Poorest Countries Are Failing and What Can Be Done About It*. Oxford: Oxford University Press, 2007.

Collins, Daryl, Jonathan Morduch, Stuart Rutherford, and Orlanda Ruthven. *Portfolios of the Poor: How the World's Poor Live on $2 a Day*. Princeton: Princeton University Press, 2009.

Conforti, Benedetto, and Angelo Labella. *An Introduction to International Law*. Leiden, The Netherlands: BRILL, 2012.

Conrad, Josph. Heart of Darkness. The Project Gutenburg. Produced by Judith Boss and David Widger. Original Publication 1899. Last updated March 2, 2018. https://www.gutenberg.org/files/219/219-h/219-h.htm.

Copi, Irving M., Carl Cohen, and Victor Rodych, eds. *Introduction to Logic*. 15th ed. New York: Routledge, 2019.

Cornell University Learning Center, "The Cornell Note-Taking System." Accessed June 1, 2019. http://lsc.cornell.edu/notes.html.

Council on Foreign Relations. "The Lasting Legacy of George F. Kennan." Interview of John Lewis Gaddis conducted by Richard N. Haass on Monday, June 4, 2012. Accessed August 26, 2019. https://www.cfr.org/event/lasting-legacy-george-f-kennan-0.

Croxton, Derek, and Anuschka Tischer. *The Peace of Westphalia: A Historical Dictionary*. Westport, CT: Greenwood Press, 2002.

Center for Research Libraries, Global Resources Network. "The 'State of the Art': A Comparative Analysis of Newspaper Digitization to date." CRL/Global Resources Network, April 10, 2015. https://www.crl.edu/sites/default/files/d6/attachments/events/ICON_Report-State_of_Digitization_final.pdf.

Cuban, Larry. *How They Taught: Constancy and Change in American Classrooms, 1890-1990*. 2nd ed. New York: Teachers College Press, 1993.

Cutler, Robert. "The Development of the National Security Council." *Foreign Affairs Magazine*. 34, no. 3 (April 1956): 441–458.

Darder, Antonia, Marta P. Baltodano, and Rodolfo D. Torres, eds. *The Critical Pedagogy Reader*. 2nd ed. New York: Routledge, 2009.

DeMartino, George. *Global Economy, Global Justice: Theoretical Objections and Policy Alternatives to Neoliberalism*. Contemporary Political Economy Series. London: Routledge, 2000.

Deardorff, Darla K. "Identification and Assessment of Intercultural Competence as a Student Outcome of Internationalization." *Journal of Studies in International Education* 10, no. 3 (2006): 241–266.

Debs, Eugene. "The Canton, Ohio Anti-War Speech." Speech, Canton, OH, June 16, 1918. Marxists Internet Archive, Marxists.org. https://www.marxists.org/archive/debs/works/1918/canton.htm.

"Debs v. United States." *Oyez Free Law Project, Cornell Legal Information Institute.* Accessed June 3, 2020. https://www.oyez.org/cases/1900-1940/249us211.

Diamond, Jared M. *Guns, Germs, and Steel: The Fates of Human Societies.* 1st ed. New York: W.W. Norton, 1997.

Dicken, Peter. *Global Shift.* 6th ed. New York: Guilford, 2011.

Donnelly, Jack. *Human Rights in Theory and Practice.* 3rd ed. Ithaca, NY: Cornell University Press, 2013.

Dorman, Shawn, ed. *Inside a U.S. Embassy: Diplomacy at Work.* 3rd ed. New York: FS Books/ American Foreign Service Association, 2011.

Douglas, Paul H. "The American Occupation of Haiti I." *Political Science Quarterly* 42, no. 2 (June 1927): 228–258.

Doyle, Terry. *Learner-Centered Teaching: Putting the Research on Learning into Practice.* Sterling, VA: Stylus Publishing, 2011.

Easterly, William. *The White Man's Burden: Why the West's Efforts to Aid the Rest Have Done so Much Ill and so Little Good.* New York: Penguin Press, 2006.

Ehrlich, Paul R. *The Population Bomb.* A Sierra Club-Ballantine Book. New York: Ballantine Books, 1968.

Eknath, Easwaran, trans. *The Bhagavad Gita.* 2nd ed. Classics of Indian Spirituality. Tomales, CA: Nilgiri Press, 1985, 2007.

Engelbrecht, Helmuth Carol, and Frank Cleary Hanighen. *Merchants of Death: A Study of the International Armament Industry.* New York: Dodd, Mead and Co, 1934.

Ericsson, Anders, and Robert Pool. *Peak: Secrets from the New Science of Expertise.* 1st Mariner Books ed. Boston: Mariner Books/Houghton Mifflin Harcourt, 2017.

Escobar, Arturo. *Encountering Development: The Making and Unmaking of the Third World.* Princeton, NJ: Princeton University Press, 1995.

Fahey, Joseph J. and Richard Armstrong, eds. *A Peace Reader: Essential Readings on War, Justice, Non-violence, and World Order.* New York: Paulist Press, 1992.

Fanon, Frantz. *Black Skin, White Masks.* Translated by Charles Lam Markmann. Evergreen Black Cat Book. New York: Grove Press, 1967.

Fanon, Frantz. *The Wretched of the Earth.* Translated by Constance Farrington. New York: Grove Press, 1965.

Faraday, Michael. "The State of The Thames." *The Times*, July 9, 1855.

Fasulo, Linda. *An Insider's Guide to the UN.* 3rd ed. New Haven: Yale University Press, 2015.

Ferrell, Robert. *Harry S. Truman: A Life.* Columbia: University of Missouri Press, 1994.

Festenstein, Matthew, and Michael Kenny. *Political Ideologies: A Reader and Guide.* Oxford: Oxford University Press, 2005.

Fields, Jeffery, ed. *State Behavior and the Nuclear Nonproliferation Regime.* Athens, GA: University of Georgia, 2014

Fisher, David. *Morality and War: Can War be Just in the 21st Century?* New York: Oxford, 2011.

Fisher, Roger, William Ury, and Bruce Patton, *Getting to Yes: Negotiating Agreement Without Giving In.* 2nd ed. New York: Penguin Books, 1991.
Foreign Policy Association. "How U.S. Foreign Policy is Made." Last updated 2020. Accessed on July 15, 2019 https://fpa.org/features/index.cfm?act=feature&announcement_id=45&show_sidebar=0.
Friedman, Thomas L. *The World Is Flat: A Brief History of the Twenty-First Century.* 1st ed. New York: Farrar, Straus and Giroux, 2005.
Freire, Paulo. *Pedagogy of the Oppressed.* Translated by Myra Bergman Ramos. London: Penguin Press, 1996.
Frieden, Jeffrey, David Lake, and Kenneth Schultz. *World Politics: Interests, Interactions, Institutions.* New York; London: W. W. Norton & Company, 2010.
Friedman, Milton, and Rose D Friedman. *Free to Choose: A Personal Statement.* New York: Avon, 1981.
Friedman, Milton. "Playboy Interview: Milton Friedman." *Playboy Magazine* 20, no. 2 (February 1973).
Fukuyama, Francis. *The End of History and the Last Man.* New York: Free Press, 1992.
Gaddis, John Lewis. *George F. Kennan: An American Life.* New York: Penguin Books, 2011.
Gaddis, John Lewis. *The Cold War.* New York: Penguin Books, 2005.
Galvan, José L., and Melisa Galvan. *Writing Literature Reviews: A Guide for Students of the Social and Behavioral Sciences.* 7th ed. New York: Routledge, Taylor & Francis Group, 2017.
Gardiner, Richard K. *Treaty Interpretation.* The Oxford International Law Library. Oxford: Oxford University Press, 2008.
Gavin, William F. *Speechwright: An Insider's Take on Political Rhetoric.* East Lansing: Michigan State University Press, 2011.
George, Susan. *A Fate Worse than Debt.* New York: Grove Press, 1990.
Gibbs, William E. "James Weldon Johnson: A Black Perspective on 'Big Stick' Diplomacy." *Diplomatic History* 8, no. 4 (Fall 1984): 329–347.
Gilbert, Martin. *The Routledge Atlas of the Second World War.* 2nd ed. Routledge Historical Atlases. London: Routledge, 2019.
Gilbert, Martin. *The Second World War: A Complete History.* New York: Holt Paperbacks, 1989.
Glenn, David. "Close the Book. Recall. Write It Down." *The Chronicle of Higher Education* 55, no. 34, A1, May 01, 2009. https://www.chronicle.com/article/Close-the-Book-Recall-Write/31819.
Gobet, Fernand, Peter C.R. Lane, Steve Croker, Peter C-H. Cheng, Gary Jones, Iain Oliver, and Julian M. Pine. "Chunking Mechanisms in Human Learning." *Trends in Cognitive Sciences* 5, no. 6 (2001): 236–243.
Goodman, John B., and Louis W. Pauly. "The Obsolescence of Capital Controls? Economic Management in an Age of Global Markets." *World Politics* 46, no. 1 (October 1993): 50–82.
Gormley-Heenan, Cathy, and Simon Lightfoot, eds. *Teaching Politics and International Relations.* New York: Palgrave MacMillan, 2012.
Gramsci, Antonio. *Prison Notebooks.* New York: Colombia University Press, 2011.

Grant, Adam. "Why I Taught Myself to Procrastinate" *New York Times*, January 16, 2016, https://www.nytimes.com/2016/01/17/opinion/sunday/why-i-taught-myself-to-procrastinate.html.

Gray, Colin S., and Geoffrey Sloan, eds. *Geopolitics, Geography, and Strategy*. New York: Routledge, 1999.

Haidt, Jonathan. *The Righteous Mind: Why Good People are Divided by Politics and Religion*. New York: Vintage Books, 2012.

Hanhimäki, Jussi M. *The United Nations: A Very Short Introduction*. 2nd ed. New York; Oxford: Oxford University Press, 2008, 2015.

Hardin, Garrett. "The Tragedy of the Commons." *Science* 162, no. 3859 (December 13, 1968): 1243–1248.

Hardin, Russell. *Collective Action. Resources for the Future*. Baltimore: Published for Resources for the Future by the Johns Hopkins University Press, 1982.

Harvey, David. *Brief History of Neoliberalism*. Oxford: Oxford University Press, 2005.

Hastedt, Glenn P. *American Foreign Policy: Past, Present, Future*. 7th ed. Upper Saddle River, NJ: Pearson/Prentice Hall, 2009.

Hayek, Friedrich A. *The Road to Serfdom*. London: Routledge & Kegan Paul, 1944.

Heilbroner, Robert L. *The Worldly Philosophers*. 7th ed. London: Penguin, 2000.

Helleiner, Eric. *States and the Reemergence of Global Finance*. Ithaca, NY: Cornell University Press, 1994.

Helleiner, Eric. *Forgotten Foundations of Bretton Woods: International Development and the Making of the Postwar Order*. Ithaca, NY: Cornell University Press, 2016.

Henig, Ruth B. *The League of Nations. Makers of the Modern World*. London: Haus Publishing, 2018.

Hertz, Noreena. *The Debt Threat*. New York: Harper Collins, 2004.

Hickey, Samuel. *The Government of Chronic Poverty: From the Politics of Exclusion to the Politics of Citizenship?* Abingdon: Routledge, 2011.

Hinojal-Oyarbide, Arancha, and Annebeth Rosenboom. "Managing the Process of Treaty Formation—Depositaries and Registration." In *The Oxford Guide to Treaties*, edited by Duncan B. Hollis, 248–276. Oxford: Oxford University Press, 2012.

Hirst, Paul, Grahame Thompson, and Simon Bromley. *Globalization in Question*. 3rd ed. New York: Polity, 2009.

Hitler, Adolph. "Address Before the Reichstag." Speech, Berlin, Germany, September 1, 1939. The Avalon Project, Yale Law School, https://avalon.law.yale.edu/wwii/gp2.asp

Hollis, Duncan B., ed. *The Oxford Guide to Treaties*. Oxford: Oxford University Press, 2012.

Hoopes, Townsend, and Douglas Brinkley. *FDR and the Creation of the U.N.* New Haven: Yale University Press, 2000.

Hobbes, Thomas. *Leviathan*. A. D Lindsay, Everyman's Library. Philosophy and Theology. London: J.M. Dent, 1928, originally published 1651.

Hoekman, Bernard M., and Petros C. Mavroidis. *World Trade Organization: Law, Economics, and Politics*. London: Routledge, Taylor & Francis Group, 2016.

Hopgood, Stephen. *Keepers of the Flame: Understanding Amnesty International.* Ithaca, NY: Cornell University Press, 2006.

Howard-Snyder, Frances, Daniel Howard-Snyder, and Ryan Wasserman. "Chapter 4: Informal Fallacies." In *The Power of Logic.* 6th ed. New York: McGraw-Hill Higher Education, 2019.

Hurley, Patrick J., and Lori Watson. *A Concise Introduction to Logic.* 13th ed. Boston, MA: Cengage Learning, 2018.

Ikenberry, G. John. *After Victory: Institutions, Strategic Restraint, and the Rebuilding of Order After Major Wars.* New ed. Princeton Studies in International History and Politics. Princeton: Princeton University Press, 2019.

International Coalition on Newspapers. "Statistics." Center for Research Libraries and ICON, 2019. http://icon.crl.edu/statistics.php.

Jackson, Robert H. *Quasi-States: Sovereignty, International Relations and the Third World.* Cambridge, UK: Cambridge University Press, 1990.

Ishay, Micheline R. *The History of Human Rights: From Ancient Times to the Globalization Era.* Berkeley and Los Angeles, CA: University of California Press, 2004.

Ishay, Micheline R. *The Human Rights Reader: Major Political Essays, Speeches, and Documents from Ancient Times to the Present.* 2nd ed. New York; London: Routledge, 2012.

Johnson, Toni. "Congress and U.S. Foreign Policy" *Council on Foreign Relations*, January 24, 2013. https://www.cfr.org/backgrounder/congress-and-us-foreign-policy.

Jolly, Richard, Louis Emmerij, and Thomas G. Weiss. *UN Ideas that Changed the World.* Bloomington, IN: Indiana University Press, 2009.

Joshi, Devin, and Roni Kay M. O'Dell. "Global Governance and Development Ideology: The United Nations and the World Bank on the Left-Right Spectrum." *Global Governance* 19, no. 2 (April-June 2013): 249–275.

Jowett, Garth, and Victoria O'Donnell. *Propaganda & Persuasion.* 7th ed. Thousand Oaks, CA: SAGE Publications, 2019.

Kant, Immanuel. *Perpetual Peace.* Project Gutenburg. Produced by Turgut Dincer, Ramon Pajares Box. https://www.gutenberg.org/files/50922/50922-h/50922-h.htm.

Kaplan, Robert D. *The Revenge of Geography: What the Map Tells Us About Coming Conflicts and the Battle against Fate.* 1st ed. New York: Random House, 2012.

Karns, Margaret P, Karen A Mingst, and Kendall W Stiles. *International Organizations: The Politics and Processes of Global Governance.* 3rd ed. Boulder, CO: Lynn Rienner Publishers, 2015.

Kaufman, Joyce P. *A Concise History of US Foreign Policy.* Lanham, MD: Rowman and Littlefield, 2014.

Kaufmann, Johan. *Conference Diplomacy: An Introductory Analysis.* Leiden: A.W. Sijthoff, 1968.

Kaufman, Peter and Janine Schipper. *Teaching with Compassion: An Educator's Oath to Teach from the Heart.* Lanham, MD: Rowman & Littlefield, 2018.

Keating, Joshua. "Why do Diplomats Still Send Cables?" *Foreign Policy.* November 30, 2010. https://foreignpolicy.com/2010/11/30/why-do-diplomats-still-send-cables/

Keegan, John. *The Second World War.* New York: Penguin, 2016.

Kennan, George. "Long Telegram" (February 22, 1946). History and Public Policy Program Digital Archive, National Archives and Records Administration, Department of State Records (Record Group 59), Central Decimal File, 1945-1949, 861.00/2-2246; reprinted in US Department of State, ed., Foreign Relations of the United States, 1946, Volume VI, Eastern Europe; The Soviet Union (Washington, DC: United States Government Printing Office, 1969), 696–709, http://digitalarchive.wilsoncenter.org/document/116178.

Kennan, George. "The Sources of Soviet Conduct" (a.k.a., "The X-Article"). *Foreign Affairs.* (July 1947).

Kennan, George F. *American Diplomacy.* 60th Anniversary Expanded ed. Chicago: University of Chicago Press, 2012.

Keohane, Robert O. *Neorealism and its Critics.* New York: Columbia University Press, 1986.

Keohane, Robert O. *After Hegemony: Cooperation and Discord in the World Political Economy.* Princeton: Princeton University Press, 1984.

Keynes, John Maynard. *The General Theory of Employment, Interest and Money.* London: Macmillan, 1936.

Kiewra, Kenneth A. "A Review of Note-Taking: The Encoding-Storage Paradigm and Beyond." *Educational Psychology Review* 1, no. 2 (June 1989): 147–172.

King, Martin Luther King Jr. "A Time to Break Silence." Speech, New York City, April 4, 1967. In *A Testament of Hope*, edited by James M. Washington. San Francisco: Harper Collins, 1986.

Kinsella, David, Bruce Russett, and Harvey Starr, Eds. *World Politics: The Menu for Choice.* 10th ed. Boston: Wadsworth, Cengage Learning, 2013.

Kissane, Dylan, and Alexandru Volacu, eds. *Modern Dilemmas: Understanding Collective Action in the 21st Century.* Stuttgart, Germany: Ibidem-Verlag, 2015.

Kissinger, Henry A. *Diplomacy.* New York: Simon & Schuster, 1994.

Knowles, Malcolm S, Elwood F. Holton, and Richard A. Swanson. *The Adult Learner: The Definitive Classic in Adult Education and Human Resource Development.* 6th ed. Amsterdam: Elsevier, 2005.

Kohn, Margaret, and Kavita Reddy. "Colonialism." In *The Stanford Encyclopedia of Philosophy.* Edited by Edward N. Zalta. (Fall 2017 Edition). https://plato.stanford.edu/archives/fall2017/entries/colonialism/.

Kovach, Bill, and Tom Rosensteil. *Blur: How to Know What's True in the Age of Information Overload.* New York: Bloomsbury, 2010.

Kratochwil, Fredrich. *The Puzzles of Politics: Inquiries into the Genesis and Transformation of International Relations.* New York: Routledge, 2011.

Krugman, Paul. "How Did Economists Get It so Wrong?" *New York Times*, September 6, 2009.

Kuzenkoff, Jeffery H. "The Impact of Mobile Phone Usage on Student Learning." *Communication Education* 62, no. 3 (February 2013): 233–252.

Lal, Deepak. "In Defense of Empires." From the Henry Wendt Lecture at the American Enterprise Institute, October 2002.

Lang, James M. *Small Teaching: Everyday Lessons from the Science of Learning.* San Francisco: Jossey-Bass, 2016.

Lantis, Jeffrey S., Lynn M. Kuzma, and John Boehrer. *The New International Studies Classroom: Active Teaching, Active Learning.* Boulder; London: Lynne Rienner Publishers, 2000.

Lamy, Steven L, John Scott Masker, John Baylis, Steve Smith, and Patricia Owens. *Introduction to Global Politics.* 5th ed. New York: Oxford University Press, 2019.

Lauren, Paul Gordon. *The Evolution of International Human Rights: Visions Seen.* 3rd ed. Philadelphia, PA: University of Pennsylvania Press, 2011.

Leith, Sam. *Words Like Loaded Pistols: Rhetoric from Aristotle to Obama.* New York: Basic Books, a member of the Perseus Books Group, 2016.

Lenin, Vladimir Il'ich. *Imperialism: The Highest Stage of Capitalism.* Great Ideas. London: Penguin, 2010, originally published 1917.

Lewis, Benny. *Fluent in 3 Months: How Anyone at Any Age, Can Learn to Speak Any Language from Anywhere in the World.* 1st ed. San Francisco: HarperOne, 2014.

Library of Congress, The. "Harry S. Truman: A Resource Guide." Web Guides. Last modified October 20, 2015. https://www.loc.gov/rr/program/bib/presidents/truman/bibliography.html

Little, Richard. *The Balance of Power in International Relations: Metaphors, Myths, and Models.* Cambridge: Cambridge University Press, 2014.

Lunsford, Andrea, and John Ruszkiewicz. *Everything's an Argument.* Boston: Bedford Books, 1998.

Maathai, Wangari. "Nobel Lecture." Speech, Oslo, Norway, December 10, 2004. The Nobel Foundation, Nobel Media AB 2020. https://www.nobelprize.org/prizes/peace/2004/maathai/26050-wangari-maathai-nobel-lecture-2004/.

Maathai, Wangari. *The Green Belt Movement: Sharing the Approach and the Experience.* New York: Lantern Books, 2003.

Magdoff, Harry. *Imperialism without Colonies.* New York: Monthly Review Press, 2003.

Mahan, Alfred Thayer. *The Influence of Sea Power Upon History, 1660-1783.* Little, Brown, 1890.

Malthus, Thomas. *An Essay on the Principle of Population as It Affects the Future Improvement of Society.* London: John J. Johnson in St. Paul's Churchyard, 1798.

Mandela, Nelson. *Long Walk to Freedom: The Autobiography of Nelson Mandela.* New York: Bay Books, 1994.

Marcuse, Herbert. *One-Dimensional Man: Studies in the Ideology of Advanced Industrial Society.* Routledge Classics. Hoboken: Taylor and Francis, 2013.

Margulis, Matias, ed. *The Global Political Economy of Raúl Prebisch.* Ripe Series in Global Political Economy. Abingdon, Oxon: Routledge, 2017.

Marshall, Katherine. *The World Bank: From Reconstruction to Development to Equity.* Global Institutions Series. London; New York: Routledge, 2017.

Martin, James. *Politics and Rhetoric: A Critical Introduction.* London: Routledge, 2013.

Marx, Karl and Friedrich Engels. "The Manifesto of the Communist Party." From the English edition of 1888, edited by Friedrich Engels (originally published in February 1848, proofed and corrected against the 1888 English edition) last updated January 25, 2005, Project Gutenberg. http://www.gutenberg.org/cache/epub/61/pg61-images.html.

Marx, Karl. *Das Kapital, A Critique of Political Economy*. Chicago: H. Regnery, 1959.
Masters, Jonathan. "U.S. Foreign Policy Powers: Congress and the President." *Council on Foreign Relations,* March 2, 2017. https://www.cfr.org/backgrounder/us-foreign-policy-powers-congress-and-president.
McClintock, Anne. *Imperial Leather*. New York: Routledge, 1995.
McCullough, David. *Truman*. New York: Simon & Schuster, 1992.
McGuire, Saundra Yancy. *Teach Yourself How to Learn: Strategies You Can Use to Ace Any Course at Any Level*. Sterling, VA: Stylus Publishing, 2018.
Mearsheimer, John. J. *The Tragedy of Great Power Politics*. 1st ed. New York: W.W. Norton, 2002.
Meisler, Stanley. *United Nations: A History*. New York: Grove Press, 1995, Reprinted 2011.
Meisler, Stanley. *United Nations: The First Fifty Years*. 4th ed. New York: Atlantic Monthly Press, 2007.
Merrill, Karen R. *The Oil Crisis of 1973-1974: A Brief History with Documents*. The Bedford Series in History and Culture. Boston: Bedford/St. Martin's, 2007.
Mertus, Julie. *Bait and Switch: Human Rights and U.S. Foreign Policy*. New York and London: Routledge, 2004.
Messner, Kate. *Real Revision: Authors' Strategies to Share with Student Writers*. Portland, ME: Stenhouse Publishers, 2011.
Miner, Horace. "Body Ritual Among the Nacerima." *American Anthropologist* 58, no. 3 (1956): 503–507.
Mingst, Karen and Ivan M. Arreguin-Toft. *Essentials of International Relations*. New York; London: W. W. Norton & Company, 2016.
Mingst, Karen A., Margaret P. Karns, and Alynna J. Lyon. *The United Nations in the 21st Century: Dilemmas in World Politics*. 5th ed. New York: Routledge, 2018.
Mitzen, Jennifer. *Power in Concert: The Nineteenth-Century Origins of Global Governance*. Chicago: University of Chicago Press, 2014.
Morris, Errol. *The Fog of War: Eleven Lessons from the Life of Robert S. McNamara*. Culver City, CA: Columbia TriStar Home Entertainment, 2004.
Morsink, Johannes. *The Declaration of Human Rights: Origin, Drafting, and Intent*. Philadelphia: University of Pennsylvania Press, 1999.
Mueller, Pam A., and Daniel M. Oppenheimer. "The Pen is Mightier than the Keyboard: Advantages of Longhand Over Laptop Note Taking," *Psychological Science*, 25, no. 6 (April 2014): 1159–1168.
National Security Council. "National Security Council Report, NSC 68, 'United States Objectives and Programs for National Security'," April 14, 1950, History and Public Policy Program Digital Archive, US National Archives. http://digitalarchive.wilsoncenter.org/document/116191.
Narlikar, Amrita, M. J. Daunton, and Robert Mitchell Stern. *The World Trade Organization: A Very Short Introduction*. New York: Oxford University Press, 2012.
Nau, Henry. *International Relations Perspectives: A Reader*. CQ Press, 2009.
Nau, Henry. *Perspectives in International Relations: Power, Institutions, and Ideas*. 7th ed. Thousand Oaks, CA: CQ Press/Sage, 2020.

New York Times, The. "Dearth of Food-A Startling View." *New York Times,* January 5, 1860. Digital Archive Accessed June 3, 2020. https://www.nytimes.com/1860/01/05/archives/dearth-of-fooda-startling-view.html.

Nisbett, Richard E. *Intelligence and How to Get It: Why Schools and Cultures Count.* New York: W.W. Norton and Co., 2009.

Noel, Terry W. "Lessons from the Learning Classroom." *Journal of Management Education* 28, no. 2 (April 2004): 188–206.

Nye, Joseph. *Soft Power: The Means to Success in World Politics.* Public Affairs, Perseus Books Group, 2004.

Oakley, Barbara. *A Mind for Numbers: How to Excel at Math and Science.* New York: Penguin Random House, 2014 (and free companion Coursera Course: *Learning How to Learn*).

Oakley, Barbara A. *Mindshift: Break through Obstacles to Learning and Discover Your Hidden Potential.* New York: TarcherPerigee, 2017.

Office of the Historian. "US Invasion and Occupation of Haiti, 1915-1934." Washington, DC: US Department of State. Last updated 2016. Accessed August 15, 2019. https://history.state.gov/milestones/1914-1920/haiti.

Office of the Director of National Intelligence. "National Security Act of 1947." Accessed March 10, 2020. https://www.dni.gov/index.php/ic-legal-reference-book/national-security-act-of-1947.

Ohmae, Kenichi. *The Borderless World in the Interlinked Economy.* New York: Harper Business, 1990.

Olson, Mancur. *The Logic of Collective Action.* Cambridge, MA: Harvard University Press, 1965.

O'Neil, Patrick H., Karl J. Fields, and Donald Share. *Essentials of Comparative Politics with Cases.* 6th AP ed. New York: W.W. Norton & Company, 2018.

Osmańczyk, Edmund Jan. *Encyclopedia of the United Nations and International Agreements.* (Volumes 1–4). New York: Routledge, 2003.

Ostrom, Elinor. *Governing the Commons: The Evolution of Institutions for Collective Action. The Political Economy of Institutions and Decisions.* Cambridge: Cambridge University Press, 1990, reprinted 2015.

Oxford English Dictionary Online. "capitalism, n.2." Accessed through the University of Colorado Library System. Accessed August 1, 2019. https://www-oed-com.aurarialibrary.idm.oclc.org/view/Entry/27454?rskey=982XHj&result=2.

Patel, Raj. *Stuffed and Starved.* Hoboken, NJ: Melville House, 2007.

Pedersen, Susan. *The Guardians: The League of Nations and the Crisis of Empire.* New York: Oxford University Press, 2018.

Peterson, Martin, ed. *The Prisoner's Dilemma,* Cambridge: Cambridge University Press, 2015.

Pettersson, Therésa, Stina Högbladh, and Magnus Öberg. "Organized Violence, 1989-2018 and Peace Agreements." *Journal of Peace Research* 56, no. 4 (June 2019): 589–603.

Popova, Maria. "Malcom Gladwell on Criticism, Tolerance, and Changing Your Mind." *BrainPickings,* June 24, 2014. https://www.brainpickings.org/2014/06/24/malcolm-gladwell-nypl-interview/.

Pevehouse, Jon C., and Joshua S. Goldstein. *International Relations*. Pearson: New York, 2017.

Polanyi, Karl. *The Great Transformation*. New York: Farrar & Rinehart, 1944.

Porter, Robert Odawi. *Sovereignty, Colonialism and the Indigenous Nations: A Reader*. Durham, NC: Carolina University Press, 2005.

Ramcharan, Bertrand G. *Preventive Diplomacy at the UN*. United Nations Intellectual History Project Series. Bloomington, IN: Indiana University Press, 2008.

Rauchway, Eric. *The Great Depression & the New Deal: A Very Short Introduction*. Oxford: Oxford University Press, 2008.

Richmond, Oliver. *Peace: A Very Short Introduction*. Oxford: Oxford University Press, 2014.

Roosevelt, Theodore. "Annual Message to Congress." Speech, Washington, D.C., December 6, 1904. A National Initiative on American History, Civics, and Service. OurDocuments.gov. https://www.ourdocuments.gov/doc.php?flash=false&doc=56&page=transcript.

Roosevelt, Franklin Delano. "Joint Address to Congress Leading to a Declaration of War Against Japan." Speech, Washington D.C., December 8, 1941. Franklin D. Roosevelt Presidential Library and Museum. A National Initiative on American History, Civics, and Service. OurDocuments.gov. http://www.ourdocuments.gov/doc.php?doc=73&page=transcript.

Rosset, Peter. *Food Is Different!* Halifax: Fernwood, 2006.

Sachs, Jeffery. *The End of Poverty*. New York: Penguin, 2005.

Saint Augustine of Hippo. *The City of God*.

Salvatore, Nick. *Eugene V. Debs: Citizen and Socialist*. 2nd ed. Urbana, IL: University of Illinois Press, 2007.

Sarfaty, Galit A. *Values in Translation: Human Rights and the Culture of the World Bank*. Stanford Studies in Human Rights. Stanford, CA: Stanford University Press, 2012.

Sasser, Jade. S. *On Infertile Ground: Population Control and Women's Rights in the Era of Climate Change*. New York: NYU Press, 2018.

Schlesinger, Stephen C. *Act of Creation: The Founding of the United Nations: A Story of Superpowers, Secret Agents, Wartime Allies and Enemies, and their Quest for a Peaceful World*. Boulder: Westview, 2005.

Seidel, Shannon B. and Kimberly D. Tanner. ""What Is Students Revolt?"—Considering Student Resistance: Origins, Options and Opportunities for Investigation," *Cell Biology Education—Life Sciences Education* 12, no. 4 (Winter 2013): 586–595.

Sen, Amartya. *Development as Freedom*. New York: Anchor Books, Division of Random House, 1999.

Sen, Amartya. *Inequality Reexamined*. Cambridge: Harvard University Press, 1992.

Serra, Narcis, and Joseph Stiglitz. *The Washington Consensus Reconsidered*. London: Oxford, 2008.

Shiva, Vandana. "Development as a New Project of Western Patriarchy." In *Reweaving the World: The Emergence of EcoFeminism,* edited by Irene Diamond and Gloria Feman Orenstein. New York: Zed, 1990.

Shiva, Vandana. *The Violence of the Green Revolution*. New York: Zed Books, 1989.
Shiva, Vandana. *Oneness Versus the One Percent*. New Delhi: Women Unlimited, 2018.
Shor, Ira. *Empowering Education: Critical Teaching for Social Change*. Chicago, IL: University of Chicago Press, 1992.
Singham, Mano. "Away from the Authoritarian Classroom." *Change: The Magazine of Higher Learning* 37, no. 3 (May/June 2005): 50–57.
Skidelsky, Robert Jacob Alexander. *Keynes: The Return of the Master*. New York: Public Affairs, 2013.
Smith, Anthony D. *Nationalism: Key Concepts*. New York: Polity, 2013.
Snyder, Timothy. *Bloodlands: Europe between Hitler and Stalin*. London: Vintage, 2015.
Sobel, Dava. *A More Perfect Heaven: How Copernicus Revolutionized the Cosmos*. London: Bloomsbury, 2011.
Spykman, N. J. *America's Strategy in World Politics. The United States and the Balance of Power*. Yale University. Institute of International Studies. New York: Harcourt, Brace, 1942, reprinted 2007.
Stage, Frances K., Patricia A. Muller, Jillian Kinzie, and Ada Simmons. *Creating Learning Centered Classrooms. What Does Learning Theory Have To Say?* Washington, DC: ASHE-ERIC Higher Education Report, 1998.
Stager, Manfred. *Globalization: A Very Short Introduction*. Oxford University Press, 2013.
Stavrianos, Leften Stavros. *Global Rift: The Third World Comes of Age*. New York: Morrow, 1981.
Steil, Benn. *The Battle of Bretton Woods: John Maynard Keynes, Harry Dexter White, and the Making of a New World Order*. Princeton: Princeton University Press, 2014.
Steger, Manfred B. *Globalization: A Very Short Introduction*. Oxford: Oxford University Press, 2003.
Steil, Benn. *The Battle of Bretton Woods: John Maynard Keynes, Harry Dexter White, and the Making of a New World Order*. Princeton: Princeton University Press, 2014.
Stiglitz, Joseph. *Globalization and Its Discontents*. New York: W.W. Norton, 2002.
Stringer, Lindsay C., Chasca Twyman, and Leah M. Gibbs. "Learning from the South: Common Challenges and Solutions for Small-Scale Farming." *Geographical Journal* 174, no. 3 (2008): 235–250.
Stokke, Olav. *The UN and Development: From Aid to Cooperation*. Bloomington; Indianapolis: Indiana University Press, 2009.
Strunk, William and E.B. White. *Elements of Style*. 4th ed. New York: Longman, 2000.
Taylor, Ian, and Karen Smith. *United Nations Conference on Trade and Development (UNCTAD)*. Global Institutions. London: Routledge, 2007.
Tinder, Glenn. *Political Thinking: The Perennial Questions*. 6th ed. New York: Longman Classics Series, 2004.
Tooze, Adam. *Crashed: How a Decade of Financial Crisis Changed the World*. New York: Penguin Books, 2019.
Thoreau, Henry David. *On the Duty of Civil Disobedience*. Project Gutenberg. June 1, 1993, originally published 1849. http://www.gutenberg.org/ebooks/71.

Bibliography

Thucydides. *History of the Peloponnesian War.* Translated by Benjamin Jowett. Amherst, N.Y.: Prometheus Books, 1998.

Truman, Harry S. "Address Before a Joint Session of Congress." Speech, Washington DC, March 12, 1947. The Avalon Project, Yale Law School, https://avalon.law.yale.edu/20th_century/trudoc.asp.

Truman, Harry S. "Inaugural Address of Harry S. Truman." Speech, Washington, DC, January 20, 1949. The Avalon Project, Yale Law School, https://avalon.law.yale.edu/20th_century/truman.asp

Tuathail, Gearóid Ó. and Simon Dalby, eds. *Rethinking Geopolitics.* London: Routledge, 1998.

United Kingdom. "Inclosure Act 1845." Legislation.gov.uk. Accessed July 24, 2020 https://www.legislation.gov.uk/ukpga/Vict/8-9/118

United Nations. *Charter of the United Nations.* Charter, October 24, 1945, 1 UNTS XVI. Accessed August 29, 2019. https://www.un.org/en/sections/un-charter/un-charter-full-text/

United Nations. "The Declaration by United Nations." Accessed on March 6, 2020 from https://www.unmultimedia.org/searchers/yearbook/page.jsp?volume=1946-47&page=36&searchType=advanced.

United Nations. 1969. "Vienna Convention on the Law of Treaties."

United Nations. "Universal Declaration of Human Rights." Dec. 8, 1948. G.A. Res. 217A (III), U.N. Doc. A/810 at 71 (1948) accessed July 24, 2020 https://www.un.org/en/universal-declaration-human-rights/.

United Nations High Commissioner for Human Rights, ed. 2014. *The Core International Human Rights Treaties.* New York: United Nations.

United Nations Development Program. *Human Development Report.* New York: United Nations, 1990.

United Nations Treaty Collection. Accessed March 4, 2020. https://treaties.un.org/Pages/Home.aspx?clang=_en.

United Nations. *The Rio Declaration on Environment and Development.* Geneva: United Nations.

United States Constitution. "The Constitution of the United States of America." Accessed March 8, 2020 https://www.archives.gov/founding-docs/constitution-transcript.

United States and Haiti. "Treaty Between the United States and Haiti," signed at Port-au-Prince September 16, 1915 Presented by Mr. Pomerene, ordered to be printed in 1922. Washington DC: Government Printing Office, accessed July 23, 2020 https://www.loc.gov/law/help/us-treaties/bevans/b-ht-ust000008-0660.pdf.

UNC Chapel Hill. "Fallacies" Accessed on March 6, 2020 at https://writingcenter.unc.edu/tips-and-tools/fallacies/.

Uppsala Universitet. Uppsala Conflict Database. https://ucdp.uu.se/.

Vick, Brian E. *The Congress of Vienna: Power and Politics After Napoleon.* Cambridge, MA: Harvard University Press, 2014.

Wallerstein, Immanuel Maurice. *The Modern World System. Vol. 1, Capitalist Agriculture and the Origins of the European World-Economy in the Sixteenth Century. Vol. 1.* Studies in Social Discontinuity. New York: Academic Press, 1974.

Waltzer, Michael. *Just and Unjust Wars.* New York: Basic Books, 2015.

Weber, Max. "Politics as a Vocation." Speech, Munich, Germany, January 28, 1919.
Washington, James M., ed. *A Testament of Hope: The Essential Writings and Speeches of Dr. Martin Luther King, Jr.* San Francisco: Harper Collins, 1986.
Weimar, Maryellen. *Learner-Centered Teaching: Five Key Changes to Practice.* 2nd ed. San Francisco: Jossey-Bass, 2013.
Weiss, Thomas G. *What's Wrong with the United Nations and How to Fix It.* 2nd ed. Cambridge: Polity Press, 2012.
Weiss, Thomas G. *Thinking About Global Governance: Why People and Ideas Matter.* Hoboken: Taylor & Francis, 2012.
Weiss, Thomas G, and Ramesh Thakur. *Global Governance and the UN: An Unfinished Journey.* United Nations Intellectual History Project. Bloomington: Indiana University Press, 2010.
Weitz, Eric D. *A Century of Genocide: Utopias of Race and Nation.* Princeton, NJ: Princeton University Press, 2003.
Weston, Anthony. *A Rulebook for Arguments.* 4th ed. Hackett Publishing, 2008.
Whitely, Bernard E. Jr. and Patricia Keith-Spiegel. *Academic Dishonesty: An Educator's Guide.* East Sussex, Psychology Press, 2012.
White, Katherine. *Strategies for Analysis: Analyzing Information for Classroom, Homework and Test Success.* New York: Rosen Publishing Group, 2006.
Wiesenthal, Simon. *The Sunflower: On the Possibilities and Limits of Forgiveness.* New York: Schocken Books, 1997.
Willis, Judy. "The Neuroscience of Joyful Education." *Educational Leadership: Journal of the Department of Supervision and Curriculum Development, N.E.A.* 64 (January 2007).
Wilson, Woodrow. "War Message to Congress." Speech, Washington DC, April 2, 1917. https://wwi.lib.byu.edu/index.php/Wilson%27s_War_Message_to_Congress.
Woods, Ngaire. *The Globalizers: The IMF, the World Bank, and Their Borrowers.* Cornell Studies in Money. Ithaca, NY: Cornell University Press, 2014.
Wong, Linda. *Essential Study Skills.* 6th ed. Boston: Houghton Mifflin, 2009.
World Bank. *World Development Report 1978.* Washington, DC. © World Bank, 1978. https://openknowledge.worldbank.org/handle/10986/5961 License: CC BY 3.0 IGO.
World Bank. *Getting to Know the World Bank: A Guide for Young People.* World Bank E-Library. Washington, DC, 2005.
Yergin, Daniel and Stanislaw, Joseph. *The Commanding Heights: The Battle for the World Economy.* New York: Free Press, 1998
Zimmerman, Barry J. "Becoming a Self-Regulated Learner: An Overview." *Theory into Practice* 41, no. 2 (2002): 64–72.
Zinn, Howard. *A Peoples' History of the United States.* New York: Harper Collins, 1980.
Zinsser, William. *On Writing Well: The Classic Guide to Writing Nonfiction*, reprint ed. New York: Harper Perennial, 2016.
Zull, James E. *The Art of the Changing Brain.* Sterling, VA: Stylus, 2002.

Index of Primary Sources

The Atlantic Charter (1941), 80–81

The British Inclosure Act (1845), 201–2

Charter of the United Nations (1945), 62–64

Churchill, Winston: "Blood, Toil, Tears, and Sweat Speech to the House of Commons" (1940), 171

Debs, Eugene: "The Canton, Ohio Speech" (1918), 151–53

Friedman, Milton: "Interview with Playboy Magazine" (1973), 29

Kennan, George: "The Long Telegram" (1947), 95–96
Kennan, George: "The Sources of Soviet Conduct" (1947), 97
King Jr., Martin Luther: "A Time to Break Silence" (1967), 189–90

Lee, Kyung Hae: "Statement at the WTO Conference in Cancun, Mexico" (2003), 44–45

Maathai, Wangari: "Nobel Prize Acceptance Speech" (2004), 190–92
Marx, Karl and Friedrich Engels: *The Manifesto of the Communist Party* (1848), 26–28
McNamara, Robert: "Foreword to the *World Development Report*" (1978), 114–15

The New York Times: "Dearth of Food--A Startling View" (editorial; 1860), 203–5

Oxford English Dictionary: "Capitalism, n.2" (2019), 25–26

Roosevelt, Franklin D.: "Address to a Joint Session of Congress Leading to a Declaration of War Against Japan" (1941), 171–72

Shiva, Vandana: "Development as a New Project of Western Patriarchy" (1990), 30

Treaty between the United States and Haiti (1915), 132–36

Truman, Harry S.: "Address to Joint Session of Congress" (1947), 97–98
Truman, Harry S.: "Inaugural Address" (1949), 6–9

The United Nations: *Universal Declaration of Human Rights* (1948), 218–22

Subject Index

active reading, 42–43
active resistance, xii–xiii
actors, 10–11, 41, 46–47, 50–55, 72. *See also* institutions
agriculture, 44–45, 48–51, 53–55, 194–95, 203–5, 210–11
American exceptionalism. *See* United States
American Revolution. *See* United States
anarchy, 139–41, 146
Anglo-Polish Agreement, 178
annotated bibliographies, 22–24, 33–35
appeasement, 88, 176, 178
Aristotle, 223, 225
Atlantic Charter, 67, 69–70, 77, 80–89
Atlantic Conference, 69
audience, 11, 45–46, 104, 223
Aung San Suu Kyi, 155
Austria, 173
Aztec Empire, 119

balance of power, 85, 89, 140–41, 173
Battle in Seattle, 52
Bloom's Taxonomy, 3–5, 9
brainstorming, 186–87
Bretton Woods Conference, 8–9
Bretton Woods Institutions, 14, 88–89. *See also* International Monetary Fund; World Bank

Brezhnev, Leonid, 35
British Inclosure Act, 199, 201–2, 210
Brookfield, Stephen, xii

Canada, 2
capitalism, 22, 25–36, 112, 121–22, 157–59, 194
capitalist class, 47, 154–59, 161–64
Cassin, René, 223
Chamberlain, Neville, 87–88, 178
Chang, Ha Joon, 123
Chang, P.C., 223
charter, 64–65. *See also* Atlantic Charter
China, 70, 119
chunking, 16–17, 167–68, 173–80, 239–40
Churchill, Winston, 67, 81–83, 88, 171–80
Cirillo, Francesco, 94
cognitive dissonance, xv
Cold War. *See* war
collective action problems, 199, 205–12
collective goods, 201, 208–9
collective security, 67, 208
colonization. *See* imperialism
communism, 10, 26–28, 117, 121–22, 194
Concert of Europe, 67–68
conference diplomacy. *See* diplomacy

Confucius, 225
Congress of Vienna, 68
Congress of Westphalia, 68
Constantine, 243
containment, 93, 98, 101–3, 118. *See also* Cold War
Cornell Method of Notetaking, 78–79
coronavirus, 1, 243
critical pedagogy, xii
Czechoslovakia, 85, 88, 173, 176

Debs, Eugene, 149, 151–64
debt, 117–18, 120, 123–24, 138, 146
debt crisis. *See* debt; economic crisis
decentralization, 34–35
democracy, xii, 10, 82, 112, 117, 195
Destroyers for Bases Agreement, 83, 88
development, 30, 33–37, 49, 51, 87, 111, 114–24, 132–36
dialogue, xii, xx
dictionaries, 10, 25–26, 31, 65
diplomacy: ambassadors, 69; chargé d'affaires, 100, 104; conference diplomacy, 68–69, 93; consulates, 100; delegate, 69; diplomatic cable, 93, 100, 103; diplomatic corps, 104; diplomatic mission, 99, 100; diplomats, 99; embassies, 100; foreign service officer, 104; peace conference, 68; plenipotentiary, 69; summit diplomacy, 68–69
Donnelly, Jack, 226
Dunant, Henri, 180

economic crisis, 120–21, 123–24, 243. *See also* debt; Great Depression; Great Recession
economic growth, 113, 120–21, 123–24
Eden, Anthony, 67
editing, 241–42
empire. *See* imperialism
encyclopedias, 10, 25
Engels, Friedrich, 26–28, 33–36, 124, 154
England. *See* United Kingdom

English School, 145
Enlightenment, 227
environment, 194–95, 205–12
etymology, 32
European Union (EU), 54
Exceptionalism. *See* United States
expansionism, 13, 14
exploitation, 36, 154, 194

Faraday, Michael, 202–3
farming. *See* agriculture
FDR. *See* Roosevelt, Franklin D.
financial crisis. *See* economic crisis
flashcards, 150
foreign aid, 13–14, 138, 140
France, 32, 173, 176–78
free riding, 207
freedom, 10, 34–35, 223, 225–30
Freire, Paulo, xii
Friedman, Milton, 29–30, 33–36

gender, 194–95, 210
General Agreement on Trade and Tariffs (GATT), 54. *See also* World Trade Organization
Geneva Conventions, 180
geography, 13–14, 49, 77, 81–89, 206
geopolitics, 13–14, 81–89
Germany, 81, 83, 87–89, 105, 145, 153–59, 167, 170–80
Gladwell, Malcom, 243
global governance, 5, 9, 64–72
globalization, 52–55, 85, 121–22, 136, 145, 242
goal setting, 200
Gorbachev, Mikhail, 243
Grabel, Ilene, 123
Great Depression, 35, 120, 121
great powers, 140–41
Great Recession, 120, 243
Greece, 14, 179
greed, 34–35
Grotius, Hugo, 70
growth mindset, xiv–xv
Gulf of Tonkin Resolution, 101

Subject Index

Haiti, 120, 129, 132–46, 208
Hammurabi's Code, 223, 225
hard power, 85
Hardin, Garrett, 209–10
hasty generalization, 112, 123–24, 169
hegemony, 14, 69, 85, 88, 120–21, 139, 156, 217
hierarchy, 50
historical context, 15, 49–50, 64, 111, 113–24, 138
historical timelines, 113–16
Hitler, Adolf, 170–80
Hobbes, Thomas, 54
Holocaust, 174, 223, 225
human nature, 34–35, 54–55, 210
human rights, 65–67, 194–95, 217–33
humanism, 227
Humphrey, John, 223

ideology, 46–47, 53, 101, 122–23, 227
illusion of competence, 80
imagination, 18
imperialism, 83, 85–6, 118–20, 136, 138, 141, 143–46, 155–56, 194, 210
inaugural address, 11–12, 14
independence movements, 118–19. *See also* self-determination
independent learning, xvi–xvii
India, 225
individualism, 34, 227
Industrial Revolution, 34, 36
industrialization, 32, 34, 36, 154
inequality, 16, 34–35, 51, 54–55, 85, 122–23, 144–46, 149, 154, 157, 160–64, 194–95
intelligence, xv
intercultural competence, 43–44
interdependence, 139
intergovernmental organizations (IGOs), 2, 12, 59, 111. *See also* specific names of IGOs such as United Nations, International Monetary Fund, World Bank, World Trade Organization
international agreements, 64–72

International Court of Justice, 66. *See also* United Nations
International Criminal Court, 231
international law, 6, 72, 99–100, 230–31
International Monetary Fund (IMF), 52, 89, 117, 120, 123, 124
international organizations (IOs), 12, 49
international system, 117, 129, 136–46, 173
international trade, 41, 44–45, 49, 52–55
internet, 43, 60–62
interventionism, 121–22
Iran, 121, 160–64, 208
isolationism, 13, 82
Israel, 121, 208

Japan, 72, 82, 85, 171–80
jargon, 21
JFK. *See* Kennedy, John F.
Johnson, Lyndon, 111
Joint Comprehensive Plan of Action (JCPA), 208
just war theory, 179–80

Kant, Immanuel, 55
Kautilya, 223, 225
Kennan, George, 93, 95–106
Kennedy, John F. (JFK), 34, 111
Kenya, 194–95
Keynes, John Maynard, 28–29, 33–36, 121–22
Keynesianism. *See* John M. Keynes
King Jr., Martin Luther, 48, 124, 155, 185, 189–90, 193–96
Korea, 44, 49, 50
Kosovo, 85
Krugman, Paul, 242–43

League of Nations, 67–68, 177–78
Learner-centered teaching, xiii–xiv, 218
Lee Kyung Hae, 41, 44–45, 47–48, 50–55, 154
Lend-Lease Act, 83, 88. *See also* United States
less developed countries (LDCs), 49–51

level of analysis, xii, 208
liberal internationalism, 14, 82
liberalism, 46–47, 55, 144–45. *See also* liberal internationalism; neoliberalism
lifelong learning, xvi–xvii
logical fallacies, 112–13, 228

Maathai, Wangari, 124, 185, 190–96
main ideas, 16, 129–32, 158
Malik, Charles, 223
Malthus, Thomas, 210
Manchuria, 173, 178
Mandela, Nelson, 82, 155
markets, 31, 33–35, 121–24, 241–42
Marx, Karl, 26–28, 33–36, 54–55, 124, 154
Marxism, 46–47, 54–55, 145, 155
McNamara, Robert, 72, 103, 111, 114–24
memory, xv, 78–80, 150
mercantilism, 82
metacognition, xix, 201
Mexico, 2, 44, 52, 123
military draft, 156–58
mind maps, 186–87
monopoly, 34
Monroe Doctrine, 155–56
Mosco Declaration, 69
Moscow Conference, 69
multinational corporations (MNCs), 52, 145
multitasking, 42
Munich Agreement, 87

national interest, 99, 140, 142–44, 146, 178–79
national security, 99–106, 136
National Security Act, 101. *See also* United States
nationalism, 12, 173, 174, 178–79
nation-state, xii, 2, 12, 173
natural resources, 86, 210–11
neoimperialism. *See* imperialism

neoliberalism, 52, 122. *See also* liberalism
Nixon, Richard, 102
Nobel Peace Prize, 185, 190
nongovernmental organizations (NGOs), 2, 12
North American Free Trade Agreement (NAFTA), 2
North Atlantic Treaty Organization (NATO), 12
notetaking, 78–80. *See also* annotated bibliography

Ohio (USA), 149, 151–58
oil, 120–21
Organization of Petroleum Exporting Countries (OPEC), 121
Orwell, George, 243
Ottoman Empire, 119
Oxford English Dictionary (OED), 25, 226

Paris Peace Conference, 67–68
passive resistance, xii–xiii
Patel, Raj, 210
patriotism, 12, 169, 173, 178
Pax Britannica, 85
peace, 185, 190–96, 223, 230
Peace of Westphalia, 68, 143
Placentia Bay, 83, 88
Plato, 223, 225
Poland, 85, 170, 173, 176–78
polarity (international system), 117, 119, 139–41
Pomodoro Technique, 94
population growth, 209–10
positive-sum games, 139, 141, 143, 146
post hoc ergo propter hoc, 112–13
post-structuralism, 46–47
Potsdam Conference, 70, 173
poverty, 115–24, 194–95
Prisoner's Dilemma, 207
private ownership, 33–36, 209, 212
procrastination, 94
propaganda, 167, 169–70, 179

protectionism, 82

racism, 174, 194, 210
Reagan, Ronald, 112
realism, 46–47, 54, 144
recall, xx, 79–80, 149–50
reflective journaling, xix–xx
relativism, 227–28
resistance behaviors, xvii
retrieval, xx, 150
revision, 241–42
rhetoric, 167, 169–70
Roman Empire, 119
Roosevelt Corollary, 155
Roosevelt, Eleanor, 223, 225
Roosevelt, Franklin D., 10, 15, 67, 81–83, 88, 89, 104, 106, 171–80
Roosevelt, Theodore, 155–57
Russia, 29, 95–97, 105, 204, 208. *See also* Soviet Union; Union of Soviet Socialist Republics (USSR)

Saul of Tarsus, 243
self-determination, 86, 118–20, 177
self-immolation, 43, 48
Sen, Amartya, 161
sheres of influence, 85
Shiva, Vandana, 30, 33–36, 124
Siddhartha, 243
social class, 149, 154–59, 161–64
social constructivism, 46–47, 145
socialism, 32. *See also* communism
social movements, 52, 194–95
Socrates, 155
soft power, 85, 141
Soong Tzu-wen, 67
South Africa, 82
South Sudan, 85
Southeast Asia Collective Defense Treaty, 101–2. *See also* Vietnam War
sovereignty, 66, 85–86, 138–40, 143–46, 173, 177
Soviet Union, 13, 16, 34, 67, 70, 97–106, 116–19, 121, 208
spaced repetition, xv

Spain, 119
Stalin, Joseph, 16–17, 67
St. Augustine, 179
Stettinius, Edward, 67
Strategic Arms Reduction Treaties, 208
structural adjustment programs, 123–24. *See also* debt; International Monetary Fund; World Bank
St. Thomas Aquinas, 179
studying, 78–79
Subcomandante Marcos, 112
summit diplomacy, 68. *See also* diplomacy
Sun Tzu, 70
superpowers, 141
synaptic pruning, xv
synthesis, 17–18

T-chart, 24, 36, 193
Tehran Conference, 69
telegram. *See* diplomatic cable
territorial integrity, 86
Thatcher, Margaret, 243
thesis statements, 129–32, 145–46
third world, 43, 49
Thucydides, 146, 179
trade. *See* international trade
Tragedy of the Commons, 199, 209–10
treaties, 132–46, 173, 231–32
Truman, Harry, 2–3, 6–17, 93, 97–98, 104, 106, 117
Turkey, 14
tyranny, 34–36, 223

Uganda, 113
Union of Soviet Socialist Republics (USSR). *See* Soviet Union
unit of analysis, 46–47
United Kingdom (UK), 32, 67, 70, 80–89, 112, 121, 124, 167, 171–80, 201–3, 210–11
United Nations (UN), 12, 59, 62–72, 99–100, 172; Declaration of, 69–70, 89; Dumbarton Oaks Conference, 67, 70; General Assembly, 224;

International Court of Justice, 66, 231; San Francisco Conference, 67, 69–70, 89; UDHR Drafting Committee, 223; UN Charter, 59, 60, 62–72; UN Commission on Human Rights, 223–24, 231; UN Development Programme (UNDP), 123; UN Treaty Collection, 65; Universal Declaration of Human Rights (UDHR), 66, 217–33

United States: agricultural subsidies, 54; American exceptionalism, 11; American Revolution, 116; Central Intelligence Agency, 101; Congress, 10–11, 13, 15, 93, 97–98, 100, 101, 106, 117, 124, 156, 171; Constitution, 15, 100, 103; Department of Defense, 102–3; Department of State, 100, 102; economic policy, 54, 123–24; foreign policy, 10–16, 67, 70, 80, 81–89, 98–106, 129, 132–46, 167–80, 225; Joint Chiefs of Staff, 102–3; National Intelligence Council, 101; National Security Council, 101; political parties, 154; President, 101–2, 157; *See also* specific names of presidents; Supreme Court, 13, 100, 155; USS Augusta, 83, 88

United States-Mexico-Canada Agreement (USMCA), 2

Universal Declaration of Human Rights. *See* United Nations

universalism, 227–28

Versailles Treaty, 69, 176–77, 232

Vienna Convention on Consular Relations, 99–100

Vienna Convention on Diplomatic Relations, 99

Vienna Convention on the Law of Treaties, 65

Vietnam, 72, 101–3, 116, 194–95

violence, 194–96

Von Clausewitz, Carl, 70–71

war, 70–72, 116–17, 151–64, 170–80; Arab-Israeli War, 121; Cold War, 10–17, 34, 71, 84, 93, 95–105, 116–19, 121; collective security and, 67; definition and causes, 70–72; Iran-Iraq War, 149, 160–65; Korean War, 116, 103; Napoleonic Wars, 71, 180; Thirty Years War, 143; UN Charter and. *See* United Nations; Vietnam War, 72, 101–2, 103, 116, 194–95; World War I, 15, 68, 116, 119, 136, 144–45, 149, 153–59, 161; World War II, 2, 13–15, 66, 72, 79, 81–89, 105, 116, 123, 167, 170–80, 217, 222–24

War Powers Resolution, 102. *See also* United States

Washington Consensus, 123–24

Weber, Max, 144

Wilhelm II, 155–57

Wilson, Woodrow, 67–68, 156–57

working class, 34, 47, 154–59, 161–64

working definition, 36–37, 71

World Bank, 52, 89, 111, 114–24

World Trade Organization (WTO), 41, 44–45, 49, 51–55, 89

World War I. *See* war

World War II. *See* war

writing, 185–88, 193

Yalta Conference, 70. *See also* WWII

zero-sum games, 139, 141, 143, 146

About the Authors

Roni Kay M. O'Dell is an associate professor and department coordinator in the department of political science at Seton Hill University. She teaches courses on international relations, global studies, comparative politics, human rights, development studies, and research methods. She advises Model United Nations teams and independent student research projects in political science and global studies. Prior publications cover subjects related to human development, the World Bank and the United Nations Development Programme, and pedagogy on teaching about inequality and poverty.

Sasha Breger Bush is an assistant professor of international studies in the political science department at the University of Colorado Denver. She teaches courses on international relations and global politics, international political economy, comparative politics, political theory, and research methods, and advises independent student researchers across multiple disciplines. Sasha researches and publishes extensively on global finance, global food and agriculture, global drug economies, and international relations pedagogy.

CPSIA information can be obtained
at www.ICGtesting.com
Printed in the USA
BVHW081918191220
595989BV00003B/5